Praise for the Haunted A

"Amazing tales."   —*Chicago* magazine

"Great reading for a stormy night."   —*Booklist*

"*Haunted America* provides a deliciously disturbing collection of stories from every state in the Union. . . . Engrossing and entertaining."
                                        —*Minneapolis Star-Tribune*

"Inject some spirit into your travels."   —*Orlando Sentinel*

"Mesmerizing, spine-tingling, and not to be missed by any folklore collection."   —*Library Journal*

HAUNTED AMERICA

BETH SCOTT

AND

MICHAEL NORMAN

A TOM DOHERTY ASSOCIATES BOOK

New York

This book is dedicated to our families
for always being patient,
and to Mark Lefebvre for never losing faith.

HAUNTED AMERICA

Copyright © 1994 by Michael Norman and the Estate of Elizabeth Scott.

Book design by Fritz Metsch

A Tor Book
Published by Tom Doherty Associates, LLC
175 Fifth Avenue
New York, NY 10010

www.tor.com

Tor® is a registered trademark of Tom Doherty Associates, LLC.

Library of Congress Cataloging-in-Publication Data

Norman, Michael.
    Haunted America / Michael Norman and Beth Scott.
        p. cm.
    ISBN-13: 978-0-7653-1967-8
    ISBN-10: 0-7653-1967-5
    1. Haunted houses—United States.   2. Ghosts—United States.
 I. Scott, Beth, 1922–1994.   II. Title.

BF1472.U6N67   1994
133.1'0973—dc20

           94-28984
           CIP

First Hardcover Edition: October 1994
First Trade Paperback Edition: September 2007

Printed in the United States of America

0 9 8 7 6 5 4 3 2 1

Contents

CONTENTS

THE UNITED STATES

The Face in the Window

The imposing Pickens County Courthouse on the town square in quiet, old Carrollton is perhaps the most unusual seat of local government in all of Alabama. There are courthouses older and larger than this two-story edifice, quite a few that harbor within their walls stories of Civil War horror and heroism, and not an insubstantial number with ghostly legends. But, for the sheer oddity and grotesqueness of the event, few can match what can be found at the Carrollton courthouse.

Embedded in the windowpane of a garret window high above the casual pedestrian is the likeness of a human face. To be exact, it is the face of one Henry Wells, an African-American man accused of burning an earlier courthouse in 1876. How and why Henry Wells's face was etched in that glass for all eternity is a story both sad and bizarre.

It begins on April 5, 1865, when Union troops under the command of General John T. Croxton burned the University of Alabama at Tuscaloosa, some forty miles east of Carrollton. General Croxton then sent a detachment of soldiers to destroy the Pickens County Courthouse at Carrollton, although why he issued such an order remains a mystery. There was no military value in the act. But the Yankees carried out their mission with soldierly precision, and the stately old building burned to the ground.

The people of Pickens County vowed to erect a new structure, despite the presence of carpetbaggers and a radical, federally installed government in the county, which made the task doubly difficult. But rebuild it they did, and for twelve years the courthouse stood, symbolizing, as one writer observed, "the return to law and order in a strife-torn land."

But all that changed on November 17, 1876, not quite twelve years after Northern troops torched the first courthouse. On that late autumn night, two men, one of whom is alleged to have been Henry Wells, a former slave, set fire to the new Pickens County Courthouse.

A newspaper of the era, the *West Alabamian*, contained an account of the fire on page three of its November 22, 1876, edition, which said in part: "The burning was unquestionably the work of an incendiary. It took fire in several places about the same time."

Henry Wells and his buddy, Bill Burkhalter, were suspects from the beginning. According to Dan Turnipseed, a Carrollton historian and an expert on the legend, Wells had been accused of raping a white woman. He was allegedly told that if he burned the courthouse all the records of his arrest would be destroyed and he wouldn't come to trial. Just who gave this "advice" to Wells isn't clear, but the fire did burn all the books and records of the probate court. However, the "dying confession of Henry Wells," published in the February 6, 1878, issue of the *West Alabamian,* contains a different account. That story quotes Wells as saying Burkhalter persuaded him to break into the courthouse to steal money. One of the men accidentally knocked over a candle left in the probate court office and that started the fire, the confession claimed. However, some doubt can be cast on the validity of the well-written confession. Wells could neither read nor write. He signed the "confession" with an X.

Burkhalter had been indicted for a series of burglaries at about the same time the courthouse burned, including ones at stores in Reform, Carrollton, and Lineburg, all in Alabama, along with three other businesses across the state line in Mississippi.

Both men fled the county before they could be arrested for the courthouse fire.

Two years passed. Pickens County built another new courthouse. Then, on January 29, 1878, Henry Wells was arrested while working on Bill McConner's plantation near Fairfield, now a western suburb of Birmingham. Wells tried to escape and was shot twice in the legs. The other suspect, Bill Burkhalter, was soon captured near Tuscaloosa.

The men were returned to Carrollton. The sheriff feared for their safety and decided to house Wells and Burkhalter and several other prisoners in a garret storeroom. There is no record that Wells was treated for his leg wounds. Word soon spread through the town that Wells, the man many thought mainly responsible for burning their courthouse, had been found. A mob gathered on the night after his arrival in Carrollton, intent on imposing their own brand of "justice."

Storm clouds rolled across the sky, bringing intermittent rain and a spectacular lightning display to the mob of whites calling for Wells's hanging. The frightened prisoner stared down from his attic cell, shouting his innocence through the half-opened window.

What happened next is part legend and part fact. A tremendous bolt of lightning struck near the courthouse. The imprint of Wells's horrified expression was said to have been permanently emblazoned on the garret window glass.

It remains there to this day.

The mob eventually dispersed. Although accounts of what finally happened to Henry Wells differ, the generally accepted story is that he died shortly after that loathsome night from wounds inflicted during his capture at Fairfield.

Burkhalter was convicted of complicity in the burglary and fire and died while serving a sentence at the state prison.

Not long after Wells's death, passersby started to notice the distinct image of a man's face on the garret window. One man described it as having a moustache and wearing a black hat.

Carrollton's Dan Turnipseed said it "looks like a negative, when someone sees it from the street." Strangest of all, he said, is that the face *cannot* be seen when looking out the window from inside. Turnipseed said the face clearly has the look of someone distressed or frightened.

In the mid-1980s the courthouse was renovated. During the cleaning operation, Turnipseed said the bottom portion of the garret window, where the face is seen, was raised so workmen could paint the sill and destroy some beehives. Even with the bottom portion of the window up, the face in the top part was perceptible.

Over the decades unsuccessful attempts have been made to remove the image from the window by washing or scrubbing the glass. In recent years the county has decided to leave the window alone.

"We don't fool with it," Turnipseed said.

In the mid-1980s, the Atlanta Center for the Continuing Study of the Shroud of Turin took close-up photos of the face in the window using a power company's truck to lift photographers to within a few feet of the image. Copies of the photographs, clearly showing the mysterious face, were sent for analysis to the Jet Propulsion Laboratory in Pasadena and to a laboratory in West Germany.

A close-up view of the window shows that the face seems iridescent with a variety of colors, somewhat suggestive of an oil slick. One supposition is that the molecular structure of the window changed over time, causing the portion of the glass with the "face" to actually take on a different composition. However, a change of this nature could be caused quickly by heating the glass. Iridescence can occur by shooting an X ray through glass. Could electrical current, such as that caused by a lightning bolt, also produce such an effect?

Gary Moore, a former student at the University of Alabama, studied the face in the window. In a report, he wrote that lightning is caused by an imbalance of electrical charges between the earth and the sky. Negative electrons in the sky are disproportionately smaller than the positive protons on earth. Lightning is really the larger number of protons rushing upward to correct the imbalanced neutrons in the clouds. Moore speculated that a human face might produce a "very high positive charge, causing protons to flow toward the sky from eyes, nose, mouth, or other features discretely, until this flow was deflected by the insulation of a window pane, which then was disfigured."

The window itself has escaped destruction at least once, during the early part of this century. Incredibly, a hail storm knocked out every window on the north side of the courthouse save the one with the terrified image of Henry Wells!

Does the ghost of Henry Wells also walk the Pickens County Courthouse? Some say he does, particularly on those nights like that of a century and more ago when thunder rockets across the late winter landscape and lightning jabs at the old courthouse. On those evenings, folks say that the figure of Henry Wells stares out of his garret cell toward the square where the mob called for his quick hanging. If he does appear, or if it is really Henry Wells's face embedded in that window, perhaps it serves as a reminder that mob violence does not bring justice, just sorrow and ruin for those on both ends of the noose.

Do Not Disturb

When the cruise ships arrive in Skagway, Alaska, entrepreneurs are waiting at the dock in this little frontier village of seven hundred souls on the Gulf of Alaska. They offer tours of the town by horse-drawn buggy, and, for the more adventurous, helicopter flights over the Chilkoot Trail where legions of prospectors perished on the grueling trek to the Yukon gold fields in the 1890s.

But there is another who waits and watches, unseen, as the passengers disembark. She peers from behind the lace curtains of a window on the top floor of the historic Golden North Hotel. Her name is Mary. But gentle Mary never goes to the dock, never even goes outside. She is the hotel's permanent, incorporeal spirit.

Mary's lover left her in 1898. The gold stampede was on and Klondike Ike, as he came to be known, went off to make his fortune. He'd come back to marry her. He promised.

But Ike never returned. The legend is that he perished in an avalanche, buried forty feet deep in ice and snow.

Ike was not alone in his fate. Untold numbers of men died in the Chilkoot Pass. Some were buried in avalanches, others fell off rock ledges or froze to death while crawling on hands and knees across slippery glaciers. Scores of others succumbed to exposure, the flu, tonsillitis, and joint pains so severe as to cause them to scream in agony as they lay dying.

This veritable trail of death, however, didn't deter the hundreds more who were consumed by gold fever. They traveled by foot, by horse, by mule, by teams of oxen, all pulling their gear on heavily loaded sleds from one camp to the next. A strong man, by himself, and in excellent physical condition, could pull five hundred pounds of freight on a good trail in level country. And always through vicious weather.

Maybe Mary heard these stories, but she believed only the ones that her Ike told her before he left: stories of Dawson—the City of Gold—where four men could shovel as much as seven thousand dollars of pay dirt a day into the sluice boxes, of how the precious ore was found everywhere along the Yukon River. He didn't tell her that permafrost made the ground as hard as rock a foot below the streambeds of the Yukon and its tributaries, or that most prospectors were doomed to failure.

When Mary learned that Ike had died, she locked herself in her room—Number 24—at the Golden North, and she secluded herself, a beautiful eighteen-year-old woman dressed in a Victorian wedding gown, a garland of flowers entwined in her long, silky hair, and slippers encrusted with pearls on her dainty feet. There she stayed, refusing to believe that Ike would not return for her. They would be married. He *had* promised.

In Room 24 Mary died. Of tuberculosis some said; others avow she died of a broken heart. Oddly, no one ever learned Mary's last name. It doesn't really matter. Her lovely visage has lingered for a century in the old hotel, wandering the corridors, unwittingly frightening an occasional guest, but doing no real harm.

More became known about Mary's ghost after Donna Whitehead and her husband, Dave, bought the Golden North Hotel in 1978. Their story was published in the 1980s. The hotel was also home to them and to their five children. They'd been told about the hotel ghost. They smiled. Nobody believes in ghosts.

The Whiteheads kept busy for the first few weeks settling into their thirty-three-room "house." A previous owner had named each room for a Skagway gold rush family, and each room contained fine antiques: mahogany highboys, oak dressers, and four-poster canopied and brass beds. Photographs of local pioneer families lined the corridor walls. The hotel also featured a restaurant and lounge.

Before long, the Whitehead children began asking their parents about the pretty lady in the long white dress. Donna paid little attention until one day, while walking into the hotel, she happened to glance up toward the third floor. Peering through a window was a beautiful, but pensive young woman. Donna knew the room hadn't been rented. She rushed upstairs, but Number 24 was empty.

Shortly afterward, summer visitors made nervous inquiries of the innkeepers. One couple asked who was coming in and out of their room in the middle of the night. Did someone else have a key to that room? Another asked why the chandelier in their room swayed back and forth. And a honeymooning couple swore that Mary had climbed into bed with them! No one ever claimed ghosts were devoid of carnal desires.

Only one guest seemed to be genuinely frightened. A man once insisted on changing rooms. In the middle of the night he had awakened fighting for breath. Something was choking him.

Finally, the Whiteheads were prompted to arrange a séance in Room 24. Mary was becoming a bother.

Local spiritualists were brought in. They made contact with the ghost, they said, and urged her to "go to the light." There, "on the other side," she'd find her Klondike Ike, waiting for her.

Evidently Mary didn't understand. She didn't go away.

Some guests prefer that Mary stay. The legend of Mary has preceded many tourists and at least a few ask for Room 24 when they check in. They're always disappointed if the room has already been reserved or is occupied. By people.

Were the Whitehead children ever frightened? No, Mary's a friendly ghost, so friendly that one of the Whiteheads' daughters opted to sleep in the bedroom next to Mary's. While the young girl never saw Mary, she sensed her presence.

In 1984, when writer Tom Carpenter interviewed the Whiteheads to gather information about their haunted hotel and how they felt about the presence of Mary, Donna Whitehead said: "I wish I could talk to her sometime. It would be nice to tell her that it's okay to haunt us. She has a home here as long as she wants."

Charlotte's Corner

Army Colonel Roy Strom was asleep in a bedroom of old Carleton House at Fort Huachuca. His wife was out of town for a few days and his daughters had returned to school.

Suddenly a loud crash from somewhere in the house startled him awake. Colonel Strom climbed out of bed and set about trying to locate the source of the disturbance. It didn't take him long. In a daughter's now-vacant room he found an Oriental jewelry box facedown in the middle of the floor. The lacquered box's five drawers were still closed. When he picked it up, the drawers and their contents spilled out onto the floor.

Colonel Strom was puzzled. The jewelry box, which he had bought for his daughters during a tour of duty in the Far East, had been sitting on a fireplace mantel a half-dozen feet from where he found it lying on the floor. How did it get there? It would have been impossible for it to have slid off and landed where he found it.

To this day, Colonel Strom, from 1980 to 1982 the deputy commander of the U.S. Army Intelligence Center and School at Fort Huachuca, calls it the most puzzling incident during his stay at the post's *haunted* Carleton House.

Built as the post hospital in 1880, Carleton House performed that role for only a few years before being turned into housing quarters for officers, an officers' mess, post headquarters, a café, and then a schoolhouse. In more recent years, the house has been the residence of the hospital commander or other officers assigned to the base.

Fort Huachuca itself dates from about 1877 and played an integral role in the Indian wars of the 1870s and 1880s. It served as advance headquarters and supply base in the campaign against Geronimo. Later the Tenth Cavalry, headquartered at Fort Huachuca, joined Gen. John Pershing's punitive 1916 campaign into Mexico to find bandit Pancho Villa. The fort was also home to the four regiments now known collectively as the "Buffalo Soldiers," all African-American army units during the nineteenth and early twentieth centuries.

In 1954, Fort Huachuca became the site for advanced testing of electronic and communications equipment. Today, the fort is the location of the Army

Intelligence Center and School and the Army's Information Systems Command. All C130 flight training for NATO forces takes place at the fort, as does some training for the Israeli air force and army.

Carleton House is the oldest building on the base. It was named after Brig. Gen. James H. Carleton, the famed leader of the "California Column" during the Civil War. When the fort was temporarily turned over to the State of Arizona from 1947 to 1951, Carleton House was used as a vacation retreat by Governors Sidney P. Osborn and Dan E. Garvey.

Tales of ghostly apparitions and peculiar incidents have been reported by several of the families who have occupied the house.

"I never believed in ghosts. And I didn't change my mind because of 'Charlotte,'" said General Strom, who has been promoted since his tenure at Fort Huachuca.

It was his wife, Joan Strom, who first attached the name Charlotte to their resident spirit. There seems to be no historical connection between the ghost and anyone named Charlotte, other than it being "a nice 1800s sort of name," Mrs. Strom said. She wanted to be able to call the ghost by name, particularly on those occasions when the family wanted to blame "someone" for mischievous activities in the house. And most people who have observed the haunting believe there is a distinctively feminine quality about the spirit.

On the very first day the Strom family moved in, the house's reputation was impressed upon them. Several local men were hired to help the moving company unload furniture. One worker in particular seemed jittery. He would carry boxes only to the front door before setting them down. His cohorts were upset with his seeming laziness.

"I'm just not going in there," he told them. "That house is haunted."

On that same day, the Stroms piled boxes in what had been the hospital's morgue, now a bedroom a few steps below the level of the rest of the house. Sometime that evening all the boxes were torn open and the contents strewn about the room.

The family dog was blamed for that piece of mischief, but Roy Strom really isn't convinced it wasn't something else.

A day or so later, Strom was home alone when the doorbell rang. He answered but no one was outside. Twenty minutes later the bell rang again. This time, he checked all four entrances to the house, each with a doorbell, but again didn't find anyone. A few minutes later, the doorbell buzzed again. Strom figured it might be some kids pulling a prank, so he raced around the house trying to catch whoever was out there. Again unsuccessful, Strom arrived at his own solution a half-hour later when the bell rang once more. He disconnected the wiring.

Four chandeliers in the cavernous knotty pine living room, formerly the hospital's ward room, also seem to cause occasional problems. A separate switch controls each pair of lights so that when all four chandeliers are lighted both switches must be flipped on. On the day the Stroms moved in, all four lights worked. But that night Roy Strom found that three of the chandeliers were fine, but a fourth refused to operate. The next morning all four worked fine once again. That pattern was repeated throughout the family's stay at Carleton House when lights suddenly developed sporadic electrical difficulties.

Soon after they moved in, the Stroms hung a number of pictures in the dining room. The adobe walls made the job difficult, but they finished the task after a few false starts. During the night all of the pictures fell down, including a solid-brass Oriental trivet. It was bent nearly in half. Roy tried and failed to straighten it by hand the next day.

"I think I can explain almost everything that happened to us in the house," explains Roy Strom, citing poor wiring for the electrical problems and weak walls for the pictures falling. He still can't understand how the brass trivet became so badly twisted.

Joan Strom sectioned off a portion of the living room which she called "Charlotte's corner." The area is perceptibly colder than the rest of the house (which Roy says is caused by its being close to a stairwell) and the chandelier overhead has always refused to work at night.

Joan thought the ghost was that of a woman who died when the house was a hospital in the 1880s. The woman may have died in childbirth, along with her newborn child. Joan believed that the ghost doesn't think her dead child was properly taken care of or buried. While she lived in the house, Joan searched fort records and a cemetery trying to find evidence of a mother and child's death, but without success. However, records were sketchy during the frontier era, or they may have been lost over the decades. Sometimes those who died were simply buried in unmarked graves.

Two other peculiar events at Carleton House directly involved Joan Strom. Early one morning, she was at a table in the kitchen when she saw her teenage daughter, Amy, walking down an adjacent hallway. Joan called out to her, but Amy didn't stop or return her greeting, which her mother thought very unusual. She got up from her desk and went into her daughter's bedroom. Amy was fast asleep, as were her two sisters. Joan doesn't think it was Amy that she saw in the hallway that morning.

One of the "eeriest experiences of Joan's life," according to Roy Strom, took place one afternoon as she carried freshly washed linen to a bathroom closet. A swirling miasma, a kind of whitish fog enveloped her. Joan said it wasn't hot or cold, dark or damp. It didn't feel like anything, she reported.

Although the legend of the Carleton House haunting has been around for many years, only a few people, perhaps including Joan Strom, have reportedly seen the ghost. One of the first sightings involves the ten-year-old son of a neighbor family who had been sent to deliver a message to the Koenigs, residents of Carleton House before Roy and Joan Strom. The boy didn't know that the house's front door was actually located at the side. Instead, he went up the front steps and knocked. He later told his parents that Margaret Koenig walked right down the hall toward him but ignored his raps. She had blond hair and wore a long dressing gown.

Puzzled by Mrs. Koenig's actions, the boy's mother later telephoned. Mrs. Koenig insisted she and her family had only just recently returned home. No one had been in the house at the time of the boy's visit. He insisted that a woman *had* been in the hallway of Carleton House.

One of Margaret Koenig's teenage daughters may also have seen Charlotte's ghost. Nancy Koenig had been out late on a date. Earlier that evening, her mother had asked her to "check in" when she returned home. Nancy got home, went into the paneled living room and saw her mother standing at the end of the hallway. "Hi Mom," Nancy called out. "I'm home." She then went to bed. The next morning Mrs. Koenig scolded her daughter for not letting her know when she got home. Nancy insisted she had and described how she had seen her mother in the hall. But it was Charlotte that Nancy may have seen.

Col. Warren Todd, his wife Nancy, and their two sons lived in Carleton House for several years, until 1988. If the Stroms took a somewhat lighthearted view of the house's ghostly reputation, Colonel and Mrs. Todd became reluctant believers that the story of Charlotte may have been something more than a story for the faint of heart.

Warren Todd was the post's hospital commander. He is a pediatrician and mechanical engineer. "I like to look at things and try to make sense out of them," he insists.

Within a month of the family's moving in, Dr. Todd's belief in rational explanations for all events was tested.

"Something happened to the hot water heater," he remembered. The unit was located in a small room under the house reachable through a door near the front steps. "I got a key, went into the room and walked about ten feet before I said, 'I don't like it in here at all.' I never got to the hot water heater. I guess you could say I was 'psyched out.' That room was the only place that I've never wanted to go into. Nothing really happened. I just said that if I didn't have to go in there I wasn't going to."

Dr. Todd said his sense of dread upon entering that isolated cellar was palpable.

According to several psychics who contacted Dr. Todd after the incident was publicized, the little child that Charlotte is said to be looking for may have been buried in that room.

Two key events while the Todds lived at Carleton House convinced them that something else could have been in the house.

The first occurred at about three-thirty one morning while Dr. Todd studied particularly late for a course in health services administration he was taking at the University of Arizona. He sat in the kitchen; the door going into the dining room was shut. A voice that seemed to come from behind the door said, "Father! Father!" Dr. Todd jerked his head toward the sound, concerned that his six-year-old son wanted something. But then he realized that his son never called him "Father," but always "Dad" or "Daddy." He listened for anything further, but went back to his studies after a few minutes of silence thinking that perhaps it was his imagination.

After only a short while, the voice, like that of a child, again called out "Father! Father!" and this time Dr. Todd jumped up from the table, shoved the door open leading into the dining room and raced for his son's room, some twenty feet down the hallway. Little Drew was safely tucked in bed, without any indication that he had been the voice in the night.

The Todds' dog, a dachshund, was never comfortable in Carleton House. He seemed to have a sixth sense that another creature roamed the place, unseen.

Nancy Todd said: "His hackles would go up for no reason at all. We would be in the TV room and he would go racing down the hallway, barking all the time. He dug a hole in the rug at one particular spot in the hallway. There was something about that area he didn't like at all. We finally had to put chicken wire over that part of the carpet. This went on the entire time we had the dog, not just for a few days. He would quiet down for a few hours and then be back at it. There was never anything any of us could see, smell, or hear that would cause him to do that. In the TV room I definitely got the feeling that somebody was standing there, or walking near me."

Interestingly, Nancy Todd didn't feel uncomfortable in the house. "I was always very secure, even though I don't particularly like being alone. It never felt eerie, and I never wished that I didn't live there."

Nancy also heard a peculiar voice in the house. "I was out on the porch very early one morning, about five. And I heard something. I looked out to see if a jogger or walker was going by but I couldn't see anyone. The only way I can describe what I heard was that it was like a computer-voice, sort of mechanical sounding. It seemed to be saying something like 'Sleep . . . sleep.' "

Her stepson lived with the family during their stay at Fort Huachuca and reported another strange encounter. The boy's bedroom was the one in the lower level, the former hospital morgue.

"He had to cross the front paneled living room, the one with Charlotte's corner, in order to get to his room," Nancy Todd explained. "Well, he had fallen asleep in the TV room and was going back to his bedroom through the living room when he looked to his left and saw a dress. There wasn't any body connected to it, just a long dress that seemed to be standing all by itself."

The boy ran down the steps and "waited for something more to happen. But nothing did," according to Nancy Todd. The next morning he drew a picture of what he had seen: a light-colored gown with ruffled edges around the sleeves and hemline. Just the type of dress a young woman on the Arizona frontier of the 1880s might have worn.

Charlotte's corner of the Todds' living room contained a rocking chair with a baby doll on it. No one ever used the chair. Mrs. Todd thought the chair and doll might help out the ghost on those lonely nights when the "search" for her baby seemed particularly hopeless. "Charlotte is like a young puppy dog," Mrs. Todd said. "She would never do anything with a lot of people in the house."

For his part, Warren Todd doesn't *disbelieve* in ghosts as much as he once did. He actually wanted to "meet" Charlotte, hoping that he could talk to her and find out what she wanted. "If it had not been for that one early-morning episode with the child's voice and with our dog's strange behavior, I would have said it's a cute story but that's all. As a medical doctor and an engineer, I would have to say that Carleton House is worthy of inspection by parapsychologists."

Ozark Gothic

His name is Michael. Those who see him never forget his striking appearance—a muscular Swede in his early twenties with piercing blue eyes, a mane of unruly hair, and a bushy blond beard. He always dresses in work clothes, befitting his job as a carpenter.

He hangs around the Crescent Hotel, in Eureka Springs, so much that he's become something of a nuisance. A laundry maid got particularly exasperated with his antics. She had a number of rooms to clean and needed a laundry cart kept in a storeroom. She grabbed the handle to pull it out, but Michael was there and he tugged back. To and fro they went, a king of tug-of-war developing between the pair. Finally, the maid gave up, stared in the direction of her tormentor and shouted, "Michael, let go! You know I've got a lot of work to do." He released his grip and she quickly started on her rounds.

What's a Swedish carpenter doing playing tricks on unsuspecting maids in an Arkansas hotel? The answer, it seems, is that this Michael is the playful ghost of a workman killed in 1884 during the Crescent Hotel's construction.

Along with Michael, the hotel's white stone walls harbor a veritable pantheon of phantoms, including a nurse, left over from its brief tenure as a hospital; a gentleman in frock coat and top hat, who occasionally shows up for a drink at the bar; and a photograph that has floated through the air.

The hotel's changing fortunes and forbidding American Gothic appearance contribute to the tales guests and employees tell of their encounters with the supernatural.

Built on the crest of West Mountain between 1884 and 1886 at the then-substantial sum of $300,000, the Crescent Hotel was a mecca for the thousands of midwesterners drawn to Eureka Springs in the nineteenth century to soak in the city's "healing waters" bubbling from the earth.

The hotel was designed by Isaac L. Taylor, a well-known Missouri architect best remembered for the Rialto Building; the Liggett and Myers Office Building and Tobacco Factory, all in St. Louis; and for his designs at the Louisiana Purchase Exposition of 1903. Financing came from several wealthy individuals, including Powell Clayton, Arkansas's Reconstruction governor from 1868 to 1870, and later U.S. ambassador to Mexico. Clayton formed the Eureka Improvement Company to seek investors and acquire land. Financial backers included a number of officials with the Frisco Railroad.

Excursion train vacations were popular during the 1880s, and the Frisco built a spur from Seligman, Missouri, to Eureka Springs to accommodate the tourists who wanted to visit the Crescent and other hotels in the area. Liveried footman would meet guests at the railroad depot and transport them by coach up the winding hillside to the Crescent's expansive portico.

Architect Taylor combined a number of styles when he designed the Crescent. Victorian–French Gothic is the best description, although the numerous towers and jutting balconies make the hotel look like an out-of-place French château. Numerous remodelings have somewhat altered its five-story exterior. The granite block walls are eighteen inches thick, but spliced together without mortar.

A massive stone fireplace still dominates the commodious lobby, and the dining room could, at one time, hold five hundred persons for a single sitting. Electric lights were included in the hotel's original construction along with baths and modern plumbing. Indeed, it seems that no convenience known to the 1880s was denied the wealthy "carriage set" clientele. Outside, sweeping lawns, gazebos reached by winding boardwalks, tennis courts, and exquisitely landscaped gardens dominated the twenty-six acres surrounding the Crescent.

The hotel flourished until just after the turn of the century, if not through profits, for they were meager, then certainly by reputation. It was among the most popular vacation retreats in the American South, frequented by the wealthy from this country and abroad. The guest book bore the signatures of dignitaries from William McKinley and Mark Hanna to Missouri's own infamous "Uncle Joe" Cannon.

From 1902 to 1907, the Crescent was operated as a summer-only hostelry by the Frisco Railroad, which leased the property. But the gradual realization that the "magic waters" of Eureka Springs held no curative powers and the changing recreation patterns of America's wealthier classes led the railroad to abandon its attempt at innkeeping.

The next sixty years were not altogether kind to the hotel nicknamed the "Grand Old Lady of the Ozarks." Various attempts were made to keep it going year-round.

In 1908, A. S. Maddox and J. H. Phillips opened the Crescent College and Conservatory for Young Women. It served as an exclusive academy for wealthy young ladies at a time when any college education for women was unusual. During the summer months, the Crescent continued to cater to vacationers. Unfortunately, the cost of running the aging Victorian monolith overwhelmed even the staggering tuition charged students. The school closed in 1924. It reopened, briefly, from 1930 to 1934, as a junior college.

By the 1920s, the automobile was transforming the Arkansas Ozarks. One estimate was that a half million people drove to the Ozarks for vacations in 1929.

A number of individuals leased the hotel for the summer seasons after the college closed, until 1937 when an Iowa-born medical charlatan, Norman Baker, turned the hotel into a hospital and "health resort."

Baker made his fortune by inventing the Calliaphone, a calliope played with air pressure and not steam. Profits from the instrument soared into the millions of dollars by 1934. He wasn't content to settle back and enjoy his fortune. Baker fancied himself a medical expert, although he had no formal training. He claimed to have developed cures for various ailments but believed that organized medicine was trying to keep his alleged breakthroughs off the market. He thought that his "enemies" were responsible for firing shots at him and throwing bombs at a radio station he started in Muscatine, Iowa.

He founded the first Baker Hospital, in Muscatine, to honor his mother and provide a venue for his controversial treatments. He later ran for governor and U.S. senator from Iowa and financed a Mexican radio station with a signal that reached most of North America.

Baker ran afoul of the law many times with his medical beliefs, including a cure for cancer. He was convicted in Iowa in 1936 of practicing medicine without a license. The American Medical Association dismissed all of his remedies.

Nevertheless, Baker purchased the Crescent Hotel and proceeded to "remodel" the structure at a cost estimated at $50,000. His changes included ripping out the distinctive, filigreed wooden handrails and balconies outside the first three floors and replacing them with concrete porches. He repainted the lustrous woodwork with garish shades of red, orange, black, and yellow, and installed himself in a penthouse office finished in purple hues.

Baker was a paranoid. He hung machine guns on the wall of his private apartment and is said to have built secret escape passages from his hotel suite and office.

Cancer patients from his Iowa "clinic" were eventually moved to Eureka Springs, where they received "Doctor" Baker's treatments, mostly the drinking of fresh spring water from the region. His patients were "home folks, one large family," he was fond of saying. He boasted that no surgery was performed, nor were X rays taken. For that his "family" should have been grateful.

Federal authorities eventually caught up with the good doctor. He was charged with several counts of using the mails to defraud the public with his medical claims. He was convicted in 1940 and sentenced to four years in Leavenworth. The hospital closed, and with it one of the Crescent's more bizarre incarnations.

The brooding old hotel, the "Castle in the Air High Atop the Ozarks," stayed shuttered until 1946 when new investors took over. After a few shaky years, the Crescent regained some of its prominence as a package-vacation destination. Major remodeling has added shine to the marble and woodwork, but the years show the effects of the hotel's century of struggle. One writer called it "seedily elegant."

It is little wonder, then, that the place has such a reputation for being haunted.

Lynn Worley probably knows as much about the Crescent Hotel as anyone. He started working there as a bellhop in the late 1970s and eventually became a manager. He has little doubt that strange and unexplained events often take place in the old resort hotel.

"I guess it was about my second year up there," Worley explains, "when I checked some people into the hotel. I put them in room 424. At about eleven o'clock that night they came down to the front desk and wanted to leave. I asked them what the problem was and they asked me if the hotel was haunted. I said I had heard rumors that it was. Well, they told me that they were in bed watching television when 'something' walked right through the room's outside door, across the floor and into the bathroom. We let them go and they found a room at another hotel in town. Later on the desk clerk there called me and said the couple had told him the story. He asked me if it was true. I said it probably was because there are a lot of strange things that go on up here."

Another room in the hotel, number 218, however, has the distinction of being called the "ghost room." Several guests have told hotel employees of encountering strange sensations and noises while staying in that room. Lynn Worley hasn't *seen* anything peculiar there, but he said it sometimes seemed "there was somebody watching me there. Especially late at night."

On one occasion, Worley wanted to show the room to prospective guests. He inserted his key into the room lock and pushed the door open. It slammed shut in his face. He mumbled an apology to the startled visitors, but eventually got it open with no further trouble.

A salesman staying in room 218 said he was shaken awake when he felt someone trying to push him out of the bed. A few minutes later he heard footsteps scurrying across the floor.

There doesn't appear to be any unusual history to that particular room. Worley does say there is a hotel legend that the wife of one of the myriad owners stayed in the room. At one point she ran screaming downstairs, crying that there was blood splattered all over 218's walls. Several people rushed up there but found that all was as it should have been.

The most persistent ghost sighting is that of a distinguished-looking gentleman with a moustache and beard, sometimes attired in formal evening wear. The mysterious stranger favors the elegant lobby and Men's Bar, an ornate room with nineteenth-century photographs on the walls and a gleaming brass foot-railing encircling the bar.

Worley can recall one particular episode involving the hirsute specter. "During the summer we had two auditors work for us because we're so busy. One of these men left the front desk to get a drink of water in the bar, after it was closed. He told me that he saw some guy sitting on a bar stool, staring straight ahead. He didn't say anything and he didn't move. Our guy left to get his partner, who was still at the front desk. They came back and spoke to the man. They thought he was drunk."

When the odd figure didn't respond, the men decided to leave him alone and return to their work. As they glanced back over their shoulders, however, the bar stool was empty.

"One of them started searching for the man. He looked around the lobby, which is about twenty-five to thirty yards across, everywhere in that area. He was even saying out loud that they didn't mean any harm, they just wanted to talk."

From the lobby, a stairway ascends to the top floors.

"The auditor who was looking around went over to the steps. The fellow at the bar was on the second-floor landing, looking down at him. He went up but as he got to the second floor he felt something push him back down. That's when he got the manager and told him what had happened."

Robert Feagins, a Kansas architect and developer and one-time owner of the Crescent Hotel, also saw what he thought was a ghost near the lobby staircase, a figure in frock coat and frilled white shirt. His black moustache stood in sharp contrast to the waxy pallor of his face. The apparition evanesced before Feagins's eyes.

Feagins saw the same figure in Room 218. He was awakened after midnight to find an intruder standing at the foot of his bed. He seemed to radiate a kind of light. It was a grim experience, Feagins told acquaintances.

The hotel's tenure as a hospital may be responsible for another ghost.

In one episode, in July 1987, a lady was leaving her room when she saw a nurse pushing a gurney down the hall. The vision—nurse, gurney, and all—vanished. When her story got around, she was told that numerous other people had seen the same scene reenacted.

A photograph taken many years ago in room 202 is the subject of one hotel legend. No one knows who took it, or why. The picture is said to contain the image of a misty figure slouched in the closet of room 202. Only the photographer was present. Unfortunately, the picture itself is now among the missing.

Whatever lives on at the Crescent also likes to frighten folks without ever making an appearance. Early one quiet Sunday morning, desk clerk Dee Chambers looked up from her desk as the French doors on the lobby's east side swept open. A rush of cold air seemed to charge across the lobby, race along the registration desk and out the nearby doors. It left scattered papers in its wake. Chambers's puzzlement grew as she realized that the east French doors were usually locked . . . and are located directly below the infamous room 218.

An antique switchboard that has since been removed caused a considerable amount of trouble—perhaps as a result of ghostly intervention. Lynn Worley said: "In the summer we would get phone calls on that switchboard coming from a basement recreation room. There was no one on the other end because the room was unused and locked. We would check it out and find that phone had been taken off the hook. There was only one way in and out of the place and the only key to the door was kept at the front desk."

Worley himself checked out the recreation room one evening to make sure all was in order. "Of course, the phone was on the hook. I picked it up, dialed the front desk and told them it felt like somebody was in the room with me. I just wanted to get out."

He locked the door, went back upstairs, but within five minutes the switchboard buzzer went off, indicating a call coming in from the same room he had just left. Worley declined to go back downstairs.

An apparition that some believe may be "Doctor" Baker has been spotted in the same vicinity as the old recreation room, near the foot of the steps going to the first floor. He seems to be lost, staring first one way and then the other before he quickly fades from view.

A psychic who visited the Crescent Hotel several years ago said the dining room was where "everybody"—meaning the ghosts—was located. Lynn Worley agrees wholeheartedly. "You can walk late at night across that dining room, and it's as big as a basketball court, and get chilled. Other people would come up to me when I was night auditor and say it felt just like there was somebody else in there."

The hotel's aged tabby cat, Morris, was once sought out by an unseen play-mate. In December 1985, Lynn Worley and a colleague, Mike Manley, were lounging before a blazing fire in the lobby's impressive fireplace. Morris started chasing around the furniture.

"We were right behind him," Worley remembers, "but we couldn't see any-thing. He was looking up in the air, batting at something. He ran toward the dining room so we let him in there. I don't know what it was he was chasing, but it went into the dining room. He came back out about an hour later and settled down."

But a short while later, the cat got back up and resumed his playful antics. Only this time, the cat went to the front door. Whatever it was he was chasing wanted to go outside. Worley let the cat—and his friend—out the door.

The Crescent Hotel continues to provide its paying guests with genteel ac-commodations in the unique surroundings of Eureka Springs, and ample op-portunities to mingle with the temporal and spectral relics of yesteryear.

All Ghosts on Deck

October 1942. The Cunard–White Star Line's majestic flagship, the HMS *Queen Mary*, has been reoutfitted and pressed into service ferrying American troops to European battlefields. At 1,019 feet and 81,237 gross tons, the *Queen Mary* had the best time for crossing the Atlantic. Speed is critical on the ship's unescorted wartime dashes across the Atlantic, between New York City and Britain.

Nearly fifteen thousand soldiers are crowded into cramped quarters as the *Queen Mary* steams off the coast of Ireland, only a few hundred miles from her destination of Clyde. She has picked up a British convoy to protect the valuable cargo of men and materials in the German U-boat–infested waters near Ireland. The Allied Command remembers all too vividly the 1915 sinking of the *Lusitania* by a German U-20 in the Irish Sea and doesn't want a similar tragedy.

And so it was that several British destroyers patrolled the waters well ahead of the *Queen Mary*, while one antiaircraft cruiser, the 4,200-ton *Coracoa*, kept a close vigil off the *Queen*'s bow. The procedures for guarding the *Queen* called for the *Coracoa* to zigzag ahead, alternating positions from port to starboard, watching for enemy submarines that might try to slip through the forward armada.

Somehow a mistake was made. Suddenly, in broad daylight, the *Coracoa* cut across the *Queen*'s bow too late for the "monster of the sea" to slow or alter course. The *Coracoa* was sliced in half. The *Queen Mary* was relatively unscathed, although a tear in her bow allowed some water to enter a forward compartment. Watertight bulkheads prevented serious damage, or possible sinking.

The *Coracoa* went under in less than five minutes, carrying 338 sailors to their deaths. Only 101 survived. Many of the deaths were from drowning since wartime restrictions prevented the *Queen Mary* from stopping to pick up survivors. A stopped ship the size of the *Queen* presented an easy target to enemy submarines.

A naval inquiry some months later found the *Coracoa* two-thirds to blame and the *Queen Mary* one-third responsible for the tragedy.

There the matter would have ended, an exceedingly sad chapter in the *Queen Mary*'s illustrious transoceanic career, if not for a peculiar twist of fate that brought the *Queen* to Long Beach, California, in 1967. She was to be made over into a permanently anchored floating hotel and resort along that city's burgeoning oceanfront.

On board the ship's voyage to retirement was one John Smith, a tall, soft-spoken sailor with sharp features and the ruddy complexion of a man at home on the sea. Now retired as the *Queen's* last chief engineer, Smith stayed aboard while the ship was being outfitted as a tourist attraction.

But what John Smith remembers most about his job on the *Queen* is not the ocean voyage around Cape Horn to Long Beach, for the trip went smoothly enough, nor the months of tedious watch as the grand old lady of the sea was stripped of her engines and made ready for paying customers. He knew that the *Queen Mary* was a relic of an earlier age, unable to compete with luxurious passenger jets. What was a top speed of thirty knots, after all, when travelers could reach Europe in a matter of hours, not days?

What bothered John Smith the most then, and does to this day, were the unexplained sounds and phantom voices he heard on the ship, all originating near the bow of the *Queen Mary* . . . in almost the precise location where the *Coracoa* had punched a hole in her iron skin nearly four decades earlier.

Smith is precise in his memories.

"The *Queen Mary* has a short bow, eight decks high, and a division a short ways after the bow, about eight feet, but it's only a partial division," Smith said, sitting in an elegant conference room aboard the refurbished *Queen*. "Then there's a full division about thirty feet back. At the bow there are six decks of vertical stairs, with very dim lighting, that go down near the bottom of the ship. It's the structural area so they can't store anything, too many girders and beams in the way.

"On the last voyage I still didn't know much about the history of the ship, not even everything the general public knew. One of my jobs was to keep the ship from sinking. I'd roam the ship with a flashlight . . . and at times I'd go up on the top deck at the bow and look down this six-deck vertical ladder. I was looking down to make sure that there was a way to get down with ropes," Smith noted, adding that his regular patrols continued for several months after the *Queen* reached her berth in Long Beach.

When he reached the bow, Smith would sometimes hear water rushing, as if pipes were breaking, or the hull had sprung a leak. Smith would descend the ladder in the forward section of the ship, but the "gurgling and rushing" sound would gradually fade away.

"I would be really mystified and wonder what I heard and where it had come from. Nothing was ever wrong, there were no problems," Smith said.

"And then I would hear a strange tapping noise. Now the ship was tied up at the pier, near the naval base, so there was no reason for this," he said. At sea, Smith realized the noises he heard would have been too quiet to have been audible above the pounding of the waves. "I definitely heard it. I checked the ship, I looked over the sides, there was no one around and no activities going on. I can't explain it."

The most unnerving experience for John Smith, however, came on the heels of that rhythmic tapping and the seeming rush of water.

Voices.

Voices as if from a distance. Smith could hear them crying, moaning, shrieking, even laughing sometimes. Always men's voices.

When that phenomenon occurred, Smith left as quickly as possible. "I know that common sense says that something structural or mechanical was causing it, but it happened again and again. Probably seven or eight times."

It was after he retired that John Smith read a history of the *Queen Mary*, including an account of the grisly collision with the cruiser *Coracoa*. Although part of the *Queen's* bow was torn open, the ship was able to continue on to Scotland for temporary repairs. It was eventually returned to Boston and dry-docked while the bow was permanently repaired before the *Queen* returned to service.

"If I had known about that, I'd say it all ties in, but I didn't know about [the collision] until years later," Smith acknowledges.

He often *felt* as well as heard something during his watches. "You'd hear the thump, then the vibration, the water gurgling and then the crying and shrieking," Smith said. "I felt vibrations, like going over a washboard. But it was always more or less in that pattern. The thumping noise always first, never clear, it seemed garbled. When one sound faded out, then another faded in. Maybe the whole thing took sixty seconds at most."

From his research, Smith knows that the mysterious voices came from the same area of the *Queen Mary* that would have struck the *Coracoa*. He believes that what he heard on all those occasions was the ghostly, albeit invisible, reenactment of that tragic disaster.

John Smith also encountered the ghost of British statesman Winston Churchill on the *Queen Mary*, or at least the remnants of smoke from Sir Winston's famous cigars.

During World War II, while the *Queen* usually carried American and Allied forces to Europe, a special stateroom was outfitted for the wartime British prime minister for his frequent trips to Washington, D.C. Sir Winston preferred to travel by ship rather than by air.

A quarter of a century later, the prime minister's old stateroom, M115, was given over as a temporary office for Smith during the *Queen's* renovation in Long Beach.

"I definitely smelled smoke in that room, cigar smoke," Smith recalls. "He had a favorite brand of Cuban cigars that they used to sell at the coffee shop on board. They probably even called them Winston Churchill cigars. Nothing smelled quite like it. But there it was. I recognized it. Right now, twenty years later, I would recognize that smell, almost more than any other."

The odor was most prevalent after hours, when everyone except Smith and a few others had left the ship.

"I could see the smoke near the ceiling. The ventilators were not operating then so there was no artificial ventilation. It all came through the porthole, or a door if it was open. And if the door was closed at night, and the porthole was shut, somehow the smoke got in there."

The smoke didn't last. It would gradually disappear, along with the cigar odor, in about ten minutes, Smith said. There was no apparent pattern. "It happened often, but not every evening. Maybe three or four days in a row nothing, then it would come again. As soon as I smelled it I would go out in the corridor and look around in each direction. I assumed that somebody maybe even blew smoke through the keyhole, but it wasn't that."

As far as Smith could tell, no workman renovating the ship smoked cigars while aboard, and certainly not the distinctive brand Sir Winston preferred.

The screams of dying sailors and the sight and smell of cigar smoke aren't the only peculiar remembrances of retired chief engineer John Smith. One of the most well-known ghost legends on the old ship concerns not people, but a handsome Irish setter dog whose barking echoes even to this day. John Smith knows the story well.

"The kennel was up on the sundeck. Unless you were a VIP like Elizabeth Taylor—she could keep her dogs in her stateroom—you would have to put your dog in the kennel during the trip. An old English gentleman always traveled with this beautiful Irish setter. Real friendly he was. He'd wag his tail when strangers came up. The dog would walk every day by his master up and down the deck. They had a regular walkway there. He didn't even need a leash, the dog would just follow and stay right with him.

"One night this dog started howling. The kennel attendant was called by security to see what was wrong. They couldn't control him and he howled and howled, and scratched at the cage which he had never done before. So the kennelman let him out. He didn't know if the dog had been injured, needed food or water, or what was wrong. The dog kept running around the kennel. It was fenced in so he couldn't get out, but he was always scratching at the exit gate. Anyway, the kennelman sent the security guard down to wake up the Englishman to bring him up to see what he could do to control the dog. They didn't really want to disturb him at three o'clock in the morning, but they had to keep the dog quiet.

"The security guard found the man dead in his room." John Smith believes the dog somehow sensed his master's death.

Shortly after the *Queen Mary* arrived in Long Beach, Smith heard what he believed was a dog barking on the sundeck. Always, the barking was indistinct, a distant baying that was directionless. It seemed to emanate from the old kennel area, yet when Smith and his colleagues got there, it seemed remote again, almost as if the spectral dog had run to another part of the ship.

Nancy Wozny was a guide and a security officer during the *Queen Mary*'s early years as a tourist attraction in Long Beach. Now an investigator for a southern California insurance company, Wozny speaks of her uncanny experiences on the ship with the assurance of one who is used to dealing with facts and details. While John Smith never saw an apparition, Wozny had an unnerving encounter with an actual ghost.

"My job as a lead guide was to close up an area after the tour. I'd turn off the tapes, or the lights, or reattach the chains, whatever needed to be done. I was pretty sure I was the last one in this particular tour," Wozny said.

The tour had taken her to the engine room. She had completed riding up the first escalator to the main deck and was halfway up a second escalator when it happened.

"I felt someone behind me. I turned around and saw a man standing behind me. I figured I'd missed somebody, or that he was crew because his overalls were dirty. He had a beard, a beautiful beard, short black hair, very round black eyes and very white skin, grossly white. And blue overalls. I kept thinking he was maintenance. I thought he came up behind me and I just must not have heard him," Wozny remembers.

The man wore no expression, looked straight ahead as if Wozny didn't exist.

"That was about two seconds from the top," Wozny said, adding that she reached the top and stepped aside to let the man pass.

He wasn't there.

Not a word was exchanged between Wozny and the man. Indeed, she turned around because she "sensed" his presence.

"I didn't feel him touch me, but I just felt I wasn't alone. He was three-dimensional. Very vivid."

Could it *have* been a maintenance man playing a practical joke on the young guide, something that wasn't all that unusual? No, answers Wozny.

"There's no place for him to go, he couldn't have reversed himself. It was my job to turn off the escalator. That's why I was doing what I was doing. I was about three steps from the top, I turned and saw him. I turned back thinking I had missed somebody, stepped aside to let him go by, and when I looked back he was gone," Wozny said.

There may be a reason for the phantom crewman's visit. According to some sources, a crew member had somehow been crushed in one of the watertight doors during the ship's heyday. His name was John Peder, although the spelling of the last name may have been different. Wozny thinks the man on the escalator could very well have been Peder.

On modern cruise ships, swimming pools are built on open decks to take full advantage of the sun. Passengers can while away their afternoons sitting in deck chairs only a few feet away from the soothing waters of a freshwater pool.

The *Queen Mary*, too, has a swimming pool, but it is as different from those found on today's ships as the opulent mahogany and brass staterooms on the *Queen* are from the relatively spartan cabins on ships that cater to tourists on a budget. The *Queen*'s swimming pool is quite small, but installed in an area the size of a gymnasium deep within the bowels of the ship. There was little reason to build a swimming pool on an open deck for a vessel plying the North Atlantic.

The pool is kept half-filled with water to prevent cracks and to show modern visitors what passengers in the 1930s considered a luxurious touch. Soft, indirect lighting casts subtle shadows on the art deco designs, lending an altogether ethereal feeling to the area. Two stairways lead down to the pool deck from a spacious entryway. Sturdy columns surround the pool, rising dozens of feet to the ceiling above. Even a diving board stands unattended at the pool's deep end.

But all is *not* quiet here. Several current and former employees say that a woman swims in that pool, a bather who could very well be a ghost.

The former guide and security officer Nancy Wozny is one who has seen the ghostly bather.

"It was almost like I had caught her in another dimension," Wozny explained. "I couldn't see her face, but I saw her form, I saw the bathing suit. But everything was absolutely void of color. She wasn't transparent, though she didn't appear before my eyes and she didn't disappear before my eyes."

Wozny was near the railing at the entrance, gazing down at the pool, when she saw the woman. "I thought she had stepped back behind the pillar. I disconnected the rope [blocking the stairs] very quickly and ran down, because I thought it was a tourist."

The startled young guide quickly looked behind the column, only to be dumbfounded by finding absolutely no one. She noted that the other doors leading into the pool area were closed, with no other way for the intruder to have escaped.

Lester Hart is a laconic, plainspoken man who works as an engineer on the *Queen Mary*. He, too, has seen a mysterious woman in the swimming pool area, but his report of what happened to him in 1983 is quite different from that of Nancy Wozny.

"I walked into the starboard [right] side of the pool and she was on the port side and just disappeared," Hart said. "From what I could tell she was thirty-five to forty years old and blond. She was in a white flowing gown, like a nightgown or maybe an evening dress with long sleeves. She was standing by the double doors, and it was as if she turned around and vanished." The doors Hart describes lead from the pool to an area of the ship known as Shaft Alley, named after the giant shafts that ran from the four, single-reduction-geared turbines, each producing 160,000 horsepower, to the immense, eighteen-foot propellers. Shaft Alley has had its share of mysterious events.

"She looked right straight at me," Hart said of the woman near the doors. "I looked at her and then she turned away, she was right at the corner of the door, a hazy image. It wasn't a person. It startled me. You hear about these things but you never expect to see them."

Hart had been working the graveyard shift when he saw the apparition at about three o'clock in the morning, but dismisses the notion that his mind was playing tricks on him.

A second incident in the pool area provided Hart with additional visible evidence of a ghostly presence. He had been working in one of the *Queen*'s maintenance shops, a dozen yards down a corridor from the swimming pool.

"I came out of the shop and it sounded like somebody was swimming in the pool. I walked up there and there was nobody around. The water was moving and on the port side, where the ladder comes out of the pool, there were wet footprints going out through the double doors that go to C deck and they stopped. Well, I turned around and started up to the next deck and there's wet footprints going up the steps. They vanished too."

More puzzled than frightened by the singular indication that someone had taken an unauthorized dip in the pool, Hart tried to find some rational explanation.

"If somebody was playing games, they weren't going to stand there and get dried off and change clothes. If they're soaking wet, the water's going to be there, but the footprints just stopped. It was just like when you get out of a swimming pool."

It's not unusual for overnight guests in the hotel section of the ship to slip into the pool area for a swim. But not this time. Hart said it took him less than a minute to walk from the shop to the pool, making it impossible, he believes, for two people—there were *two* sets of footprints—to exit the water and run off.

Two other factors make a human explanation questionable. The incident occurred between two and four o'clock in the morning, certainly very late for anyone to be roaming the ship. Also, an alarm system, installed to prevent unauthorized persons from entering certain sections of the ship at night, would have been triggered if someone had left the pool to go topside. Hart himself tripped the alarm during his search for the mysterious intruders.

According to Richard Kerlin, a spokesman for the *Queen Mary*, a woman passenger drowned in the pool during the 1960s. Who she was and under what circumstances she died are not known, but that fact alone makes the sightings of a ghostly bather even more plausible.

Tough, direct, no-nonsense. Those words fit the character of Tom Hennessy, a veteran reporter and columnist for the *Long Beach Press-Telegram* with the solid build of a former prizefighter. He is a newspaperman of the old school, hard-bitten and often cynical, a figure who seems to have stepped from the pages of Damon Runyon.

Hennessy brought his notebook and skepticism aboard the *Queen Mary* one night several years ago to check out the oft-repeated tales of ghostly sightings. He went away not entirely convinced that there wasn't something to them.

"I had been hearing these ghost stories, and most of them seemed to be connected with locales on the ship where people had died, or had come to some violent end," Hennessy explained. "So, I had arranged to be locked up in two of these places, the swimming pool area and then what's known as Shaft Alley."

The reporter spent about a half-hour, alone, in each place in the middle of the night. Guards had locked all the doors and activated the electronic alarms to prevent anyone else from entering.

His vigil near the swimming pool proved uneventful. He found a dressing room light blazing, but that he attributes to a forgetful tour guide or bad wiring.

Shaft Alley proved to be a different story. Hennessy doesn't completely accept the notion that what happened to him there proves the *Queen* is haunted, but it left him with lingering questions.

"I started along the catwalk [in Shaft Alley] and I passed an oil drum. I walked down to the end and I came back and there were two oil drums there. I said to myself, now, there must have been two at the very beginning, except I didn't know that for sure. I wondered about that.

"The other thing that happened was that I heard very distinctly a voice and I was able to make out a few words, something like 'Close the door.' Later on there was a noise, which seemed to be almost like a voice, except as I would approach it, it would die away. Then as I would leave I'd hear it again. But at one point I distinctly heard words. I told this to the guard later on. I said it must have been a voice coming through the ventilation system and he told me we were two decks away from where anybody was. He also said not to worry, I wasn't the first person who heard this sort of thing."

Hennessy is still a skeptic about ghosts and moving oil drums, allowing himself to say only that his investigation of the *Queen Mary* was "an interesting experience." He continues to be intrigued by the stories and admits some of them "are really tough to explain."

Veteran *Queen Mary* security officer Billy Thompson echoes those who can't explain the phenomena.

"The pool is an amazing place because all of those doors around it are on the alarm. Anybody that sets foot through those doors triggers the sensors. The alarms would go off at night, we'd go in there and there was no one. We even staked it out, to see if, maybe, somebody's down there trying to steal something."

Thompson and other guards would hide in the old dressing rooms or showers hoping to catch the culprits. They never did, and, if one is to believe the accounts, probably couldn't if they tried. So far as is known, a ghost has never been captured.

"All of a sudden alarms would go off," Thompson said of his late-night hunting expeditions, "and yet nobody's there. We saw water on the floor by the pool where it was dry before, and the water's moving."

At other times, Thompson would edge even closer to the pool so that all he had to do was look around a corner to get a clear view of anyone swimming. Then he would hear a splash, as if someone had jumped in the water. He quickly thrust his head out and although the water was roiling, the pool was quite empty.

"You figure that one out," Thompson challenged.

Inexplicable activity is not limited to the *Queen Mary*'s first-class swimming pool, Shaft Alley, escalators, or bow. Nor does it appear that the hauntings are always deliberate, occurring numerous times in a single place. Sometimes the acts are random, more indicative of "traditional" poltergeist activity.

Ellie May is a waitress of long standing aboard the *Queen*. She has worked over the years in all of the ship/hotel's dining areas, including the elegant main dining salon where sumptuous Sunday brunches are a Long Beach tradition, and the Pig 'n' Whistle, a quaint tavern modeled after an old English pub.

"I've seen plates fly clear across the room and break all to pieces for no reason," Ellie May said. "They landed right in the middle of the floor." The early morning hours, before the restaurants opened to customers, were the times when she witnessed most of these events.

"There was me and a gal named Peggy, she's not here anymore, and she was standing right by the steam table. I thought that poor child was going to faint right there. I was talking to her and 'it' just lifted them up and threw them like a Frisbee. About three of them, just a few seconds apart, from the steam table to the middle of the room, about ten feet."

In late spring 1989, Ellie May had a second encounter with poltergeist activity. Shortly after she arrived for work at five o'clock in the morning, Ellie May heard the scream of a waitress in a workroom near the Pig 'n' Whistle.

"Somebody tried to pick up the table where she was sitting," Ellie May said.

"It just started shaking and she screamed at the top of her lungs. She was scared to death. I came in and found the pictures on the wall upside down, the clock hanging upside down by the front door. I just put them back, but the chef told me I should have had a camera so I could tell security about it."

Ellie May finds it impossible to believe that the other waitress or someone unknown could have caused either bit of mischief. She was usually at work a few minutes before five, preparing for the day's customers alone or with another early-arriving waitress. It would be extremely difficult for an intruder to get in without Ellie May's knowledge.

Shawn Duke is a former guide who did quite a bit of exploring on the old passenger liner to satisfy his interest in its intriguing history. He found one section that caused him to listen more attentively to the tales told by other employees.

"That was up in the bow of the ship, just after [behind] the bos'un's locker," Duke said. He visited that room frequently, but never experienced what he felt on one particular day.

"It was cold, meat-locker cold. It was a hot day and ships' hulls are not air-conditioned. They get very hot in the summer. I didn't stay that day, I went in and came right back out."

Duke described that part of the ship as a working area for crew members. It's off-limits to visitors and normally locked. The sudden cold struck Duke as being more odd than frightening. But, he still can't explain what could have caused such a plunge in temperature inside the hull of an enormous ship on a simmering summer day.

Among the entertainments for day visitors and overnight guests aboard the *Queen Mary* hotel are tours of various parts of the ship. Brave souls can venture through haunted Shaft Alley and the nearby first-class swimming pool, or they might wish to view a furnished luxury suite as it was decorated in the 1930s. On either tour, cheerful guides explain the intricacies of life among the well-to-do travelers of a half-century ago.

What they may *not* explain is the case of the disembodied voice Nancy Wozny heard as a chief guide some years ago.

On this day, it was Wozny's assignment to trail each tour group, shutting doors and turning off lights in the suite exhibit as the last of the tourists passed her way in order to prevent anyone from getting lost or, even worse, vandalizing the exhibit.

Nancy Wozny was listening to the tour guide explain the luxuries of first-class passage when she was startled out of her reverie.

"I thought it was a joke being played on me," Wozny said. "I was in the suite exhibits. The tour guides were on one side of the wall to that area and they were to bring the group around past me. I was going to go ahead and lock the front doors after them. I was listening to her talk about the suite exhibit, I had my clipboard in my hand, and I leaned against the wall. Just as I touched it came 'Nooooo!' The hair stood up on the back of my neck, but I thought it was my supervisor who'd crept up and was trying to scare me. I reeled around to hit him and he wasn't there."

In fact, no one was there who could have uttered that single, clear, frightening word—"Noooooo!" The voice came from directly behind her, at the instant she touched the woodwork. "The voice sounded human because I thought it was my supervisor," Wozny remembered. A wall phone nearby proved that it wasn't her boss. "I ran to the phone and I called him and he answered it." That would have been five decks down and a thousand feet away, she estimates.

Nancy Wozny filed that incident away until a friend of hers, now deceased, had a strange experience in the same suite exhibit area.

Wozny explained that her friend was standing near a three-way mirror on hinged doors that opened into a small room. Suddenly, the doors started to rattle and then flew open. Two beams of light, like a pair of headlamps, bounced up and down in the dim, closetlike room.

"She was hysterical when it happened," Wozny said. Once she got the woman calmed down, Wozny said they began comparing notes and realized they had both encountered these unknown forces in approximately the same place in the suites exhibit. That's when they started telling other employees of their experiences.

"I'm not spiritual, I don't necessarily believe in these things, but I know what I saw and I can't explain it," Wozny said.

She definitely believes the frightening story told by two other guides who came to her in tears one afternoon. Both had been on the engine room platform in Shaft Alley when they distinctly heard a man clearing his throat, as if he wanted to call attention to himself. Only they couldn't see anyone else to pay attention to! When a chain hanging from a ceiling pipe started to arc through the air, the pair fled.

"They both saw it and they were both hysterical. They wouldn't go near the area again," Wozny said. "It scared them to death."

The engine room is near the watertight door where, legend has it, Queen Mary crewman John Peder was crushed to death. Coincidence? Or the desperate attempt by a trapped spirit to make contact with the world of the flesh?

The HMS Queen Mary, along with Howard Hughes's nearby wooden airplane, the Spruce Goose (which flew only once, for a short distance), enjoyed a popularity on the Long Beach waterfront equaled by only a few other southern California attractions. Each year thousands of tourists queued up to tour the grand dame of the seas, spend a night or weekend luxuriating in one of the exquisitely decorated stateroom suites in the Queen Mary Hotel, or partake of a sumptuous Sunday brunch in the elegant first-class dining room.

Her engines have long since been removed and permanent gangplanks and cables anchor the ship tightly to a visitor's center, but the Queen Mary still exudes a majesty, an almost palpable sensation of power in repose. A visitor need not even shut his eyes to imagine the gleaming black and red hull splitting the turbulent whitecaps as the ship raced across the ocean, heavy black smoke pouring from her triple smokestacks as she tried to outrace the inexorable passage of an era.

The ghostly crewman on the escalator, a bather who refuses to leave the pool, echoing voices of doomed sailors, and all the other peculiar phenomena are also part of the Queen Mary's captivating legacy. And so it should be, that a ship which touched so many lives should harbor secrets beyond the ken of mere mortals.

POSTCRIPT: Press accounts in mid-1992 asserted that the *Queen Mary* might be out of business by the end of the year, unless a new buyer could be found for the luxury liner.

Although the City of Long Beach paid over $400 million to purchase and restore the ship nearly three decades ago, it has been a money loser ever since, despite being the city's number one tourist attraction. The Walt Disney Corporation reportedly lost $7 million annually after taking over the ship's management in 1988. Disney had offered to continue operating the restaurants and shipboard leisure facilities until a new buyer, if any, could be found. The hotel closed on October 1, 1992.

On December 22, 1992, the Long Beach City Council voted to take over the *Queen Mary* from the independent Harbor Commission, which had wanted to sell the ship to a group of Hong Kong investors.

A nonprofit corporation was formed in January 1993 to operate what is now called the Queen Mary Seaport, a fifty-five-acre park which includes the ship, a British-themed shopping center, and a children's playground. While Disney had charged almost eighteen dollars to tour the ship and the adjacent *Spruce Goose* (now moved to an Oregon aviation museum), admission to visit the ship and its numerous exhibits is now free. The city hopes to make up for the lost gate revenue through income generated by the *Queen*'s restaurants, bars, and hotel, which have all reopened.

The grand old lady of the high seas—and her ghosts—seem to have cheated oblivion once again.

Little Girl Lost

Kim Gilbert sipped a mixed drink and chatted with her friend Stephanie Smith at a cozy table for two near the glowing embers in a large stone fireplace. The bar in the Brookdale Lodge, where the two sat, had just closed for the night. It was two-thirty in the morning.

Kim is the resident manager and head bartender. Her parents own the grand old central California tourist hotel. Stephanie Smith was a cocktail waitress there. Both women laughed and chatted about the evening just past and some of the characters they'd encountered.

Adjacent to the barroom is the lodge's main lobby. The fireplace next to which Kim and Stephanie sat fronts on both the lobby and bar. An open hallway leads from the lobby to the bar entrance as well as to several other rooms, including the spectacular Brook Room, which features a stream running through it.

The women's first drinks sat barely touched on the table separating them, their casual conversation about their patrons and Kim's plans for renovation of more immediate interest. One of Kim's management rules limits all employees, herself included, to two drinks per night when on duty.

As Kim glanced around the dimly lit bar she couldn't help but be pleased that in just over six months, she and her parents were well on their way to restoring the grandeur that was once Brookdale Lodge. Beginning in the 1920s, the lodge had served as a popular resort for San Franciscans, located as it is near Boulder Creek, in the scenic San Lorenzo Valley a dozen miles inland from Santa Cruz. The lodge fell on hard times in more recent decades and had been closed for six years. Kim's father, San Francisco police officer Bill Gilbert, bought Brookdale Lodge and eight acres in 1990 for a reported $2 million. The Gilberts are long-time real estate investors.

Despite her hectic schedule, including responsibilities as the parent of two young children, Kim had succeeded in reopening the lodge's bar and most of the guest rooms. A loyal cadre of office staff, waitresses, and motel employees were enthused about Brookdale's "new" look.

Seated next to the faint glow of the fireplace's single smoldering log, Kim occasionally glanced through the mesh screen of the open fireplace into the lobby. Several lamps cast a warm glow across new carpeting. An antique Victorian oval ottoman, covered in red velvet, graced the center of the lobby. Several lighted display cases held old news clippings about the lodge and numerous autographed pictures of Hollywood stars, many of whom once frequented it. The front door had been locked for several hours; bar patrons used a separate entrance.

Abruptly, something in the lobby caught Kim's attention. It was a slight movement coupled with a faint rustling, as if someone was walking across the lobby.

Someone was. That's what startled Kim Gilbert. No one should have been out there, including her children, who had been tucked in upstairs bedrooms hours before.

"I looked out and thought that Melanie was up. I wondered what she was doing standing in front of the display case. She's four years old and would never just walk out there and stand. She would have walked directly into the bar and sat on my lap," Kim said.

"People have said to me, 'Oh, come on, it was probably a silhouette from the fire.' But there's no way I'm going to mistake a shadow for my child."

Although it was late at night, the lobby was illuminated by three separate lamps. She could clearly see all of the lobby.

"I looked up because out of the corner of my eye I saw something. And I heard a kind of pittering, too. I think that sound was what caught my attention. When I looked out, she was walking in kind of her own world, like nobody else mattered. She was walking around, but she never faced me, I never got to see the front of her face. Her back was always turned to me. Even when she was sideways, she was looking down at the floor the whole time. Like she was looking for something on the floor. Then she walked right into the case."

And disappeared.

Kim still believed it was her daughter, Melanie, who had somehow slipped downstairs from her second-floor bedroom. "I wondered what she was doing there, standing in front of the case. She knows where I am and would have come directly into the bar. I didn't hear a door open, either."

The child Kim saw had shoulder-length blond hair fixed in a flip curl. She was about six years old and dressed in what appeared to be a long dress or nightgown.

The entire episode lasted a scant few seconds. The child appeared as a three-dimensional figure, but Kim said she wasn't "as solid as you or I." The fire screen Kim was looking through, coupled with the soft lighting in the lobby, produced a kind of otherworldly quality to the child. Yet she was certain, at first, that it was her daughter.

She also had the sense that by sighting the little girl, she was intruding on some private scene. "Looking back I can say that I did feel strange. There was something weird about looking out there seeing her. It just didn't feel right."

After the girl seemed to vanish, Kim quickly got up and checked the lobby. Finding no one hiding anywhere, she ran upstairs to check on her children. "At the time it didn't occur to me that it was anything but Melanie," Kim remembered. "That it was anything out of the ordinary. It first hit me when I started going up the stairs and the door up there was locked. I thought either Melanie is hiding or I saw something really strange down there. I unlocked the door and the first thing I saw was her laying in bed. I went up to her and poked her. I looked in her eyes to see if she was faking. But she was sound asleep."

How did Kim explain to Stephanie what had transpired?

"When I came back I tried to explain it to her, but she just said 'Oh, wow!' " Kim couldn't quite get across to her friend what had just transpired.

"Never did it scare me, though, never. I came back down here and I sat and had my other drink with Stephanie and talked. That was it."

Kim Gilbert was very perceptive. What she saw that night in the lobby of Brookdale Lodge was not her daughter, nor anyone she knew. What she apparently saw was Sarah Logan, a child of six or so. Old-timers know all about the little girl. They describe her precisely as Kim saw her. The problem here is that little Sarah has been dead for nearly seventy years.

Soon after its completion in 1923 by developer Dr. F. K. Camp, Brookdale Lodge became one of the premier resorts in California. Politicians such as Herbert Hoover and Cordell Hull, and wealthy industrialists and Hollywood stars— including Marilyn Monroe, Joan Crawford, Tyrone Power, Rita Hayworth, Hedy Lamarr, and Mae West—stayed at the sprawling redwood resort during summer vacations. A world-class trout stream (President Hoover fished it), the towering redwoods, a lively nightlife in nearby Santa Cruz, and a relaxed lifestyle were the attractions for the famous and near-famous.

The lodge is on the site of an earlier wayside, the Brookdale Hotel. A prominent local developer and district judge, John Logan, built the original hotel in the 1880s to attract vacationers. He was a devout Christian who forbade smoking and drinking in his rooms. The judge's most famous legacy, however, is the loganberry, which he developed while living in the area.

According to a published history of the community of Brookdale, by 1905 the tiny village was the second most popular resort destination in California. Each summer, trains would disgorge upwards of seven hundred families—nannies and pets in tow—for the "season." Most were from San Francisco and Oakland. Many stayed at the old Brookdale Hotel and, later, Brookdale Lodge.

During the succeeding years, the lodge changed owners several times. Dr. Camp sold it to A. T. Cook and W. G. Smith. A consortium of San Franciscans bought it in 1951.

The attractions of Brookdale Lodge to generations of vacationers are obvious. A rambling, almost Bavarian-style design gives the lodge a Continental flavor. Native redwood and stone construction were used throughout. The exterior looked suitably weathered to blend in with the rugged terrain.

The lodge's most famous attraction is the Brook Room, a football-field-sized dining- and ballroom actually built *over* Clear Creek. Unique grated openings allow the water to flow in and out of the room. The natural streambed runs through a depression in the center of the room; a bridge connects the two sides of the room. Balconies that can be used for dining overlook the large hall.

The Brook Room is not the only unique feature at the lodge. Until 1972, the lodge had an indoor, kidney-shaped swimming pool. A drowning that year forced its closure. Below the pool was the "Mermaid Room," a bar that featured a large window for underwater viewing of the swimmers.

Brookdale Lodge burned to the ground on October 24, 1956, the third major fire in the area that year. The loss at the lodge was estimated at $200,000. It was rebuilt to its original specifications and reopened a short time later. Sadly, old records and photographs of the lodge were destroyed in the fire.

The owner during the 1950s, a man named Barney Morrow, also owned the Brookdale Inn, a popular restaurant directly across the street from the lodge. Morrow jointly operated the two properties for several years.

There are, of course, numerous legends connected with the lodge and its intriguing history, some of which involve ghosts, and there are others that, though not supernatural, are equally fascinating.

One such tale involves a secret tunnel. According to manager Kim Gilbert, a construction crew rebuilding the driveway in front of the lodge in 1990 accidentally discovered the old tunnel when one of their machines started sinking into the ground. Gilbert said the tunnel was about seven feet tall and supported with beams. Though no one ventured inside, it appeared to run from the lodge to the former Brookdale Inn directly across the highway. She had no idea where the entrances to the tunnel were located in either the lodge or the inn, which the Gilberts also own.

Kim Gilbert believes that the inn may have been a bordello in the 1920s and 1930s, or a supply depot for illegal whiskey. Women and booze might have been secretly transported between the inn and lodge without alerting local officials.

She said that another legend holds that men would watch "the girls" swim in the lodge's pool through the underwater window in the Mermaid Room. The women allegedly had numbered tags on their backs which the men would use in identifying their choice for an evening's entertainment.

There is little in the way of verification for these tales and most others connected with Brookdale Lodge, since most records were destroyed in the 1956 fire, or, in the case of supposed illegal prostitution and bathtub gin, no records probably existed anyway.

The existence of the tunnel, however, does hint at some mysterious enterprise. How else to explain such a sophisticated, secret underground passageway linking structures just a hundred yards away from each other?

During the 1960s and 1970s, the owners of Brookdale Lodge tried to maintain its once-glorious reputation, but two devastating events hinted at darker days to come.

The 1972 drowning of a thirteen-year-old girl in the swimming pool precipitated its closing. Without the unique indoor pool, there was one less reason for vacationers to stop there.

Then in 1982, Clear Creek roared over its banks following torrential rains and flooded the lodge. Mud caked the floor, and debris littered nearly every square foot of the building.

Brookdale Lodge finally closed in 1984 and would remain locked until Bill and LeAnn Gilbert reopened it in 1990.

Actually it was Kim's mother, LeAnn, who seemed to be the driving force in their family's purchase.

"My mom fell in love with the place," Kim recalled. "She was going on and on about it. She told my dad and me all the time that there was somebody guiding her" to buy the resort complex.

Bill Gilbert worked twenty-two years on the San Francisco police force on assignments ranging from beat cop in the notorious Tenderloin district to traffic commander, according to his daughter.

But the family's roots in the Brookdale community are quite deep. Kim's grandparents owned a cabin outside Brookdale. She recalls visiting the area many times as a child.

During their first year of ownership, the Gilberts spent well over $100,000 refurbishing the lodge and remodeling over one hundred condominium units and motel rooms. The main lobby and bar were finished first, followed by the Brook Room and the Fireside Room, the latter a large hall used for weekend dances and private parties. The Brook Room is especially favored by wedding couples for their receptions.

The Gilberts hoped to turn the old Mermaid Room and the swimming pool into a health club and fitness center.

From the moment Kim Gilbert moved to Brookdale from San Francisco, where she was a recent graduate of San Francisco State University, she had heard the stories and legends connected with the haunting of Brookdale Lodge.

"At first I thought it was probably some spooky, creeped-out place that would suck the people in as they came by," Kim said with a laugh, making the lodge sound like a cross between *The Amityville Horror* and a Charles Addams cartoon. "Now I don't feel that way. I used to work, go up to my apartment and sleep. I didn't even go around to look at everything. But I always had an eerie feeling that I was being watched. There's definitely a feeling that something happened here. Now people always say to me that they know that I'm part of the lodge now. I tell them not to say that. It's like my ghost will be floating around here some day! I just want to be normal."

Her encounter with the little girl in the lobby was not the first solid indication that ghosts roamed Brookdale Lodge.

"Walking through late at night I've seen shadows, I've heard footsteps a lot. My kids weren't up and it wasn't cats, either. I've heard voices. Many times I've heard voices, especially in the Brook Room.

"Whether the creek's rushing, or whether it's dead calm, you hear those voices, people are talking. There's the clinking of glasses and plates."

Music, too. "I heard that twice," Kim said. "Once when I was sitting on the dance floor [in the Fireside Room] I heard very faint music. I heard it, too, in the pool room. Big band music, like Tommy Dorsey." Because she heard it only twice in the first year and as it was very late at night, she doubts that it was coming from a radio or passing vehicle.

Kim is very specific about the night stalkers in the old lodge. "It's somebody walking very slowly, very methodically. Everywhere. But especially upstairs in the conference room. Definitely. You hear it up there a lot." The conference room is off a second-floor hallway in the main lodge. It's used now for small parties and meetings.

Although Kim isn't ready to finger ghosts as the only source of problems in her establishment, she's hard pressed to explain the noises. One evening when the phantom feet were particularly loud, she investigated. "I took three guys up there [to the conference room] with me. Nobody was in there. There could be some secret entrance where a hobo gets in, but as far as I know there's not. I checked. You never know though, he could have it blocked off." However, no one has reported seeing any *earthly* strangers skulking through the premises.

Several employees share Kim's suspicion that it's haunted. She told of one employee, whom she described as a "real straight arrow," running into the bar late one night. He had heard the clinking of glasses and rattling of dishes in the Brook Room. His eyes were like china saucers as he described what he'd heard.

Malcolm, a burly native Hawaiian, is a maintenance man who doubles as the hotel's security guard. He said that one evening he opened the door to the old Mermaid Room. Big band music came from within. It's his belief that the lodge is a "museum" filled with old life that is not yet through with living.

A former employee told Kim that as he started work one morning about nine o'clock, he heard a conversation taking place in the bar. The speakers sounded Chinese. He walked over to look through the closed barroom door windows, since the bar wasn't yet open for business. He saw that it was empty.

One of the front-office staff took her boyfriend to explore some of the old rooms. As they made their way through a dank passage that connects a women's bathroom with the swimming pool room, the woman's boyfriend grew increasingly uncomfortable. Finally he stopped. He had walked into an icy cold spot. Something touched his arm and he couldn't move for a few seconds. The couple beat a hasty retreat.

A similar experience befell Kim and *her* boyfriend in late March 1991.

"We walked into the conference room," Kim recalled. "All the chairs were set up. There was a smell. It just smelled like people were there, like people smell when they're in a crowd. I felt very unwelcome. It was a very heavy presence. It wasn't evil at all, just like, well, we shouldn't be here right now because 'they're' here. The weirdest part is that the lights would not come on."

"Let's get the hell out of here," her boyfriend said, leading the way out.

The Gilberts rent the conference room to various groups, but there hadn't been anyone using it for some time. The next morning Kim made a point of returning. The room was pleasantly empty of any bad smells and the lights worked perfectly.

There are three specific places at Brookdale Lodge that Kim Gilbert is afraid of. One is the "crowded" conference room. The others?

"I can't stand being in that damn pool room. There's something about that room I do not like," she emphasizes. The 1972 drowning that caused the closing of the pool may still reverberate in another dimension.

The Brook Room with its cold mountain stream and multiple dining terraces is the third area Kim tries to avoid. Perhaps with good reason.

"There's a room off to the side of the Brook Room that I have a horrible feeling about," Kim confesses. "I just don't like it at all."

It's in the Brook Room that several sightings of a little girl ghost—perhaps the same one Kim saw in the lobby—and a phantom woman have taken place. As far as she knows, the smaller, adjacent room she has such fear of has no evil history. But she can't be sure.

"Judge Logan had a niece who drowned in the Brook Room pond sometime in the 1920s or 1930s," Kim said, citing one of the lodge's most powerful legends.

"I'm assuming other people have seen a little girl in the Brook Room, especially on that second balcony." There are several small dining alcoves overlooking the main room.

The most remarkable story of the Brook Room ghosts involves a young couple planning their wedding reception at the lodge. They had stopped in one afternoon in November 1990 to look over the facilities.

"Actually it was about the same time that I saw her [the child ghost] in the lobby, so I wonder if she was active then," Kim recalled. "The couple were sitting at the far end of the Brook Room facing the windows. Actually the whole place is windows. They looked up toward one of the windows and saw this child running around a balcony. They actually got up and told us that somebody's kid was in there. Now that area is closed off to the public. No one was supposed to be in there."

No one was. When members of the staff accompanied the couple back to the Brook Room, nothing was found to indicate a child had been there. The couple said the little girl never looked up and looked as if she was playing her own secret game.

It also seems possible that the child's mother is a wandering spirit at the lodge.

"A woman has been seen in there," Kim said. "And they've been seen together, the mother holding the girl. People have reported that they've seen this woman walking across the creek, in the air. I can't figure that out. Maybe there was a bridge that went directly over the creek and followed it downstream a long, long time ago. She's always dressed in a long gown. The psychics we've had here said it's the mother come back for her. The girl died a traumatic death and will stay forever, or until she's told that she's dead and needs to go on."

So far that hasn't happened. The process of "cleaning" the lodge of all its ghosts might take some time. According to psychics Kim has consulted, there are forty-nine entities haunting Brookdale Lodge!

Only a few of the entities have had names tied to them. In addition to Sarah, psychics told Kim that there's a woman named Mary residing there and someone named George, a lumberjack.

"George stands in the back of the conference room," Kim said matter-of-factly. "He's also out back chopping wood. I found out recently that there was a woodcutting knoll back there. So apparently he's in two places. Maybe he's bringing in wood."

Kim doesn't know who "Mary" is. "Just a woman," she proposed.

Joslyn Chisholm, a thin, nervous woman who works at the lodge as a cocktail waitress, described for Kim her amazing experiences in Room 46, one of the motel rooms. She worked at the lodge in exchange for rent.

Chisholm said that at night objects and shapes would fly across the room. Ballroom dancers swirled about, their faces leering at her as they floated by. Various ghostly forms periodically materialized next to her as she sat on the bed watching this bizarre carnival. Although most of the people were vague forms, several faces were very clear.

One face was that of a little boy, about twelve or thirteen. He reminded Chisholm of her brother. He was "curious" about her, she said. He would stare at her almost eye to eye.

Other faces were far more horrible: a man with his left eyeball hanging loose on his cheek, another with a ghastly knife wound across his face. "But they didn't hurt me," Chisholm emphasized. "What I saw always seemed like a party. They were testing me all the time, showing me who they were."

Once she felt someone sit on the bed next to her and stroke her arm.

Kim Gilbert says Chisholm is reliable.

"I was making these jokes with her about him [the boy], but she was dead serious. I knew she wasn't lying."

The motel rooms adjacent to the lodge were not built until the 1970s. However, they replaced old tourist cabins that dated to the turn of the century. Kim suspects that the boy Chisholm saw and that the psychic identified may have been molested and killed decades ago in a cabin that stood on the site of Room 46.

Kim had other clues that Brookdale Lodge contained mysteries.

"The first couple of weeks I was here, I had a real sweet gardenia smell following me around," she said. "It was just overwhelming. I don't own a bottle of gardenia perfume." Nor did anyone else who worked at the lodge.

Unlike perfume, which might linger for a moment in the air as the wearer passes and then dissipates, the perfume that Kim sniffed seemed to follow her.

"It was right with me, followed me up to my apartment but then it would stop at the door and leave. You couldn't smell it when you went into the apartment, it would stop directly at the front door."

The lingering odor always occurred at night, and she noticed its periodic presence for about two weeks. Oddly, she often caught the scent in the Brook Room, where the child drowned and the ghostly mother is reported. It would last anywhere from twenty seconds to twenty minutes, depending upon where Kim was and how long she spent in a particular room. The suddenness with which the smell always evaporated amazed her.

In January 1991, Kim asked Sylvia Browne, a well-known San Francisco psychic, to investigate the hauntings at Brookdale Lodge. Browne sent two associates, John Davis and Kristin Brumm, both Gnostic ministers from the Church of Novus Spirits.

The pair conducted a ninety-minute tour of the lodge. Brumm occasionally sprinkled holy water in some of the rooms, carrying a 35mm camera around her neck. "Just in case," she told a reporter.

None of the reported forty-nine ghosts materialized during the tour. Davis told a reporter that the lodge was a typical haunted house in which any ghostly entity probably died a violent death and couldn't find its way to "the other side."

"They [Davis and Brumm] didn't do much," said Gilbert. "They lit a candle and said a few . . . words and told them [the ghosts] to go on to the light. I didn't see anything, I didn't hear anything, I didn't feel a damn thing. In fact, I thought the only thing I did feel was that the next day there was a lot of tension around here. I could feel it and I thought that was bad. We shouldn't have had them [Davis and Brumm] come here. The ghosts are pissed off. Everywhere I went, it was just like I was being watched."

An incident the day after the visit by Davis and Brumm may or may not have had any connection with the exorcism, but Kim calls the coincidence "bizarre."

"Somebody tore the paneling off one of the windows going from the Brook Room to get inside the Fireside Room," Kim said. "It was completely torn off the hinges, the window torn open. There was no evidence of anyone being in there. They tried to find fingerprints, but nothing. Think the ghosts were trying to tell me something? Like 'Don't ever bring psychics here again and try to exorcise us, lady'?"

Through all of her brushes with the spirit world in the old California lodge, Kim Gilbert has maintained a positive outlook. She dismisses those who accuse her of creating the stories to promote a struggling business.

"Some people look at me as if I am doing this as a publicity stunt. I've heard that many times. But I would never embarrass myself to be in a publicity stunt saying I've seen things. It's very real, but I keep a sense of humor about it. I try to find a lot of humor, but it is serious. I've seen these things and I've felt things many times. I just go with it. It's part of life. I want to see something right in front of me, I want to touch it."

With forty-nine ghosts to choose from, it seems certain Kim Gilbert will continue to encounter many entities. And perhaps reach out to touch some of them.

The Spirits of Bradmar

When Robert A. Bradley, a Denver physician, went downstairs one morning in his historic brick country home he had no idea that the experience would change his life forever.

Dr. Bradley often enjoyed an early morning smoke before the rest of his family awakened. Taking a cigar from its box, he ambled into the drawing room to use a lighter kept on a heavy, marble-topped table. As he reached for the lighter, his hand closed on empty air. The lighter had risen and was floating away! After it had traveled about a foot it returned to the table and fell silently on its side.

The astonished doctor examined the lighter. Surely one of his three sons had played a practical joke on him. But how? There were no wires attached or any other visible means of propulsion. Dr. Bradley experimented with the lighter by pushing it over and each time it hit the table with a loud clank.

That was the first of a series of unexplained incidents that would soon be witnessed by every member of the family.

They all went shopping one Saturday and returned to find the reception hall of their home in shambles. A wrought-iron trellis had been wrenched from a stone planter and the plants themselves uprooted and thrown around the room. The carpeting, covered with dirt, resembled a Roto-tilled garden. Oddly, there was no evidence that the house had been broken into.

That night after the children were in bed, Dr. Bradley, his wife, Dorothy, and Siegwalt Palleske, a foreign languages professor who was staying with them, were watching television. The only illumination came from the television set and a light in the adjoining entry hall.

Suddenly, Mrs. Bradley thought she saw a movement out of the corner of her eye. Turning toward the plant beside her, she noticed one leaf moving up and down. The windows and doors were all shut and there were no drafts. As she watched closely, she saw that no other leaf moved! She said nothing.

A moment later, the house shook with a terrifying noise. Professor Palleske leaped to his feet and ran. The Bradleys followed. They searched the entire house, but could find no cause.

It had been an incredible day that left the family exhausted yet sleepless, tossing and turning while trying to figure out what had happened.

The Bradleys were determined to find the answers. They combed libraries for books on psychic phenomena to which they devoted every spare moment in reading; joined study groups where they met persons who had witnessed similar unexplained incidents; participated in discussion groups on the paranormal; attended lectures and séances with a variety of mediums.

The Bradmar haunting began as a case of serendipity. A realtor, knowing of Dr. Bradley's interest in architecturally distinctive houses, telephoned him one spring morning in the 1960s to say that a splendid old English Tudor country home was available; in fact, it had been on the market for some time because of its condition. The previous owner, a woman who had been bedridden for seven years, had been unable to maintain it, and recently vandals had wreaked havoc upon it. Would the Bradleys like to see it anyway? They would.

They saw and they bought. Dr. Bradley loved the beautiful stained glass windows, the rich blue slate roof with its many tall chimneys and gables, and the walls of handmade bricks. The manor house, which they would call Bradmar, was framed by ancient cottonwood trees set on four acres of lawn. It was a perfect place for a growing family. Best of all, Dr. Bradley would still be close to his city office.

The restoration took many months of painstaking work by a crew of workmen under the direction of Karl Vogel, an interior designer and relative of Dr. Bradley. The man was a bachelor who had recently moved to Denver, and the Bradleys invited him to live with them as soon as they could move into the house. Karl was experienced in house restoration, and the Bradleys felt fortunate to have a competent person in charge.

One afternoon while Karl was busy at the house, a former caretaker dropped by to see how the restoration was going. He seemed pleased that a family would be moving in. Then, as he glanced around, he said casually, "You know of course that the house is haunted."

No, Karl hadn't heard that, nor did he have any interest in the supernatural. But he was courteous and listened to the old man's story.

"It seems as how everyone in these parts knows the story," the stranger began, "and I believe there's something to it. An elderly woman was the last one to live here. Long before her death she told her relatives and friends that when she died she wanted her casket to be placed in front of the fireplace of the great hall. At that moment, she said, she would split one of the two large cross beams overhead. She even told them which one. Well, sir, the split occurred exactly as she had predicted, and those present in the room say they heard the crack." He paused and shook his head. "It's hard to understand these things." Karl admitted that it was.

After the caretaker left, Karl went into the great hall and studied the overhead beam. It was the strangest one he'd ever seen. A series of small cracks had occurred in the center of the wood, running the full length of the beam. No crack extended to the outer edge as would logically be the case.

Karl dismissed it with a shrug. He had more important things to think about.

When fall arrived the restoration was still unfinished. Mrs. Bradley went to enroll her sons in their new school, but was told that the children had to be *sleeping* in the house before they could be admitted.

The Bradleys considered how this might be done while the boys jumped with glee at the thought of living in the woods in an unfinished house. It might be the greatest adventure of their lives. Dr. Bradley suggested that he and Karl take turns spending nights at Bradmar with the boys.

Karl's turn came first. When he met the Bradleys the next morning his face was ashen. He asked if either one of them had been to the house at any time during the night.

"Of course not," said Dr. Bradley. "Why do you ask?"

Karl straddled a sawhorse and told his story. He and the boys had slept in one room because the floors in all the other rooms of the house were being sanded. After the boys had gone to sleep, Karl sat on the edge of his bed, smoking a last cigarette.

Suddenly, he heard the back door slam. Soft footsteps shuffled from room to room. The sound changed as the footsteps reached the marble floor of the hall. Karl waited for someone to call him. No one did. After several moments he heard the footsteps retreating to the back of the house. The back door opened and slammed shut. Karl went to the window to see who was leaving. No one was in sight. And the only entrance to the property was a single driveway, half a mile in length. Karl doubted that anyone could have come into the house, but he couldn't doubt the reality of what he'd heard.

A week later while Karl was staying with the boys, he again heard the back door open and slam shut. The same sound of soft footsteps shuffled through the main floor rooms. This time Karl was determined to catch the intruder. When the footsteps reached the great hall Karl stepped onto the balcony that overlooks it. The hall was flooded by the light of a full moon. But no one was there!

Karl gripped the handrail of the balcony and shouted the name of the former owner. "Is that you down there?"

The footsteps stopped. "I'm trying to restore your beautiful home," he yelled, "and if you don't like what I'm doing, speak up now!"

Karl said later that he did not know what he would have done had there been a response. He stood frozen to the spot until the footsteps grew faint and the back door slammed shut. From that moment on he was a believer in the paranormal.

On one occasion the Bradleys invited Dorothy's mother to visit them. The elderly woman woke up in the middle of the night, hearing footsteps coming down the hall. She assumed it was her daughter coming to check on her to be sure she was covered. Although it was summer, the night was cool.

The woman heard the bedroom door open and close and footsteps approach the bed. Moonlight streamed through the window, but she couldn't see anyone. Then the footsteps moved to the dresser, and someone or something pulled the drawers open as if looking for something. After the drawers were pushed in, the rocking chair began to creak. She learned in the morning that her daughter had not been in the room.

Dr. Bradley has a theory that both small children and elderly persons who have arteriosclerosis of the brain can tap into the subconscious level, without dependence upon hypnosis or alteration of consciousness through meditation.

As a test, he grouped his mother-in-law's great-grandchildren around her at a table.

"Boy, did that table ever tip!" said the doctor. All sorts of spirit communications resulted, including the name of his mother-in-law's lover of many years ago—much to her embarassment.

Electrical problems are inherent in haunted houses, and Bradmar was no exception. Lights went on and off by themselves. Later the Bradleys would learn that the builder of the house had never gotten along with his wife. They argued constantly. She kept the heavy drapes closed and all the lights off. He stumbled into the furniture and turned the lights on. Was the couple still in the house? Dr. Bradley felt that they might be, that their spirits had come back to find out whether the new family was restoring or altering the place. He felt they were probably delighted to witness a restoration.

Yet the erratic behavior of the lights continued. It became so annoying that an electrician was called in to inspect the wiring. He said it would all have to be replaced.

One day Mrs. Bradley was standing in the center of a room when a bare yellow bulb overhead came on. "Who turned on that hideous light?" she called, then realized there was no one else in the room. She walked over to the wall switch and found it in the "on" position. She snapped it off and called Tom, the electrician, who was working elsewhere in the house. When she explained what had happened, Tom said, "That's not possible."

"Of course it's not," said Mrs. Bradley, "but it happened."

Tom shrugged his shoulders and returned to his work.

After the wiring job had been completed, the Bradleys invited friends over one evening to show them through the house. In one wing not a single bulb would light. The next day, Tom spent all morning trying to find the source of the problem. Finally, in desperation, he yanked a piece of wiring out from a conduit. The wires that he had painstakingly braided were now unbraided and the conduit disconnected!

Another day Professor Palleske was up on a stepladder using an electric hand sander to sand some woodwork. Mrs. Bradley was working nearby. Suddenly, she heard a scream and a crash. She found the professor sitting on the floor and holding his head.

"Someone hit me!" he yelled.

"That's impossible, Sieg," said Mrs. Bradley. "There's only the two of us here."

He groaned. "I know. Am I bleeding?"

He wasn't, but there was a small red area on his forehead. He said that the minute he was "hit" the sander stopped. A short circuit would have burned his hand, not his head.

Mrs. Bradley took the sander downstairs to Tom and asked him to check it. He took off the casing, turned it over, and it worked. When he put the casing back on, the sander did not work. He repeated this routine several times with the same results. The sander simply refused to work with its casing on and, in this inoperable condition, it was returned to the rental store.

The family soon noticed that there was a significance to some of these electrical problems. Lamps that turned themselves on usually presaged bad news, but always with a favorable outcome.

Once, lights came on by themselves at four-thirty for three consecutive mornings. A short time later, the children suffered serious illnesses, but regained their health.

A light that went on in the afternoon gave twenty-four-hour warning of an injury to Professor Palleske's father.

Again, a bedroom lamp lit in the daytime and four hours later the water pump failed.

Another day the huge brass chandelier that hung from the ceiling of the great hall began swinging. Within two hours a message arrived that a relative with a severe illness had been hospitalized. A complete recovery resulted.

Water also is a puzzling phenomenon in haunted houses. Faucets often turn themselves on and off at will. At Bradmar a relative entered the house one morning and was hit on the head by a blob of water. The water hadn't yet been turned on! The man got a stepladder and climbed high enough to reach the ceiling of the room. It was completely dry.

Such pranks are usually attributed to a poltergeist or "noisy" ghost that is heard but not seen. It may break dishes, upset furniture, strip linens from beds, and do all manner of annoying things. It is commonly thought to be associated with the presence of an adolescent in the house. Parapsychologists believe that the turbulence and energy force of the teenager are somehow transferred to inanimate objects.

But the Bradleys couldn't accept that theory. In their book, *Psychic Phenomena: Revelations and Experiences*, they write: " . . . the physical happenings . . . have been associated in our minds with definite purposes, definite meaningful events or ideas . . . They seem in our case to be intelligence-directed, and of a higher level than pre-adolescent capriciousness.

"The second theory, therefore, the one which seems more likely to us, is that these physical happenings were effected by deceased people manifesting via psychokinesis and utilizing this power for a purpose."

The Bradleys never doubted that a surviving subconscious mind had split the beam. Nor did they doubt that the footsteps Karl had heard without anyone visibly present had come from the spirit world. They would be heard again, this time by Mrs. Bradley and her sister, Mary.

On a New Year's Eve the two women were visiting upstairs long after the other family members had gone to bed. Karl was out at a party. At 12:30 A.M. the women heard footsteps on the carpeted area of the dining room hall, then the sound of Karl's leather heels on the marble floor of the great hall. He'd be up in a minute to tell them about the party. But why was he returning so early? Had something gone wrong? The footsteps started up the staircase, then retreated.

"He's gone to the kitchen for a cup of coffee," Mrs. Bradley said.

"Did he float there?" asked her sister.

Mrs. Bradley looked at Mary and realized there were no footsteps in the kitchen. Nor anywhere else. Silence enveloped the house. The women went on to bed. In the morning Karl said he'd arrived home at 4:00 A.M. and that the party was great.

Although the Bradleys never saw a ghostly figure in their house, others apparently did. On a number of occasions, the family opened their home to tourists, charging a small fee to be donated to local nonprofit institutions. Some visitors said they saw phantoms flitting in the hallways, and once a group of children reported seeing a woman in a window. She was not real. Dr. Bradley invited "spirit" photographers to come down from Canada, but they couldn't capture anything on film.

Marital problems not connected to their supernatural experiences caused Robert and Dorothy Bradley to divorce in the late 1960s. In 1970 Dr. Bradley remarried and, ten years later, sold Bradmar because the couple no longer needed a thirty-three room house.

The buyers, friends of the Bradleys, reported continued poltergeist activity, with items, especially jewelry, disappearing from one place to reappear in another. After living in the mansion for only a short time, the family sold it. It takes a special kind of person to live in a haunted house.

A Revolutionary Haunting

Monuments to America's Revolutionary War heroes adorn the landscape in countless New England villages and counties. From Boston Harbor to Fort Western in Maine, where Benedict Arnold and his men mustered for their march on Quebec in 1775, inland to historic old Fort Ticonderoga and Saratoga, patriot homes, battlefields, and birthplaces mark the intense interest Americans have in that bloody fight for independence.

One of the emerging nation's first martyrs, Nathan Hale of Connecticut, is just such a Revolutionary hero, a soldier-spy whose exploits are known to countless schoolchildren. Though his life was short, his valiant efforts on behalf of the patriot cause are still held up as a model of unselfish bravery. Several monuments commemorate his life. A boulder marks Halesite, near Huntington, New York, the place where it is believed he was captured by the British.

In South Coventry, Connecticut, is the remarkable Hale Homestead, where Nathan was born in 1755, the sixth of twelve children of Deacon Richard and Elizabeth Strong Hale.

The Homestead today is open to the public, administered by the Coventry Historical Society for the Antiquarian and Landmarks Society of Connecticut. The home and grounds are evocative reminders of the colonial era where costumed docents guide visitors through the intricacies of eighteenth-century life.

Tourists may not know, however, that the colonial Hales must have been more attached to their home than even they suspected. The Homestead is reputedly haunted by the ghostly visages of Nathan Hale's own family.

The story of the Hale Homestead must begin with the Revolutionary hero himself. Ironically, Nathan Hale could have avoided the great conflict. A graduate of Yale College at the age of eighteen, the calm, pious young man with remarkable athletic skills accepted a teaching job in East Haddam, Connecticut, in 1773. By all accounts, Hale was quite a good teacher. He moved to New London the next year and began what he probably assumed was going to be a life of teaching and scholarship.

It was not to be.

Hale was excited by the ideals embodied in the American Revolution and volunteered to fight in July 1775, one month after his twentieth birthday. He was commissioned a lieutenant by the Connecticut assembly and joined colonial troops in driving the British from Boston.

When His Majesty's forces invaded the New York area, Hale, by now a captain, marched with colonial troops to drive the Redcoats from their new encampment. He was a daring and resourceful soldier, commended by his superiors for many acts of bravery. On one occasion, the captain's men captured a British supply ship from under the cannons of a British war vessel.

The ragtag American soldiers, however, were growing dispirited. General Washington's troops were facing disintegration in New York. Soldiers began to desert, slipping away from their posts. The commander in chief needed information about British troop movements in order to prepare his tactics, and he needed it badly. He turned for help to an elite fighting force, the Rangers. Washington asked their commander to find a volunteer who would penetrate the British lines to collect intelligence on enemy positions, tactics, and troop strength.

Captain Nathan Hale had been awarded a place in the small Rangers outfit after he captured the British supply ship. On the Rangers commander's second call, Captain Hale stepped forward to take the dangerous assignment.

Disguised as a Dutch schoolmaster, a role ideally suited to his background, Hale successfully crossed British lines and gathered the vital information. But the young patriot-spy was captured by British troops on September 21, 1776, as he attempted to make his way back to the American side. Historians believe a British Loyalist cousin may have betrayed him.

Hale was tried as a spy before Gen. William Howe, the British commander, and sentenced to hang on the following day. Calm and courageous even as the noose was dropped over his neck, Captain Hale asked for a Bible and gave the executioner, a Major Cunningham, a letter to his family. The British officer denied him the Bible and ripped up Hale's last letter.

So just three months after his twenty-first birthday, Nathan Hale met his death. His reputed final words have been included in history books for decades: "I regret that I have but one life to lose for my country."

Contrary to that tradition, however, he probably didn't say those words. According to a recently found war diary penned by British captain Frederick Mackenzie, who witnessed Hale's execution, the young soldier's final words were: "It is the duty of every good officer to obey any orders given him by his commander-in-chief." Mackenzie's record of what Nathan Hale actually said is not as stirring as the oft-quoted passage cited above, but certainly still befitting the man's stoic nature.

In the same year Nathan Hale lost his life, 1776, his widower father, Deacon Richard Hale, faced a daunting challenge. How to provide room for his own twelve children and a cluster of pretty teenage girls brought into his life by the widow he had married in 1769?

Born at Newbury, Massachusetts, in 1717, Deacon Hale had moved to Coventry in the 1740s. He bought a large farm and married a local girl, Elizabeth

Strong, in 1746. To that union were born twelve children, eight boys and four girls. Mrs. Hale died in 1767 following the birth of her last child. Little Nathan was twelve.

Two years later, in 1769, Deacon Hale married Abigail Cobb Adams, the widow of Captain Samuel Adams. She brought to the marriage several teenage girls. One of them, Sarah Adams, married John Hale, one of Nathan's older brothers.

Deacon Hale rebuilt the mansion as a two-family house shared by father and son, and their wives, who were also mother and daughter. As the children of this blended family grew to adulthood they moved away, although several members of the family lived on at the Homestead for several decades.

The haunting of Hale Homestead has been documented since at least 1914. In that year, the great American antiquarian, George Dudley Seymour (1859–1945), purchased the vacant Hale Homestead and spent the rest of his life making it a centerpiece in his quest to immortalize his favorite American hero, Captain Nathan Hale. He also came to believe the Homestead was haunted.

Indeed, one of the first documented ghost sightings involved Seymour himself. He had completed the acquisition of Hale Homestead in the spring of 1914 and embarked on a journey to visit it. He and a friend took a train from New Haven to Willimantic where he then rented a buggy to take them to South Coventry. Heavy rains had turned the roads to muddy ruts. Both men were tired from the long trip.

Seymour recorded his impressions of the Homestead in his diary:

"Isolated, dilapidated, unpainted, and vacant, the [Hale] house presented a forlorn picture, heightened on the inside by streamers of paper falling from dampened walls . . . [Seymour's friend] jumped out of the buggy and ran to the window, and what should he see but Deacon Hale's ghost looking out of the [schoolroom] window to see who had arrived. As my friend put his face against the pane, the Deacon stepped back to the inner end of the room and vanished into thin air. My friend was so jarred by the apparition that he did not mention the matter to me for hours. I must say that the Deacon's ghost never appeared again to my knowledge."

A patent attorney by profession, Seymour probably did more than any other single person to make Nathan Hale famous. He not only "collected" houses associated with the Hale family, but also commissioned artist Bela Lyon Pratt to sculpt a new statue of Hale. There were three already in existence, but Seymour disapproved of them. Pratt's statue is now almost universal, gracing the headquarters of the FBI and CIA, the Chicago Tribune Building, Phillips Academy in Massachusetts, and three Connecticut cities. A miniature version is at the Hale Homestead.

Seymour also successfully campaigned for Nathan Hale's portrait on a postage stamp. Bela Pratt's one-and-a-half-cent stamp carried his portrait from 1925 to 1938. Interestingly, there is only a "shadow portrait" of Hale extant, so Pratt's statue and stamp are, to some extent, imaginative likenesses.

But George Dudley Seymour was also keenly aware that not all history is to be found in dusty tomes. He collected all manner of legends and stories connected with Nathan Hale, indeed he seems to have been addicted to writing down nearly everything he thought or heard—including accounts of the ghosts at Hale Homestead.

Local residents told Seymour that the ghost of Lydia Carpenter, one of the Hale family's servants, "was said to be always listening to catch scraps of household gossip." It may also be Lydia who has been seen sweeping the upper hall toward morning, and she may be the woman in white who putters around the kitchen at an early hour.

In addition to Deacon Hale, Seymour found that another member of the Hale family had been sighted at the Homestead.

Seymour wrote that the ghost of one of Nathan's brothers, Lieutenant Joseph Hale, "who was confined, it was said, in one of the British prison ships off the Jersey coast . . . came home to die, and his ghost clanked his chains in the great cellar of the house."

However, more recent research casts doubts on Seymour's account of Joseph Hale's war service. He served in the Lexington alarm with several of his brothers (six Hale sons fought for the patriot cause) and was a Knowlton Ranger with the rank of lieutenant when he was captured at Fort Washington, New York, where a musket ball grazed him. That was on November 16 or 17, 1776, barely two months after his brother's execution.

Whether Joseph ever was confined to a prison ship is unknown, but he certainly didn't "come home to die." Records indicate that he was exchanged for a British prisoner and was serving as a lieutenant in Colonel Ely's regiment by 1777. He met Rebeckah Harris, the daughter of prominent judge Joseph Harris, in New London and married her on October 21, 1778. They returned to Coventry, where they bought a house near his father's farm.

In 1784, he became "low in consumption," a term used in those days to describe tuberculosis. He died that same year, leaving his young widow with four small children born during the Revolution.

George Seymour wrote that Joseph "was assigned the northwest chamber of his father's house" during his final days. According to a historian at the Hale Homestead, it is possible that Joseph did "come home to die" in 1784, even though he had a house nearby. His widow and children lived at the Hale Homestead following his death.

There are two additional candidates for ghostdom at the Homestead—John and Sarah Hale, Nathan's older brother and stepsister who were married, lived, and died in the house.

John Hale emulated his father in many ways. Born in 1748, he died shortly after Deacon Hale in 1802. Like his father, John became a deacon in the Puritan Church in Coventry, and served in various public offices. From 1791 to 1802, he was a delegate to sixteen sessions of the Connecticut General Assembly. He served as justice of the peace, town clerk, and treasurer for many terms between 1786 and his death. Earlier, he, too, had been a lieutenant in the Revolution's Knowlton Rangers.

He continued to live at the Homestead after his marriage to his stepsister, Sarah Adams Hale. Their only child was stillborn. Sarah died a year after her husband, in 1803, at the age of fifty.

Another person who believed the Homestead is haunted, perhaps by the ghosts of John and Sarah Hale, was Mary Elizabeth Campbell Griffith, of Manchester, Connecticut. Her late husband, Harold Griffith, was the Hale Homestead caretaker for George Dudley Seymour.

Mrs. Griffith moved to the Homestead in 1930. She lived in the building's ell for many years. Her two daughters were born there.

In an oral history of the Hale Homestead collected in 1988, Mrs. Griffith recalled one perplexing episode:

"It was early in the morning. Harold [Mr. Griffith] was out milking. Everyone else was in bed. I heard somebody come down the back stairs. I didn't even look. I asked Harold when he came back, and he said no, he hadn't been in the house at all . . . Clump, clump, clump, it was so plain. I never could explain that. . . ."

George Seymour believed the house was haunted, Mrs. Griffith said. But she seemed to excuse that eccentricity by adding, "He'd been to England, and liked that sort of thing. . . . "

According to Mary E. Baker, Hale Homestead administrator, staff members have not seen any ghosts nor found evidence of their presence.

"However, we strongly believe in bringing history to life," she said. "Sometimes that includes bringing the people who lived here back for a few hours for special programs. This is done at Halloween time and on special weekends when the Nathan Hale Fifes and Drums put on colonial encampments and battle reenactments. On such occasions, 'Nathan Hale' himself can sometimes be seen here, trying to recruit men to join the militia, or signing autographs with his feather quill pen for children. Even on ordinary days, it is not uncommon for one of the Hale family members to be on hand."

But not all of them may be visible.

Dead Man's Tree

Three sixth-grade girls in Dover, Delaware, may be the youngest ghost hunters in the country, and possibly the youngest to investigate a haunted governor's mansion. But Michael Castle, former governor of Delaware, believed in the ghostly legends that swirl around the state's official residence, "Woodburn"—an eerie two-hundred-year-old estate—and that is why he agreed to let Holly Forbis, Taryn Morrow, and Faith Truman of the Warner Elementary School of Dover spend the night of May 7, 1985, in the executive mansion.

Accompanied by their teacher, Connie Malin, the youngsters arrived with a Ouija board, a tape recorder, a video camera and monitor, and a stuffed dog to capture the attention of the child ghost who is said to live in the house.

Governor Castle told the group that in January 1985 at his inauguration party at Woodburn, several women guests had complained that something was tugging at their dresses, but when they turned around no one was there. One woman felt that a little girl lingered in a corner of the room, but no one could be seen.

The governor said that in March a second-floor window kept opening by itself all night and setting off the burglar alarm. Security guards said no one was near the window.

The children were impressed. Perhaps they could solve the mystery. They toured the house and then set up their equipment. By 11:00 P.M. the camera, which had been in perfect working order, wouldn't focus.

"The pictures were clear on the monitor, but you couldn't focus through the lens," the teacher said. "When the girls filmed themselves with the objects they'd brought, they appeared transparent on the monitor, while the props were normal."

The tape recorder failed to operate and the Ouija board yielded nothing.

The equipment failures were especially baffling.

In the morning the girls said they weren't frightened, but were made uneasy by the painting of a woman who they said smiled at them a couple of times as they worked.

Woodburn is Delaware's first executive mansion, purchased by the state in 1966 for $65,000. (Before that time governors provided their own living quarters.) The brick house, on an acre and a half of land on Kings Highway, was built in 1790 by a Charles Hillyard, whose great-grandfather had been given a tract of three thousand acres by William Penn.

On days when the mansion is open to the public, some visitors come to see the exquisite Georgian furnishings, or perhaps sit outdoors by the reflecting pool in the boxwood garden. But many more come in hopes of catching a glimpse of one of Woodburn's four ghosts.

The small girl in a gingham dress apparently shares the house with two others: a gentleman spirit in eighteenth-century garb complete with knee breeches and ruffled blouse drinks wine from a decanter left on a sideboard, and an elderly dinner guest is still trying to find his way to the dining room. Outdoors, close to the house, the ghost of a Southern slave raider inhabits a massive tulip poplar.

Nothing is known about the child ghost, but the others have been authenticated.

In the middle of the nineteenth century the house was occupied by Dr. and Mrs. M. W. Bates. On one occasion Lorenzo Dow, a famous traveling Methodist minister, was a houseguest. As Dow started downstairs to breakfast he was startled to see, on the staircase landing, an elderly gentleman wearing knee breeches, a ruffled shirt, and a white powdered wig. Dow nodded and continued on downstairs. When he reached the breakfast room, Mrs. Bates asked him to lead the family in prayer.

"But shouldn't we wait for your other guest?" said Dow.

"There is no other guest," snapped Mrs. Bates.

Dow was not easily put off and went on to describe the "person" he'd seen.

Mrs. Bates was visibly upset, and after the meal was over, she asked Lorenzo Dow not to relate the incident to anyone. He learned later that the apparition he'd seen bore a strong resemblance to Mrs. Bates's father, who had been dead for many years. Dow was never again entertained at Woodburn.

Although the description of the ghost that Lorenzo Dow saw parallels that of the tippling ghost, who can know if it's the same specter? The late Gov. Charles L. Terry Jr., during whose administration the state bought Woodburn, talked sometimes about a wine-drinking ghost.

"They used to fill bottles of wine for the ghost," Terry told a news reporter, "and in the morning the bottles were empty. One time, a servant swore he saw an old man in colonial costume sitting there in the dining room, slowly drinking wine."

In the 1870s George P. Fisher, a college student, lived in the house. One Christmas he brought a classmate home with him for the holidays. On the first night the two men sat up late swapping stories and making plans for their brief vacation.

At one o'clock they went off to bed—Fisher to his room and the guest to the adjoining room. Before Fisher was undressed he heard a thud in the next room. Throwing open the door between the rooms, he found his friend sprawled unconscious on the floor.

What had happened?

After the man had been revived he told Fisher that he had just entered the room with his candle when he saw, by the dim light, an old man hunched in a chair by the fireplace. To his horror, the man arose and shuffled toward him. The student remembered nothing more. The men searched the room thoroughly and found no evidence of any living thing.

Years later, after George Fisher had become a judge, he enjoyed telling this story. The room his classmate had occupied was the bedroom of Woodburn's builder and first resident, Charles Hillyard. Some believe that Hillyard may have stayed on in the home he loved in life.

The cellar and the Dead Man's Tree command the most interest from visitors. In pre–Civil War days Woodburn was a station on the Underground Railroad. Runaway slaves, trying to escape to the North, were hidden in various cellar rooms, and some of them died there. Is it their death cries that are sometimes heard? Or only the moaning of the wind on a stormy night?

The gnarled old poplar known as the Dead Man's Tree, or Hanging Tree, grows close to the house. Reputed to be more than two hundred years old, it has been split twice by lightning. Legend has it that one night Southern raiders reached Woodburn and attempted to capture the slaves in the cellar to sell them back to their owners. But Daniel Cowgill, the master of Woodburn, drove the raiders off—except for one man who hid in a hollow of the ancient tree. His head somehow became stuck in the hollow and there he died.

Today, children do not loiter while passing Woodburn after dark. They say that you can hear a man groaning inside the tree, and that by the light of a full moon you can see him.

The Shadow

The ghosts of several former residents roam the rooms of Washington, D.C.'s historic Octagon House. Two died horrible deaths there. Screams shatter the night air, heavy footsteps tramp the top floors, and lights blink on and off with no one near the controls.

The magnificent Georgian mansion, at New York Avenue and 18th Street NW, was built in 1801 by Col. John Tayloe III. A horse breeder with a three-thousand-acre plantation in Mount Airy, Maryland, Tayloe also wanted a city home. His close friend, George Washington, convinced him of the bright future in the nation's capital. Besides, Mrs. Tayloe was eager to live near her friend Nelly Custis, of Mount Vernon.

The Tayloes were thrilled with their new home one block from the White House. It was a stimulating time in the federal city, with statesmen meeting the challenges of government by day and relaxing by night, many of them at gala parties in the Tayloes' Octagon House. Ann Tayloe loved to entertain. Her guest register regularly included the names of many of America's founding fathers—James Madison, James Monroe, Thomas Jefferson, and Andrew Jackson.

Colonel Tayloe couldn't recall being happier. At his wife's balls he often stood quietly beside the mantelpiece in the ballroom, watching his elegant daughters waltzing with one partner after another. They would marry well. Of that he was certain.

But the War of 1812 destroyed his dreams. One of the girls fell in love with a dashing young British officer. Her father hated the British and refused to allow the suitor into his house. Father and daughter argued loudly and repeatedly.

The girl ignored Tayloe's warnings and continued to see her young man until late one particular night when she returned from a tryst. She quietly entered the house, removed her shoes and tiptoed up the grand staircase that rose from the ground-floor rotunda to the third floor. Suddenly her father loomed above her, staring down from the top landing. They exchanged heated words, their voices growing louder with each hurled accusation. Then came a shriek as Miss Tayloe plummeted over the banister to her death.

Colonel Tayloe was outwardly inconsolable over his daughter's death. Whether she fell accidentally, committed suicide as a final, desperate slap to her father's obstinacy, or was murdered by Colonel Tayloe himself must remain speculation. He insisted to his own death years later that the girl's fall was an accident.

But on nights when the wind is particularly piercing and rain slaps against the aged walls the girl's restless spirit reenacts the death scene, complete with screams and the sickening thud of a falling body. The shadow of a candle moves up the wall by the staircase in precisely the same fashion as if it were held in the slim fingers of a young lady returning from a late, illicit rendezvous.

Soon after Miss Tayloe's death, Colonel Tayloe moved his family back to their plantation. He tried to assuage his grief—or guilt—by working from dawn to dusk with his horses. He spoke little to his wife or his fourteen surviving children.

In Washington the fighting blazed. On August 24, 1814, the British burned the White House, leaving it a smoldering ruin and leaving President James Madison and his wife, Dolley, homeless. The Octagon was spared the flames, probably because it flew the flag of France. Mrs. Tayloe had insisted that the French minister occupy the Octagon in her family's absence. But now, a presidential home was needed. Colonel Tayloe offered his mansion as an executive residence until the White House could be rebuilt. The Madisons accepted the offer and Mrs. Madison, following in Ann Tayloe's footsteps, entertained frequently and lavishly.

At the end of the war the Tayloes returned to their city home. But tragedy wrought by Colonel Tayloe's fiery temper and unforgiving nature would strike again. A second daughter fell in love with a man of whom her father disapproved. He refused to allow a marriage. She eloped but quickly regretted her decision and returned home seeking her father's dispensation.

The colonel was not a forgiving man. The two met on the staircase and exchanged words, the young girl beseeching her father to excuse her foolish mistake and he, in turn, rebuffing her every plea. Apparently, Colonel Tayloe angrily shoved his daughter aside and she lost her footing. She fell headfirst down the stairs and landed in a crumpled mass of crinoline at the foot of the steps. She was dead, her neck broken in the fall.

This second, unfortunate Tayloe daughter may be another ghost in the Octagon House. On certain days a shadow marks the death spot on the floor of the great rotunda, and persons crossing the hall at that place unconsciously walk around an invisible object lying there. Perhaps they feel a cold spot or sense the presence of the tragic Miss Tayloe.

A rug at the foot of the staircase is often found turned back at one corner, and heavy footsteps pace the third floor when no one is up there. Colonel Tayloe may be walking off his sorrow, or guilt, at his role in the deaths of two of his children. He died at the age of fifty-seven.

Other mysterious presences have been reported in the Octagon House. For more than a century thumping sounds came from within a wall, but no source was ever found until workmen making house repairs removed a portion of that wall. As they removed a section of the old plaster, the skeleton of a young girl fell to their feet. Each bony fist was clenched as if she had died knocking on the walls. After the skeleton was properly buried the sounds ceased.

And the girl's identity? Legend has it that a British soldier murdered a young servant girl after a lover's quarrel and stuffed her body inside a hollow wall.

Ann Tayloe died in 1855, and the house was rented to a succession of tenants. No one stayed long because they said the place was haunted.

During the Civil War, five men arranged to stay overnight in the mansion to prove that the ghost stories were groundless. They were soon disturbed by the rattle of a sword, heavy footfalls from the top floors, and terrible moans and sobs. They fled.

In 1902 the American Institute of Architects purchased the property and restored the badly deteriorated house. It is now a National Historic Landmark open to the public. Yet, in spite of the restoration and thousands of prying tourists, the ghosts remain. Visitors sometimes feel another person standing close behind them on the floor where the servants slept, but when they turn around no one is there.

The ghost of Dolley Madison, wearing the plumed turban that she favored in life to make herself appear taller, glides through the rooms. And the delightful scent of Dolley's lilac perfume often fills the drawing room.

During the 1950s the Octagon's caretaker, James Cypress, lived in the house with his wife. One day Mrs. Cypress became ill and her husband sent for a doctor. After the physician arrived he told Cypress that he'd met a man coming down the staircase. The doctor said he paused to stare at the stranger because he was wearing an American military uniform of the early 1800s. There was no such person in the house.

Alric H. Clay was superintendent of the Octagon in the early 1960s. He was an earnest young man who scoffed at ghost tales. But one night in February 1963 he had an experience he could never explain. A late party took place in the mansion and, after the last guest had left, Clay switched off the lights and locked the house for the night.

At 3:00 A.M. Washington police called Clay to report that the doors of the Octagon were open and all the lights were blazing. Clay and a Mr. Woverton accompanied police officers in a search, but all was in order. The men shut off the lights, again locked the doors and left.

At 7:00 A.M. the officers made another check of the house. The lights were burning again and the back door was unlocked. Yet Clay was the only person who possessed a key to that particular door. Again a search found no evidence of uninvited guests.

The phenomenon of the lights was not new to Clay. One night in 1962 he'd been driving past the Octagon and saw the lights on. He unlocked the back door and went to the basement where the light controls are. While down there he heard a man's heavy footsteps striding across the main floor. Flashlight in hand, Clay climbed the stairs cautiously. Clay checked through all the rooms and tried the doors. Everything was in order. Alric Clay was the only *living* person in the house that night.

Despite the numerous ghostly legends, Octagon guides are reluctant to answer questions about the house's spectral history. They prefer to point out the architectural uniqueness of the house and its significance as a meeting place for the individuals who helped shape American history.

But should you catch the odors of cooking, or the scent of lilacs, or sense a slight chill at a certain place in the rotunda, you'll know that the Tayloes, or perhaps the Madisons, are still in residence.

The *Other* Tenants at 1600 Pennsylvania Avenue

President John Adams and his wife, Abigail, were the first occupants of the White House. During Adams's presidency (1797–1801), the capital moved from Philadelphia to Washington, a struggling hamlet built mostly in a swamp. Pennsylvania Avenue was unpaved, and frequent rains turned it into a quagmire. Although the White House itself was only half finished, Mrs. Adams cheerfully tolerated the noise and confusion of workmen coming and going. She was as fond of pomp and ceremony as Martha Washington had been, and, in spite of the inconveniences, held memorable receptions and dinner parties. Indeed, her invitations were highly coveted.

But one immediate problem presented itself—where to hang the family wash. The White House was inadequately heated, and a number of the rooms were cold and damp. Mrs. Adams finally decided that the East Room was the warmest and driest place in her august home, and that's where the clotheslines were strung.

And *that* first lady has never forgotten.

The ghost of Abigail Adams is seen hurrying toward the East Room, with arms outstretched as if carrying a load of laundry. She can be recognized by the cap and lace shawl she favored in life.

Although Abigail Adams is the "oldest" ghost ever to have been encountered at the White House, she is by no means the only former occupant to occasionally wander its halls and great rooms. The home of the American chief executive has been the site of so much intense life it seems only appropriate that from within its walls come stories and legends of presidents and first ladies who linger . . . after life.

Dorothea Paine "Dolley" Madison was one of the most popular first ladies to have presided in the White House. She was born in 1768 and became the wife and young widow of John Todd, a Quaker lawyer of Philadelphia. In 1794, at the age of twenty-six, she married James Madison, who became, in 1809, fourth president of the United States.

Dolley's wit and charm and her ability to remember faces endeared her to everyone. But she never liked to be crossed, as the legend of *her* ghost bears out.

When the second Mrs. Woodrow Wilson occupied the White House, she ordered gardeners to dig up the familiar Rose Garden. They never turned a spade. Dolley Madison had planned and built that garden! Her ghost arrived in all her nineteenth-century finery to upbraid the workmen for what they were about to do. The men fled. Not a flower was disturbed and Dolley's garden continues to bloom today as it has for nearly two centuries.

The Rose Room is believed to be one of the most haunted spots in the White House. It contains Andrew Jackson's bed, and if we are to believe the testimony of those who have felt his presence, "Old Hickory" himself still dwells in his former bedchamber. And well he might.

In 1824 Jackson ran for president against John Quincy Adams and two other candidates, garnering the most popular and electoral votes, but not a clear majority; the election was decided by the House of Representatives, which chose Adams. In 1828 Jackson finally won the presidency, but he never forgot nor forgave his enemies. Bitterly resentful over his earlier defeat, he removed two thousand former office-holders, replacing them with his own appointments.

Twenty years after Jackson's death, Mary Todd Lincoln, a devout believer in the spirit world, told friends that she'd heard him stomping through the White House corridors and swearing. Still settling old scores?

Through the years White House staff members have reported feeling uncomfortable in the Rose Room. Lillian Rogers Parks, a seamstress, had a particularly frightening experience. In her 1961 book, *My Thirty Years Backstairs at the White House*, Mrs. Parks wrote:

"I remember that when I was working at the bed in the Rose Room, getting the spread fixed for Queen Elizabeth, I had an experience that sent me flying out of there so fast I almost forgot my crutches. The spread was a little too long, and I was hemming it as it lay on the bed. I had finished one side, and was ready to start the other, when suddenly I felt that someone was looking at me, and my scalp tightened.

"I could feel something coldish behind me, and I didn't have the courage to look. It's hard to explain. I went out of that room, and I didn't finish that spread until three years later."

Mrs. Parks also recalled a strange story told to her by Cesar Carrera, valet to Franklin Delano Roosevelt. Carrera said he heard someone calling his name one day in the Yellow Oval Room. The voice seemed to come from a distance, saying, "I'm Mr. Burns." At first, Carrera thought someone was playing a joke on him, but he learned later that a man named David Burns had given the government the land on which the White House was built.

A similar story surfaced during the Truman White House years when a guard heard a soft voice calling, "I'm Mr. Burns." Thinking that Secretary of State James Byrnes was calling down from upstairs, the guard went searching for him. He found out later that Secretary Byrnes hadn't been in the White House that day.

On April 9, 1865, Robert E. Lee surrendered his Confederate forces to Ulysses S. Grant at Appomattox Court House, Virginia. Although the last Rebel troops would not surrender until May, the Civil War was effectively over. The Union had held. But, a weary President Abraham Lincoln would not live to see the triumphant march of the Army of the Potomac through the streets of Washington. Just five days later, on April 14, 1865, he was shot by a Southern sympathizer, John Wilkes Booth, in Ford's Theater. He died the next day.

Psychics believe that President Lincoln has never left the White House, that his spirit remains to complete the business of his abbreviated second term and to be available in times of crisis. For seventy years presidents, first ladies, guests, and members of the White House staff have claimed to have either seen Lincoln or felt his presence.

The melancholy bearing of Lincoln himself, and several instances of eerie prescience on his part, only add to the legends of the Great Emancipator's ghost.

The lanky president had paid fanatical attention to even the most minute details concerning the Civil War and felt personally responsible for its outcome. His background was Southern, leading some critics to accuse him of traitorous acts. Mary Todd Lincoln had brothers who fought for the Southern cause. By the time of his 1864 reelection, deep lines etched his face and heavy black circles underlined his eyes. During his five years as commander in chief, he had slept little and taken no vacations. There may have been more to his sadness than even he would admit. Lincoln dreamed of his own death.

Ward Hill Lamon, a close friend of the president's, wrote down what Lincoln told him on an evening in early 1865:

"About ten days ago I retired very late . . . ," the president told Lamon. "I soon began to dream. There seemed to be a deathlike stillness about me. Then I heard subdued sobs, as if a number of people were weeping. I thought I left my bed and wandered downstairs.

"There, the silence was broken by the same pitiful sobbing, but the mourners were invisible. I went from room to room. No living person was in sight, but the same mournful sounds of distress met me as I passed alone . . . I was puzzled and alarmed.

"Determined to find the cause of a state of things so mysterious and shocking, I kept on until I arrived at the East Room. Before me was a catafalque, on which rested a corpse wrapped in funeral vestments. Around it were stationed soldiers who were acting as guards; and there was a throng of people, some gazing mournfully upon the corpse, whose face was covered, others weeping pitifully.

" 'Who is dead in the White House?' I demanded of one of the soldiers. 'The President,' was his answer. 'He was killed by an assassin.' "

It was not the first time that Lincoln "saw" his own death. Soon after his election in 1860, he'd seen a double image of his face reflected in a mirror in his Springfield, Illinois, home. One was his "real" face, the other a pale imitation. Lincoln's superstitious wife, Mary Todd Lincoln, did not see the mirror images, but was deeply troubled by her husband's account of the incident. She prophesied that the sharper image indicated that he would serve out his first term. The faint, ghostlike image was a sign, she said, that he would be renominated for a second term, but would not live to complete it.

* * *

President Lincoln's morose acceptance of his own mortality was never more apparent than on the morning of his tragic visit to Ford's Theater. He summoned the Cabinet to the Council Chamber. The president's face was grave.

"Gentlemen," he began, "before long you will have important news."

The Cabinet members pressed him to reveal what information he had, but Lincoln demurred.

"I . . . I have no news, but you will hear tomorrow." He hesitated, his chin cupped in his bony hands. "I have had a dream, the same dream that I have had three times before. I am in a boat, alone on an ocean. I have no oars, no rudder. I am helpless. Adrift." The president seemed to be speaking as out of a reverie.

He scanned the questioning faces before him, then stood up and shambled out of the room. It was possibly the strangest Cabinet meeting ever called by a president of the United States.

That night President Lincoln was shot in the back of the head with a single bullet fired from a derringer as he watched *Our American Cousin* at Ford's Theater. He died at 7:22 the next morning, April 15, 1865.

A train bore Lincoln's body home to Springfield. That solemn procession has given rise to another persistent legend surrounding Lincoln. Each year, on the anniversary of that journey, so the story goes, two ghost trains slowly travel the rails between Washington and Illinois. Aboard the first train a military band plays a funeral dirge. Before the smoke of the locomotive clears, a second steam engine follows silently behind, pulling a coach bearing a coffin containing the body of President Lincoln. The ghost trains never reach Springfield.

The shock felt by the nation upon the death of its sixteenth president took years to wear off. Children, too young to have understood the implications of the tumultuous years of the Civil War, saw their parents' bereavement and wanted to learn more about the man from Illinois. Newspapers responded to this need by reprinting numerous stories about Abraham Lincoln's early years. Most were true. Others contained more fable than fact.

It is true that tragedy had stalked Lincoln long before his first presidential term. His beloved mother, Nancy Hanks Lincoln, died when her son was nine. When Lincoln's first love, Ann Rutledge, died of typhoid fever, he lapsed into a melancholy that may have led to his emotional breakdown a few years later.

In 1842, at the age of thirty-three, Lincoln married Mary Todd, but the union was not a particularly happy one. Mary had a mercurial temperament and a strong belief in the supernatural. It was her influence that led to her husband's interest in spiritualism, although he always regarded it with some skepticism.

The Lincolns had three sons, but only Robert Todd lived to adulthood. Edward died at age four and young Willie succumbed to a fever during his father's first term as president. Lincoln was shattered by Willie's death and often visited the crypt where the child was buried. He would sit there for hours, weeping copiously. At Mrs. Lincoln's urging, séances were held at the White House with the hope of communicating with their dead sons. The results of these séances were not entirely satisfying, and it's believed that Lincoln attended only two of them.

During the administration of Ulysses S. Grant, however, a member of the household staff claimed to have seen Willie and to have conversed with his spirit. In the Lyndon B. Johnson presidency (1963–69), Lynda Johnson Robb occupied the room where Willie had died, and later, where the autopsy on Abraham Lincoln had been performed. This was also the room in which President Truman's mother died. Mrs. Robb wrote to the authors of this book that, although she'd never seen a ghost in the White House, "I did live in a room where lots of sad things took place!"

Liz Carpenter, press secretary to Lady Bird Johnson, told author John Alexander that Mrs. Johnson believed she'd felt Lincoln's presence one spring evening while watching a television program about his death. She noticed a plaque she'd never seen before hanging over the fireplace. It mentioned Lincoln's importance in that room in some way. Mrs. Johnson admitted feeling a strange coldness and a decided sense of unease.

This disquieting apprehension has been felt by others. Grace Coolidge, wife of Calvin Coolidge, the thirtieth president, was the first person to report having actually *seen* the ghost of Abraham Lincoln. She said he stood at a window of the Oval Office, hands clasped behind his back, gazing out over the Potomac, perhaps still seeing the bloody battlefields beyond.

The ghost of Lincoln was seen frequently during the administration of Franklin D. Roosevelt, when the country went through a devastating depression and then a world war.

When Queen Wilhelmina of the Netherlands was a guest at the White House during that period she was awakened one night by a knock on her bedroom door. Thinking it might be an important message, she got up and opened the door. The top-hatted figure of President Lincoln stood in the hallway. The queen fainted. When she came to she was lying on the floor. The apparition had vanished.

Eleanor Roosevelt used Lincoln's bedroom as her study. Although she denied seeing the former president's ghost, she admitted to feeling his presence whenever she worked late at night. She thought he was standing behind her, peering over her shoulder.

On one occasion, Mrs. Roosevelt's secretary, Mary Eben, encountered Lincoln's ghost sitting on the bed in the northwest bedroom. He was pulling on his boots, as if in a hurry to go somewhere. The startled young woman screamed and ran from the second floor. Other staffers of that era said they'd seen Lincoln lying quietly on his bed of an afternoon.

Seamstress Lillian Rogers Parks detailed in her autobiography a mystifying experience that she had one summer day in that same northwest room. It had just been freshly painted and she was putting it back in order. The White House was almost empty because the Roosevelts had gone to Hyde Park, taking most of the maids with them. As Mrs. Parks worked, she kept hearing someone coming to the door, but she never saw anyone. In fact, the second floor was deserted.

After an hour of listening to the tromping, Mrs. Parks went searching for the source. On the third floor she found a houseman. She asked him why he kept pacing the second floor. He shrugged his shoulders. "I don't know what you're talking about," he said. "I haven't been on that floor. I just came on duty. That was Abe you heard."

During Harry S Truman's administration, his daughter, Margaret, slept in that area of the White House and often heard rappings at her bedroom door late at night. Whenever she checked, no one was there. She complained to her father and he said the "noises" must be due to dangerous settling of the floors. He ordered the White House completely rebuilt. It was a propitious decision. The chief architect, Major Gen. Glen E. Edgerton, told President Truman that the building had been in danger of imminent collapse! Had the ghost of Lincoln tried to warn the Trumans that the president's home was ready to fall down?

Thirty years after the rebuilding of the White House, the Lincoln Bedroom was still regarded as a spooky place. Susan Ford, daughter of President Gerald Ford, said publicly that she believes in ghosts and during her stay in the White House she had no intention of *ever* sleeping in that room.

Stories of a ghostly President Lincoln wandering the corridors and rooms of the White House persist, but are not officially acknowledged. The gangly prairie lawyer with the black stovepipe hat and the long, sad face was the kind of man around whom legends naturally collect. If one were to believe in ghosts, one would have to believe that the benevolent spirit of Abraham Lincoln, our greatest president, still watches over the nation he fought so gallantly to preserve.

The Vestigial Projectionist

Foster Finley was the ideal employee. He arrived early, stayed late, and looked upon his job as a second home. No one ever complained about Foster or criticized the quality of his work. He was, said a man who used to work for him, "the nicest guy you'd ever want to meet."

But you wouldn't want to meet him now. He's been dead for over a quarter century. Gone, but certainly not forgotten. And not unseen. Foster Finley—Fink to his friends—is still on the job, as a ghost.

To understand Fink Finley, his devotion to his employer and the reason he haunts the earth, the investigator must appreciate *where* he spent his life: a palatial show palace known as the Tampa Theatre. Fink was a projectionist at the theater from 1930, four years after it opened, until he died on December 17, 1965, of a heart attack while at work in his booth above the balcony.

Designed by the dean of movie-palace architects, John Eberson, Tampa Theatre embodies all of the frills and embellishments of theatergoing in the early twentieth century. The design is an eclectic blend of Italian Renaissance, Greek Revival, and "Florida Mediterranean" styles. The interior boasts statues, reproductions of famous paintings, dozens of gilt-edged mirrors, intricate tapestries and banners, terra-cottas, and copper and brass jugs. A ceiling painted to represent a deep blue sky with hundreds of twinkling stars arches across the auditorium, complementing perfectly the Moorish pleasure garden scene below. Above the right organ grille is a peacock figurine, Eberson's trademark.

Promoted as "The South's Most Beautiful Theatre," the Tampa movie palace certainly lived up to its reputation. It held fifteen hundred seats and boasted a twenty-piece orchestra, a "Mighty Wurlitzer" organ, and ten thousand light bulbs! An early photograph shows a sign prominently displayed reading "COOLED BY REFRIGERATION"; the theater had the first commercial air-conditioning in Tampa.

Nearly from the beginning, Foster "Fink" Finley was as much a part of the atmosphere at Tampa Theatre as the gargoyles leering down from their perches in the lobby or the uniformed ushers who guided patrons to their seats. A short, slightly balding man with a cigarette always dangling from the corner of his mouth, Fink spent thirty-eight years projecting Hollywood films from the era of D. W. Griffith to that of Stanley Kubrick.

"He traveled by bus and never drove," Bill Hunt, one of Fink's former colleagues once told a reporter. "He wore glasses, was immaculately attired. He always wore a suit, tie and hat to work, then he'd change when he got to the booth. He shaved there." Hunt was the man who took Fink home on the day in 1965 when he fell ill.

For five decades, Fink watched as the parade of American motion picture history unwound on his projectors. The theater was Tampa's "premiere showplace" until suburban movie theater complexes began to nibble away at attendance in the 1960s. Ironically, Fink died just at the time "his" theater started to decline.

Another longtime employee, Syd Morris, related in a 1978 newspaper interview just how devoted Fink Finley was to the theater. "Ol' Fink used to come to work at seven or eight in the morning and get his cup of coffee. The theater didn't even open until one in the afternoon in those days. He practically lived there."

Fink, however, was not an easy man to get along with, nor did he have many friends. His colleagues knew he was married and had other family in the city, but he rarely spoke of anything but his work. He kept to himself, fussing over his projector.

"In those days, there were two projectionists," Morris said. "Fink would watch over his machine and another man would watch his. Fink's partner could be throwing up and he wouldn't touch the other machine."

Tampa Theatre was restored in the late 1970s by the Arts Council of Tampa–Hillsborough County, which now manages and programs it. The City of Tampa maintains the theater, used now for a variety of theater, music, and dance events. The Tampa Film Club shows over one hundred films each year in the theater.

Far above the main floor, at the very top of the balcony, small windows reveal the presence of the projection room. Even when the auditorium is fully lighted, it is a dark and gloomy chamber. A narrow passageway leads to doors to the booth. Inside, there is space for little more than the enormous 35mm motion picture projectors, a couple of chairs, and a workbench. It is most certainly *not* a place one would want to spend hours upon end, yet it seems that Fink was extremely comfortable within its narrow confines.

Not unexpectedly, the projection booth figures in many of the stories about Fink's ghost. Angel Altuzarra, for instance, was one longtime employee who believes Fink has stayed behind. Angel worked his way up from custodian to operations foreman in the years 1979–1985. Although he never actually *saw* Fink floating around the projectors, Angel had several eerie experiences. The most perplexing episode involved a knife.

"I had this knife in a [belt] holster. I would slip the holster strap and the knife popped out into my hand. Well, I lost it one day. I got quite upset because after a couple of days I couldn't find it. Now I'm an expert at finding stuff in that theater. And, believe me, that theater is an expert at losing things. You'd put something down and you might not find it where you put it. It's really strange.

"Well, I had seen on a TV show that if you asked a ghost to return something, then you'd find it again. And that's what I did. I was looking down from the mezzanine toward the stage when I asked for the knife's return. Nothing happened. But then I turned around and there it was."

Angel spotted the knife on the carpet against the wall near the projection booth. The knife was leaning against the wall with the blade out. He had looked around that area several times in the preceding days.

"I was pretty shaken up," Angel recalled. "I just picked up the knife, put it away and left for the day. It convinced me there was a ghost in the theater."

Angel's encounters with what he believes is the ghost of Fink Finley weren't limited to the projection booth, however, especially on those long nights when he was alone in the theater cleaning up after a concert or film showing. He remembers, for instance, the time Fink poked him.

"I was there by myself mopping the floor in the lobby. About twelve midnight. I got tapped on the shoulder. I massaged my shoulder because I thought it was a muscle contraction. It must be, I thought. Well, I kept on working and I got tapped on the shoulder again. And again. And again. About five times within about thirty seconds, and always from the same direction. I just went nuts!"

Just off the main lobby is a staircase that descends to a hallway with offices and public rest rooms. Angel encountered *something* there, in more ways than one. "I had come out of the men's room and felt a cold wind, but without the wind. No blowing. Like a feeling of fear all of a sudden. I felt as if I walked right through someone, or somebody took my soul away. It was weird, very scary." It is clear that Angel believes he accidentally walked right through Fink, or what was left of him.

But there was another incident that truly frightened Angel Altuzarra. It literally drove him out of the theater.

Angel had been on the job about three or four months. A Sunday afternoon. Quiet. The streets in front of the theater were deserted, as was the theater itself. Angel had ridden his bicycle to work and was adjusting the gearshift mechanism near the locked front doors, getting ready to head for home. And then . . .

"I heard chains dragging. Like a heavy chain being pulled across the terrazzo floor. It wasn't like someone was trying to attract attention, just dragging it along. I was holding the bike in my hands and thought about going back into the theater to find out who the heck was making that noise. But I was just too scared to do it."

Less than a minute after Angel first heard the chains, house manager Gary Jordan showed up at the locked outside door. The sound stopped. Angel told Jordan about the incident and asked him to wait a few seconds. "It'll happen again, I'm sure of it," Angel told Jordan. It didn't. Angel left posthaste after it became apparent the phantom chains had stopped their rattling.

Fink's last partner, Bill Hunt, told a reporter about an episode that gave him a "strange feeling." Hunt was among the first to voice suspicions that the old theater was haunted by Fink's ghost. A few years after Fink's death, Hunt walked into the projection booth through one of its two entrances. He started to close the door behind him, but he felt someone pulling back on it. Hunt thought his current partner had quietly come in behind him, but no one was following him.

Some projectionists have reported the door between the booth and the generator room opening and closing while they have to watch the film closely for the cues signaling when to switch projectors. They hear a surge in generator noise, indicating the door opened, but it's never open when they can look in that direction. One worker almost quit when the power switch was turned off while no one was near it.

Box office manager Denise Darby believes in Fink's ghost. According to an interview she gave a newspaper reporter, Denise was never able to explain what happened to her while she was alone one Sunday afternoon. Ironically, it was the same day of the week on which Angel Altuzarra heard the rattling chains in the lobby.

As Denise walked through the auditorium, a door in front of her opened and shut, as if someone had walked through. Her first thought was that someone had opened another exit door, causing air pressure vacuum to force the door nearest her to open. Upon checking, however, she discovered all the other doors were locked and chained as usual. "It took me aback for a second," she said. That may have been an understatement.

In 1984, *Tampa Tribune* reporter Warren Epstein gathered three men and two women one evening to "investigate" the haunting with a séance late one evening. The movie showing that night was *Mutiny on the Bounty*. When the intrepid group gathered after the audience had left, house manager Gary Jordan told them not to be concerned if the lights flickered on and off. That was not uncommon, he said. Jordan snapped off the main lights and left the five sitting on the stage.

Within a few minutes, the group all had the intense feeling of being watched by someone. According to theater employee Pat McElroy, one woman "got so scared she ran out into the lobby. She thought she'd be safer out there, but the lights in the lobby were also turned off." The numerous Gothic gargoyles staring down from the walls and dim lighting made the lobby even gloomier than usual.

The young woman stayed out there for the rest of the time the group was in the theater. "When they were done," McElroy said, "this woman was very upset. She thought she had seen something move in the mirrors out there. In two of the mirrors she said she knew she saw something move. The hard part for her to believe was that she was the only one in there. There wasn't anyone else walking through. It is the type of place that when the lights are off your imagination can go wild. Even in the daytime, I dread walking through here." The woman also heard faint strains of old music or, she said, what may have been the theme from the "Bugs Bunny Show." The lobby should have been deadly quiet at that hour.

Epstein and the other three "ghost catchers" remained in the theater's auditorium. They tramped up to the balcony and Fink's old projection booth, asking all the while for the ghost to put in an appearance. One man said it seemed as if someone were sitting in the empty seat next to him. He also heard what seemed to be one of the auditorium seats being opened. A woman in the group said she sensed, more than saw, someone walking in front of the stage.

The group eventually gave up, found the woman who had unwisely chosen to sit out the séance in the lobby, heard her curious story and left for home. They

seemed neither convinced nor unbelieving that Fink Finley's ghost haunted the
theater.

Pat McElroy, the assistant to the theater's director, emphasizes that no one
yet has seen Fink peering out from his old projection booth or wandering up
the balcony aisle. She loves the ornate theater and its history, but the same
statues, pillars, and mirrors that cause visitors to exclaim in wonder make her
slightly uncomfortable as she rambles alone through the endless passages and
stairwells. That and the prospect of a chance encounter with Fink Finley.

McElroy hopes someone does see something, ideally one of the visiting show
business stars who give frequent concerts. Like Harry Anderson, the comedian
and star of television's "Night Court," who has performed at Tampa Theatre.

"Harry joked about our theater, he loved it. He thought it was the prettiest
place he'd ever been. But he asked about a ghost and we told him there was
one. He kidded around about how his dressing room was way down in the back.
He hoped that no one came knocking on his door so that when he opened it
nothing was there. He was pretty funny."

Perhaps Fink was off in a corner somewhere, chuckling. And planning just
how he would introduce himself to Harry Anderson the next time he visits.

On the Old Kolb Farm

Katherine and James Tatum have always considered themselves rational, practical, stable people. They have a solid marriage, travel widely both in the United States and abroad, and have a wide circle of friends. James is a retired U.S. Army officer. Katherine is an accountant who is, she said, "used to analyzing the cause and effect of things in my work."

Therefore it was frustrating when they weren't able to find a "normal" explanation for an extraordinary series of events that thrust them into a mystifying series of encounters with the supernatural.

The Tatums had been looking for just the right community in which to retire. After traveling the world courtesy of the army, the couple first settled in Florida after James retired. However, the extremely hot summers there soon persuaded them to look elsewhere. They also missed the change of seasons of more northern climes. That's when they discovered Marietta, Georgia, and a new housing development that was being built on what was known as the Kolb Creek Farm, a tract of land that had been under cultivation since well before the Civil War. Amid the wooded, rolling hills, Katherine and James Tatum were among the first families to build a house in the exclusive subdivision. They moved to Kolb Ridge Court in 1986, just down the road from the original log-sided Kolb Creek farmhouse, which had been preserved for its historic significance.

For the first year the Tatums thoroughly enjoyed their lovely, two-story, contemporary-style home. They often entertained new acquaintances in Marietta and old friends who dropped in for visits. Their idyllic retirement was not to last.

"A little over a year after the house was built, we began to experience strange events," Katherine Tatum remembers. What came to transpire was over a half dozen events so perplexing they would be "hard for anyone to believe . . . unless they experienced it themselves," Katherine said.

The first came in the middle of a quiet night.

"My husband and I had gotten up to go to the bathroom at the same time, about two-thirty A.M.," Katherine said. "Our bedroom is upstairs. My husband used the bedroom bath and I went into the hall bath. The bathroom door was open. I saw a man walking down the hall in front of the open bathroom door. I assumed it was my husband looking for me since I was not in bed. I called out to him. He didn't answer. I thought he'd gone downstairs to search for me and had not heard me call out to him. When I got back to our bedroom James was back in bed. He wouldn't have been able to go back to the bedroom without passing me again."

Although she was startled to see James in the bedroom after she thought she had seen him going downstairs, the peculiarity of the event didn't immediately strike her. "I asked if that was him in the hall. He said it wasn't. I asked if he had heard me call out to him. He had, but he knew I was in there and couldn't figure out why I kept calling out."

Katherine then told her husband that she had seen someone going down the hall toward the stairs. James grabbed a gun he kept next to the bed and quickly checked all the windows and doors in the entire house. There was no sign that anyone else had been in the house.

That upset Katherine Tatum even more. "After that it was almost impossible for me to go to sleep. I spent the rest of the night going over and over the incident. I came to realize that when the man walked past me there had been no sound, as you would normally hear whenever someone is walking down the hall."

The more she concentrated on the figure she had seen, the more she remembered. The man—for she was quite convinced it was a male—had his head slightly tilted. He seemed to be wearing a coat of some sort and a hat.

The man was in shadow because a high-intensity floodlight on the side of their house was throwing light through a window directly opposite the hallway bathroom. "He was a solid figure. I couldn't tell what he was wearing because I was on the dark side of him. He was walking like he was going somewhere, not shuffling. And he was swinging his arms as he went by. Like he had someplace to go."

Katherine even briefly followed after the figure, calling out all the while since she still believed it was James. There was no answer, and by the time she had gotten to the top of the stairs whoever it was had disappeared. That's when she turned around and returned to the master bedroom . . . and found James settled back in bed.

"I became afraid," Katherine said. "I started trying to rationalize what had happened. What did I see? That's when I realized I didn't hear anything when the figure went by."

What did James think of his wife's encounter with a phantom? "At first he thought somebody was in the house. And then he didn't know what to think. But he knew I couldn't get back to sleep once I found out that it was not human."

Not human.

Two simple words, but for Katherine Tatum they spelled out what seemed almost impossible—their new house in suburban Marietta was not quite what it seemed. And yet Katherine's common sense and work experience told her to look for the logical explanation, the facts behind this bizarre nightmare. But before she could reach a satisfactory answer, other, equally perplexing episodes caused the couple almost to question their own sanity.

Approximately a month later, James Tatum undertook a small carpentry project involving a pull-down type of attic stairs. Every time the stairs were pulled down from the ceiling, the bottom posts dug into the hallway carpeting. He was going to bolt a board across the bottom to prevent any further damage.

Katherine Tatum takes up the account:

"He had his tools and a power drill up there. One time I called him for dinner. He laid the drill to the side and came down, intending to go back and finish later. Well, he forgot about it and started watching a television program. Later on I went upstairs to our bedroom to lie down and read. I had turned away from the bedroom door when I heard the drill. It was real loud, as though someone was playing around with it, turning it on and off. I thought that my husband was trying to scare me with it. I tried to ignore it and continued to read my book. After a while I had had enough of his 'playfulness' so I ran out to the hallway."

The drill lay on its side, propped up against the wall just as James must have left it several hours before. Katherine knelt to touch it and found it cold. She ran down the stairs to find her husband. He looked around, but came up with nothing.

"He was sympathetic," Katherine said, "yet not quite able to believe me. I was one shaky woman."

The house was quiet for several weeks and Katherine Tatum almost believed the earlier episodes were an aberration, somehow explainable if only she could figure them out.

"I had just about gotten over the drill business," Katherine said, "when I went upstairs to watch television one night. I was completely engrossed in a TV drama when I began to hear what sounded like static electricity in the middle of the room. A kind of popping in the air."

She turned off the television set to concentrate on what was causing it. Try as she might, however, there didn't appear to be any clear source for the mysterious sound. But as she walked around the room looking, the noise seemed to move toward her.

"I backed up clear to the corner and it came right up to my face. I had no alternative but to duck under and run down the stairs to my husband."

The noise stayed in the room and did not follow her. At Katherine's insistence, James checked through the room, but by this time all was quiet. Whatever had caused Katherine's fright had vanished.

"This began to make me quite fearful of what was happening in our home," Katherine remembers.

A few days later, the Tatums left on a long-planned two-month vacation to the West Coast and Alaska. Although the trip was unconnected with the peculiar events in their house, Katherine, in particular, felt a desperate need to get away for a while.

"When we returned home everything was quiet. I was hoping that it was the end of it. It wasn't," she said.

The Tatums were readying themselves for a short trip to Florida several weeks after their return from the West Coast when Katherine had a *physical* encounter with the ghost.

"I was in a rush to get things picked up and packed away. We were going to drive our motor home to Florida the next day. I was bent over putting a casserole in the microwave when I felt two distinct tugs on the bottom of my blouse. I turned around, thinking that it was my husband. He was outside."

Although this was the only time Katherine felt "touched" by their house's invisible occupant, she did have other physical reactions to the haunting.

"I always felt a cold spot in the upstairs hallway and one of the guest bedrooms. I would feel the hair stand up on the back of my neck in the bedroom. It almost felt like I was infringing upon someone else's room," she recalls. Katherine had a desk in that guest bedroom at which she would sometimes work but, she said, "I don't linger. It's just not comfortable for me, yet it's a very comfortable room."

James Tatum had been only indirectly involved in the strange goings-on at his home. He never doubted his wife's veracity, yet he didn't have any explicit proof of the events his wife described. All that would change in early 1988 in a series of occurrences with a small angel bell the couple kept in a second guest bedroom.

"My husband gets up quite early each morning," Katherine explains. James would usually dress and go downstairs for coffee and to read the morning newspaper in the family room. His wife stayed in bed.

"I ring the little angel bell that we keep in the guest bedroom whenever I need him," Katherine said. "The family room is so far away that it's difficult for him to hear me when I call out. It's easier for him to hear the bell. One morning he heard the bell ringing and came upstairs. But I was still asleep. He couldn't figure it out."

When Katherine awoke later, James told her the bell rang that morning. She denied ringing it and, indeed, to James it seemed totally out of character that his wife would pull such a prank. He jokingly told her that the "ghost" was behind it. A few days later, the couple weren't laughing anymore.

"It happened again, and he ran up the stairs. As soon as he hit the top step the bell stopped. He looked in the guest bedroom and the bell was still in there. He started back down the stairs when the bell rang again, as if he was being teased," Katherine said.

That morning at breakfast, James told his wife that he had no intention of running up the stairs again when the bell rang unless the couple could adopt some sort of code. He wanted to be sure it was his wife whose hand held the bell. Katherine told him she would ring the bell three times to let him know that it was she.

"You know what happened, of course," she said. "The next time it rang, it rang three times. He checked on the bell again. And it started ringing as he left the room. After that he told me that if the bell rings again, he wasn't going to answer. He said you'll have to come and get me. The bell never rang again."

James realized at that point that what was happening couldn't be explained in any rational manner.

The "ghost" remained dormant for some four months. The couple believed whatever was responsible for the activities had left the house. In May 1988 their hopes were dashed.

Katherine Tatum was again the center of the incident: "I had gone upstairs to read before going to bed. It was quite late, and my face was turned away from the door so that I could read by the bedside lamp. My husband keeps a little wooden bowl on the chest of drawers so that he can put his pocket change in it before going to bed. I heard the money dropping into the bowl a coin at a time. I turned to look at him, but he wasn't there. Yet I could hear the change being dropped in the bowl. It was just as clear and as loud as can be."

She ran downstairs to find James, but by the time they got back to the bedroom all was quiet. "He was ready to shoot it," Katherine said. "But I told him you can't shoot something you can't see. Whatever we have in this house, everything it does seems to be some sort of teasing. As long as I'm alert and looking for something to happen, it doesn't. It seems to happen only when I forget about it, or I'm engrossed in something else."

An incident involving a pack of Tums and a glass of water Katherine keeps on a tray on her night stand is an example of the "teasing" nature of the haunting. It was late evening and Katherine had just turned off the bedside lamp. James was still downstairs. "First I could hear the tray moving around and the glass being lifted up and put back down. I knew exactly what was going on. It was like listening to a bunch of rats playing around," she said. "And then when I didn't turn over [to look], the Tums started dropping down on the tray—one, two, three, four, five, just like that." As soon as she started paying attention to the annoying noises, they ceased nearly as suddenly as they had begun.

The Tatums rarely told anyone of the bothersome events they experienced. However, two of their longtime friends may have had an inadvertent brush with their prankish spirit. James and Katherine had arranged to "house-switch" with the couple—they would stay at their house in Florida for a week while their friends visited the Atlanta area by staying in the Tatums' Marietta home. Neither James nor Katherine told them they thought their house was haunted.

"About two months later we were talking to them on the telephone when I asked if anything strange had happened to them while they stayed here," Katherine said. "He [the husband] said, 'Ahhh!, so that's what it was.' I asked him to explain what he meant. He said something very odd had happened and he wondered what had caused it."

It seems that three nights after the Tatums left, the visiting couple were jarred awake in the guest bedroom very early in the morning by a very loud, persistent ringing. Though it sounded like an alarm clock, they couldn't determine where it was coming from. Eventually they found it was an electric alarm clock in the master bedroom. Somehow, it had gone off this one time. Seventy-two hours *after* the Tatums had left.

The next morning, the husband, an electronics technician at Walt Disney

World, examined the clock but couldn't figure out what had made it ring in the middle of the night.

In their phone conversation, Katherine told their friends about the inexplicable events in their house and said it was probably another example of the mischievous spirit.

Katherine and James Tatum found a possible explanation for the ghostly activity in their house in local history books. Not only is their house located on a very old homestead, but the area was the site of Civil War combat. The Battle of Kolb Farm took place at about the same time as the more famous Battle of Kennesaw Mountain, Georgia, during which thirteen thousand Union troops under the command of Gen. William Tecumseh Sherman stormed Confederate forces dug in across the mountain. Sherman failed to dislodge Confederate general Joe Johnston's troops, and lost several thousand men in the process. It didn't deter him, however, from continuing his march toward Atlanta.

The skirmish at Kolb Farm is a footnote in history books, but for Katherine Tatum its legacy may account for all of the inexplicable events she and her husband endured. The quick, probably painful death of a soldier over a century ago might provide a clue to the haunting. The lingering presence of one who died so suddenly may still be embedded on the land upon which the Tatums built their home. Katherine can't be sure that the man she saw in her upstairs hallway was a soldier from the Civil War, but so far it's the only reason she can come up with for the haunting on the old Kolb farm site.

"It's hard for anyone to believe this phenomenon unless they experience it themselves. It's mostly aggravating, but I do get frightened when it happens. It just doesn't make sense."

The Night Marchers

In an unearthly procession they march by, chanting ancient Hawaiian words long forgotten in company with a single, pulsating drumbeat. Some say it looks like a silvery cloud of dust moving along the roadway. Vague forms issue from the swirling smoke, each carrying a light as they move toward the *heiau*, the most revered of places in Hawaiian lore.

This is a Night of *Kane*, between the twenty-seventh and twenty-ninth of the month of a new moon.

The spirits are walking.

The Night Marchers are among the living.

It is also a dangerous time. A human observer is in mortal danger should the Night Marchers catch the odor of his body. A cry of *"Oia"* (Kill him!) will arise from the Marchers' vaporous lips, and the life of the interloper is forfeit. But if the witness should have a relative among this procession of the undead, and if the ghost sees his kin, a spell will be cast over the human that will prevent the Marchers from seeing him. His life will be saved.

Tales of the Night Marchers are among the most persistent of ghost stories in the Hawaiian Islands. On Molokai, but particularly on Oahu, where there are many sites associated with the old temples and healing stones known as *heiau*, Night Marchers on a Night of *Kane* are much to be feared by those knowledgeable in the Old Way.

Listen to some of the stories collected by writer Antoinette Withington:

A Caucasian physician who practiced for many years in the islands saw the ghostly procession many times. He often spoke of the strange sight to a young woman of his acquaintance. She did not believe him. Then on a Night of *Kane* he persuaded her to accompany him to a hillside near an old *heiau* and there they waited. As midnight passed they were still alone. As they prepared to return to their car the old physician suddenly called out, "Wait! Be still! They are coming!"

His young friend picked up the account: "I was amazed to see a long line of people slowly moving up from the water and steadily climbing the hill. They appeared strange, as though touched with a shimmering radiance. Each figure carried a light. I could almost see their faces through the darkness. They were chanting in old Hawaiian. Then we heard the drums. I was never so terrified in my life. Never again will I say that I do not believe what I have been told about these sacred things."

Earlier in his life, the physician asked geologists to examine the area where he saw the procession, and also the water from which the figures seemed to emerge. He wanted to find out if phosphorescence or some other natural explanation might account for the "spirit lights," as he called them. The scientists found nothing unusual. Neither could they account for the sounds like chanting voices or beating drums.

On the island of Molokai, a young boy who would grow up to become a prominent Hawaiian official first heard the mysterious drums on a night before the Fourth of July.

He had gone to bed quite early that night. The steady beat of a drum awoke him sometime later. He thought it was Molokai's fife and drum corps serenading in the neighborhood, as they sometimes did on summer evenings. The drums did not stop, however, and he got out of bed to ask his grandmother, who was still up, what it might be that he heard. She told him it must be the fifes and drums, but the child insisted it didn't sound anything like that. A short time later the corps did come around and play outside their house. The grandmother asked them where else they had played that night. Nowhere, the leader said, this was the first house they visited. Then the boy and his grandmother knew that he had heard the Night Marchers near the old *heiau*.

It is unusual for a *haole* (Caucasian) to see this ghostly procession. It is even more unusual that a *haole* should witness such an event at a Honolulu resort hotel. But that's what happened to one woman tourist. She told the writer Antoinette Withington what happened on two successive nights:

"I had gone out by the ocean before retiring to look at the water, and on both nights I had seen strange lights along the shore. The first night I saw only the moving lights, but the next night they seemed to leave the water and I saw that they were figures, and like a procession they walked along the beach and on toward Diamond Head."

A Hawaiian historian said there was a famous *heiau* on the slopes of Diamond Head, and the Marchers were probably headed there. The tourist was very fortunate to have seen such an event, he said.

On the Big Island, the Hawaiian Historical Society recorded a sighting of the Night Marchers that included the most famous of Hawaiian kings. It was recounted by a "very trustworthy" individual:

"As he was walking along Mahikiwaina Road, the solemn procession was seen to approach. Kamehameha the Great, attended by his officers and warriors in imposing array, marched along the ancient highway. Near to the king marched his *ilamuku*, or master of ceremonies, club in hand. Our traveler, knowing it was death to be discovered by this officer, dropped to the ground and crawled to a place of concealment in the woods which lined the road. From this point he saw the procession go by. Overcome by terror he was glad to escape unhurt, a living witness to this exhibition of the supernatural."

George Nawoakoa was an old Hawaiian with many stories of the Night Marchers. With his wife he lived in a house at a clearing in a cane field several miles outside Honolulu. Though he was reluctant to speak of the healing stones at Wahiawa—such spiritual matters would not be understood by a simple *haole*— he did reveal that once he saw the ghostly procession. "A person has to be right in here to see a procession," he said pointing to his heart.

He continued speaking: "I was coming home alone along the road. I had been to a neighbor's. It was getting toward dark. There was a little new moon but it did not affect the darkness. As I said, I was walking along alone when suddenly I saw something strange ahead of me, coming toward me. It seemed like a cloud of dust, but it shone like silver. It was then that I looked at the moon and knew that it was not that which made the shining.

"When I looked longer it seemed to me it was smoke—and just then I saw the people and I knew it must be a procession. I had heard that if the people in the procession caught sight of a living person that person might drop dead or the procession would disappear instantly. I crouched down by a big stone along the side of the road and they did not see me. There were old people and young ones. My young cousin had died a year before and I looked to see if she might not be with them, but I didn't see anyone I knew. They were all so white and strange. But they went right on to the old *heiau* and I heard the drums beating. We sometimes hear them now. The old people believed that the spirits of the dead sometimes came back to the *heiau* and had a celebration. I never saw it but once."

Should one be out on a Night of *Kane* to search for the Night Marchers, two locations on Oahu seem to present the greatest chance for success. *Heiaus* are found outside Wahiawa, near Interstate H2 and close to Schofield Barracks, and it is there that ghostly processions have been reported. A second possibility is an old road a few hundred yards up from the beach near Waialee where the Night Marchers used to cross on their way from the sea.

But remember the warning: Keep the wind in your face, lest they detect your scent. And never let them see you. Or you might be invited along on their everlasting march.

Eddy's Place

Sharon McKlusky, a Boise housewife and mother, was tired after a particularly stressful day. She fed her three children their supper, then drew a hot bath. Water always had a calm and soothing effect upon her. She had just settled into the tub when the bathroom light went off. A second later, the light came back on and the bathwater turned ice cold!

Later, Sharon told a newspaper reporter that she had felt suspended in space, that the experience seemed unreal.

But that was only one of many "unreal" incidents in the old frame house at 200 East Idaho. It was believed to have been built in 1895 by the grandfather of the late Frank Church, who served in the United States Senate from 1956 to 1981. The elder Church and his wife, Mary, raised five children in the house. Their five-year-old son, Clair, died a tragic death here from drinking turpentine he found in the garage.

After Mr. Church died in 1922, his widow and an unmarried daughter, Evangeline, remained in the house. Eventually Evangeline inherited the house and stayed on until her death in 1953. That same year Domingo Aldecoa and his wife bought the house to use as rental property. And they had many renters; most moved out after the first month.

Sharon moved in during 1970 and stayed for three years. She knew nothing of the history of the house, but she liked its spaciousness. The children had separate bedrooms and there was plenty of room both indoors and outdoors to play. It was much better than being cooped up in a tiny city apartment. Besides, the rent was reasonable. Sharon felt extremely fortunate.

Yet, the longer she stayed the more certain she was that something was wrong with the house. Sometimes while standing between the door of a bedroom and the door to the attic she felt a tingling sensation as if an electrical current had surged through her body.

Shapeless forms moved across the walls, doors opened and closed by themselves, and radios clicked on and off and changed stations with no one near them. Sharon's children seemed not to notice anything unusual and she said nothing that might frighten them.

Then one day she heard a child's plaintive voice call out, "I'm Eddy." It had seemed to come out of the walls. One of the children who had either lived in the house or visited there at one time was named Elmer Edmond. Although the little ghost child didn't materialize, Sharon began to feel "vibrations" whenever it moved through a room. She determined not to try to communicate with it. The little boy's presence was announced by the tinkling of a tiny bell that sounded like no other bell Sharon had ever heard. The bell rang on and off for six months, then stopped. The Church family had kept a harp in the parlor. Was that what Sharon heard?

One night a voice cried out, "Help!" Sharon froze in bed and prayed that the voice would go away. It did. For six months there was no supernatural activity.

Sharon's children loved the house and often invited their friends to spend the night. Sharon was happy because they were. Maybe there was nothing frightening about the house after all; perhaps she had imagined the tingling, the bell ringing, and the voices. She had been tired and upset when she moved her family into the house, and decided her imagination had run away with her. It hadn't.

Late one night Sharon was lying on the sofa in the living room. Two sets of sliding doors divided this room from the dining room on one side and the parlor on the other. All the doors were closed. Suddenly, letters began to appear across the bottom of one door. They came slowly, one after the other, but Sharon, too startled to move, recalled seeing only an *a*.

A round ball of light then floated across the room and as it twirled at high speed Sharon saw the sweet, smiling face of a little boy in the center of the light. It vanished as quickly as it had come.

But it reappeared several nights later when Sharon, two girlfriends, and the brother of one of the girls were visiting. They sat in the living room, a candle burning on one of the end tables. All of a sudden a rush of cold air blew through the room and extinguished the candle. The young man yelled that a ball of white light was whirling toward him. He ducked and saw the light pass through a wall. No one else had seen anything.

Sharon still was not at ease on the second floor. Every time she stood in the doorway of the bedroom that faced the attic door she became frightened for her children's safety.

One afternoon when the mother and her three-year-old son were sitting in the backyard, he exclaimed, "Look, Mama! Little boy in attic window!" Sharon saw nothing but the sun reflecting off the glass.

When they went back inside, her son led her to the bedroom across from the attic door and said, "He died there." Sharon didn't know who he meant, and he said no more.

The family didn't use that room for sleeping because Sharon's older son had tried to sleep there the night they moved in and awoke screaming that he couldn't breathe. He said something was choking him.

Sharon stored trunks and suitcases in the room and some of the children's toys that they played with infrequently. One afternoon, needing a sweater out of a trunk, she stepped into the room and saw a little boy in one corner and a small woman in a white dress bending over him. Were they Eddy and his mother? Sharon backed away.

Later, a friend of Sharon's named Judy, who had psychic ability, entered the room and saw a bed in one corner and curtains at the windows. She saw Eddy, who she said was harmless, but she also saw a bedridden old man who she said was evil. Judy said his ghost created the chills that swept the house. Was he the one who had called for help?

In 1972 Sharon rented rooms to two girls. The extra income would be welcome, and besides, little psychic activity was occurring. The renters were pleased and Sharon and her children enjoyed having them in the house. All went well until March 1973, when a man needing a place to stay approached Sharon. She explained that her rooms were all rented, and when he asked about bunking in the attic she told him that the house was haunted by a child ghost who "lived" in the attic. The man laughed.

The next day he moved a bed and all his gear into the attic. That night he felt uneasy and kept a light burning. The second night disaster struck. At 6:00 A.M. the man awakened in the midst of an inferno. The entire attic was on fire, but he was able to escape by jumping out a window. Although his injuries were not serious, he spent some time in the hospital.

Before the fire department could bring the blaze under control it had destroyed the second floor also. Firemen listed faulty wiring as the cause, but Sharon and her close friends were convinced it was astral arson. Had Eddy resented an interloper in his living quarters? And what role had the evil old man played in the fire?

The McKluskys and their two women roomers found a suitable house to rent and began the process of clearing out everything that could be salvaged.

Jim, one of Sharon's friends who had scoffed at her superstitious fears, offered to clean out the basement. As he started down the wooden stairway, he screamed that a step had broken. He plunged to the basement floor.

Seconds later, Jim, bruised and shaken, sat up and glanced at the stairway. There was no broken step!

On March 15, 1973, bulldozers leveled the remains of the old Church house.

The Music Room

THE TIME:
A spring night in the early 1920s

THE PLACE:
Pemberton Hall, Eastern Illinois University

She screamed. No one heard. The wind was high and rain lashed the windows of the old building, blotting out all other sounds.

In the morning, Jenny found her friend's bloodied body in the third-floor hallway, slumped against the door of the room they shared. Fingernails had clawed the door, leaving crimson trails.

Jenny wept.

Today, no one is alive to mourn the victim, but students at Eastern Illinois University in Charleston know her story.

They say her name is Mary. That she'd been practicing the piano late at night in the music room on the fourth floor of this old residence hall when she was bludgeoned to death by a crazed custodian wielding an axe. That the murderer was never apprehended. That it happened seventy years ago. And they add, with a bit of pride, that Mary has never left "Pem" Hall. Her spirit remains, gliding silently through the rooms, locking and unlocking doors, turning stereos and television sets on and off, busying herself with myriad mundane tasks—an ethereal housemother watching over the 225 women students who occupy the hall.

Patty O'Neill is one who can vouch for Mary. She believes she was visited by Mary in the spring of 1981.

Midterm exams were at hand and O'Neill had stayed up to study until early in the morning. Her roommate was already asleep. Before turning off the lights, O'Neill went to lock the door, but a recent rainy spell had swollen the wood to such an extent that she couldn't shut it all the way. The coed decided against slamming the door and awakening her roommate. The women of Pem Hall were trustworthy, she reasoned. They looked after one another and respected a person's privacy. Doors were routinely left unlocked, at least during the day.

O'Neill left the door unlocked and climbed into bed. She turned over with her back toward the door.

"I was in a very light sleep when I got an awful feeling that someone was watching me," she recounts. "As I turned over to look, I glanced at the lighted digital numbers on the clock. It was two-fifteen A.M.

"I saw a figure standing by the side of my bed dressed in something like a long nightgown or robe. She stood there for several seconds, then turned away and walked toward the door.

"She opened the door and started to leave when she turned around with one hand on the door and looked back at me for several more seconds. She left, closing the door behind her. . . . "

In the morning, O'Neill checked with other residents and learned that in two nearby rooms *locked* doors had mysteriously opened several times during the night although no students claimed to be up and about.

O'Neill had been living in Pem Hall for three years before she had this encounter with the ghost. She never saw it again. And she doesn't believe she was dreaming.

Is it possible another resident had entered her room by mistake, or on some nefarious mission? The door was unlocked, after all. The identity of the intruder, mortal or otherwise, was never determined.

Although few students admit to seeing Mary, many have had experiences they couldn't explain. Lucy O'Brien and several companions discovered that all the shower curtains in the communal bathroom had been closed. A short time later, they found the curtains were open and a heavy chair had been moved. No water had been running in the showers and they'd heard no one enter or leave the bathroom.

No one pays much attention to stereos, television sets, and radios playing in the residence hall. Not even when they operate all by themselves. But one night Pattie Hockspiel and her roommate, Deanne Radermacher, had an unsettling experience. Both were awakened from a deep sleep by a whispering voice saying either "Hi" or "Die." The women weren't sure which word it was, and they couldn't figure out where it came from.

Another "Pemite" reported hearing the faint sounds of a piano coming from the fourth floor late one night. That floor is locked and off-limits to students. However, there *is* a black upright piano there, along with sagging upholstered furniture, an ancient floor-model radio, and some storage bins. Wall studs form unfinished rooms. Not a comfortable or inviting place to be, unless perhaps you are a ghost.

Students say a shadowy figure sometimes exits through hallway doors into a stairwell, only to vanish before their eyes. Is it Mary? Or one of Mary's "neighbors"? The women believe that at least three other ghosts "live" with Mary on the fourth floor of the ivy-clad building.

A saucy "pin lady" in a long white gown taps on doors at night, begging for safety pins. One night several girls followed her to the fourth-floor landing, where she disappeared.

A "lounge ghost" overturns furniture in a rec room every few years in the middle of the night. In 1976, Nancy Vax, a sophomore student, recalled the resident director who found all the lounge furniture tipped over and the room in total disarray. The director ran to get help to clean up the mess. When she returned the room had been restored to perfect order.

Another spirit makes nightly rounds to lock any unlocked doors.

Are these ghosts separate entities or only various manifestations of Mary?

And most important, is there any truth to these stories?

Shirley Von Bokel, a resident of Pem Hall in 1992, told the authors that she has reservations about the ghost business, yet her door swings open when no one is there. "Everybody still talks about Mary," she says, "but I'm not sure if her spirit is around my room because people are always coming and going."

Doris Enochs, Pemberton Hall counselor from 1970 to 1980, says the story of Mary is not true, "but the upperclassmen keep it as a tradition to pass on to incoming freshmen. Everyone who tells it adds more and more to it."

Mrs. Enochs thinks the story had its genesis in the death of Mary Hawkins, a dorm counselor from 1910 to 1917. A plaque in the hall's lobby honors her. However, the woman did not die in the hall, but in a hospital. Further, there are no records of any murder or other unusual death in Pem Hall.

Although Mrs. Enochs does not believe in ghosts, she did tell a news reporter, "Some weird things happen there." She did not elaborate.

Stella (Craft) Temple was a 1921 resident of Pem Hall. She had a different perspective on the ghostly tales.

"Those myths have no origin in dead dorm counselors or murdered coeds either," she told student news reporter Karen Knapp.

Temple recalled a thirty-year-old student named Euterpe Sharp who was studying psychology and was much interested in hypnotism. According to Temple, Sharp used to hide in the janitor's closet next to the restroom and jump out at the girls as they walked by. In time, no coed would walk the halls alone; they traveled in groups of threes or fours.

Temple said that Sharp wasn't really strange, but "she had different interests than the rest of us. Her eyes were crazy." Temple contends that the ghost legends originated from Sharp's frightening prowls through the halls.

Journalist William M. Michael was less concerned with determining the origin of the ghost legend than with finding a good Halloween tale for his newspaper. Michael, a lifestyle writer for the *Decatur Herald and Review* before his retirement in 1988, spent a night on the fourth floor of Pem Hall. All reporters had heard the fantastic rumor about the attic: that it had been partitioned into beautifully furnished rooms whose closets were filled with elegant gowns, presumably worn by the numerous ghosts.

On a brisk October afternoon, Michael climbed the stairs to the "murder" floor. He carried his sleeping bag under one arm. Fifteen Pem Hall residents followed him.

"You're not *really* going to sleep up there?" one asked.

Michael shivered. Yes, indeed, he was going to sleep there—all night. "The wind whooshed around the gables, rain rattled against the roof, huge leafless trees shook. The air felt heavy and musty," he wrote.

"I found the music room where I would spend the night. A light in the closet was burning. Who had left it on? How long ago? Mary? Are you here? My courage began to falter, but then I remembered that Mary is a good ghost—prankish but the non-hurting type," his account read.

Michael noted the dingy furnishings, including the ancient piano. He spread out his sleeping bag on an old leather couch that had no cushions, and settled down to await his spectral visitor. He had just started to doze off when he heard voices—human voices. Michael jumped up and hid behind the door. When it opened, he jumped out from behind it.

The curious coeds screamed and giggled and asked to see the rest of the attic. Thus, William Michael's career as a Pem Hall tour guide was launched. Several more groups of women made their way up the dark stairs that night. All were disappointed to find a vast unfinished area and a less than attractive music room whose floor was covered by a dirty green rug. To please them, Michael spun ghost stories until the wee hours.

Alone at last, he slept fitfully.

At a quarter past three he was jarred awake by a pungent smell. Mary? He squinted into the darkness. The odor of the old couch had awakened him; he hadn't been aware of it before.

At dawn, the bleary-eyed newsman packed up to leave. As he made his way out of the hall, students crowded around to ask if he'd seen Mary.

"No." He shook his head. "I didn't see Mary. But I sure saw a lot of non-ghosts," he said, looking at his audience. He added that he was disappointed to have missed Mary, "but deep down I didn't think I would have . . . a ghost of a chance . . . of meeting her anyway."

Although William Michael's ghost search was uneventful, his visit to Pem Hall brought him a different distinction. He told the authors that he believes he and the late distinguished actor and folk singer, Burl Ives, are the only two men to have spent some time in the women's dorm.

Burl Ives attended Eastern Illinois University from 1927 to 1930. Legend has it that the singer visited a Pemite one evening and was seen crawling out a lower-floor window shortly before dawn the next morning.

In 1986 Burl Ives received an honorary doctor of humane letters degree for his many years of dedication and financial support to Eastern Illinois University. Later, the Burl Ives Art Studio Hall was dedicated to him in the spring of 1990.

Some day Eastern Illinois University might see fit to award their famous ghost similar honors. In absentia, of course.

The Stump

The worn, narrow dirt trail to Stepp Cemetery begins at a curved rock wall near the edge of Old State Highway 37 in Morgan-Monroe State Forest. The path winds up a short hill, skirting a broad, brushy thicket, through massive oak and poplar trees, to emerge at the graveyard.

Fewer than twenty-five headstones remain. All of the markers are old; no one has been buried there in a very long time. Faded plastic flowers are strewn over some of the simple graves. It is a peaceful atmosphere. Along the south boundary there is a row of broken, lichen-covered tombstones, including one on which the years have erased the name and the dates. The barely visible outline of sunken earth is less than three feet in length. A child's grave. Nearby is a small stump in the shape of a chair.

It is here, on this crude "throne," that the ghost of an old woman sits each night—watching . . . and waiting. Oddly, no one seems to be able to attach a name to the mysterious female specter.

One popular version explains the woman's presence in this manner:

"Forty years ago, a woman in the area had a child that was struck and killed by a car. She buried her baby in Stepp Cemetery. The woman had the tree next to her child's grave cut down and the stump shaped into a chair so that she might sit in it and protect her child from any strangers that entered the cemetery. When she is not in her chair, she puts a curse on it to protect the grave. If anyone sits in the chair, or even touches it when she is not there, that person will die one year later to the day."

Presumably, it is the woman's ghost that has taken over the chore of guarding the small grave.

Other "witnesses" to the ghostly guardian are more precise. She has long white hair, is quite old but not ugly, and always dresses in black. A strange, triangular mark anoints her forehead. The woman rarely accosts any visitors, preferring to sit on the stump swaying back and forth with her imaginary baby in her arms.

Folklorists at Indiana University in nearby Bloomington have collected some of the other more popular stories for the origin of the ghost. Some believe:

• During the 1950s a girl was killed and her body dumped in Stepp Cemetery. The girl's mother comes to the cemetery nightly in search of the killer. If he runs, he will die as the girl died; she was stabbed and beaten beyond recognition.
• During a drive in the state forest, a girl told her boyfriend that she did not love him anymore and would not see him again. He shoved her from the car. She was never seen again. Several days later, the girl's mother also vanished in the same area. When couples go into the forest in search of the girl's body, her mother's ghost secretly checks their car to see if her daughter is in it.
• A mysterious woman in black visits the grave of her small daughter every midnight. She disinters the girl's corpse and holds it through the night.

This last story may be poignant to mothers who have lost children. A woman who lived near the state forest, and who lost an infant son years ago, said: "If I hadn't been afraid somebody would see me . . . being so close to the road and all . . . I'd have dug him up [from Stepp Cemetery]. I just wanted to see him again so bad."

Although Morgan-Monroe forest rangers will tell the visitor the cemetery was begun by area families, a defunct religious sect called the Crabbites may have had some early connection with it. This peculiar religion conducted services that included speaking in tongues, snake handling, and sex orgies. One longtime resident of Monroe County wrote that her father had been called to the cemetery late one evening to help break up one particularly frenetic Crabbite sexual rite. He had to use a bullwhip to restrain the lascivious congregation.

The tales of Stepp Cemetery have also taken on some of the characteristics of modern horror folklore.

In every state of the Union, tales are told of "The Hook," a nefarious being who skulks about lovers' lanes waiting to pounce on unsuspecting couples. He is generally described as an escaped convict who can be easily identified: he has a steel hook where one of his hands should be. The lovers generally learn of the man's escape over the car radio and decide to leave their isolated location. At home, they find a steel claw—The Hook's hand—imbedded in their car door. They escaped just in time!

The Stepp Cemetery "Hook," however, is a woman, and she is not an escaped convict:

A woman and her small son were involved in a horrible automobile accident. The boy was killed and buried in Stepp Cemetery. His mother's hand was smashed in the accident and replaced with an iron claw. The boy had always been afraid of the dark. His mother decided to watch over the grave each night. She continued to do so until her death, and her ghost now sits on that stump. But she is extremely shy, fleeing when a car approaches as she shakes her hook at the intruders. Her only companion is a ghostly white dog.

Written accounts of encounters with the ghost of Stepp Cemetery are scarce. The legends rarely include actual physical encounters with the ghost. However, several late-night visitors claim to have been frightened by something, including a teenage girl who remembered the following harrowing experience:

"Connie and Jeanne and I went out to Stepp Cemetery. They had told me stories, but I had never been there. I really didn't want to go, but they talked me into it. I really didn't believe the stories.

"I wouldn't get out of the car, but Jeanne finally got out and said we should just walk around. Anyway, after a while, we got back in the car and started to drive out. Right where the road curves and goes back to the highway, we suddenly heard the wind, like things rushing through the trees. It was really dark, too. I was driving, and then, right in the middle of the road, there was this image, rippling right in front of the car. And the car lights went off. The motor died, too.

"We all screamed, and I closed my eyes. Connie started to cry.

"We locked the doors and rolled up the windows. We all tried turning the key, but the car just wouldn't start. We could hear the wind on both sides of the road. The image drifted on across the road. Then, all by itself, the car started. No one had touched the ignition. Connie wanted to get out and look at the battery and engine, but I wasn't going to let anybody out of the car. We took off!"

Those girls later told an interviewer they never again ventured into Stepp Cemetery.

We are left, then, with speculation. However, there does exist that strange, twisted tree stump, just right for sitting. It is real. But is there a ghost? Does an old woman come back at night to protect her child's cold tomb?

Is it only the occasional teenager who sits on that "throne"? Or, is there another *thing* that perches there in the blackness . . . ?

Phantoms of the Opera House

On the night of August 15, 1986, Sue Riedel took the stage of Dubuque's exquisite Grand Opera House. The theater was packed for the opening night of *Tintypes*, a musical of George M. Cohan songs from the turn of the century. Riedel welcomed the audience and told them that in 1904 the great Cohan himself had performed on this historic stage during the Grand's heyday as a legitimate theater.

Suddenly, all the lights in the building went out except for those on stage! Electricians hustled along corridors, checking fuse boxes, searching for frayed or broken wires. All seemed in order, but the lights would not come on.

Nevertheless, true to showbiz tradition, the performance went on. If patrons complained about the lack of aisle lights and dark restrooms, their grumblings went unheard. In fact, the thundering applause following the performance assured the Barn Community Theatre that it had found a real home at last. Live theater had returned to Dubuque, to stay.

But with it, some say, came ghostly players who have yet to understand that the curtains have closed forever on their soliloquies.

The community theater company, established in 1971, had performed originally in a barn. Riedel, a speech and drama teacher at Hempstead High School, became artistic director and longed for the day when the troupe could find a permanent home.

Their wish came true in 1986 when a group of dedicated aficionados of live theater bought the Grand Opera House and worked for months renovating it.

Built in 1889–90 at a cost of $65,000, the Grand was known as Dubuque's "temple of the muses," presenting opera, ballet, and minstrel shows, all on a scale rarely seen in the Upper Midwest. The immortal Cohan joined the likes of Sarah Bernhardt, Ethel Barrymore, and Lillian Russell on the list of stars who trod the boards of the Grand.

But with the advent of moving pictures, interest in live theater declined, and in 1928 the beautiful brick and sandstone building became a movie theater. And so it remained for the next thirty-nine years.

By the early 1990s, the Barn Community Theatre was staging eight shows each year in the restored Opera House and rented the building to other groups when its own rehearsals and plays were not in progress.

The Grand is a busy place now, made busier by a complement of ghosts. Or so it is said. Many persons have reported hearing voices on the empty stage, floorboards squeaking when no one walks on them, doors of unoccupied rooms opening and closing, tape recorders turning themselves on, and lights flashing when no one is near the switches.

That electrical problem on *Tintypes'* opening night has never been solved. It wasn't unique. During one production, spotlights rose up and down by themselves, and one particular spotlight kept falling from its batten.

Yet Sue Riedel, for one, oddly enough pays scant attention to this phenomenon. She is often at the Grand until the early morning hours rehearsing lines on the empty stage. She locks up, but when she arrives back the next morning, lights she had turned off are aglow. She knows very well that no one else has been in the building, so her cheery "Good Morning!" to the empty auditorium seems directed toward her unseen companions.

When the Barn Community Theatre first moved into the Grand, company members found a "ghost light" in the attic. They described it as a lamp with a bare bulb on top that was set on the stage at night to light the theater for "whatever" may be there. Historically, members said, the lamp was left burning because people thought that without illumination they saw "things."

"Theater people are very, very superstitious," Riedel cautioned. Had ghostly thespians "retired" to the attic of the Grand, taking their light with them? Although the lamp has been removed and the attic is used for costume storage, "presences" from the past tarry in the old theater.

Here, then, are a few of the stories told by persons who believe they've brushed against "another world" at the Grand Opera House.

Helen Johnston, a retired teacher, is the office manager of the Grand. She works nine to five Monday through Friday and is often the first person in the building. One morning in 1986, shortly after the Barn players took over the building, Johnston was walking upstairs to her office when she heard noises on the stage.

"I looked to see who was down there," she remembers. "It was very dark, but still I could see that nobody was there. It wasn't a scary feeling, and I'm not a brave person. I really don't know why I wasn't scared. The office is at the back of the balcony and when I got out there the voices were gone. Two years later, I had the same experience."

Johnston is also the theater's accompanist. Her piano is in the orchestra pit, but is moved onto the stage occasionally for a production. And that's where Johnston is most uncomfortable.

"I just feel that there's a presence behind me whenever I play up there," she said.

*   *   *

Sue Lynch-Huerta, like Helen Johnston, has heard disembodied voices in the vicinity of the office. Early one morning she went up there to catch up on some paperwork.

"When I got to the office door," she began, "I heard all these voices and I thought there was a board meeting going on. The voices were predominantly male, but I couldn't make out any words. I knocked and nobody answered so I walked in. Empty.

"Then I heard the voices coming from the stage. I went out onto the balcony and hollered, 'Hello! Who's there?' I flipped on the lights. Nobody was around.

"After that experience, I decided to talk to the ghosts. I tell them, 'Hello, it's me again. I'm just here to do some work in the office.' I'm never frightened. It isn't as if your hair stands on end and you feel terrible vibes coming at you. But then, I grew up in a 150-year-old house where things moved in the night all by themselves. I guess you might say I'm used to it. I don't think the ghosts are hostile. I think they're happy souls who found a place they enjoyed so much they decided to stay."

Anyone who has built a stage set appreciates the difficult assignment craftsmen in this line of work have, and doubly so when a cold wind heralds a ghost's arrival. Bill Stark, the set builder at the Grand Opera House, volunteers his time, but whenever that cold air tickles his skin he tells his coworkers, "I'm leaving right now. They're here again!"

Stark isn't sure who "they" are, but he knows he doesn't like to be distracted from his work. He always returns later to finish the job at hand.

Sometimes it doesn't even take a chilly breeze to tell Stark that something's amiss. For instance, during a rehearsal of *The Follies*, Stark was upstairs making a videotape of the performance.

"My camera suddenly went haywire," he said, "focusing in and out real fast and real blurry."

Stark went downstairs and found, to his surprise, that a woman was also taping the show and she was having the same problem he was having.

"I'm upstairs and she's downstairs," he went on. "Neither one of us knew that the other was taping."

Although Stark quit taping after his camera malfunctioned, he claims that a picture of a "ghost" appeared on a section of the videotape before the camera troubles. He said it made "a believer out of one guy who never believed in ghosts."

Stark recalled that on another night during the run of *The Follies*, its director from Minneapolis had a run-in with an errant light switch. "One night she and several others turned the lights out, and when they got to the door and turned around the lights were on. It happened twice so the third time she said, 'We're going to turn these lights out and we're going, regardless.' So that's what they did."

The next night the last group out reached to switch off the lights but they went off by themselves. Seems to happen all the time at the Grand Opera House.

*   *   *

Jim Meyer has been associated with Sue Riedel since the early days of the Barn Community Theatre. He calls himself a "jack of all trades," filling in as a company dancer, running the popcorn concession, ushering, taking tickets, even cleaning the theater. When a job needs doing, Meyer is there to do it. He, too, has had some perplexing experiences, especially his first one. It was plain frightening.

"I was painting the front drop with my back to the auditorium," he said. "I was alone. Suddenly, I heard beads clanking. It sounded like a nun walking across the stage. You know how in Catholic schools you can hear the nuns coming a mile away by those beads? Well, I turned to look and as I did I got a blast of cold air. Every hair on my arm and head stood right on end. Well, I put the lid on the paint can and walked out the door and locked it. I was still holding the wet paint brush! I cleaned it at home."

Meyer's account dates to 1986, the year the Barn Players moved into the Grand. He didn't know anything about ghosts then. Within a year, however, he would have another strange encounter.

"Just before Christmas of 1987, I was in the lobby putting up Christmas decorations. I was on one side of the lobby. All my boxes were on the floor on the other side by the ticket booth. I was up on a ladder hanging a wreath and something shoved a box. It went all the way across the lobby."

Meyer shouted, "Knock it off! I haven't got time to deal with you now."

There were no more tricks, and Meyer finished his decorating.

Cathy Breitbach began choreographing musicals for the Barn back in 1988.

"I kind of laughed," she said of the stories she heard about the haunted theater. "I don't believe in ghosts."

Yet the day came when she wasn't so sure.

"We were onstage rehearsing *Gypsy*," she said, "and were well into all the dances. Now my music tapes are never where they're supposed to be. I always have to rewind and find the right song because I've often got ten numbers on one tape.

"Everybody was lined up onstage and we were ready to go. I walked over to my tape recorder to rewind it . . . but it turned on—and right to the song we needed.

"I'll never forget that. I thought at first the knob on the machine was loose from all the jumping onstage, but that wouldn't have moved the tape to the exact song that we were doing."

Breitbach said the machine has never since malfunctioned. And she has second thoughts about ghosts.

Jeff Schneider is a newcomer to Dubuque and a novice actor. He said he is also a psychic. In December 1990, he and a friend were doing a photo session at the Grand.

"When we finished," Schneider said, "I felt like someone was standing right behind me. I turned around and saw a man about five feet seven inches tall with orange-colored hair. At the same time I heard the name 'David.' I knew he wasn't a living person. I figured he'd been part of the theater at one time, maybe an actor. But I didn't have any problems with him; he didn't scare me." Schneider would see "David" several times over the coming months.

In January 1991, during a rehearsal for *Anything Goes*, Schneider said he caught glimpses of people in the back of the theater, although no one was out there.

"They appeared like little flashes. I remember an older man with white hair and a white beard stood behind the last row of seats. He wore a tux. I don't know who he was. Although I wasn't really frightened, he kind of bothered me. I wasn't comfortable with him."

Schneider also "saw" two women, one in her thirties and one in her forties, in rear seats with a young man about thirty. They seemed to be attired in old-fashioned clothing. Schneider thinks they are part of the "spiritual residue" that he says is "all over the place."

"The energy here is really strong," Schneider emphasizes. "You can feel it when you walk in. You *know* that there is something here in this theater."

Even some who have no direct connection to the Grand agree that mysteries abound in the great edifice at 135 Eighth Street.

In the early afternoon of February 10, 1988, businessman Dick Landis stopped by the theater to buy tickets for *Gypsy*.

"The lobby was empty," he recalls, "or at least it was empty to the human eye. I looked behind the ticket counter, but no one was there so I turned to leave. At that moment, the door between the hall and the ticket counter slowly closed and latched. Then, after a few seconds, the door between the hall and the lobby opened, paused, and went partially shut again. I have to wonder if I was truly alone in the lobby."

A Dubuque attorney who prefers to remain anonymous had a similar experience. He entered the theater late one night and saw the concession stand door open and close. Feeling certain that someone was in the building, he went home and got his dog. The pair returned to the theater and searched it top to bottom. They turned up nothing tangible.

Sue Riedel herself recalls an incident that took place during a rehearsal for a children's play one summer.

"One of the little girls said to me, 'Who rehearses before our group? I heard singing on the stage when I came in but I didn't see anybody.'"

Riedel calmly assured the child that it must have been some other group using the theater. In fact, the children's play was the *only* show being rehearsed at the time.

The Dubuque Police Department gets few reports today that something "funny" is going on at the Grand Opera House, but it was not always so. When the building housed a movie theater, cleaning women sometimes called the cops when they heard voices as they went about their nightly chores. Police sweeps never found the source.

Today, the Barn Players accept their haunted theater with a certain nonchalance. "We love our ghosts," says director Sue Riedel. "They don't do anything scary. They don't make things fly around. We just hear them and see things that have happened as a result of them."

Truly, they are the unseen phantoms of the opera house.

The Surgeon's Legacy

The two-story white bungalow resembles many others in El Dorado, Kansas—at least on the outside. Inside it is far different. But Clark Richardson could not have known there was anything wrong with the house when he bought it in 1967. The four bedrooms would provide ample space for his growing family, and the children would enjoy the large yard shaded by magnificent old trees.

One night, after they'd lived there for a month, twelve-year-old Karen went upstairs to bed. She had just turned off her bedside light and closed her eyes when she heard her mother coming up the stairs. The footsteps resounded on the polished hardwood floor, then stopped at the foot of Karen's bed.

"Is something wrong, Mom?" the youngster said sleepily.

Her mother didn't answer. When Karen turned over there was no one there!

Karen rushed downstairs to find her mother reading in the living room. No, Mrs. Richardson hadn't been upstairs, nor had anyone else. Karen's father suggested that the noise had been caused by the house settling—except that it had been built in the 1890s, and any settling would have occurred years ago.

Several days later Karen was in her bedroom when the closet door opened and slammed shut with no one near it. She rushed into her sister's room, the only other room on the second floor, and found Hilary standing wide-eyed in the center of the room, watching *her* closet door opening and shutting by itself.

The girls were frightened, but decided to say nothing to their parents.

Soon the girls' dresser drawers opened and closed of their own accord. Karen and Hilary would come home from school and find all the drawers pulled out to their full extent. The window shades too were always raised, although the girls pulled them down each morning before leaving for school. And there was no one in the house all day.

Or was there?

After the girls told their mother about the incidents in their rooms, the three began seeing the image of a large, tall man. He would appear for just an instant in different parts of the house, and then vanish. Sometimes the women would catch a glimpse of him leaving a room.

They were not upset, only curious about the ghost's identity and what it wanted. Not until two years later did Mrs. Richardson mention the matter to her husband. He laughed and said she and the girls were crazy. "You've been seeing too many movies."

A short time later mother and daughters were out of town visiting a relative for the weekend, leaving Mr. Richardson home alone. He'd been asleep for only a couple of hours when he was awakened by slamming and banging noises, and footsteps running back and forth upstairs. (He and his wife occupied the master bedroom on the first floor.) He became so unnerved by the commotion that he leaped into his clothes, ran from the house and sought refuge in an all-night diner. There he sat drinking coffee until the sun came up.

When his family returned, he was overjoyed to see them and, although he talked little of his experiences alone in the house, he never again chided his wife and children about their moviegoing.

In 1973, the Richardsons sold the house and moved to another town. The buyer, a widow with three children, installed floodlights immediately and a burglar alarm system to keep away prowlers. She left the following year.

The house changes hands frequently. One family stayed only five months because they said there was something "wrong" with the house.

And what was wrong with the house? The Richardsons investigated its history. They learned that a prominent surgeon had built the house, lived and died there. Because there was no hospital in Butler County until the turn of the century, the doctor often performed surgeries in the basement. Recuperating patients stayed upstairs.

Are those discharged patients of a century ago still gathering their clothes from the closets and dresser drawers? And does the old surgeon still make his rounds?

It seems possible.

Old Things

The Conjure Chest

An elegant mahogany veneer chest of drawers, hand-carved by an African-American slave 150 years ago, resides in the Kentucky History Museum at Frankfort. Crafted in the Empire style, the chest has glass knobs on its four drawers. Nothing about its outward appearance gives any hint that tragedy has stalked its existence. That it's known to historians as the "conjured" chest.

Two decades before the Civil War, the family of one Jacob Cooley lived a sumptuous life as wealthy Southern planters. Jacob owned many slaves and farmed thousands of acres. He was also an evil, despicable man who frequently beat his slaves for the slightest infraction of his stringent rules.

Jacob Cooley ordered one of his slaves, an excellent furniture maker named Hosea, to construct a chest that would be used for his firstborn child. For some unknown reason, Jacob was angered at Hosea's finished product and beat him so savagely that he died a few days later.

Cooley's slaves, led by an old "conjure man," placed a curse on the chest for all future generations. One drawer was sprinkled with dried owl's blood, and a "conjure" chant was sung. All those associated with the chest would fall within the curse's evil power.

Although Jacob Cooley himself evidently escaped the malevolence, his descendants were not as fortunate.

The baby for whom the chest was built died soon after birth. The chest was in his nursery. His brother inherited the chest, and he was stabbed to death by his personal servant.

Jacob Cooley had another son, John, who inherited one of his father's many plantations. The young man led a serene bachelor's life until a vivacious young woman, barely out of her teens, came into his life. Her name was Ellie and she soon married John, nearly three times her age.

The couple inherited the conjured chest. Knowing of the tragedies that had befallen her husband's siblings, she put the chest in an attic.

Meanwhile, Jacob Cooley's youngest daughter, Melinda, eloped with a waggish

Irishman named Sean. With nowhere to live, Melinda turned to Ellie. John and Ellie had done well and had accumulated several farms in Tennessee. They turned over one of these to Sean and Melinda to work.

While Melinda bore her young husband a brood of children and worked from sunrise to sunset, Sean came to loathe the dullness of farm life.

Ellie Cooley tried to help, but Sean's rebuffs made her presence unwelcome. To try to bring some beauty into Melinda's dreary existence, Ellie sent over her father-in-law's chest. It had been in her attic for a very long time and nothing had happened. She'd almost forgotten the chest's legacy. Perhaps the "curse" was only a lot of talk.

Within days, Sean deserted his wife for the bright lights of New Orleans. Melinda was disconsolate. She took to her bed with an "ailment." There, Melinda soon died, an exhausted, gray-haired woman barely out of her thirties.

Shortly after his wife's death, Sean was struck in the head by a steamboat's gangplank and died.

The conjure chest had claimed its third and fourth victims.

The couple left many orphaned children. John Cooley was given the job of traveling to Tennessee to assign the youngsters to other family members. The youngest, a baby named Evelyn, ran up to him, her tiny arms outstretched. John took her to live with his own family in Kentucky.

Little Evelyn grew into a beautiful and intelligent young woman. When she turned sixteen, Evelyn passed an examination that provided her with a teaching certificate with which she took over a one-room schoolhouse.

She met and married a Scotsman, Malcolm Johnson, barely two months after she began teaching.

As a wedding present, Ellie presented her niece with Jacob Cooley's handsome chest. And the evil passed to a new generation.

Evelyn Johnson had children and even adopted a young orphan, a girl named Arabella.

The curse was all but forgotten. Evelyn had the chest but didn't find it necessary to use right away. However, after Arabella married some years later, Evelyn put the girl's bridal gown in the chest. Shortly thereafter, Arabella's husband suddenly died.

That was the beginning of a series of horrible events visited upon Evelyn and Ellie. Arabella's child died after her baby clothes had been put in the chest.

Evelyn's daughter-in-law, Esther, married to her oldest son, put her wedding attire in the chest. She died.

Evelyn's Aunt Sarah knitted a scarf and gloves to give her son for Christmas. While walking along a train trestle, he fell off and was killed a few days before Christmas. Two other tragedies befell Evelyn's immediate family—a son-in-law deserted his wife and a child was crippled for life in a bizarre accident.

Yet Evelyn's husband, Malcolm, was a success. A small man, always courteous to those around him, he parlayed a shrewd Scottish sense of thrift into a burgeoning business empire that, at its height, consisted of mills, houses, a coal yard, wharf, and dry goods store.

Malcolm was an extraordinarily wealthy man when he died. Despite her material comfort, his wife was haunted by the memories of those around her who were struck down or stricken in some other way by hardship. She took her own life.

Eleven persons. The "conjure" chest was taking its toll.

As the twentieth century unfolded, the chest was inherited by Virginia Cary Hudson from her grandmother, Evelyn Johnson. Mrs. Hudson thought tales of the "curse" were hearsay.

She was wrong.

Her first baby's clothes were put in the chest. She died. Another's child's clothes were tucked in a drawer and she contracted infantile paralysis. Another daughter's wedding dress was stored there, and her first husband ran off. A son was stabbed in the hand. He had clothes in the chest.

A friend of the family put hunting clothes in it. He was shot in a hunting accident.

And so it went. Sixteen victims, all of whom had one thing in common: some of their personal clothing had been put in the conjured chest.

Mrs. Hudson wanted to put an end to the curse. She found what she hoped would be the solution in the form of an old friend of hers, an African-American woman named Annie.

Annie understood curses and conjures. The spell cast by Hosea's faithful companions would be broken only when three conditions were met. First, Mrs. Hudson would have to be given a dead owl without her having to ask for one. Second, the green leaves of a willow tree had to be boiled from sunup to sundown. The dead owl had to remain in sight. Third, the boiled liquid was then to be buried in a jug with its handle facing east, toward the rising sun, below a flowering bush.

A stuffed owl given to Mrs. Hudson's son by a friend accomplished the first requirement. Mrs. Hudson plucked leaves from a nearby willow tree and boiled them in a large, black pot. The owl kept watch from a kitchen counter. At dusk, old Annie and Mrs. Hudson took the jug and, with its handle pointed east, buried it beneath a flowering lilac bush outside the kitchen window.

Annie said they would only know if the curse had been broken if one of them died before the first full days of fall.

Annie died in early September. The seventeenth, and last known victim.

The final private owner of the conjure chest was Mrs. Hudson's daughter, Virginia C. Mayne. Though she may have been skeptical of the curse, and knew fully the story of its "lifting" by Annie and her mother, she never stored *anything* in the chest and kept it hidden in her attic.

The Kentucky History Museum has it now. Mrs. Mayne donated it to the museum in 1976. According to museum registrar Mike Hudson, "The chest is in storage in our vaults, awaiting the time when it fits into a new exhibit." Supposedly, the curse has been removed.

Has it? Tucked safely in the top chest drawer is an envelope . . . with a cluster of owl feathers inside.

The museum isn't taking any chances.

Witch Leah

The old woods known as Lapland, near Battletown, Kentucky, is a dangerous place to visit. Locals advise you to venture through the dense forest with a knowledgeable guide and then only in the fall or winter, when the deadly rattlesnakes are in hibernation.

But there may be another reason to be cautious in the old forest. The ghost of Leah Smock, an accused witch who died mysteriously 150 years ago, haunts the old cemetery in the Lapland woods that holds her mortal remains. Some claim Witch Leah is the oldest haunting in all of Kentucky.

A reliable sighting came from a hunter several years ago who told a longtime area resident that he believed he had seen Leah's ghost hovering near her grave in the abandoned Betsy Daily Cemetery.

The apparition had long black hair, he said, and was swathed in a white robe set off with black ties at her waist and throat. A purple light seemed to envelop the incomplete form.

The life of Leah Smock is hard to separate from the legend that has grown up around her. The facts are sparse. She was born about 1818, reputedly the daughter of another powerful Kentucky witch. As a child, she preferred to be alone, strolling for hours upon end in the woods searching for fruit and berries to eat.

She had few friends and seldom visited other neighborhood children. Once, while she was playing at a neighbor's, their black cat began to scratch wildly at the walls. When the front door was opened, it ran screeching from the house, never to be seen again.

Leah was also a seer. She often "predicted" the deaths of critically ill people. As she was frequently right, her reputation for "knowing" the future spread through the frontier community. It's *not* known how many times her predictions were wrong!

Her death on August 21, 1840, is also shrouded in uncertainty. Some accounts say she starved to death in the woods. Other reports have it that she was burned to death when her house caught fire. Her twenty-two years on earth, however, live on in the ghost legend that continues to this day among the older residents of Meade County.

Several years ago, an area resident led a reporter and two companions to Leah's grave. Battling through the dense underbrush, pistols at the ready to thwart any belligerent rattlesnakes, they found the old hilltop cemetery deep within a grove of trees. Forsaken for decades, the graveyard's seventy or so plots were covered with pine needles, leaves, and moss. Leah's grave was the only one with a pointed headstone. Nothing stirred there; it was still daylight.

The visitors did find one peculiar detail during their visit. Shortly after Leah Smock died, locals who claimed to have seen her ghost piled a two-feet-high stack of small boulders on her grave. To keep her in her coffin, they hoped. For over a century, that pile of stones had remained intact.

On this day, however, the rocks were in disarray. About half of them had been removed. By whom? For what purpose?

The witch-ghost Leah Smock surely knows the answer.

Bloody Polly

Frances Clara Brown was a strikingly beautiful woman. Tall and slender at age eighteen with a sweet disposition and gentle face, she had flaxen hair that framed a creamy complexion set off by large, expressive brown eyes. She lived with her father, Frederick Brown, her mother and brothers and sisters in a log cabin a few miles from Lancaster, in Garrard County. Mr. Brown had brought his family to the rough Kentucky wilderness from Maryland in 1815.

He soon turned their frontier cabin and few acres into a large, thriving plantation. His mules broke the earth for crops, and a mill built with his own hands separated hemp from flax for spinning.

Life was good until the day Harry Geiss showed up.

Now Frances Clara had a sister, Polly, two years her elder. With black hair, flashing eyes, and a fiery temper, she usually got her way.

Polly's worst fear was becoming an "old maid." Women usually married by their late teens in that era, so her prospects were already looking dim.

When Harry Geiss came along—single and evidently on his way to becoming a prosperous merchant—Polly Brown set her sights upon him. They became engaged, but it wasn't long before his attentions turned toward her younger sister, Frances Clara. Perhaps Polly's temper made the young bachelor have second thoughts. But it was soon evident to everyone in the neighborhood that handsome Harry Geiss would soon marry vivacious "Fanny Clary" Brown.

Apparent to all, that is, except Polly Brown.

She was enraged at the thought of losing Harry Geiss to her sister. Her devious mind created a scheme so horrible that years passed before its full impact was known.

The fateful series of events began one morning when the merchant Geiss set out for Maysville, Kentucky, on the Ohio River. There was no transportation to the deep wilderness surrounding Lancaster, so goods were transported from Philadelphia to Maysville, where they were off-loaded and toted to the outlying pioneer communities. Geiss periodically made the several-hundred-mile round-trip, taking several days to complete the journey. On this day, however, as he bade farewell to Frances Clara, he had no way of knowing that it would be the last time the two would ever be together.

A few hours after Geiss's departure, Polly Brown found her sister weaving. Polly cheerfully persuaded her sister to accompany her to a Mrs. Brassfield's, there to examine a new quilt pattern the woman was completing. The two young women plunged through the thick forest. In a grove of papaw trees Polly remarked that Frances Clara's hair was coming loose. She would pin it up, she said, guiding her sister to a log.

Frances Clara should never have turned her back. As soon as she did, Polly Brown drew a hatchet from beneath her skirts and, grasping her sister's hair firmly in her left hand, brought the sharpened blade down in a mighty swing at her sister's pale neck.

Blood spewed from severed arteries. *Chop . . . chop . . . chop.* Blow after blow rained down on helpless Frances Clara, her sister crazily swinging the bloody hatchet in a murderous rage. Frances Clara cried out for mercy, but her screams were quickly silenced. Polly didn't stop until her sister's mangled head rolled off her lifeless torso.

The murder had been carefully planned, savagely executed. Polly Brown had picked a particular part of the forest in which to carry out her deed. She dragged her sister's remains to a nearby sinkhole and buried them in the soft earth, being careful to obliterate any signs of a struggle or blood. So meticulous had been her scheme that she had secreted a change of clothing nearby so as not to call attention to her own bloodstained garments.

In a field some distance away, three young slaves—Abe, Tom, and Pomp— heard Frances Clara's screams. "Polly, don't kill me!" she cried. Abe, the oldest, dashed forward and hid behind a bush. He saw Polly inflict the final, mortal wounds. Quickly fleeing, he told his companions what he had seen. He made them swear never to reveal what had occurred. All three were fearful they would be blamed for the murder.

For the rest of the day, Polly Brown quietly gathered up her sister's saddle, good clothing, and personal effects from their home and stashed them in another area of the forest several hundred yards away from her sister's dismal grave. She calmly returned home and awaited the discovery of Frances Clara's absence. The murderess had an explanation for that prepared, too.

As twilight descended, Frances Clara's parents did indeed wonder where their daughter was. Polly slyly stepped forward and offered the opinion that she must have run away with Harry Geiss as he had left for Maysville that morning. She pointed to the fact that Frances Clara's saddle and "Sunday clothes" were missing, sure signs that Geiss had persuaded her to leave with him. The hint of a self-satisfied smile must have slipped across Polly's face. She knew that it would be days or weeks before Geiss returned with his merchandise. By that time, she hoped, her rival would have been forgotten and Harry Geiss would turn his attention to her.

Polly Brown's plan would have succeeded but for a macabre discovery by several small boys a few weeks later. Sent to gather papaws in the woods, Claiborne Lear, Joshua Comely, and Sammy Johnson were startled by a wild pig chewing at something on the ground. When they got closer, they were scared witless to see that the pig's snack was actually a thin, white hand sticking out of the sandy soil.

The boys raced home to tell their parents of the awful discovery. Within hours, several dozen neighbors had gathered at the papaw patch. They unearthed the remains of the headless Frances Clara Brown. Her parents reburied her on the plantation grounds.

The whereabouts of Frances Clara's good clothing and saddle puzzled the Brown family. A psychic, a man named Ramsey who lived in nearby Lancaster, predicted that the missing items would be found precisely 440 yards south of the Brown home. Family friend Thompson Arnold measured out the distance and found the material only a few inches below ground.

The devious plan hatched by Polly Brown succeeded in keeping anyone from suspecting her, but failed at winning Harry Geiss's affection. He eventually left town.

The owners of the slaves grew suspicious. They recalled that the youths had been working near where Polly's body was found. Eventually, Tom and Pomp were arrested and jailed. Perhaps someone overheard one of them talking about the murder, or maybe they were confused by Abe's orders to keep quiet. Whatever the reason, they were tried for murder. The only evidence was presented by their jailer, who claimed to have heard one of them say, "The first lick didn't kill her."

Justice was nonexistent for African-American slaves, and any pretense of fairness a mockery. The boys were found guilty on December 13, 1820. Tom was hanged on January 7, 1821. Pomp was sent to the gallows two weeks later. Nothing is known of Abe's fate.

Polly Brown didn't raise a hand to prevent the tragic hanging of two innocent young men. The blood of three persons now stained her hands.

It was all too much even for the twisted mind of Polly Brown. Her family moved away to Indianapolis, leaving only her behind. It isn't known why. Perhaps it was her turning toward herbs as cures for disease, or her long walks in the woods—particularly near the old papaw trees where her sister's body lay for so long.

She moved into a small cabin when the Brown farm was purchased by Josiah Burnside. Mr. and Mrs. Logan Harris lived there and more or less looked after her.

One night many years later, Polly Brown was returning through the woods after a visit with a sick "patient." Her herbal medicines were popular on the frontier, where a physician might be hundreds of miles distant. On this evening, however, even the strongest drugs would not have helped her. Coming at her was the ghost of Frances Clara, her arms outstretched as if to grab at her tormentor. The apparition's neck was a bloody stump.

Polly turned and ran, shaking uncontrollably at the sight of her reanimated sister. When she stumbled into the Harris cabin babbling about Frances Clara's ghost, the couple immediately put her to bed. From that night forward, Polly Brown descended into a mania from which she never recovered. Eventually she was chained to her bed after she was caught attempting to break into her old home. Her gray hair fell in long, unkempt strands about her shoulders; her once dancing eyes grew dull and sunken. Mr. and Mrs. Harris could only keep her in a rough-sewn sack dress.

The truth was eventually learned. As she lay dying, Polly Brown confessed to the murder of her sister, and expressed her sorrow for the wrongful deaths of Pomp and Tom. She amazed Mr. and Mrs. Harris by appearing completely lucid on her deathbed.

Josiah Burnside and his wife Almira raised a large family on the old Brown plantation. Regular appearances by the ghost of Frances Clara became a part of the family's tradition. She would playfully pull covers from the bed or rush through the front door, slamming it as she entered. The soft rustle of her skirts could be heard ascending the stairs to her old loom room.

The last vestiges of the Brown homestead reportedly burned to the ground in about 1940. Did the ghost of Frances Clara Brown vanish with the last of her old home? Most of the folks in the neighborhood think so, but others—well, other people familiar with the tragic tale just aren't so sure. They think Frances Clara is still out there somewhere, looking for her head.

Ghost Lovers

Old Noel Sympson wasn't known for spreading wild tales. He was a fisherman who sometimes made extravagant claims about the "one that got away," but there was nothing even remotely sinful in his yarn-spinning.

That's why the story he told one day at Greenfield's Store was so improbable that the local philosophers gathered around the wood stove thought he'd taken to drink. Or worse.

"Better change your brand of whiskey, Noel," they hooted. "Ain't no ghosts on the Barren River—ain't go ghosts anywhere—and you well know it."

He left the little store a few miles from Bowling Green, but told the hecklers he would return with another eyewitness. And so he did, about a week later, this time with Hosiah Hathaway in tow. Both men claimed to have seen a boy and girl, ghostly lovers, floating down the Barren River in a small boat. They tried to get up a company to prove their statements.

Only Schoolmaster Lindley could be persuaded to accompany Sympson and Hathaway back to the river. The trio boarded Sympson's rowboat at sunset and floated off downstream. They slipped past cedar trees clinging to the steep banks while bats swooped low to pick off tasty dragonflies dancing on the water's surface. The stream narrowed so that strands of quivering sycamores formed a canopy over the water.

At last they came to an area known as Hammel's Cliff. While Hathaway rowed and Sympson kept a sharp lookout ahead, the schoolmaster peered back upstream. He suddenly gave a sharp cry and collapsed in the bottom of the boat. Bearing down on them in the dusky twilight was a translucent skiff being rowed by a wan, black-haired young man. Admiring his muscular physique was a blond young woman, her skin as white as milk, with her back resting against the bow of the boat, her arms draped atop the gunwales. She was smiling at her beau's effortless rhythm with the oars. The opposite shore was clearly visible *through* them.

Neither the girl nor the boy took any notice of the three men watching their ghostly progress. The phantom rowboat made no sound as it swept by. As quickly as the skiff appeared, it abruptly stopped. The girl stood up and put her arms around the young man. The boat quickly vanished beneath the surface. Nary a ripple stirred the calm waters.

Days later, Lindley began asking around if anyone might know who the ghostly boaters might have been. The Widow Overton nodded her head knowingly when she heard the question. Yes, she told the schoolmaster, they must have been Harry Stonewall and Annette Bellmont. The couple had eloped and had been seen setting off in Annette's boat on the Barren River.

They were last observed near Hammel's Cliff in the spring of 1825.

Shadow of the Unknown

The Cumberland Lake region of south-central Kentucky is rich in tales of the supernatural. Perhaps it is the mountainous terrain and isolated settlements that give rise to such beliefs, but stories of ghosts and hauntings are plentiful.

Eddy Pierce had an eerie experience several years ago that he recounted for writer Helen Price Stacy.

Pierce and his wife had just finished supper when their telephone rang. A man's deep voice advised him that if he would meet him at a certain house not too far distant, Pierce might find one of the best ghost stories ever.

He jumped in his car and headed for the abandoned farmhouse, one that he had passed many times before. The man met Pierce at the front door, and guided him inside. To his amazement, Pierce found oil lamps lighting rooms furnished in turn-of-the-century style.

Suddenly, the soft rustle of skirts and a slight cry caused him to glance at the staircase. Coming down was a lovely girl in a long dress with petticoats.

Pierce's nameless host explained that the girl had lived in the house with her widowed mother. When she remarried, her husband began beating her daughter in frequent drunken rages. Then one day he killed her with a sharp blow to the head.

The girl's mother accepted her husband's explanation that the girl had fallen from a horse. Or at least she didn't ask questions of her brutal spouse.

"But the girl's soul has never rested in peace," the man told Pierce.

He watched as the man and young woman walked out the front door. Pierce rushed to follow, but they'd vanished. Pierce knocked on the door of a lighted farmhouse across the street to ask if he might use the telephone. He called his wife to bring his camera.

Minutes later, as the couple walked toward the house, they noticed that all the lights had been turned out. The front door, which Pierce had left open, was now firmly closed. He put his shoulder to it and after several tries finally forced it open. The rooms were empty. Dust covered the floor and windows, massive cobwebs hung from the ceiling. There was no sign of the furniture and lighted lamps Pierce had seen only minutes before.

The farmer at whose house Pierce had telephoned his wife said he had seen only Pierce go into the house. He had not seen any lights through the window.

Eddy Pierce never solved the mystery of what happened to him that night. To him it always remained the time he walked into "the shadow of the unknown."

The Devil Lived in New Orleans

New Orleans. The Crescent City. A paradise for lovers of Creole and Cajun cuisine, hot jazz and vibrant nightlife. The sights and sounds and smells of this most exotic of all Southern cities are unlike those of any other place on earth. It is said that even the angels leave here with tarnished wings.

The ghosts and haunted places of New Orleans are also unique. The stories have a definite strain of the macabre, yet their undeniable romanticism attests to the duality of this city's personality—the mysterious, chilling legacy of voodoo and slavery, and, at the same time, the glamour and excitement typified by Mardi Gras and the revelries of Bourbon Street.

Take the case of Marie Laveau, for example.

When she died on June 15, 1881, Marie was New Orleans's most famous voodoo priestess. Her grave in St. Louis Cemetery Number One, on North Rampart Street, is on a popular tour sponsored by the aptly named Voodoo Museum. Curiously, her tomb is often marked with little x's drawn in the brick dust, while shells, coins, and beads are strewn around its base, along with occasional flowers and scribbled notes. The offerings are left by those seeking Marie's intercession, with a special charm . . . or curse.

Unfortunately, their devotion to the dead voodoo queen may be misplaced. Many folks believe that Marie is actually buried in an unmarked grave in St. Louis Cemetery Number Two; it's really Marie's *daughter* in the tomb at the first cemetery.

Whichever grave holds the remains of Marie Laveau *mère*, it is indisputable that her life has passed into New Orleans legend. Fact and fiction have blended to create a figure of almost mythic proportions.

Those New Orleans historians who believe there were, indeed, *two* Marie Laveaus, mother and daughter, say Mama Marie died in the early 1880s. Her place was taken by her daughter, also named Marie, who had her own voodoo practice until the turn of the century.

But others cling to the belief that only one Marie Laveau existed.

Their Marie was born sometime in the early 1800s and was practicing voodoo as early as 1830, in Congo Square. Her home was at what is now 1020 St. Ann Street. African Americans, Cajuns, and Anglos flocked to her door to ask special favors. From charms that cured diseases to love potions, poisons, and spells, Marie could accommodate almost any request. A portrait of her in the House of Voodoo, 739 Bourbon Street, depicts her as a wrinkled old hag with blazingly white hair. One long strand curls down the side of her face and ends in a serpent's head at her neck.

What may be most fascinating, however, is the legend that Marie never really died, in a palpable sense anyway.

Reports have placed her ghost in the vicinity of St. Louis Cemetery Number Two on several occasions. One man said he was slapped by her as he walked by the graveyard.

Her old home on St. Ann Street has been the subject of tales of wild voodoo ceremonies practiced by the ghostly Marie and her followers.

Curiously, another house may also harbor Marie's ghost. In the late 1980s, a family that lived on Chartres Street told reporters that their house contained "a diaphanous form" that seemed to hover in the living room near the fireplace. The house was built in 1807 by Pierre de La Ronde. According to legend, Marie Laveau lived there for some time. Also, a murder may have been committed under its roof, according to psychics consulted by the owners.

The owner of the house told the newspaper writer he wasn't sure the ghost was that of Marie Laveau. "In New Orleans the ghosts are part of the package. We just move in and they usually make room for us," he noted serenely.

However, it may not be all that difficult to contact Marie Laveau. One legend has it that she turned herself into a large black crow when she sensed that she was dying. That bird can be seen still flying noisily around her final resting place.

If you're fortunate enough to see Marie herself, and want her to perform a small miracle, be forewarned. She will expect to be paid well for her services. Whatever you do, don't disappoint her. Death does not rob a voodoo priestess of her powers to command the forces of darkness.

The Devil's Address

The ornate mansion at 1319 St. Charles Avenue was to be avoided at all costs. At this address, the Devil once took up residence in New Orleans.

Built sometime in the 1820s, the so-called Devil's Mansion took form, according to legend, literally overnight. Satan needed the house for his beautiful young mistress, a Madeleine Frenau.

So quickly did the house go up, however, that each room was at a different level—steps led up or down to every room. Even so, the mansion was outfitted with the best Satan's money could buy. Crystal chandeliers hung above carved mahogany furniture, while the finest dinner china and silverware were set for visitors who never came. Strangely, no servants were ever employed there. Not even dust dared gather in the Devil's own kingdom.

Mademoiselle quickly tired of being left alone to wander the lifeless rooms while the Devil plied his "trade" on the wicked streets. Sometimes he would be gone for several days at a time.

In time, she found another lover. His name was Alcide Cancienne, a vain and handsome Creole man who found in Madeleine such physical pleasure as he had never known. Again and again he came to St. Charles Avenue to lose himself in Madeleine's charms. Alcide was unaware that he had a rival who would stop at nothing to destroy the illicit liaison.

One day Alcide was particularly morose. As was the couple's habit when the Devil was away, they were eating dinner in the elegant dining room. Madeleine asked him the cause of his melancholy. He told her of his experience a few hours earlier. On the sidewalk outside the mansion he had been accosted by a dark-haired man attired in a great cape and top hat. The stranger asked him if he knew Madeleine Frenau. Alcide said truthfully that she was his lover. He was on his way to see her at that very moment.

The stranger laughed merrily and said that he, too, was her lover but that he had grown tired of her. Alcide could have her, but on one condition. The couple could leave with a million pounds of gold, the stranger promised, if Alcide promised to change their names to "Monsieur and Madame L."

Alcide told Madeleine that he was puzzled as to what the L stood for. She evaded answering for a few moments, but at last acknowledged that the L symbolized Lucifer. To leave St. Charles Avenue they would have to become the "Devil's couple."

Despite the conditions, Madeleine begged to leave with Alcide. She had had enough of the Devil's insatiable depravity.

Alcide just laughed at her. He had no intention of taking Madeleine anywhere. The Devil was right. He, too, was growing tired of her. And she was growing old, he added. There were many other younger and more beautiful women he could have. Besides, a mistress would never make a proper wife.

Mademoiselle Frenau was furious. She grabbed a long cloth napkin and before Alcide could act she had twisted it about his throat, crushing an artery. Blood spewed from the dying man's mouth, soaking Madeleine's hands and gown. Alcide slid off the chair and fell in a heap on the lush carpet, a pool of blood forming beside his head.

For the rest of the night, Madeleine tried to wash the blood from her body and clothing. It would not go away. At last the Devil returned from his rounds. Madeleine told him of the events, but he simply chuckled in merriment. His plans were progressing nicely, he thought.

He hoisted Alcide's corpse over his shoulder, grabbed the struggling Madeleine by the arm and climbed to the roof. Grinning, he told Madeleine that he had not had a decent meal all day. With that he began to devour Alcide's body, leaving only a few bloodied shreds of skin. He threw those to the alley below for the hungry neighborhood cats. His hunger still not satiated, he turned to Madeleine. . . .

For many years the three-story house stood vacant, its bottom windows barred, moss growing on the pillars. A family finally moved in during the 1840s, but with them came the ghosts of Madeleine and Alcide. It was always the same. In the dining room, a large table would materialize. Seated at it were the diaphanous figures of the young couple. Soon there was a scream and Madeleine's ghost lunged for the deceitful Alcide. As she twisted the napkin around his throat, the entire scene faded away. That family, and many others after it, found the horrible scenario too upsetting to stay for long.

The only family to stay was Charles B. Larendon and his wife, Laura Beauregard Larendon, the daughter of Civil War general Pierre Gustave Toutant-Beauregard. The Larendons saw the ghostly murder take place many times, but grew to accept the Uninvited Ones. They loved the house and remained for many years. Sadly, the Larendons' infant daughter died there. Mrs. Larendon passed away soon after. Charles remained a virtual recluse, keeping meticulous diaries of his experiences there. It was he who was responsible for gathering the house's incredible early history.

A Mrs. Jacques and her family later lived in the Devil's Mansion, but the haunting overwhelmed them. Not only did the spectacle in the dining room frequently turn up, but often there was the acrid smell of smoke when no fire was set in one of the numerous Italian carved fireplaces, doorknobs would be twisted by unseen hands, and disembodied footsteps raced up and down the hallways.

To passersby familiar with the house, the weirdest sight of all was the head of the Devil himself embedded in the gable. Some said it was simply a hideous gargoyle made of stone or bronze, but those who really knew said it was the head of the living Devil himself. How did they know? If you watched carefully, the eyes would follow your path and its lips would pull back in a snarl, revealing long, spiked teeth soaked in human blood.

The house was demolished many decades ago.

Buyer Beware

Would you knowingly buy a haunted house?

And if you did, how would you go about appeasing the resident specters?

In New Orleans, making peace with the nearly departed can be an all-consuming chore because, it seems, almost every old house in the city harbors its share of ghostly tenants. Quite a few have become designated historic sites or museums, so the ghosts can wander unimpeded, knowing their routines won't be upset.

The strikingly austere Le Pretre House, at the corner of Dauphine and Orlean streets, for instance, would come with a sultan and his five translucent wives— if it were on the market. In 1792, the sultan and his comely retinue were all murdered in their sleep. Despite that definite end, their ghosts continue partying well past midnight on certain dismal nights.

At the French Quarter's Hermann-Grima Historic House, 820 St. Louis Street, resident ghosts are of a kindly nature. On chilly mornings, they will light the fireplaces and scatter the pleasant essences of lavender and roses about the parlor.

For the sheer number of ghosts in residence, however, the Beauregard-Keyes

House, 1113 Chartres Street, is the clear winner. It's hard to ignore the clattering footsteps of an entire phantom army regiment!

Gen. Pierre Gustave Toutant-Beauregard leads the invisible Rebels in a reenactment of the 1862 Battle of Shiloh in the various rooms of his magnificent house. The soldiers materialize out of the paneled walls on those foggy, moonlit nights reminiscent of the bloody Civil War battle. General Beauregard, of course, went down to bitter defeat in the final minutes of the Shiloh bloodletting.

Why the good general chooses to reenact his worst hour in his former New Orleans mansion rather than at the original battlefield is anyone's guess.

A local historian said there is another legend at the Beauregard-Keyes House. Dancers and a fiddle player stage ghostly soirees in the ballroom.

Interestingly, caretakers deny that anything unusual has ever been documented. Nevertheless, the Beauregard-Keyes House is a strong contender for the city's most haunted mansion.

A house in the 700 block of Royal Street is noted for the beautiful female ghost that walks across its roof. And she's an X-rated wraith at that!

The girl was a young slave who fell in love with a handsome Creole lad. He promised to marry her if she would prove her love by spending the night on the roof of his house. Naked.

On a cold December night, she obeyed his bizarre demand, for she was hopelessly in love with the man. She stripped off her clothing and lay down on the roof. Her fiancé found her frozen to death the next morning.

Neighbors say the young woman reenacts her fatal devotion whenever December nights turn especially chilly; her nude form is clearly visible against the moonlit sky.

La Maison Est Hantée

The French and Spanish in the old Quarter knew the place all right. *La maison est hantée,* they whispered. The house is haunted. And not just any house. This address, 1140 Royal Street, is the most notorious haunted house in all of New Orleans, and perhaps in all of Louisiana as well.

On Royal Street was the 1830s home of Madame Delphine Macarty Lalaurie, a monstrous purveyor of torture and death wrapped in the guise of a beautiful, sophisticated society belle known throughout the city for her lavish entertainments and grand balls.

The most famous names in early New Orleans frequented Madame Lalaurie's salon. New Orleans raconteur and author Lyle Saxon said that as late as the 1920s Madame's old mansion was "the largest and finest in the neighborhood, rich and beautiful in detail."

But her public demeanor was a hideous charade. Lurking behind the charming smile and crinoline skirts was the soul of a sadist, a woman who reveled in unspeakable cruelties and slow, agonizing death; the exact number of helpless slaves ripped and sliced apart on her instruments of torture will never be known. Madame Lalaurie may have been the most prolific murderess in early American history.

Those unlucky enough to have heard or seen the ghosts of her victims claim they are far removed from anything else the supernatural world might inflict upon the living. The twisted, translucent forms are missing limbs, or a length of intestine might dangle from a gaping stomach wound, maybe an eye or a pair of lips might be sewn shut with heavy black thread. Blood spews from the severed buttocks of one particularly hideous specter.

For a few unfortunate pedestrians, a casual stroll past 1140 Royal Street has included witnessing the suicide of a young African-American girl as she plummets from the mansion's roof, her dying screams lingering in the still, humid night air. The terrible suddenness of the event is not lessened by knowing it is all a ghostly reenactment of an actual suicide. Some say it was murder.

The house of Madame Lalaurie is old enough to harbor many ghosts. One tradition is that it was built in 1773 by Jean and Henri de Remairie on land they received through a royal grant from the French Crown. The forty-room mansion passed through various hands until it was inherited by Delphine de Macarty. She was married three times, the last to Dr. Leonard Louis Nicolas Lalaurie in 1825.

Other historians, however, point to conflicting legal records. A court record seems to show that Madame Lalaurie bought the site in 1831 and had the house built and ready for occupancy in 1832. Old City Hall records declare that Louis and Delphine (Macarty) Lalaurie bought the house from Edmond Soniat du Fossat on August 13, 1831.

Believe what you will of the mansion's origin, Doctor and Madame Lalaurie's magnificent house was all that early New Orleans society could have wanted in a center for lively galas.

The exterior of the three-story mansion, though almost plain to the point of severity, is graced by delicate lace ironwork around the second-floor balcony and by street-level arched windows.

If the outside was undistinguished, the interior was lavish even by the excessive standards of the antebellum South. The house was made for grand parties. Mahogany doors with hand-carved panels of flowers and cherubic human faces opened to parlors and dining rooms lighted by crystal chandeliers aglow with hundreds of candles. Fireplaces taller than a man warmed almost every room, while the finest products of eastern and European furniture makers rimmed the walls. Fabrics of satin and velvet were draped in dazzling array from the walls. Guests dined on delicate European china.

The charming and beautiful Madame Lalaurie knew how to impress New Orleans society, and they, in return, made her mansion on Royal Street reverberate with hundreds of voices laughing in earthly delight. Night after night the pampered rich in their slippered feet strode through the front portico and across the marble floor of the entrance hallway and preened before the great, gilded mirrors. Their attentive hostess bustled about the rooms seeing to their comforts.

But beneath the veneer of sophistication was the cursed institution of slavery, practiced with special gusto by Delphine Lalaurie.

Attending to the house and its luxurious furnishings were dozens of slaves. A small girl helped dress Madame, another dusted the downstairs rooms and served the petits fours. A man whose name may have been Carlos fetched Madame's foodstuffs. Another slave was the wine steward and still others washed Madame's clothes, or swept the courtyard. One had the exclusive task of bathing Madame's favorite poodle!

Ironically, it was Madame Lalaurie's personal maid whose suicide gave the public its first inkling of her mistress's secret life.

Her name was Lia. She leaped from the mansion's roof one afternoon. Her body smashed into a long banquette on the sidewalk outside the house, missing by only inches a startled passerby who alerted authorities.

Before Lia's suicide, there had been some quiet conversations about how Madame's servants seemed never to stay long in her employ. The parlor maid would be replaced by a new young girl with no explanation as to her whereabouts, or the slave who groomed Doctor and Madame's horses suddenly disappeared from the stable—never to be seen again.

Understandably, Madame Lalaurie had a very difficult time explaining away Lia's death. Suspicions were raised, but after all, Madame insisted, the girl was nothing more than a piece of property to be used or gotten rid of. And yet . . . the first whisperings of unease from Madame's old friends were being heard. A few party invitations declined, a dinner abruptly canceled, a night at the theater called off . . .

On April 10, 1834, however, all doubts about Madame Lalaurie were expunged. The full story of Madame Lalaurie's cruelties was revealed in particulars so disgusting that people from the shores of Lake Ponchartrain to the Old Spanish Trail talked about it for decades.

On that otherwise pleasant spring day, a small fire brought the city's fire brigade to the mansion. An elderly black woman, who herself may have started the fire in a desperate attempt to attract attention, begged the firemen to unlock the door leading to a garret apartment. Human beings were captives up there, she cried.

At the top of the uppermost flight of stairs they found the room—Madame Lalaurie's chamber of horror. Even the most hardened of the firemen cried out in anguish at the depravity of anyone who could have created such an abomination.

The April 11, 1834, edition of the *New Orleans Bee* reported the event in the typically verbose style of nineteenth-century journalism:

"The flames having spread with alarming rapidity, and the horrible suspicion being entertained among the spectators that some of the inmates [sic] of the premises where it originated were incarcerated therein, the doors were forced open for the purpose of liberating them. . . . Upon entering one of the apartments, the most appalling spectacle met their eyes— seven slaves more or less horribly mutilated, were seen suspended by the neck, with their limbs apparently stretched and torn from one extremity to the other. Language is powerless and inadequate to give a proper conception of the horror which a scene like this must have inspired. We shall not attempt it, but leave it rather to the reader's imagination to picture what it was. . . .

"They had been confined by her [Madame Lalaurie] for several months in the situation from which they had thus providentially been rescued, and had been merely kept in existence to prolong their suffering and to make them taste all that the most refined cruelty could inflict. . . ."

It was left to witnesses other than the *Bee*'s anonymous reporter to catalogue the tortures found in Madame Lalaurie's secret chamber.

All of the victims were naked and chained to the walls. Some of the women had their stomachs sliced open and their intestines wrapped around their waists. Other females were covered with black ants, supping on gobs of honey spread over their bodies. One had had her mouth stuffed with animal excrement and then sewn shut.

The men were in even more hideous condition. Fingernails had been ripped off, eyes poked out, or buttocks and ears sliced away. One poor soul hung lifeless from his shackles, a stick protruding from a gaping hole that had been drilled into the top of his skull. It had evidently been used to "stir" his brains.

Several had their mouths pinned shut.

One man had his severed hand stitched to his stomach.

All of the prisoners wore heavy iron collars about their necks and their feet were in shackles, according to one newspaper account.

The torture had been carefully administered so as not to bring quick death. Nevertheless, some of the slaves had apparently been dead for some time. Others were unconscious. One or two were crying in incomprehensible pain, begging to be killed and thus relieved of their agony. At least two of those rescued died of their injuries later in the day.

Just how many slaves were found in Madame's torture chambers during and after the fire is not certain. Some of the servants who had "vanished," or supposedly been sold to other owners, actually never made it out of the house.

While Madame Lalaurie's grisly hideaways were being searched, and the small fire doused, she apparently stayed in the mansion. But even in the slave-holding South of the 1830s, her barbarism was too much for the city.

The New Orleans *Daily Picayune* detailed what happened next in an 1892 history of the events:

"A silence fell upon the faubourg, but it was the ominous silence that precedes the outburst of the smouldering wrath of an outraged public. During the morning, an idle crowd hung about the Lalaurie mansion, the numbers increased towards midday and by evening the throng was so dense that standing room was almost impossible upon the pavement. They hissed and hooted and some cried out for satisfaction. Madame Lalaurie did not mistake the meaning and conceived and executed a bold plan for flight.

"Promptly at the hour at which she was accustomed to take her usual drive her carriage drove up before the door and madame, dressed in her usual elegant style, stepped out upon the sidewalk and entered the vehicle. In a second more the horses were going at full speed over the clean, smooth shells of Bayou Road. Madame was taking her last drive in the fashionable quarter, and it was a drive for life itself. It took but an instant for the crowd to recover from her masterful stroke of audacity, and in another moment they were at her back, yelling and hooting and screaming: 'Stop that carriage!' 'She is running away!' 'Drag her out!' 'Shoot her!' 'Shoot the horses!' but in vain; the coachman drove furiously on; the horses went at a break-neck speed; they had borne their mistress before and would not fail her now, and fashionable New Orleans stopped its carriages and watched in black amazement. . . .

"Mrs. Lalaurie, it is said, took refuge for ten days near the spot where the Claiborne cottage stands in Covington, whence she made her way to Mobile and thence to Paris."

Madame Delphine Lalaurie's eventual fate is in dispute. The *Daily Picayune's* history of the Lalaurie mansion states that she lived all her final years in Paris, in a handsome mansion that, like its New Orleans predecessor, grew to become a favorite of the cultured and elite of the city. She died, the newspaper said, "in her own home, surrounded by her family."

Another account, however, published in the 1940s, alleges that Madame Lalaurie secretly returned to New Orleans some years later and settled in a home "on the Bayou Road." She called herself "the Widow Blanque." A record may actually exist showing a "Mrs. N. L. Lalaurie" freed a slave in 1849 in that same district.

Whenever the fiend of Royal Street finally came to rest, there is no record of any legal proceedings being taken against her for the crimes she so wantonly committed. And nothing shows that she ever again saw her New Orleans mansion.

The same cannot be said of those she butchered.

The ghosts swirling about 1140 Royal Street have been the stuff of legend virtually from the day Madame Lalaurie's carriage pulled away from her front door for the last time.

A local agent, apparently on the instructions of Madame herself, placed the mansion on the market. Records indicate that it was sold in 1837 to a man who kept it only three months. He was plagued with strange noises—cries and groans and rattling chains—so that he was unable to spend a single peaceful night there. The nameless gentleman also tried to rent out various of the two-score rooms, but tenants only stayed a few days. Neighbors reported seeing the front door swing open on its own and windows rise up and down without assistance.

A furniture store and barber shop may have also occupied the premises, but again for just a very short time.

One particularly unnerving episode took place above the old stables some years after Madame Lalaurie fled for her life. A black servant was spending the night there when he was suddenly awakened by someone choking him. Bending over him in the dim light was a pale woman with black hair, a terrible look of anger on her face. She had his throat firmly in her grasp. As he was nearing unconsciousness, another pair of hands, black hands, appeared and pried the woman's fingers from his throat. Both the assailant and the servant's savior faded away in the murky darkness.

Following the Civil War, Reconstruction found the Lalaurie Mansion turned into an integrated high school "for the girls of the lower district."

In 1874, the notorious White League succeeded in forcing the black children to leave the school. Later, a segregationist Democratic school board made the school for black children only, but that lasted only a year.

After a period of vacancy, the Lalaurie mansion again found itself the center of society when an English dance teacher opened a "conservatory of music and fashionable dancing school" in 1882.

However, the resident ghosts seemed to have had other ideas.

All went well for several weeks. The teacher was very popular, drawing the best young ladies and gentlemen of New Orleans society. A newspaper wrote of that wistful time: "Music and light and laughter filled the great apartments, and it was pretty of a spring evening . . . to watch the girls in their light and graceful costumes flitting about the great rooms and over the broad balcony to the measured strains of music, while the voices of a tenor or contralto trilled through the apartments and floated out upon the dreamy street."

The dream ended abruptly. A local newspaper apparently printed an accusation against the teacher, perhaps alleging improprieties with one of his young charges, just before a grand soiree was to take place at the mansion. Students and guests stayed away and the school closed the next day. The spirits hanging about the old mansion undoubtedly danced well into the night at such wonderful news.

Not everyone was driven out of the haunted mansion. Rumors of lost treasure at 1140 Royal Street surfaced in 1892 after the death of Jules Vignie, the eccentric offspring of a prominent French family.

Vignie lived in the Lalaurie house virtually unnoticed in the late 1880s and early 1890s. Indeed, those who had known Vignie after the Civil War were surprised at the news; they had assumed him dead long before. He was a studious collector of antique furniture, fine paintings, and bric-a-brac of all sorts, and had worked for a prominent New Orleans auctioneer for years.

Vignie's body was found on a tattered cot in the attic by neighbors curious at recent signs of activity in the house. They were amazed at the beautiful furnishings Vignie had managed to acquire. A bag containing several hundred dollars was found near his body. Quick searches revealed another two thousand dollars secreted in his mattress.

Vignie's possessions were sold off and the house stayed vacant until immigrant Italian families sought housing in the Old Quarter. The Lalaurie Mansion became an apartment complex for several dozen families. For many of them, their lives in the Lalaurie mansion were anything but peaceful. The ghosts would not be stilled:

• A towering black man wrapped in chains confronted a fruit peddler on the staircase and then vanished on the bottom step.
• Strange figures wrapped in shrouds flailed away with riding crops.
• A young mother screamed when she confronted a white woman in elegant clothes bending over her sleeping infant.
• Stabled mules died mysteriously after being visited by a white-robed woman, dogs and cats were found strangled and torn in two. And always, always the groans and screams from the attic rooms.

It was never easy to keep tenants in the old house, and that was made even more difficult after one owner decided to perform some remodeling.

Workmen discovered several skeletons under the old cypress floors. The remains were found not in orderly graves, but as if they had been dumped unceremoniously into the ground. Well, the owner tried to reason, the house had been built on old Spanish and Indian burial grounds. True enough, but his response was dismissed when authorities said the bones were of relatively recent origin, certainly buried after the house was built.

What was found, officials concluded, was nothing less than Madame Lalaurie's own private graveyard. She had removed sections of the house's floor, dug shallow graves and thrown the bodies of her tortured slaves in them so as to avoid having to answer for their deaths. The mystery of the sudden disappearance of Madame's slaves was finally solved.

The twentieth century has seen the mansion on Royal Street renovated and become, for now, a favorite sight on tours of the Old French Quarter.

Mainely Ghosts

Nell Hilton is the oldest ghost in Maine.

Born before the Revolutionary War, young Nell marched to the beat of her own drummer. She soon grew to resent the strict, Puritan atmosphere of Plymouth, Massachusetts, in which she was raised. In 1740 she persuaded her father to move to Jonesboro, Maine. There Nell found the unfettered life she craved, romping through the woods and making friends with the Passamaquoddy Indians.

But one night Nell's father found his vivacious daughter making love to a Passamaquoddy brave, and in one glancing blow, dispatched him with a hatchet. Despite Nell's frantic screams, Mr. Hilton scalped the interloper.

With her lover dead, Nell turned on her father, crying that he had just killed the man she was to marry. Mr. Hilton ordered her out of his house. "You can spend the rest of your life with them," he shouted. And that's just what Nell Hilton did.

For the next thirty-five years, Nell succeeded in living between two worlds. She made friends with Indians living in French Canada and the American colonies. She often acted as a translator for the French traders who dealt with the Passamaquoddy and other tribes. There is even some evidence that Nell was a schoolteacher in New Brunswick and Maine.

Nell's special gift, however, the one that gives her a noted place in Maine folklore, was her ability to foretell war. After the French Acadians were driven from Nova Scotia by the British in 1755, legend has it that Nell correctly foretold the war that followed. She advised the Indians to remain loyal to the French. They apparently showed more honesty toward the Indians than did their British adversaries.

The next twenty years of Nell's life are obscure. She apparently resurfaced in her old hometown of Jonesboro sometime in 1775. Tensions that would erupt in the Revolutionary War a year later were already simmering. She is said to have warned the townspeople that war was imminent, outlining what would become the Battle of Lexington and the eventual Patriot victory that culminated in the British surrender at Yorktown.

Nell Hilton would not live to see that happen. She was captured by the British in 1777. Because of her French and Patriot sympathies years before, the Tories had enough "evidence" to convict her as a spy. She was hanged at St. John, New Brunswick, on March 1, 1777.

As she stood on the gallows, she vowed to return on the anniversary of her death at the "prophecy rock" near Hilton's Neck whenever war threatened America. It's said that her ghost reappeared prior to the War of 1812, the Mexican conflict of 1846, in 1861 before the Civil War, and then preceding the Spanish-American War of 1898 and World War I. Nothing is known about her appearances before World War II, Korea, and Vietnam. And no one apparently saw her March 1, 1990, ten months before Operation Desert Storm in the Persian Gulf.

Perhaps even ghosts become tired of war.

A Remarkable Monument

Col. Jonathan Buck was many things. Patriot. Magistrate. Progenitor of an old Maine family. Founder of Bucksport. By most accounts he was a moral, straightforward man often called upon to settle disputes of varying severity.

But did he also have an evil side? Did this man known for his probity once send an innocent person to the gallows? And could this mistaken death have produced a curse whose effects are visible to this day?

These questions are at the center of a controversy over just what produced the peculiar, leg-shaped outline on Colonel Buck's monument in a cemetery near the town he founded, Bucksport, Maine. Nearly fifteen feet high, the granite obelisk is clearly visible along U.S. Highway 1, about eighteen miles south of Bangor. The name "Buck" is etched on the front. An inscription on the side reads:

COL. JONATHAN BUCK
THE FOUNDER OF BUCKSPORT
A.D. 1762
BORN IN HAVERHILL, MASS. 1719
DIED MARCH 18, 1795

Soon after the monument was erected by Colonel Buck's descendants in 1852, what seemed to be the contours of a human leg appeared just below the name "Buck." Despite repeated attempts to excise the image, it remains vivid to all who visit the cemetery.

The truth behind the "witch's curse," as local townspeople call the legacy of Jonathan Buck, is wrapped in mystery and legend. The various tellings of the tale vary with the speaker or writer. Some are in agreement as to basic facts, while others are wildly divergent from what is known about the life of Colonel Buck. All constitute one of the most fascinating of all Maine traditions. What follows is an attempt to recount the most prevalent myths to see how they square with the probable truth.

Colonel Buck was born in Massachusetts, though not at Haverhill as the monument states. He gained his military title in the Revolutionary War and moved to Maine sometime late in the eighteenth century. One version of the Buck legend draws upon his early Massachusetts life:

A woman had been accused as a witch and Colonel Buck was asked to preside at her trial, a rapid affair in which the defendant was presumed guilty and quickly condemned to death. Before she was hanged, however, the woman looked at Colonel Buck and placed a curse on him. A newspaper account from 1899 recounting the Buck legend had the woman uttering these words: "Over your grave they will erect a stone that all may know where your bones are crumbling into dust . . . upon that stone the imprint of my feet will appear and for all time . . . will the people from far and near know that you murdered a woman. Remember well, Jonathan Buck, remember well. . . ."

This "witch's curse" is the most popular form of the Buck legend. However, there is no record of a witch being executed in Maine. Even in Massachusetts, where Colonel Buck was born and lived for many years, the last of the infamous witch trials took place nearly thirty years before his birth.

Another version, alternately placed in Massachusetts and Maine, provides another connection between a human leg and Colonel Buck:

It seems that Colonel Buck—called "Judge" Buck in this account—was a severe and unforgiving administrator of justice. The grisly remains of a woman were found near town. One of her legs had been neatly sawn off. Under pressure from alarmed townsfolk, Buck hauled in a "suspect," a mentally impaired hermit who lived in a shack at the edge of town. He was given a perfunctory trial and sentenced to death. The recluse looked at Buck and swore that the image of the dead woman's missing leg would appear on Buck's tombstone as a sign of this miscarriage of justice.

This, too, doesn't quite fit the facts of the case. Colonel Buck was only a justice of the peace and did not have the power to condemn anyone to death. No historical record exists to show that he was a judge in Massachusetts before moving to Maine.

In 1913, Oscar Heath, a former resident of Bucksport, wrote a sensational version of the story called "Jonathan Buck, His Curse." Heath added a new twist to the old tale. His story was "narrated" by the *son* of the "witch." The accused was not hanged, Heath wrote, but rather burned at the stake. The child witnessed his mother's horrible death, including the gruesome sight of her burning legs falling off her torso. He grabbed one of her charred limbs and struck Colonel Buck with it.

Poet Robert P. Tristram Coffin added to the Buck legend in a 1939 verse titled "The Foot of Tucksport," a thinly disguised reference to Bucksport. Coffin's main character was "Colonel Jonathan Jethro Tuck."

A boy, the witch's son, also figures prominently in Coffin's poem. The woman accuses "Colonel Tuck" of fathering her child. No crime is committed by her, but rather it is the intolerant townspeople who fall upon the hapless woman and drag her away after she shouts her accusations against the colonel in the town square:

They dragged the crone to her poor hut,
They tied her to her door,
They brought and heaped the withered boughs,
Against the rags she wore.

The thunderhead touched on the sun,
And a shadow came,
Just as Colonel Tuck bent down
And touched the boughs with flame.

Coffin has the dying woman condemning the colonel with her last breath:

"And so long as a monument
Marks a grave of thine
So long shall my curse inscribe
Thy tombstone with my sign!"

Folklore and sensationalism aside, is there any truth to the witch's curse of Jonathan Buck? Or is he just the victim of a bad press?

Colonel Buck apparently was highly moral, with a clear sense of right and wrong. A stern man, many would say. He was respected by his neighbors for his military exploits. His election as justice of the peace was doubtless a result of the high esteem in which he was held.

Could there have been the proverbial skeleton in Buck's closet? It's possible. Though he was never formally selected as a judge in Massachusetts, it's conceivable that in the absence of proper authorities in the region he was asked to preside at a trial by virtue of his military rank. Who knows what may have happened? Perhaps he did confront someone accused of witchcraft, or other heinous acts, and did participate in that person's execution.

What cannot be disputed is the eerie outline of a human leg on Colonel Buck's monument a few feet from his final resting place. Most of the curses have the leg showing up on Buck's actual tombstone, but this seems to be a small error. After all, what is a few feet for a curse that is two hundred years old?

As long as the monument stands, passersby will look and wonder if the late Col. Jonathan Buck is still plagued by a witch's last words.

Cyrus

Cyrus was the night clerk for many years at the historic Kennebunk Inn. He was an elderly gent, quiet and conscientious, who could often be found at his desk in a room behind what is now the hotel's bar. Cyrus's life was devoid of eccentricities. Now that he's dead, however, Cyrus could be making up for all of that. His ghost may be the cause of mischief sometimes reported at the inn.

Built as a private home in 1791, the three-story, clapboard Federal-Victorian building changed hands several times before its conversion to an inn called "The Tavern" in the late 1920s. The inn was expanded to sixteen rooms in 1940 by Walter Day and renamed the Kennebunk Inn. During this era Cyrus was employed by Mr. Day.

Arthur LeBlanc bought the place in 1980, added a half-dozen rooms, and passed the word that the old lodge was haunted.

According to writer Robert Ellis Cahill, "Cyrus" was a nickname first given to the resident ghost by a waitress, Pattie Farnsworth. In bringing up supplies from a food locker in the cellar one day, she told owner LeBlanc that the name "Cyrus" came to her. She said he lived under an unfinished set of steps that led from the cellar floor to the ceiling.

The ghost made himself known in distressing ways. A waitress carrying a tray of stemware saw one of the glasses rise several inches into the air and crash to the floor. Several diners witnessed the incident. The waitress took the rest of the day off.

A bartender named Dudley also encountered Cyrus. Late one August evening, a German, hand-carved wooden mug sailed from a shelf behind the bar and struck Dudley on the side of his head. A lump on the barkeep's skull seemed to support his allegation, according to those who spoke with him later.

Angela LeBlanc, the owner's wife, found out quite by accident that waitress Pattie Farnsworth's intuition about their ghost's name was prescient. One day as the LeBlancs and several friends were discussing Cyrus's recent antics, a stranger showed up at the bar. Apologizing for intruding, he asked if Cyrus was still around. He was the resident ghost, Arthur LeBlanc explained. The elderly visitor shook his head. He said he'd lived at the inn as a young man just prior to World War II and Cyrus was the night clerk at that time. In fact, he continued, Cyrus had his desk in a room directly above the basement's unfinished staircase!

Coincidence? Or evidence of a haunting?

Cahill, an author and collector of Maine ghost stories, tried to discover the truth when he stayed at the inn with three friends. Although Cahill didn't hear or see anything, one of his companions asleep in the same room was kept awake by a raspy, moaning voice. Another of Cahill's friends wanted to use the bathroom in the early morning hours. He changed his mind when a chilling breeze enveloped his legs as soon as he stepped out of bed.

Yet the man assigned to stay in Cyrus's old room didn't feel or hear anything unusual.

In nearby Kennebunkport, former president George Bush's occasional vacation home, the picturesque Captain Lord Mansion Inn harbors quite a different specter.

In 1978, a young bride on her honeymoon was understandably upset when a woman attired in a nightgown glided across her bedroom suite and vanished.

Despite some effort, no one has been able to explain who the intruder might have been, or why she was still hanging around the inn.

Windham's Ghost Tower

In the village of South Windham, a few miles southeast of Sebago Lake, a poltergeist is said to ring a bell even though it is no longer there to be rung!

The house on Windham Center Road originally belonged to the Gould family—famous as statesmen and writers. Near the house is a large outbuilding, open on the ground floor so that farm equipment could be easily driven under cover. There is an enclosed second floor for storage and, in one corner, a tower juts heavenward.

On the second floor, and in the tower, footsteps are sometimes heard skittering across the squeaking floorboards. According to legend, the bell that was once housed in the tower was used to sound alarms in the War of 1812 and for raids during the Indian wars.

Whoever the ghost might be, his warnings have long since ceased to cause alarm in neighborhood residents.

E. A. Poe and Guests

At three in the morning a man with a walking stick strides through the small, walled-in Westminster Churchyard at the corner of Fayette and Greene streets in West Baltimore. He is dressed all in black with a black fedora on his head and a neck scarf pulled up high over his face to mask his features. He is a man with a purpose and he knows the route well.

At the grave of Edgar Allan Poe, the nocturnal visitor leaves a bottle of cognac and three red roses. After kneeling for a few moments, he arises, tips his hat and leaves.

The odd ritual has been carried out on Poe's birthday—January 19—for nearly fifty years. One year a note accompanied the offerings:

Edgar, I haven't forgotten you.

There was no signature.

Although there is some evidence that Poe's ghost haunts his gravesite, the man in black appears quite real. It is certainly fitting that a mystery continues to swirl about the American writer most associated with tales of the macabre.

No one knows who the phantomlike visitor might be, or where he comes from. In fact, Alexander Rose, a historian of Baltimore's Edgar Allan Poe Society, has been quoted as doubting that the tributes are the work of one person.

So has Jeff Jerome, curator of the nearby Edgar Allan Poe House. Jerome recalled seeing a white-haired man one year while other observers at another time saw a thin man with black hair kneeling at the grave.

Could they be father and son? Had the old man died, leaving his son to carry on? Or was he too ill that one year and had asked a friend to take over the task? Is the mystery man a distant relative of the American poet? The questions are endless, the answers elusive.

Obviously, the man is an aficionado of Poe's horror stories. The possibility exists that two different men appear at different hours on the same night because two graves must be monitored—a small one in the back of the burial ground where Poe's body rested for twenty-six years, and the larger one in front where he was reburied in 1875.

Although he declined to be interviewed for this book, Jerome has been quoted as saying that if he has his way, the visitor's identity will never be known, and should it become known to him somehow, it will never be revealed. Common decency dictates that a mourner at a gravesite be left alone with his private sorrows—even if the dearly departed has been gone nearly a century and a half!

Interestingly, public opinion may be on Jerome's side. He has received numerous telephone calls from Baltimore residents requesting that no attempt ever be made to approach the visitor.

From time to time, Jerome himself has been suspected of being the dark stranger in the night. He denies the allegations, asserting that as a city employee he would lose his job over such shenanigans. Furthermore, the visitations began in 1949, before Jeff Jerome was even born.

But in an attempt to squelch the rumors, Jerome invited seventy people to gather in the graveyard at midnight on January 19, 1983. They celebrated the writer's 174th birthday with a glass of amontillado, a Spanish sherry featured in one of Poe's famous short stories, and a reading of his poems. At an hour and a half past midnight, the celebrants were startled to see a man dash around the cemetery's east wall, his frock coat flying. He was fair-haired and carried a gold-topped cane like the one Poe favored. Cognac and roses were discovered on Poe's original grave.

Jerome told a reporter on this occasion, "This is a nice mystery, and there aren't many mysteries left." Poe, the maker of such exquisite mysteries, would certainly agree.

Yet Jerome did permit one freelance photographer to try to capture one of the elusive visitors on film. Backed by $17,000 from *Life* magazine, Bill Ballenberg rented infrared night-vision photo equipment. Then, from inside Westminster Hall, the old brick Presbyterian church that abuts the cemetery, Ballenberg activated a radio signal that triggered the camera when he saw a figure approaching.

The picture appears in the July 1990 issue of *Life*. Although somewhat indistinct, it shows the back of a heavyset man kneeling at Poe's grave. The face can barely be discerned, shadowed as it was by the tilted hat brim and the fact that the man faced the tombstone. A cane rested against the stone.

"No one else will be allowed to photograph the visitor," said Jerome at the time. "This was a once-in-a-lifetime chance."

Mortal visitors come and go—even at the midnight hour. And maybe the ghost of Edgar Allan Poe does too.

Legend has it that his apparition occasionally hovers near the original gravesite and prowls the catacombs beneath the church, which provided much of the material for his gruesome stories. However, chances of seeing his ghost are slim. Although the Poe family is a very old and aristocratic one from Baltimore, the writer himself was not a native son and spent only a few early years in the city. Why should he return there in unearthly form?

Poe was born in Boston and was only passing through Baltimore when he died under mysterious circumstances. His wife had already died of tuberculosis and

Poe was on his way to New York to meet his beloved mother-in-law and take her to Richmond, Virginia, where he planned to marry his childhood sweetheart.

Four days after reaching Baltimore, Poe was found barely conscious in a gutter on East Lombard Street. He was rushed to the Church Home and Hospital and, while he lay dying, he sweated and trembled and screamed the name "Reynolds!" over and over again. His mother-in-law said he knew no one of that name. Poe died in the hospital on the seventh of October, 1849. He was forty years old.

Some said Poe's death was caused by alcohol; others thought he'd been drugged because the clothes he was wearing were not his. Was it pneumonia? Encephalitis? An acute psychotic state? At least twenty-two versions of the writer's death have been put forth—all of them as horrific as his stories.

Ironically, it had been in Baltimore in 1829 that Edgar Allan Poe struggled to begin his literary career, living in the house of his aunt, Mrs. Maria Clemm, mother of Virginia, his cousin, whom he married six years later. Poe's grandmother also lived in the small, unheated, and sparsely furnished house. Here, Poe was plagued by poverty, illness, and debt, and the ignominy of producing what some critics of the time called "hack" work. His attic room is accessible only by a narrow, winding staircase that leads to a doorway so tiny as to require an average-size adult to crawl through it.

Although Poe's ghost hasn't been seen in the house, psychics have felt hot and cold spots, a phenomenon allegedly indicating the presence of spirits.

In 1980, a local radio station held an unsuccessful séance in the little house at 203 North Amity Street. However, something *did* happen before daylight.

Curator Jeff Jerome recounted the story in a later published account of the event:

"I locked up when everyone left and went home. The next morning, as I was coming up the stairs, I felt a cold draft. When I got upstairs I discovered all the windows had been opened from the inside—even though the outside shutters were all locked. There are only two keys to this place: one for me and one for my boss, and she was in England at the time. How else could those windows have been opened?"

Maligned in life. Maligned in death. Schoolchildren learn that Edgar Allan Poe was the father of the American horror story and a great poet. They also learn that he was an opium addict, an alcoholic, a pervert, and a madman who talked to invisible people.

Today's scholars dismiss these charges as myths first perpetrated by Rufus W. Griswold, editor of *The Poets and Poetry of America*. After Poe criticized the work, Griswold set out to destroy the writer's reputation. As Poe's literary executor and first biographer, Griswold was in a position to do much damage. He succeeded.

The facts: Poe tried opium, a legal drug at the time, but his stomach couldn't handle it. He was able to tolerate only a glass or two of wine at a sitting. He did marry his thirteen-year-old cousin, hardly a perversion in his time, when young women married very early. And talking to invisible people? Perhaps there is something to that. Were his cries for "Reynolds!" a mark of delirium?

Griswold wrote Poe's obituary. It begins:

"Edgar Allan Poe is dead. He died in Baltimore the day before yesterday. This announcement will startle many, but few will be grieved by it."

Griswold is all but forgotten. But still the mourners come to the little grave-yard in Baltimore.

The Proud Lady

Midnight. Rufus Frost and Evan Randolph stood on the deserted stone pier at Baltimore's harbor. A ribbon of moonlight unrolled across the water and a gentle breeze rocked an old frigate in its berth. The ship had been christened the *Constellation*. That was two hundred years ago. As the United States Navy's first ship, she's now a national shrine permanently moored in Baltimore. Everyone calls her "the proud lady."

Some say the *Constellation* is also haunted.

Frost and Randolph were determined to find out. Together, they peered through the open gun ports, but the night watchman refused to let them board the frigate. Visiting hours were over.

Randolph grew impatient. Weren't ghosts supposed to show themselves? Make some noise? A sign of some kind?

"C'mon, Commodore, do somethin'!" Randolph shouted. "It's late and we want to get t' bed."

At that moment, something slapped the water and the twenty-foot-long wooden fenders rocked violently between ship and pier; water cascaded down the vessel's starboard side. The men grabbed each other, then raced back to their hotel.

At family reunions Frost and Randolph would joke that their ancestor, Commodore Thomas Truxton, commander of the U.S. frigate *Constellation*, had thrown a cannonball at them but missed on that strange night in 1975.

The cannonballs did not miss on the day in 1799 when the ship captured the French frigate *L'Insurgente* near the island of St. Kitts in the West Indies. It was the first major sea victory for the United States Navy in its quasi-war with France, and Commodore Truxton was widely praised for his skillful seamanship.

But Truxton was also feared by his crew. He ran a tight ship and gave no quarter to any crewman inattentive to his duty. So it was that in the sea battle with *L'Insurgente*, Neil Harvey fell asleep at his watch. As punishment, Lt. Andrew Sterett was ordered to run the hapless crewman through with a cutlass; then after the capture of the French vessel, Harvey's body was tied to the muzzle of a broadside cannon and blown to bits.

But the murdered seaman may never have left the ship. His ghost, affectionately known as "Neil," is said to prowl the decks of the *Constellation*, searching for his merciless captain—and maybe his own scattered remains.

Repairmen have reported hearing strange moans and cries coming from belowdecks on the supposedly empty ship, but when they investigate they find nothing.

James L. Hudgins, director of the ship in 1976, told a reporter, "One time, I switched on the alarm system, turned off all the lights and locked up for the night. The next day, the place was still locked from the inside, but the lights and a radio were on."

Hudgins also recalled the story of a delighted priest who claimed he'd been given a tour belowdecks by an old salt who volunteered information about the ship's history and explained various pieces of equipment. When the priest came topside he congratulated the tour guides for providing such a knowledgeable man as the one who had shown him around.

The guides were puzzled. They had sent no one below to give any tours.

When Sybil Leek, the famous English medium, visited the ship she claimed to have picked up vibrations from three spirits: a captain, a sailor, and an apprentice seaman, all of whom had died violently.

Commodore Truxton died alone and bitter after Thomas Jefferson, a French sympathizer, assumed the presidency from John Adams. Little more is recorded of Lieutenant Sterett. And the hapless Neil Harvey? Perhaps Ms. Leek sensed his spirit. Who can say?

The blood of countless seamen has flowed over the wooden beams of the old ship. The cannon are silent and, of course, dead men tell no tales.

Alfie

Alfie is every mother's dream. When parties are held in the house he stays in the background, and sometimes waves good-bye to departing guests from an upstairs window. Whenever a first-time visitor comments on this lovely child, Peg and Joe Roberts smile. They have five children, but Alfie is not one of them. Alfie is not real.

He came with the house, but the Robertses aren't sure who he is. In their traditional New England farmhouse, built in 1831, many persons have lived and died, and the ghosts of some remain. They glide like shadows across the original wide pine floorboards and watch Joe working in the basement. He feels their presence, but sees only quick, darting movements out of the corner of his eye.

Joe and Peg bought the house in 1965. It is snugged against a mountainside outside Wilbraham, and its five acres are filled with flowers and magnificent old trees. Additions to the original structure afforded plenty of space for the Robertses' growing children, and the price was right. Yet, from the moment the real estate broker showed the couple the house Joe felt that something was wrong with it. He heard odd noises and remarked, "The damn place is haunted." The broker smiled and said that all old houses creak and groan, but she admitted later that she was afraid to go out there after dark.

The Robertses learned that the previous owner was a working woman who lived alone in the house with a large German shepherd. One day while she was at work the neighbors saw the dog leap through a second-floor window, taking the window frame with him. No explanation for the dog's behavior was ever given.

Nevertheless Joe and Peg were determined to have the house. They knew it was just the right place for them. The children—four boys and a girl—were less certain.

Shortly after they moved in, little Joey said a boy had come into his room in the middle of the night and looked at his trains. Only the upper part of the body was visible and it glowed in the dark. The other children never saw it at any time.

Joe started to research the history of the house, but found that records were either missing or incomplete. He did learn that the house had been built by a Dennis Ely and that a family named Morgan owned it for many years. Eventually he was put in touch with several highly recommended psychics.

During one séance a medium learned that the phantom child's name was Alfie. He was nine years old when he died in the house in 1898. He had broken his neck in a fall down the back stairway. His father was serving in the army at that time. A child, possibly Alfie, had been born in the house on June 15, 1888, the same day that an elderly woman named Mary Morgan died there. Mary was rather an eccentric lady who wore an old farmer's hat on her head and wove rugs in a downstairs room. She may have been Alfie's great-grandmother, but this relationship cannot be documented.

However, Joe said that every year on June 15 while the children were growing up, the turbulence in the house became "very hairy." Balls of light half the size of a basketball glided back and forth across the ceilings of the children's rooms. Wind-up toys stored in a toy box started up by themselves, the *vroom, vroom, vrooms* being distinctly heard. And the running footsteps of a child were heard when all the Robertses' children were in bed.

At another séance participants felt a dog under the table rubbing against their legs. The family did not own any pets at that time. One psychic said it was Alfie's dog, "Dodo." He loved it dearly and it went everywhere with him. The psychics decided against trying to free the earthbound spirits of Alfie and his dog because the house was filled with warmth and happiness—a comforting place for a little lost boy and his dog.

Joe and Peg were saddened by the little ghost they couldn't see, and they were not afraid. When their own children were young, however, the couple longed to spend an evening out, but they seldom did. Peg could never get a babysitter to come more than once. "Too noisy," they all said.

It was. One morning Joe was awakened at three o'clock by a sound outside the open bedroom door. He sat up but saw no one in the pitch black of the hall. But when he cupped his hands to his ears he heard it clearly—the *bump, bump, bump* of something going down the staircase. He didn't get up to check, but in the morning he told his wife that "the most intelligent mouse in the world was rolling agates down the stairs." Was Alfie playing with his marbles?

On another morning after Joe had gone to work, Peg was awakened by whistling and the sound of boxes falling off the hope chest in the bedroom. She snapped on the light. Nothing had been disturbed.

Joey was home alone and heard footsteps going back and forth in the hallway to the bathroom. He was too frightened to leave his room.

Peg says the footsteps are always present. "If I'm downstairs I would hear somebody upstairs, or if I'm upstairs I'll hear someone come in the door and walk around. We keep the doors locked out here during the day if I'm upstairs, but I come down and check to make sure nobody has gotten in. But they're never around."

Yet one night Joe's nephew thought there was definitely someone there. A musician in a band, he often stayed overnight with his aunt and uncle if he'd been playing in the area. Joe warned him that the place was haunted, but said he was welcome to sleep on the downstairs couch. The young man scoffed at the idea of ghosts, but did accept the invitation . . . until the night he heard someone unlock the front door at two o'clock, close it, and walk through the house.

He leaped up, snapped on lights and hollered, "Who's there?" No answer. The door was still shut and locked. That was the last night the fellow ever slept in the house.

Joe said that for a while, exactly at 11:00 P.M. each night, "the front door went *boom* like somebody kicked it." Then it stopped suddenly. "It can get frightening, you know. You can feel it. You get that prickly feeling in your skin, in your hair. You know something's around."

Although the house is set back only ten feet from the country road, the door is secured by three locks and a deadbolt. Nevertheless, some people will not visit the house after dark. It is in a rugged and isolated area, intimidating to those not used to rural places.

In grade school the Robertses' children were embarrassed when other children wrote compositions on "The Haunted House." Everyone knew which house it was. Joe and Peg say that their children, now grown, are still not completely at ease in the house.

As a teenager Sharon suffered from the phenomena more than her brothers. Her father said she "seemed to be scared to death. And 'they' bothered a lot of her girlfriends too. She had slumber parties and a lot of girls wouldn't come back."

One warm summer night the girls ran outside in their pajamas, and as they glanced back at the house Sharon cried, "Oh gee, my father is watching us!" A light, similar to a flashlight's beam, was traveling through the house. When the light vanished, the girls ran back inside. Peg and Joe had slept soundly all night.

On another occasion one of Sharon's friends was in bed when she heard knocks on the floor all around the bed. Then the bed began to shake all by itself. The girl never slept, nor did she ever attend any more of Sharon's nighttime parties. Joe learned that many years ago a twelve-year-old girl had died of rheumatic fever in the room.

Peg said the phenomena seem to come and go. There may be a lot of activity for several weeks, and then nothing for a while except the ordinary noises of an old house. Curiosity seekers come sometimes expecting to witness something out of the ordinary, but Joe tells them that you don't program those things; they just occur. Then the visitors go away disappointed.

Many times people ask how the family can stay in the house.

"What are we supposed to do, sell the house?" asks Joe. "This is our home."

It does seem to Joe and Peg that as the children got older there was much less activity. Yet it is unpredictable.

When son Greg came home on leave from the navy one time he left his television set blaring away in his room on three consecutive nights. His mother confronted him.

"Greg, how could you be so tired you don't even turn that TV off?"

"Well, Mom," he began, "there's so much noise in this room that I turn the TV on so I don't hear it and eventually I fall asleep." He mentioned too that someone had been knocking at his door in the middle of the night. No one in the family had been up.

His mother understood. She and her husband are frequently awakened by three raps on the headboard of their bed. The raps always presage the death of an elderly relative.

Sometimes an odor will announce a death. One day everyone was sitting in the living room and saying it smelled just like a hospital. Peg smelled nothing, but the next day she learned that a young boy down the road had died of leukemia at the time the family had detected the odor.

January brings lilacs, the heavy perfume of the flowers filling the house. Joe can't explain it. Although there are a few lilac bushes on the land, they are old and seldom bloom. And certainly not in mid-winter!

The family pets are extremely sensitive to the unexplained phenomena in the house. Many refuse to go into certain rooms and all, except one cat, cannot be dragged into the cellar even through the outside door which is at ground level. A psychic once told Peg and Joe that the house was part of the Underground Railroad by which slaves escaped north before the Civil War. She said a slave had died in the basement, but Joe never found any proof of the existence of an underground railway in their area.

One female dog refuses to enter the living room at certain times. She stands in the doorway and gives a very low growl and the hair bristles all the way down her back. This occurs usually in the daytime.

At one time the family kept parrots, and Joe set up a tape recorder near their cages to see if they would speak in an empty house. One did. It gave a telephone number, and when Joe called the number it was a cemetery in New York State where William C. Morgan, one of the original owners of the property, was buried!

Sharon also has had a number of peculiar experiences with tape recordings. She used to sing in a band and practice in her room, always taping the sessions to be certain she was singing on key. Many times in playing back a tape she heard someone else singing with her!

When Sharon got married she wore a beautiful, old-fashioned wedding dress that had been worn by the deceased mother of Peg's best friend. By coincidence, Sharon was married on the anniversary of the woman's death. After the evening ceremony and reception, a few close friends were invited to join the Robertses back at the house.

Peg had given the door key to Sue and David, a neighboring couple who had agreed to go in and start the coffee. As the couple drove down the road they remembered they'd forgotten the key. David started to turn around, but Sue shouted, "Stop! Sharon's already there. I just saw her in the window. She has the wedding dress on!"

The living room light was on because the family never leaves the house in darkness. When David knocked at the door the figure vanished.

Joe and Peg have *seen* only one ghost in the house, a "harvest ghost" who shows up in the fall. He wears boots and an old black hat and tramps through the dining room into the kitchen. They think he's William B. Morgan, who farmed the land for a number of years.

One of the many psychics who has toured the house described this ghost to Peg and Joe. The woman didn't know the Robertses; she just went through the house and wrote down all her impressions before talking to the couple. Peg says her description of the farmer's ghost matched exactly the figure that she and her husband see.

Ghost lore has it that a cold spot may be felt before a ghost appears. The family periodically feels a cold spot partway up the stairway. Peg says that a psychic who has been to the house several times told her to blow smoke into the cold spot and the apparition would take form. But whenever Peg walked into the cold spot she never had a cigarette with her. By the time she'd run downstairs to get one and be back upstairs the cold had left. Peg decided that the ghost did not want to be seen. The chill moved from place to place, usually hovering near the bathroom. Often at large parties a guest would holler, "I'm in the cold spot!" Others would hurry upstairs, but neither see nor feel anything.

However, one person was badly frightened in the bathroom. Joe recalled a cook-out one day that was attended by about a hundred people. A young newly married man asked Joe if he could use the bathroom. When the fellow returned, he was pale and shaken. "There's something wrong with your bathroom," he said.

"Peg just cleaned it," Joe replied.

"No, that's not it." The guest hurried off and hasn't returned.

Although Joe never learned what had frightened the young man, he himself has been ill at ease on a number of occasions in that room. There is a crashing sound like beams falling, "very, very loud noises, like a person dropping a piano in the attic," Joe explained. "Sometimes I think the roof has fallen in." He has looked many times for the source of the noise, "but there's nothing up there."

One night at 1:30 A.M., Joe was in the bathtub when somebody knocked on the door. He figured it was one of the children and called, "Come in." Nobody did. He got out of the tub, wrapped himself in a towel and opened the door. No one was in sight.

Another early morning when Joe was in the tub he heard people arranging furniture downstairs, drawing chairs away from the table on the bare floor, then pushing them in. He wondered what Peg was doing down there. Nothing. She was asleep. As soon as Joe stood at the top of the stairway the noises stopped. He no longer goes downstairs at night.

After Joe set up a tape recorder with an ultrasensitive microphone in the kitchen, it picked up a lot of distinguishable household noises. Once he heard dishes being washed and was grateful for the help because his wife had been tired and had let the dishes go. Unfortunately, they were still there in the morning.

Another time the microphone picked up the *"clink, clink, clunk, clunk"* of someone putting dishes away in the cupboard. There was nothing to be put away. Joe thinks Mary Morgan is still at work.

One fellow told Joe the noises were caused by the house settling. "It hasn't settled in the last hundred years," Joe replied. "The foundation is three feet thick and sitting on hardpan." Joe knew. Soon after they'd moved in he had to use a pickax to dig a ditch to install drain tile.

Besides, everyone in the family is acquainted with the usual creaks and groans of an old house. Floorboards don't squeak in sequence. "When the boards squeak in sequence, it's footsteps," Joe said.

One of the strangest phenomena in the house concerns a painting that apparently cannot be photographed. The local high school once had a television program called "The Blueberry Project" in which students themselves produced a video show. Knowing about "the haunted house," one group wanted to do a show on it and Joe agreed.

The students did a story on the whole house, but the picture they wanted for the final scene they couldn't get. Peg said they tried four times with the video camera and got nothing on the tape. The picture is a semiabstract painting showing two hands thrust through a broken window. It was done by a family friend and it hangs over the fireplace. After realizing that the failure to get the picture on tape was *not* a joke, several girls became hysterical.

The program, without the close-up finale of the picture, was shown that night on the school channel. It concludes, "Joe believes in ghosts. Do you?"

The Wrong Apartment

In 1972 Merry Lee Schwander, a young working woman in Grand Rapids, was looking for a quiet, comfortable place in which to live. She found it, or so she thought, in a mansion on Heritage Hill. The handsome postbellum house, of Georgian Revival style, had been divided into apartments. Merry and a roommate chose one on the second floor. It was a mistake.

One night, shortly after she'd moved in, Merry awoke from a deep sleep to see a huge head projected on the ceiling of her room right over the bed. A young man with blond hair smiled down at her! Merry, too startled to scream, pulled the bed covers up under her chin. The gigantic head moved slowly across the ceiling and vanished.

On another night, Merry's bedroom was flooded with blinding light, as if a thousand floodlights had been turned on. Terrified, she leaped out of bed and ran to get her roommate. When the women returned, the room was in darkness.

But the most chilling incident occurred early one morning when Merry felt a presence near her. She turned her head. An old woman was lying on her back beside her! The face was deadly white and wrinkled and, as she breathed noisily through her open mouth, her whole face seemed to contort in agony. Merry screamed and stumbled out of bed. By the time she and her roommate had returned to the bedroom, the bed was empty. Only a slight depression in the pillow remained.

In 1973 the women moved out.

News of the haunting spread and efforts were made to learn everything possible about the history of the house. It had been originally an eight-room residence with the kitchen in a rear shed. In later years, different owners added more rooms and the massive, imposing front pillars.

James T. Phillips, founder and owner of the Grand Rapids Clock and Mantel Company, bought the mansion in 1880 and lived there until his death in 1912. Later, a Dr. John F. Burleson bought the house and he and his family occupied it until driven out by a fire in 1934. One of the Burleson daughters was said to be a spiritualist.

For a brief period during the 1940s the mansion was used as a nursing home for elderly women, and in 1952 it was purchased by an investor who partitioned it into apartments. It remained as income property until 1973, when Merry Lee Schwander and her roommate fled.

In November of that year, Ward Paul and Chuck Schoenknecht bought the house jointly, intending to restore it to its former grandeur.

One night, shortly after their first Thanksgiving in the house, Chuck was almost asleep when he heard footfalls on the staircase—soft at first, then louder as they neared the upper hall. They stopped outside his bedroom door. Chuck was certain that the house had been broken into, possibly by two prisoners who had escaped earlier that day.

Chuck had no weapon. He grabbed his shoes, slipped one on each hand, then sat on the edge of the bed waiting for the door to burst open. Minutes ticked by while Chuck's eyes were riveted on the doorknob. It didn't turn. Finally, he dropped the shoes and threw open the door. No one was there—nor anywhere else in the house.

On another night Chuck was pushed by something and Ward's big toe was jerked as he lay reading in bed.

The men were perplexed, but put aside their concerns in order to devote themselves to the restoration of the house. They tore out the apartment partitions, steamed off wallpaper to expose the gas jets, and installed gaslight fixtures in every room except the kitchen. They sought out period furniture and bought nineteenth-century paintings and sculpture to lend authenticity to the house. Modernists might have found the house garish, but it suited Ward and Chuck—they liked the old-fashioned ambience.

As soon as the decorating was finished, the thumpings and vibrations began. Floors, beds, tables, lamps, all seemed to be in constant motion, and, although Ward and Chuck searched the house from top to bottom, they never discovered a cause.

The couple had many friends and often invited them to stay overnight. Every guest was kept awake by heavy footsteps, bangings, and the scraping noise of furniture being dragged across the attic floor. Although guests may have been disturbed, they weren't frightened because they all assumed their hosts were working up there. They weren't!

The vibrations increased daily, shaking pictures off the walls, but leaving hooks and wires intact. Wastebaskets spewed their contents, and once a shattering explosion overhead disrupted a dinner party. Everyone dashed upstairs, but found nothing. Then came a misty figure floating up the stairs and vanishing.

When the furnace failed one night, Ward and Chuck put their sleeping bags on the living room floor. But they never slept. The floor creaked as footsteps circled the men all night long.

Three years later, in 1976, Ward saw their ghost, or at least one of them. In the living room, an elderly man in an Edwardian-style brown tweed suit appeared one night by the fireplace, gazing down at the hearth. He had an open, friendly face—the face of a person you'd like to know. But as Ward approached him, he vanished.

A few nights after that, Ward started up the stairway to go to bed. When he reached the landing, he glanced down at the entry hall. There stood the man in the brown tweed suit, semitransparent this time, with a bowler on his head and a cane under one arm. The ghost looked up, tipped his hat, and left—right through the closed front door!

Ward and Chuck figured the ghost must be that of James T. Phillips, who died in the house in 1912. As chief executive officer of the clock and mantel company he founded, Phillips always dressed nattily, and was known to wear a bowler and carry a cane. Had he returned to check up on the restoration of his beloved home? If so, he must have been satisfied because he was never seen again.

Yet Mr. Phillips's disappearance had little effect upon the poltergeist activity in the house. In 1977, Rick Smith, a friend of the owners, moved in as a tenant. Ward and Chuck enjoyed having another person living with them, and the rental income helped with the expenses of maintaining the mansion.

Rick was an art student who used an upstairs room as a combination bedroom-studio. Here he kept his drawing board and paints and did his homework. But something resented his presence. On one occasion, after he'd gone to bed his door slammed shut. When he got up and looked at the door it was open three inches. No breeze or draft could have opened the door.

Loud noises from the attic distracted Rick from his work, and once he screamed, "Shut up!" Seconds later his paint cup rose in the air, turned upside down and dumped its contents on his head. As the artist wiped the red paint from his hair, his T-square took flight and slapped him across the back!

At three o'clock one morning Rick was awakened from a sound sleep by a tapping noise that came from inside his chest of drawers. He got up, turned on a light and opened the drawer. Silence. He shut the drawer, snapped off the light, and went back to bed. The tapping resumed. Rick was determined not to play a game with whatever was in the drawer. He learned to sleep with the drawer open and the light on.

Rick had three Siamese cats who slept at the foot of his bed. One hot summer night when he was reading in bed and the cats were curled up at his feet, he felt a cold chill descend upon him. Suddenly, the cats awoke and stared at a spot above the door. Then their heads swiveled in unison as if following something across the ceiling. Rick saw nothing.

Whatever presences are in the house tease the homeowners and their guests, but haven't turned sinister—at least not yet. Still, Ward and Chuck are prepared. Each bedroom is equipped with a just-for-the-fun-of-it warning system to be used by guests in case of a visitation: a huge police whistle and a glass of water on the bedside table. (Ghosts are known to fear water.) So far, the only casualties have been broken water glasses knocked over in the dark!

Although Ward and Chuck are mostly amused by the poltergeist antics, they still wish that Mr. Phillips would come calling again. They'd like to get to know this gracious gentleman in the brown tweed suit. Ward says, "He's just a really nice old guy."

A Lonely Grave

ANNIE MARY

BORN

OCT. 14, 1880

DIED

OCT. 26, 1886

FATHER AND MOTHER, MAY I MEET YOU IN YOUR
ROYAL COURT ON HIGH

TWENTE

That simple epitaph is just the beginning of a hauntingly sad account of the little girl who lies beneath a weathered, granite tombstone on a windswept hillock a few miles southwest of New Ulm, Minnesota.

A four-feet-high, eighteen-inch-thick stone and mortar wall surrounds little Annie Mary's grave. Inside the wall, which measures no more than fifteen feet by twenty feet, broken glass, rotting tires, and knee-high weeds attest to the single grave's desolate condition. Rusted hinges at a gap in the wall give evidence that once a gate allowed the visitor entrance. Bramble bushes claw at the cracked mortar, a few elm saplings and tufts of prairie grass the only other vegetation of note.

Over the grave, nothing grows.

A towering ash close by casts furtive shade in an otherwise endless vista of tended fields and scattered farmsteads.

Who is this child who died so young, so long ago? To answer that question is to pursue a fascinating account of madness and despair, and one of the most poignant ghost legends of southern Minnesota, for it is said that Annie Mary Twente sleeps uneasily in her pine coffin.

For nearly a century, stories have been told of a small, furtive figure in white wandering forlornly near the gravesite. Automobile lights have suddenly failed on a nearby gravel road, a young boy climbed the ash tree once and fell out for no apparent reason, and though the temperatures may soar into the nineties, the tombstone and the air around it are always cold. In the dead of winter the stone is warm to the touch.

Adding to the melancholy of the place is the horror that Annie Mary Twente may have been accidentally *buried alive*.

Annie Mary was the youngest of five daughters born to Richard and Elizabeth Twente, the pioneer homesteaders who carved a 160-acre farm from the verdant prairie of Albin Township, where the grave is located. They bought the land for $1,150 in 1884.

Much of the fascination attached to Annie Mary may be due to her father's aberrant personality. To those who knew him, Richard Twente was an enigma. He was born in Pendleton County, Kentucky, in February 1855. A man of great physical and mental prowess, Twente was also feared by his Protestant neighbors because he did not share their religious beliefs—some say he was a Mormon—and was so erratic in his behavior that it is difficult to separate the real man from the myth that has grown up around him.

Some facts from his life are indisputable. He was a skilled builder who single-handedly designed and raised an innovative granary in 1885 now listed on the National Register of Historic Places. Wagons were brought through the doors and onto a scale where they could be weighed so Twente could keep accurate records of all his agricultural harvests. The wagon was then tipped so the grain fell into buckets attached to an intricate belt system. The grain was carried to one of seven bins on the upper levels. So sturdy was the building and its storage system that it was used until the mid-1970s by the present owners of the farm.

A one-hundred-foot, three-level barn, built upon a foundation of immense hand-cut stones and put in place by Twente; a two-story hog house; and an elevator with separate chutes so crops could be easily divided into various loads are all still standing, products of his amazing knowledge of mechanics and astounding construction abilities. Incredibly, there is no evidence that Twente was ever schooled in these subjects.

The meticulous notes he kept of his crops and harvests, weather conditions and soil temperatures were used as the basis of a 1918 pamphlet he copyrighted about the planting of fruit trees, rhubarb, and strawberries in northern climes.

Richard Twente also harbored mood and behavior swings so severe they may have been symptoms of paranoid schizophrenia or manic depression.

According to one source, Twente once piled his wife and daughters into a horse-drawn sled and set off across the frozen prairie. His wife convinced him to turn back after pleading with him that they would all freeze to death before reaching their destination, unknown to all but Twente himself.

His actions seemed to grow increasingly odd after Annie Mary's tragic passing in 1886.

The circumstances of her death are shrouded in legend. Most people agree that she died of "lung fever," an old-fashioned term for pneumonia. She was buried in Iberia Cemetery, some miles away from the Twente farm. The location did not please her father. He disinterred her and reburied her on the highest hill on his farm, and there she now rests. Uneasily.

It is at this point that the known facts collide with the *legend* of Annie Mary Twente.

One widely circulated story was that Annie Mary fell from a hayloft and lapsed into a coma. Her parents believed she was dead and buried her on the hill. A few days later, her father persuaded neighbors to help him unearth his daughter's coffin because he thought she was still alive. They found the poor child on her side, strands of her own hair clenched in her fists. Her eyes were fixed wide in horror as she realized too late there was no way out. Scratch marks on the inside of the coffin showed where she had clawed at her tomb.

There is nothing in the *known* record to verify that Annie Mary had been mistakenly buried alive. Her initial burial at Iberia Cemetery and subsequent removal to the family farm may have given rise to the legend. However, several neighbors of Richard Twente's reportedly told friends that he had, indeed, unearthed the coffin at least once when he thought her corpse had been stolen.

The child's death may have led her father deeper into the abyss of mental illness. On November 19, 1887, slightly more than a year after Annie Mary's death, Richard Twente was committed to the St. Peter State Hospital. He thought neighbors were pilfering his possessions, and an especially nasty episode must have led authorities to have him confined. Three months later he was released, but within a few days shot a horse for no reason. He was taken back to St. Peter for a short time and again released. But this time he began taking potshots at his neighbors. At the age of thirty-five, Richard Twente was confined a third time to the St. Peter facility.

Incredibly, the authorities at St. Peter allowed Twente his freedom, allegedly because of his "strange" religious beliefs and his promise that he would leave the region. He was released, but he didn't move away.

And what was Elizabeth Twente, Annie Mary's mother, doing all this time? What little is known of her indicates that she continued to farm the land and raise her girls when her husband was locked away at St. Peter. She had been born Elizabeth Hanker in Germany in March 1859 and married Richard when she was only seventeen. As Richard's mental condition grew more unpredictable she moved in with her daughter, Elizabeth, and her family near Maynard, Minnesota. A descendant of the Twentes said Lizzie "couldn't stand to live" with her husband. She died in 1936 at the age of 77.

Twente sold his farm in 1918 to the ancestors of the current owners of the property, and two years later bought some "worthless" land in Canada. He apparently moved there without his family. It was while chopping wood at his Canadian homestead that he collapsed from a heart attack and died on November 7, 1922. His remains were brought back to Maynard and buried there in the Methodist Cemetery. Richard and Lizzie Twente are buried side by side.

The legend of Annie Mary Twente causes a steady flow of visitors to the isolated hillside. Some are teenagers attempting to prove their bravado by visiting the gravesite, while others are lured by the prospect of seeing the ghostly little girl. Quite a few are simply interested in a most unusual monument to a never-forgotten child.

Earlier in this century, Annie Mary's grave was carefully tended, with fresh flowers planted each spring and a peony bush blossoming each summer with vibrant colors. A gate with a big brass lock prevented livestock from straying inside the unique graveyard.

Today, the grave is sadly neglected. The gate and lock are gone, peonies and fresh flowers have given way to scraggly saplings and scattered weeds. Trash litters the enclosure. The tombstone itself has been dragged away several times, each occasion marked by more chipping and cracking of the old stone. Once, some morbidly curious vandals succeeded in shoveling away two feet of dirt above Annie Mary's coffin. For some unknown reason they fled before unearthing her remains.

Most of the trouble is blamed on "hoodlums" who don't respect cemeteries, according to some neighbors. The demands of full-time farming, coupled with the easy access to the grave, make caring for it properly a difficult task. The current owners do their best to see that it isn't unnecessarily disturbed.

A pastor at the Lake Hanska and LaSalle Lutheran churches once suggested that Annie Mary's remains be taken to a regular church cemetery and reburied. He said her isolated gravesite had been desecrated and the child's memory ought to be treated with more respect. The suggestion was not met with enthusiasm by the farm owners. Annie Mary's legend is part of the area's history; to move her would destroy part of their heritage.

What of Annie Mary's ghost? Does she also prefer to remain under the spreading ash tree, on the hill where she used to romp?

Old-timers in the region seem to be skeptical of the ghost tales. They attribute most of them to flights of fancy by giddy teens, or natural phenomena that only *seem* mysterious in the eerie moonglow of a country night.

But there *have* been those few times when visitors say nature or prankish children couldn't possibly be responsible for what they saw at the gravesite.

Not too long ago, a farmer plowing the nearby field at twilight caught a glimpse of something near the grave. At first he thought it was a deer. But the longer he looked, the more the form took on the shape of . . . Well, he said the ghost of Annie Mary was out there that night. And that was enough to make him stop plowing and head straight home.

City of Ghosts

Columbus is an old town on the Tombigbee River in eastern Mississippi, a handful of miles from the Alabama state line. As with most river towns in the South, the community's earliest prosperity came from shipping cotton from the region's numerous plantations down the Tombigbee to Mobile. The state capital was moved from Jackson to Columbus during the Civil War. Confederate President Jefferson Davis visited in 1863.

Today the city of twenty-five thousand is best known as the home of Mississippi University for Women, Columbus Air Force Base, and Mississippi State University in nearby Starkville. Along with the outward signs of progress, Columbus has not forgotten its past. The city has done a remarkable job of preserving its beautiful antebellum homes. They are open each spring for a pilgrimage that attracts thousands of tourists. Inside at least five of these gracious mansions are friendly ghosts, unwilling to leave their ancestral haunts.

Miss Nellie

The most famous ghost in Columbus is that of a kindly lady who lived almost all of her life in the 145-year-old antebellum home called Errolton. Her name was Nellie Weaver Tucker, the only daughter of the home's builder, prosperous Columbus merchant William B. Weaver.

Nellie's life spanned the period from before the Civil War to the 1930s. Her father spent a small fortune to build the 1848 Italianate mansion, with its six soaring fluted columns, and delicate arches across the roof of the front veranda. The interior was no less grand. Twin parlors were graced with dazzling chandeliers that reflected in exquisite mirrors, while plaster medallions of acanthus leaves enlivened the ceiling.

Into this luxurious life Miss Nellie brought a lively sense of adventure and a ready laugh. She was a critically praised actress in Columbus amateur theatricals and gained the reputation of being the "belle of the ball" at any party she attended. As a teen, she attended the Columbus Female Institute, today's Mississippi University for Women. Her domestic skills were impressive. She was an expert seamstress, reputedly able to mend a dress or design a gown with equal aplomb.

Among the suitors who eagerly sought her hand was one Charles Tucker, a young man she first saw as a volunteer fireman battling a fire in the city. She thought he looked awfully romantic with his sooty face and soiled clothing. From the moment she laid eyes on him, Miss Nellie confided to her girlfriends, she knew he was the man for her.

Charles Tucker and Nellie Weaver were married on February 28, 1878. So happy was the young bride that she etched her name—NELLIE—with her diamond engagement ring on the window glass of the south parlor.

Sadly, their bliss would be short-lived. For reasons unknown, Charles left his young wife and their daughter, Ellen, a few years after their marriage.

Mother and daughter remained at Errolton. To help support her daughter and herself, Nellie started a private school for the children of her friends in one of the old servants' houses. Her grandchildren would later be raised in that same old house.

But the modest incomes from the school and other family members were not enough. By the time Miss Nellie died in the 1930s, Errolton had fallen into disrepair. She had spent most of her last years rocking on the front porch, telling stories of the old days to anyone who came by to listen. The sad state of the house escaped her attention.

Mrs. Erroldine Hay Bateman bought the house in 1950. An accomplished painter, she set about, with the help of her son Douglas Bateman, to repair the decades of neglect and vandalism. She is the one who named the house Errolton.

During the renovation, Mrs. Bateman found the etched word NELLIE in the pane of glass in a west window of the south parlor. She assumed quite correctly that Nellie Tucker had idly scratched it on the window when she, and the house, were young.

Mrs. Bateman's son had known Miss Nellie during her last years. "She knew everything that was going on" in the city, Douglas Bateman told a newspaper reporter. "All kinds of stories of skeletons in the very best of closets." It was through Douglas's friendship with one of Miss Nellie's grandsons that Mrs. Erroldine Bateman had been persuaded to buy the house.

Not much attention was paid to the etched name. Just another chapter in the legend of Miss Nellie. Unfortunately, a workman dropped a ladder against the window during the renovation and shattered it. The window was replaced and life went on.

By the mid-1950s, the restoration was complete and Errolton regained its fame as one of the city's finest homes. Douglas Bateman lived there with his wife, Chebie, who was adding her own touches to the historic showplace. One of those additions was a lovely sofa she had recently reupholstered and placed under a window in the south parlor. On a day when the sun was particularly bright, she started to close the drapes when she noticed scratches in the glass. When she looked more closely, the name NELLIE was easily detected. It was in the same scrawl, in the same window, and in the same place as the original. But the original window had been broken years before!

Was it the ghost of Nellie returning to announce her pleasure with the restoration? The Batemans are reasonable, responsible people not given to superstitious beliefs. Douglas is a former newspaperman and owner of a local bookstore. Chebie is director of the Columbus Public Library. "If it wasn't Miss Nellie who scratched her name in that windowpane," they have said, "we don't know how it happened."

There are no other signs of a ghost in Errolton. Should the house be open during pilgrimage time, you can see and judge for yourself if a name etched in glass is enough to convince that Miss Nellie's legacy lives on.

The Lost Child

At first Mrs. Robert Snow thought the voice belonged to one of her own children. She was walking across an upstairs balcony at Waverly, about six miles outside Columbus, when the clear voice of a child cried out.

"Mama! Mama!"

Mrs. Snow looked down, half-expecting to see one of her own youngsters, but she was quite alone. The voice was sweet, like that of a young girl of perhaps four or five years of age. It pulled at her heart, too, because whoever it was sounded quite alone and frightened, as if she had been looking for her mama for a very long time.

The Snow family had been living in Waverly for about two years when the child's voice was first heard. Mr. and Mrs. Snow discovered the magnificent, abandoned mansion years earlier when they owned an antique store in Philadelphia, Mississippi. No one had lived in Waverly for nearly fifty years. The year was 1962. So dense was the undergrowth leading to the mansion that the family had to literally hack a path to the sagging front porch.

As the renovation moved along, the Snows' new neighbors passed along all the ghostly legends. About the mysterious Indian riding a stallion in the fields nearby. Or the ghostly music and gentle laughter from Waverly's darkened ballroom.

The Snow family discovered that those images could certainly be accounted for. If one believed in the legends.

The Indian might have been the ghost of Maj. John Pytchlyn Sr., actually the orphaned son of an English couple who had been reared by the Choctaw. Although he grew to be a wealthy and powerful businessman, he never forgot the Indian ways he adopted as a child. He was buried near the present site of Waverly.

That there should be ghostly parties at Waverly is no surprise as well. The builder, Col. George Hampton Young, reared six sons and four daughters in the mansion. In the parlor is a wedding alcove where several of his children were married. Waverly was the social center in the neighborhood, with parties and dances a near-weekly ritual in the spacious rooms.

The identity of the little girl that Mrs. Snow heard, however, is a mystery. All of Colonel Young's children reached adulthood. It may be a child sheltered at Waverly during the Civil War, or one who arrived during the turbulent years of

Reconstruction. Colonel Young provided refuge for many homeless families following the war.

The little girl's plaintive cries continued for about five years. She would seem to follow Mrs. Snow around the house, often calling out as if to remind her that she was still there. Sometimes the child cried in the night. Once, one of Mrs. Snow's children came into her parents' bedroom to say that she had heard the girl and wondered if she was quite all right. She had sounded distressed.

There were other signs of the child's presence. The imprint of a child-size body would be found on a four-poster bed in an upstairs bedroom. That was usually in the summer, when it appeared that the spirit child had come in from a hard day of "play" to take a short nap.

And then one day she was gone.

Mrs. Snow was in the kitchen. Suddenly, from the emptiness, the child cried out "Mama! Mama! Mama!!" so close that Mrs. Snow thought she could have reached out to her—if there had been anything to touch. The child sounded especially upset.

Mrs. Snow spoke aloud to the girl, the first time she had ever done so, to ask what the trouble was. There was no reply, then or evermore.

Mrs. Snow hoped so much for her return that the bed upstairs stayed freshly made up. Just in case the motherless little girl ever needed a place to rest.

The Valentine Ghost

Should you be passing through Columbus on February 14, consider what might be happening at Hickory Sticks, an 1820s-era home on Seventh Street. The Valentine Ghost could have taken his annual walk.

The spirit was given that most unusual name by an owner, Mrs. Robert Ivy, because he took his short, midnight strolls during the second week of February, on or around Valentine's Day. He was quiet the rest of the year. How did they know "it" was a "he"? The steps were slow and ponderous, Mrs. Ivy said, like those of a heavy, old man.

Mrs. Ivy's first brush with this annual promenade came shortly after she moved in with her husband, Robert.

"Robert had an out-of-town . . . meeting," Mrs. Ivy told a writer some years later. "I stayed here because [her son] was little. In the night I thought I heard a burglar. I thought I heard footsteps, but I didn't get up because I knew the house was securely locked."

Mrs. Ivy's sister was staying with her and heard the same thing.

She told her husband about the footsteps, but he attributed them to her being in a "new" house. The next year, Robert went to the same meeting at about the same time and the footsteps occurred again.

The annual disturbance took on a set routine: the ghost always took about the same route—up from the old wine cellar, through the hall past the master bedroom, thence up the stairs to the old log cabin room, so named because it was part of the original log home around which the mansion had been built. He was never heard coming back down.

Because Mrs. Ivy didn't know the identity of their "guest," she nicknamed him the Valentine Ghost because of the time of year he came around.

One year Robert didn't attend his annual meeting and heard for himself the ghost of Hickory Sticks.

"Things were quiet until along toward the middle of Valentine's week," Mrs. Ivy recalled. "Late one night my husband and I sat bolt upright in bed at almost the exact instant. Our Valentine Ghost was slowly, very slowly mounting the stairway and then he entered the log cabin bedroom directly over our room and the door closed." Robert Ivy jumped out of bed to search the house but turned up nothing at all.

Mrs. Ivy suspects their visitor may be a former owner returning to look after the place. One possibility is Robert Haden, the first mayor of Columbus, who planted vineyards on the grounds and dug a cellar when he owned the house in the 1840s.

It's all right with Mrs. Ivy if the ghost is Mr. Haden. He's friendly, comes back only once each year and doesn't bother anyone at all. What would make her sad is if he decided *not* to make his annual inspection tour.

Strange Sights

At the house known as Temple Heights there is a pleasant but noisy ghost. Doors open and close and voices float from vacant rooms, as if a radio or television had been left on. That's never the case, however.

A visitor staying in an upstairs bedroom awoke with a fright one night. Through the open door, she saw a bright ball of mist cross the hallway and float up some stairs.

Another caller allegedly captured a similar ball of mist . . . on film! He was photographing an antique sofa in the parlor with a Polaroid camera. A family cat was posed on the sofa looking to the side. When the image appeared, a patch of light was hovering in the air near the cat. The light hadn't been visible to the naked eye. A second photograph showed the same manifestation.

The owners of Temple Heights think their ghost is a young woman who lived there a long time ago. The Harris family bought the house in the 1840s from its builder, Richard Brownrigg. A daughter, Mary Harris, was married in the parlor. She lived there as a young bride for only three months before her untimely death.

He Comes by Day

Wisteria Place is haunted by a man who rushes up the walk to the back door on some mysterious errand . . . but only during daylight hours.

During the early 1970s, owners Mr. and Mrs. Harris Wallace reported that the strange man's peculiar habit wasn't discussed among family members for a very long time. Each had individually seen the white-shirted figure scurrying past the east kitchen window toward the door, but hadn't wanted to mention it to other family members. Upon comparing notes, they found their experiences quite similar—they had seen the man and each had quickly gone to the back door and yanked it open. No one was ever there. The visits might occur several times a week, or cease for months at a time. It was always an unpredictable haunting.

Three deaths have been documented at Wisteria Place, beginning with the original builder, William R. Cannon, in 1858. He lived there only four years before he died, a perfect candidate to be a ghost concerned about his architectural legacy.

The Curious Visitors

Inside the small story-and-a-half house in the historic Mississippi River town of Ste. Genevieve, Jules Valle was recuperating from surgery. An eye that he had injured many years before in a boxing match had to be removed. But Jules wasn't bitter about the loss; on the contrary he had much for which to be grateful.

Jules had retired from business in St. Louis, and moved to this quiet village where he had relatives. He and his wife, Anne-Marie, thirty years younger, worked hard to restore their historic home, the charming Creole-style Guibourd House at 1 North Fourth Street, and to refurbish the lovely garden enclosed by a rose-colored brick wall.

Now, as night came on, Jules lay back against the pillows of his bed. A breeze carried the sweet, heavy fragrance of honeysuckle through the open window of the bedroom.

Suddenly, Jules felt a tap on his shoulder. He turned over. Three little old men stood beside his bed, nodding and smiling down at him. They were dressed in heavy, woolen shirts, but their bodies ended at their waists. Jules wasn't frightened, only perplexed as to who these ghostly visitors were and why they had come to visit him on that summer night in 1939. For want of a better answer, he decided they had come to wish him a speedy recovery.

As the trio faded, Jules felt cheerful and confident about his future. He would live for ten more years. When Jules told his wife about his visitors, the couple suspected that the sudden appearance of the three was entwined with the long and colorful history of Ste. Genevieve, the oldest town in Missouri.

Creole families from present-day Illinois crossed the Mississippi River in 1750 to establish farms in the rich bottom lands, and a settlement was soon organized. In 1763, the Treaty of Paris assigned the territory west of the river to Spain. Ste. Genevieve became a reluctant outpost of the Spanish Empire. A garrison was established, but regular troops were stationed there only at intervals. Then in 1803, Ste. Genevieve and all of Missouri was acquired by the United States in the Louisiana Purchase. In 1812, the village was included as part of the Missouri Territory.

The Guibourd House predates territorial days, having been built about 1784.

The first owner of record was Jacques Dubreuil Guibourd. A native of Angers, France, Guibourd went to the French side of Santo Domingo (now Haiti) as secretary to a wealthy planter. During the slave insurrection there in the late 1700s, he was saved from death by his valet, Moros. The servant sealed Guibourd inside a large keg which he carried on board a ship bound for Philadelphia.

Arriving safely in the port city, Guibourd met French merchants from Ste. Genevieve who had traveled to Philadelphia by horseback to buy supplies. Delighted to find men with whom he could communicate, Guibourd decided to accompany them back to their home. He liked the little French community from the moment he saw it and arranged to buy the house which still bears his name.

Guibourd married Ursula Barbeau, daughter of the commandant at Prairie Du Rocher, the French fort across the river, and the sister of Jules Valle's great-grandfather. The Guibourd family occupied the house from 1806 until 1906. Although Jules and Anne-Marie knew little of the Guibourd family, they did recall that two of Guibourd's descendants had been associated with the house in tragic ways. Miss Victorine, whom everyone called Miss Vickie, died in the bedroom occupied by Anne-Marie. And one of Miss Vickie's brothers, a doctor, committed suicide in the house following a bank failure.

Soon after the Valle's were settled into the house, Mrs. Elizabeth Heins, a psychic and close friend of Anne-Marie's, came to call. After walking through the house, she said that Spanish had been spoken there. She was correct. When the town was under the flag of Spain the Guibourd House had been the social center for the Spanish officers.

Jules wondered if the ghostly old men had been Spaniards. Anne-Marie didn't care who they were; she said she felt presences all through the house. They were only the most recent in a long line of mysterious encounters.

Anne-Marie once employed a maid named Dora Williams. Dora was a conscientious worker with a delightful personality, and a close bond developed between the two women. Dora went quietly about her work each day, and at night retired to her room and bath, which were upstairs over the kitchen and the dining room.

After Dora died, Anne-Marie heard footfalls overhead and knew they were Dora's. She heard them only once, but various maids who worked in the house after Dora's death heard footsteps many times in the servants' quarters when no one was there.

Dogs in the household were also keenly aware of supernatural elements. The Valles' Scottish terrier, named Dusky, sometimes cringed with fear and whined to get outdoors. Anne-Marie never discovered the reason for the dog's fright, but she thought maybe he was seeing phantoms of animals who had once lived in the house.

On two occasions, a playful collie named Jamie acted as if he were seeing another dog in the house. Each time he stood at the living room door and growled softly as he always did when strange dogs approached. His tail hung straight down, wagging slowly to signal friendship. Anne-Marie found nothing outside that could have caused the dog's reaction.

Before acquiring Jamie, Anne-Marie had owned another collie, Peter, who had died in the house. A family friend, Helene, had been extremely fond of Peter and he of her. Helene was a houseguest of the Valles' when Jamie first behaved so strangely. Anne-Marie felt that Jamie was seeing the ghost of Peter, who had come back, she thought, because Helene was in the house.

Anne-Marie was never frightened in the house until one night in the middle of March 1949. Jules had died in January of that year. Anne-Marie was living on alone in the house. On that winter night, she was awakened by banging and crashing sounds coming from Jules's bedroom. It was as if the heavy furniture were being picked up and heaved against the walls, the whole house seeming to shake under the impact. Anne-Marie heard showers of glass striking the bare, polished floor of her husband's room. Every lamp and picture was surely smashed.

Yet no one could have broken into the house. All the windows were locked and the doors bolted.

"Listen to me, whoever or whatever you are!" Anne-Marie screamed. "You are *not* going to frighten me. You are *not* going to drive me from my home. Now, get out!"

The commotion stopped and Anne-Marie went back to sleep. In the morning she went directly to her husband's room. The furnishings were all intact; not one piece had been moved. A quick search showed nothing in the house had been disturbed.

What had Mrs. Valle heard? Poltergeists threatening to take over the house, she said. And she always maintained that if she had succumbed to fear, they would have done just that.

Anne-Marie lived on in the house until her death in 1972. She'd never been happy in Ste. Genevieve, but the terms of her wealthy husband's will required that she remain in her adopted town. Jules left his entire estate to her.

After Anne-Marie's death the house was donated to the Foundation for the Restoration of Ste. Genevieve to be turned into a museum, which it is at present.

In 1983 Kristine Basler, a native of Ste. Genevieve, was hired as manager of the Guibourd-Valle house. The ghosts that frequented Jules and Anne-Marie Valle let Ms. Basler know they were still around.

On a cold December afternoon of that year she was in the cellar flushing deer hides. To flush a hide is to clean it of all remaining flesh; it is done on a fleshing beam. The cleaned hides would be made into buckskins to be worn at the Jour de Fête, a celebration held each August to commemorate the early days of Ste. Genevieve.

Kristine had just finished cleaning her fifth hide when she heard music coming from upstairs—a classical tune, baroque in style, played on either a piano or a harpsichord. The same piece was played over and over, eight or more times. Kristine pictured a little girl practicing, but no one else was in the house. She got up and walked through the basement. The music seemed to come from the front of the house, but stopped as abruptly as it had started. Kristine resumed her work. Suddenly, a male voice shouted, "Hey!" Kristine dashed upstairs. Everything was in order. She peeked out the front window. The street was empty. Later she learned that a musical family had lived in the house from 1906 until 1931, and the mother was said to be a pianist.

On March 1, 1984, Kristine moved into the two-story rear portion of the house that was originally the slaves' quarters. After she was settled, she acquired a Victrola that soon began behaving in a strange way. It turned itself on and off, and whenever she lowered the needle onto a record, the turntable began spinning so fast that the record couldn't be played. The vibrations even shook a nearby box of records. Then the phenomenon stopped as abruptly as it had started. Anne-Marie had had a Victrola.

Kristine believed that at certain times and in certain places the house gave off "bad vibes." While conducting tours she admitted to feeling ill at ease in Jules's bedroom, and at night she does not enter it at all. She added that, given the possibility of poltergeists, she had never slept in Anne-Marie's bed, and the only time she tried sleeping in the attic she was back down in her own bed by 4:00 A.M. "It was just uncomfortable," she conceded.

Many houses alleged to be haunted have electrical problems, and the Guibourd-Valle house is no exception. One night a bulb in the dining room chandelier blinked off while Kristine was sitting in the room. Thinking the bulb was loose, she got up to tighten it in the socket. But before she touched it, it lit up and the bulb next to it went out. Sometimes Kristine thought a light had gone out when it hadn't. "It's more like a shadow passing by," she said. And she pays no attention anymore, especially when leading a tour group through the house.

Animals are said to be especially sensitive to paranormal activity, but Kristine's cats seemed not to be bothered by anything in the house. Kristine said that some people have told her that cats keep spirits away. She hopes that is true.

The Guibourd-Valle House is open daily 10:00 A.M. to 5:00 P.M. An admission is charged.

Spirits of the Little Bighorn

When night winds blow across the grassy plains and purple shadows darken the bluffs of the Little Bighorn River, the ghosts in blue coats and in warpaint walk among the living.

This is Little Bighorn Battlefield National Monument in southeastern Montana. Here, on June 25, 1876, troops of the U.S. Army's Seventh Cavalry, commanded by Lt. Col. George Armstrong Custer, were cut down by Sioux and Cheyenne warriors inspired by Sitting Bull, chief of the Hunkpapa Sioux. It was in popular parlance Custer's Last Stand, and, ironically, the Indians' last stand also. The West was steadily being opened up to settlement by the white man. With Sitting Bull's arrest in 1881 and confinement to the Standing Rock reservation in North Dakota, Indians were mostly restricted to reservations.

Although details of that dramatic battle can never be fully known because no white man survived and no Indian dared to speak for fear of reprisals, impressions of the battle linger. For decades, visitors and park personnel have reported seeing apparitions of both Indians and cavalrymen, and hearing frightening screams of men in the throes of grisly death.

Mardell Plainfeather, a Crow Indian employed as a park ranger and Plains Indian historian, has never forgotten a mystifying experience she had a decade ago.

She has her own sweat lodge near the river and in 1982 had allowed an old man to use it. After he finished his rituals of religious purification, he stopped by Mardell's place to ask her to check the lodge before she went to bed to be certain that the fire was out.

Mardell drove to the lodge with her four-year-old daughter, Lorena, in the car with her. After pouring water over the hot stones in the lodge, she stepped outside. Something moved on the bluff above her.

"There, silhouetted against the sky, were two warriors on horseback," she said. "I knew they were warriors because I saw their feathers and shields. As I stood watching, one of them lifted himself up from his horse. They were looking down at me, sixty or seventy yards away."

The moon was bright and stars stretched from horizon to horizon; there was no mistaking the men or horses. Mardell got back into her car, but said nothing to her daughter. She did admit, however, that she drove home faster than usual.

In the morning, the ranger was back in the area to check for stray horses. That was part of her job. Indians living adjacent to the park keep horses, but they are not permitted on the battlefield.

She climbed the bluff upon which she had seen the mysterious horsemen the night before, but found nothing to indicate that horses had ever been up there; nor were there any bushes or trees whose shapes might have suggested a configuration of horse and rider at night. Then, as she gazed out past the cottonwood trees along the river and beyond over the endless plains, she got the strong feeling that the warriors she'd seen were either Sioux or Cheyenne and that they'd meant her no harm. Mardell prayed and left an offering of tobacco and sweet sage for the spirits of all the dead.

Christine Hope had a different, yet no less frightening, adventure into the world of the unexplained. During the summer of 1983, Christine worked as a student intern at the park. She enjoyed welcoming the many visitors and giving tours and talks; her small apartment at the edge of the battleground cemetery was quite comfortable.

One night, after an exhausting day, Christine fell asleep on her living room couch. Sometime after midnight she awoke with a sense of dread unlike anything she'd ever experienced. The room was deep in shadow, save for a ribbon of moonlight streaming through an uncurtained window illuminating her easy chair across the room.

A man was sitting there.

Christine's mind raced. She was trapped. Alone. Strangely, the man seemed to pay her no attention. Nor did he move. She noticed that he was dressed in modern attire, yet his hair was cut differently from most men. Yet there was something vaguely familiar about it. Then she realized his haircut closely resembled that of soldiers who'd fought in the Battle of the Little Bighorn and whose photographs she had closely studied. The quiescent visitor had a light beard and a handlebar mustache, and his eyes were wide and filled with terror.

Christine was too numb to move, repelled, yet oddly captivated by the fear in his eyes. Within a few seconds he was gone.

Christine pulled herself off the couch and turned on every light in the apartment. She cautiously examined the chair by the window. It was now just a comfortable-looking chair, one in which she had sat scores of times reading or thinking. Nothing about it suggested the presence of a soldier frozen in time.

The young park intern slept fitfully for the rest of the night, relieved when dawn finally came. Later that day she and ranger Tim Bernardis planned to explore the section of the battlefield known as Reno's Crossing, deep in the Little Bighorn River valley. At that place Maj. Marcus A. Reno and his besieged troops had been forced to retreat from the advancing warriors. (Custer had already been annihilated.) Pulling back into the cover of trees along the river, Reno lost control of his command. His terrified soldiers plunged into the river, striking out for the opposite shore. Few made it. The water ran red with the blood of men and horses. Their screams echoed against the bluffs. The wounded dragged their broken, bloodied bodies up the sagebrush-covered hill, only to be cut down by the Sioux and Cheyenne fighters.

As the couple retraced the route of Reno's men late that fall afternoon, Chris-

tine stopped suddenly at a single marker by the water's edge. It was the place
where 2d Lt. Benjamin H. Hodgson had fallen. He'd been a member of Company
B of the Seventh Cavalry. Christine stood silently by the memorial for a long
time. Tim noticed her interest, but said nothing.

Back at the visitor's center, Tim took out a book containing the pictures and
military histories of the men who had died in the Battle of Reno's Crossing. He
pointed to a photograph at the top of a page.

"Here's Hodgson's picture," he said to Christine, standing at his side.

She drew back. The blond beard and the flowing mustache were unmistakable.
She told Tim, in detail, about her experience of the previous night, and he said
the ghost could certainly have been that of Hodgson; he must have died an
excruciating death. In fording the river, he had taken a bullet in the leg and his
horse was killed. Grabbing a stirrup thrown out by another soldier, he was
dragged through the water to the opposite shore. Although bleeding profusely
and barely conscious, Hodgson clawed his way up the bank. Halfway up he was
shot and killed. His body rolled down to the water's edge.

As the story of the young woman's night visitor spread among park employees,
few were surprised. Weird things happen with some regularity at the battlefield.

An old stone house, by the burial ground, is built in the center of the site where
Custer's troops fought the Indians. Constructed in 1894 as a home for the first
caretaker, it has long been regarded as one of the most haunted places on the battleground. In fact, the Crow Indians called the cemetery superintendent "ghost
herder." They thought his job was to keep the ghosts from ranging beyond the
monument fence. They were free to roam by night, but the raising of the American
flag each morning signaled the restless spirits to return to their graves!

When park ranger Al Jacobson and his wife, Florence, moved into an apartment in the stone house, an Indian woman told Florence that something "bad"
would happen to them there. The Jacobsons had heard all the ghost tales about
the house and smiled indulgently. But by and by they weren't so sure.

Jacobson told reporter Mitchell Smyth, "We've been in a room when we saw
the doorknob twist open—but there was no one at the door. And there have
been unexplained footsteps.

"One night I was showing some home movies. The apartment upstairs was
empty, but I heard someone cross the floor up there. I ran upstairs, but found
no one. No one could have got out except by the stairs which I came up."

But the most peculiar incident in Jacobson's apartment had to do with a
chicken. His wife had just taken it out of the freezer when "a high-pitched whine
went right through the apartment," Jacobson said. "She put the chicken down;
the noise stopped. She picked it up again and the noise came back. She knew
something was wrong and she threw the chicken in the garbage."

Jacobson has wondered ever since if the "ghosts" were protecting his family
from eating a diseased chicken.

The experience of Ruth Massie is equally baffling.

Ruth's husband, Michael Massie, served as a park interpreter during the summer of 1983 and the couple lived in one of the apartments in a fourplex near
the stone house, which stood empty that year. Ranger/historian Mardell Plainfeather lived in one of the other apartments in the complex. Late one evening

Mardell drove past the empty stone house and noticed lights burning on the second floor. Her first thought was that maintenance men had been working up there and left the lights on. She also knew the lights sometimes had a habit of turning themselves on and off and she didn't want to check the house by herself. She knocked at the Massies' door and asked Michael to go with her. He told her to go on home and he'd check the house himself. She gave him the key and went to her apartment to await his report.

Massie searched both floors. The house was empty. He snapped off the lights and had just stepped outside when his wife came racing toward him, screaming his name. She'd been watching television when the picture suddenly went blank and a strange voice came through the set. The voice said, "The second floor of the stone house." Ruth was terrified that something had happened to Michael.

In the morning, Mardell and the Massies tried to find a cause for the disembodied voice. There seemed to be none. Radios used occasionally on the job were all locked up in the visitors center that night, ruling out the possibility of an errant transmission.

The incident remains unexplained. Massie assumed it was a paranormal experience.

Visitors sometimes report meeting ghosts on the battlefield. In one case, a man from New Orleans disappeared for several hours and when he reappeared, in a state of shock, told rangers that he'd been transported back in time and had relived the battle!

His story is reminiscent of the experiences of two English schoolteachers, Miss Moberly and Miss Jourdain, who were somehow transported back to 1789 France while on a visit to the Petit Trianon gardens of Versailles . . . in 1901! The women described houses, landscapes, and costumes not seen in over a century. They wrote about their adventures, and their belief that they even encountered the tragic queen Marie Antoinette, in a book entitled *An Adventure*.

The vaults at the Little Bighorn Battlefield park contain uniforms, boots, rusted rifles, and various other artifacts of the battle. And, according to those who've seen the vaults, they are eerie places indeed. When the wife of a park superintendent in the 1920s visited one of them, she said that a clammy hand reached out to seize her. She never went back.

James Thompson, a guide some years ago, was examining bloodstained clothing in one of the vaults. Suddenly, he felt dizzy and was seized by panic. He told friends later that he was convinced he was getting a "psychic echo" from a fallen soldier.

Is it possible that something reached out to Thompson from the clothing? Maybe some individuals with psychic powers can "see" into the life of a dead person merely by holding an object once owned or used by the deceased. The object gives off vibrations that the psychic can "pick up" or "feel."

Earl Murray, in his book *Ghosts of the Old West*, explains the theory as it relates to the frontier:

> . . . all living things give off electromagnetic impulses, or vibrations— psychic traces that are left behind even after death. These unseen force

fields are often referred to as imprints. Such imprints are transferred, especially during a state of intense emotion, from the personality of the living being to an inanimate object. These imprints apparently remain attached to the inanimate object indefinitely.

The imprints, according to psychics, reveal themselves to people who can read them much the same as motion picture film on a screen; the psychic's mind is the screen upon which the imprints are projected. The imprints are not as clear as film, and are caught only in fragments, but they do represent a series of images that can be interpreted by the psychic's mind and conveyed through normal conversation.

Old spurs, boots, rifles, arrows, empty cartridge casings, and similar artifacts have the potential to unlock secrets from the historic past.

Psychic Howard R. Starkel unlocked some rather astonishing facts about the Battle of the Little Bighorn. From 1979 to 1981 Starkel worked with historian Don G. Rickey Jr. When given an iron spur by Dr. Rickey, with no indication of where it had come from or who had worn it, the psychic turned it slowly in his hands for a few seconds. Then, he began to relive a battle:

"I was hurt; this was found in a desolate area," he began, pointing to the spur. He said he was with other people and they were being pursued by people on horses. He was trying to get across a stream to climb the bluffs. The spur, he said, was lost on the south side just after he'd crossed the river. Its owner was killed at the top of a ridge.

Starkel described the setting in such rich detail that Dr. Rickey was astonished. He was certain he was listening to an account of the Battle of Reno's Crossing. Yet in 1876, the U.S. Army had issued brass spurs to its troops, *not* iron spurs such as that held by psychic Starkel. It was a museum discard that the historian had picked up to add to his own collection.

Yet the mystery of this apparent historical discrepancy between what Starkel claimed and what was known of military issue equipment was quickly resolved. Records show that a contract surgeon named J. M. DeWolf accompanied the regiment. As a civilian, Dr. DeWolf had to outfit himself and would likely have chosen the more common iron spurs rather than the military brass ones. The surgeon had been wounded and killed after crossing the Little Bighorn River. And the marker where he fell is located near the top of a ridge!

Was Howard Starkel merely building upon information he already had about the battle? He apparently knew nothing of the Battle of the Little Bighorn and, in fact, claimed no knowledge of any Indian war. And he'd never been to Montana.

Yet that single iron spur held an unexplained form of energy that gave the psychic a direct link with a man who had died at Reno's Crossing over one hundred years earlier.

Every year over a quarter-million tourists from all over the world make their way to the Little Bighorn Battlefield. They come to reflect upon the heroism and tragedy, the victory and defeat when two cultures clashed on a single summer day on the Montana plains. Most visitors don't imagine that those long-dead warriors may be much closer than they realize.

Miss Anna

Hastings, Nebraska, is a pleasant city of some twenty-three thousand persons. Within its city limits, one finds Hastings College, some half-dozen tree-shaded parks, the site of the Adams County Fair, and the Hastings Museum, noteworthy for a natural history collection, frontier memorabilia, and a small planetarium. The town is situated in south central Nebraska, about twenty miles south of Interstate 80.

The folks in Hastings are not given to pretension or hyperbole; thus their belief in events of an allegedly supernatural origin is not intense, if it is there at all.

So the story of sixty-something Burton Nelson, a lifelong resident of Hastings who describes himself as the "fairly stable" father of four grown sons, is even more remarkable. He may be the only man in Hastings to have seen a ghost *and* be willing to talk about it.

This, then, is Burton Nelson's story. It's about a woman he encountered, long after she had died. Her name is Miss Anna.

Anna C. Peterson passed through life virtually unnoticed. She was one of those quiet, private persons, a cipher even to those who worked with her at Mary Lanning Hospital in Hastings. A city directory in 1935 listed her as a mangle operator in the hospital laundry. That's the machine that presses clothes after they've been laundered.

Not much else is known about her. She never married, or at least there is no record of her taking a husband. Where Miss Anna came from, and where she died, is a mystery. She seems to have been one of those ladies of years past who were charitably called spinsters.

Yet there is a hint of oddity, and sadness, about her unremarkable life. She was friendly and very kind, with a special affection for little babies. Today Miss Anna might well have become a single parent by adopting a child. In the 1930s that, of course, was unthinkable for an unmarried woman, and, as they said, one without prospects.

Miss Anna's death may have been at an early age, perhaps while she was still in her late thirties or early forties. The cause is another mystery. Perhaps it was

disease. But there might be another answer. This woman who loved children
may have become pregnant. No man wanted to call her his wife, but that didn't
stop someone from taking advantage of Miss Anna's genial disposition. If someone did father Miss Anna's baby, then what? There is no record of her ever
having married. Did she move far away and have the child? Did she, or her baby,
die in childbirth? This woman who led such a simple life left many large questions unanswered.

What little we know of Miss Anna is due to the remarkable events that took
place during the early morning hours of a day in 1962. That's when Burton
Nelson "met" his first ghost.

"I awoke about three A.M. during a rainstorm to see a woman with her back
to me standing by our baby's crib," Nelson said. "She was a distinct shape with
a white misty form who looked just like an ordinary woman. Except that I could
see through her. I could see the baby's crib about ten feet away and our cat
sleeping under it on the floor, as well as the wall behind her. She was patting
our baby's back. She turned her head towards me and smiled. I smiled back at
her."

Nelson was not afraid. When the ghost looked at him, he said, her wan smile
made it clear she wasn't going to hurt anyone. But then, most extraordinary of
all, this sad woman seemed to communicate with him. She had lived in the
house during the 1930s and loved babies. But she had never married and her
greatest regret was not having any children of her own. Nelson also knew somehow that her name was Anna C. Peterson and that she had worked at Mary
Lanning Hospital.

"It never entered my mind to be scared or to wake up my wife next to me,
that's the crazy part of it," Nelson recalls. "I also got the feeling that she either
had taken her own life or had died in less than happy circumstances. She was a
quiet, private, lonely woman who loved babies. That's all I knew about her."

Nelson described the apparition as being of medium height, of a solid build,
but not fat. She had dark brown eyes and brown hair pulled back into a bun. A
"nice-looking lady," Nelson said, in her late thirties or early forties. Although
the figure appeared in a white mist, Nelson said she wore a green uniform-type
dress, with dark stockings and black oxford-type shoes.

The ghost didn't say a word. Nelson didn't initiate a conversation.

"She smiled and seemed to radiate kindness and love. I felt rather comfortable
with her. In fact, I felt if anything was ever going to go wrong in that house . . .
she would be the first to tell me. I smiled and lay back down and went to sleep."

The next morning, as Nelson told his wife about the "weird dream," he quickly
realized it wasn't a delusion or mirage. He recalled a car passing on the rain-
slickened street outside, its lights playing across the bedroom walls. He heard
the alarm clock ticking.

Neither Burton nor his wife told their four children about the night visitor.
Burton made up his mind to keep a pencil and paper in the kitchen cupboard
so that if the woman showed up again, he could record what he saw. In this way
he would be sure it wasn't a dream because he would have to walk through the
living room into the kitchen to get to his writing material.

He didn't have long to wait.

"Not more than a week after that," Nelson said, "I woke up at about the same time in the morning. It was raining outside again. I saw her standing by the crib, stroking the baby's back. The baby was kind of restless. It was obvious to me that she was trying to soothe him back to sleep, and as before I was not afraid. I got out of bed, walked to the kitchen and sat down to write all that I had seen, when it was, and how I felt about it. When I went back to bed she was gone and the baby was sleeping calmly. I felt good about her."

Burton Nelson never again saw the apparition.

Over the following days and weeks, however, Nelson realized that the bedroom he shared with his wife—and a ghost—had another peculiar characteristic. Two side-by-side, built-in closets without doors stood at one end of the room. A thin partition separated the closets, yet one was always warm and the other always quite a bit cooler. Further, the family's cat steered clear of the cool closet, even when Nelson's young boys tried to keep it in there. The cat always curled up on the floor of the warm closet, even on the hottest summer day.

Nelson thinks Miss Anna "lived" in the cool closet.

Burton Nelson and his family moved to another house shortly after the ghost's final appearance. He pushed the incident to the back of his mind for several years, yet he couldn't help but wonder if there was any connection between the woman who had "identified" herself as Anna C. Peterson and a real woman who may have lived, and perhaps died, in Hastings.

Nelson decided to start a search for her at the Adams County Historical Society. He was doing "family research," he told the librarians. He thought they might be suspicious of someone looking up a ghost's lineage.

His efforts were soon rewarded. He found an Anna C. Peterson listed in the Hastings city directory, living at the house in which Nelson had seen her, for the years 1935 and 1937. City directories were only published every two years in that era, so she might have been in the house from as early as 1933 to as late as 1939, Nelson estimates. The first directory listing for her was in 1922, but at a different address, and then again in 1924 and 1926, also at different residences. During the 1920s, her occupations were listed variously as a clerk in a store, then a laundress, and finally a mangle operator at the hospital laundry. Oddly, Anna Peterson disappeared from the city directories between 1926 and 1935.

Nelson did not find a telephone listing for her anytime between 1920 and 1950, indicating perhaps that she always rented rooms in a house and shared a telephone with others. From 1939 on, Nelson could not find her name listed anywhere. Nor could he find her obituary. He looked through city cemetery records but couldn't find her grave listed. He assumes she may have been from another small town in Nebraska and had been buried there.

Mary Lanning Hospital seemed the next logical place to direct his inquiries. Nelson went there to ask about employment records for the years 1920 to 1940. He was told they had been thrown out years ago. However, the woman he spoke to directed him to a retired hospital employee who might be able to answer his questions. She had worked at Mary Lanning during the years Anna C. Peterson had been employed there.

It was during his visit with the elderly lady that Nelson's memory of the ghost he had seen was firmly linked with a real person.

"She remembered Miss Peterson quite well," Nelson said. "She said she was a quiet, private person who worked very hard in the laundry, right alongside this retired employee. Miss Peterson was a friendly person, a kind woman who had never married but simply adored babies. She described her as I had seen her, especially the dark eyes and hair. She had long hair, but kept it pulled back into a bun for safety around the mangles. She wore it that way away from work also. She told me that during the 1930s, all the housekeeping or laundry women wore a green uniform dress with the dark hose and black shoes. Miss Peterson was not a social person and rarely dressed any other way as far as she knew.

"I got up my nerve and asked her when she died. The woman said she thought it was in the late 1930s when she was still fairly young. She remembered that no one seemed to care to talk about it. Something was not right but yet she couldn't tell me exactly what. I asked if Miss Peterson might have taken her own life. Well, she said she couldn't really say for sure and anyway that was 'nothing to be poking around in now.' I got the feeling she knew more than she was ever going to tell me."

The old lady told Nelson that the thought of Anna Peterson dying so young made her sad even decades later, especially knowing how much she loved babies and yet never having had one of her own. Nelson didn't press her for more information and left. The woman died shortly after revealing what she knew of Anna Peterson.

Burton Nelson was satisfied with the information he was able to gather. He knew that the ghost he had seen was a kindly, simple woman who couldn't give up her love for little babies, even in death. She meant no harm to anyone living.

"I don't know what it was or why, but I know it happened to me," Nelson affirms. "I still don't understand what was entirely involved. But Miss Anna C. Peterson made a believer out of me."

Of Treasure Tales and Murdered Men

A. J. "Jack" Davis just never learned that crime doesn't pay. He robbed stage-coaches and trains, killed men who got in his way, and even taught Sunday school and ran phony businesses as covers for his illicit gains. But it was all for naught. He ended up with his backside full of buckshot.

Although Davis is long dead, his ghostly presence reportedly lingers in Six-Mile Canyon, east of Virginia City, where he buried much of his still-missing loot.

Davis was an easterner who arrived with the first Comstock speculators in 1859. From the beginning, Davis led a double life. To most of the people in Gold Hill, where he first settled, Davis was the owner of a livery stable and recorder of claims in the Flowery Mining District.

He found that to be an ideal cover for his preferred avocation—robbing the bullion wagons on Geiger Grade. Davis even had a small bullion mill in Six-Mile Canyon. After he stole the gold bars and coins from the wagon trains, he melted them down and passed it all off as having been processed at his own mill. The proceeds from the sale of "his" gold were buried somewhere in the desert canyon.

Davis succeeded in his duplicitous life for nearly a decade, including a stint teaching Sunday school in Virginia City, until he failed in an audacious attempt to rob the Verdi train on November 4, 1870. He was captured, tried in a Reno court, and sent to state prison in Carson City for ten years.

A year later Davis found himself in the middle of a big prison break at Carson City. He didn't join the rebellion. Instead he helped guards identify the ringleaders of the breakout. Warden Frank Denver publicly thanked Davis for his help, and on February 17, 1875, he was released after a successful petition drive urging that he be granted parole.

He returned to Virginia City and for almost two years led an apparently law-abiding life. But then he pulled up stakes in July 1877 and headed for Eureka, about 250 miles to the east.

Jack Davis hadn't mended his outlaw ways.

On September 3, 1877, Davis and two accomplices surprised blacksmith William Hood as he worked at the Willows stage stop, forty miles south of Eureka.

The Davis gang tied him up and waited for the Eureka stage and the Tybo Mines cash payroll it would most certainly be carrying.

Unfortunately for them, Davis and his confederates hadn't reckoned that aboard the stage when it pulled into the Willows would be Wells Fargo agents James Brown and Eugene Blair, guarding driver Jack Perry and the payroll. The three outlaws ordered the men down from their seats. Davis put a revolver to Blair's neck. That's when Agent Brown grabbed his shotgun and pumped a load of buckshot into Davis's backside. Agent Blair was wounded by shots from one of the other outlaws. But the gang, minus Jack Davis, fled into the hills.

Davis survived long enough to be put aboard the next morning's coach for Eureka. He died en route and was buried in Eureka. Blair recovered from his injuries.

The legend of Jack Davis's ghostly treasure in Six-Mile Canyon first surfaced a few weeks after he was killed. When word reached Virginia City that Davis was dead, fortune seekers began to look for the cache of buried loot. Rumors of its existence had been prevalent for years around the tough mining district. Davis had steadfastly refused to divulge its location, or even admit to its existence, even after his 1870 robbery conviction. Estimates of its value ranged up to several hundred thousand dollars, all of it in melted-down gold coins and bars.

The first men to venture into Six-Mile Canyon didn't stay long. They told a remarkable tale of how a giant, ashen-faced specter rose out of the parched earth just after sunset and screamed at them. Shots from their rifles and revolvers didn't faze whatever it was they saw. The thing then rose in the air, propelled by wings that suddenly grew out of its body.

After that boisterous account, few others dared to look for the lost treasure. However, Dan DeQuille, an editor on the *Territorial Enterprise*, wrote that the whole ghostly episode was very probably a hoax. A group of Davis's cronies had rigged up a sheet on a wire which they yanked into the air when anyone came into Six-Mile Canyon. They also provided the shrieks and hollow laughter the frightened men reported.

Not true, said one of the men who had actually "seen" the giant creature. He claimed to be a hardened pioneer who couldn't be scared off by flapping sheets and phony screams. But, neither that man nor any of the other treasure hunters ever went back into Six-Mile Canyon to look for the Davis gold.

Davis's two compatriots did escape the botched Willows robbery, and it's possible he had told them the location of his buried "earnings." The men could have been responsible for creating the legend of the haunted treasure to keep the curious away. But how would that explain other travelers who said weird sights and sounds were not unusual in Six-Mile Canyon well into the twentieth century?

The treasure is thought to be there still, undisturbed for a century and a quarter. All you have to do is look for it. If you dare.

Face in the Fire

The official cause of Lee Singleton's death was listed as self-poisoning. That's only partly true. What really killed the Eureka miner was guilt. And a ghost.

By all accounts, Singleton was one of those faceless men who went west to make his fortune following the Civil War. Details of his life are sketchy. He was born somewhere in Maryland in 1841 and served in the Confederate army, where he was wounded several times. When Southern forces surrendered at Appomattox Court House in 1865, Singleton hired on as a laborer for the Union Pacific Railroad.

The first reports of him in Nevada are from 1869 when he showed up in Hamilton during the great White Pine rush. From there he moved on to Eureka in 1871. The Eureka Consolidated Mining Company took him on as a charcoal furnace tender later that year.

Singleton had the misfortune to be teamed with a mean Irishman named John Murphy. A bully who loved taunting smaller men, Murphy mercilessly razzed the slightly built Singleton about his Southern heritage and other alleged shortcomings. Murphy finally went too far when he slammed a fist into Singleton's face as the men worked together one night. Singleton quietly vowed to kill his tormentor.

Murphy continued to laugh at Singleton's weakness until early one morning when his sordid taunting was finally silenced. The men were alone. The boss hadn't come on his final rounds and the ore haulers had made their last delivery. As Murphy bent to scoop charcoal into the furnace, Singleton quickly grabbed a shovel and slammed it into the Irishman's skull.

The quiet Southerner shoved Murphy's body through the furnace door and into the roaring flames. Within minutes, the corpse was reduced to a bucketful of ashes.

Lee Singleton never had a day of peace after that night.

He was able to convince his boss and coworkers that Murphy had left early that night. That he was never seen in town again was attributed to the fact that he had no family or relatives nearby. He'd probably grown weary of tending furnaces, Singleton said, shrugging.

Singleton must have wished with all his heart that Murphy *had* left town of his own free will.

Within a few days he was seeing Murphy's face glowering at him from the furnace's flames. He stared so hard into the furnace that he developed lead poisoning from the gaseous fumes and had to quit the mining company. He then developed a partnership with several friends to harvest wood for the smelters, but when the pine forests were at last depleted he left Nevada. John Murphy went with him.

Singleton spent the next five years trying to rid himself of the ghost's presence. He found his way to Wisconsin in 1872, working at the lead mines near Mineral Point. But the blast furnaces were irresistible to him, and each time he stared into the flames, John Murphy's laughing face was there.

Singleton fled as far as the Pittsburgh steel mills, but it was no use. Murphy continued to haunt him. In 1876, he returned to Eureka, Nevada. The mining furnace had been taken down, but Singleton calculated precisely where it had stood, and where Murphy had been crouching when his skull was crushed.

It was all too much. Singleton bought a small quantity of laudanum, a poisonous opium derivative, rode to his old cabin in Culver Canyon and prepared to end his life. Before he did, however, he took several sheets of paper and wrote out the story of how John Murphy's ghostly face would not leave him. If he met Murphy in death he would ask the Irishman's forgiveness. He tucked the note in a book, placed it on a rafter and swallowed the poison.

The body wasn't found for several months, and the note lay undisturbed until a new occupant of the cabin found it in early 1877. The *Eureka Sentinel* printed sections of the fantastic story on April 18, 1877. John Murphy's ghost found revenge.

There is an ironic footnote to this ghost story. Lee Singleton's ghost now haunts his old Culver Canyon cabin.

Ocean-Born Mary

In the Centre Cemetery of the village of Henniker a weathered headstone, decorated with the traditional urn and weeping willow, reads:

IN MEMORY OF WIDOW MARY WALLACE WHO DIED
FEB. 15 A.D. 1814 IN THE 94TH YEAR OF HER AGE

At the base of the stone a plain rectangular sign says:

OCEAN-BORN MARY

The visitor may be puzzled until he learns the story of Ocean-Born Mary, one of the most popular and best-loved legends of New England.

In 1720 a small sailing vessel named *Wolf* filled with Scotch-Irish emigrants left Londonderry, Ireland, to reunite passengers with relatives in Londonderry, New Hampshire. As they neared the New England coast they were overtaken by a band of Spanish pirates. The buccaneers scrambled aboard the defenseless ship, stripped the passengers of their jewelry, seized their trunks of clothing, and then, on the command of their captain, Don Pedro, prepared to murder everyone. Screams rose as the pirates unsheathed daggers and drew their cutlasses.

But, suddenly, Don Pedro raised a hand, signaling his men to back away. Beneath the cries of the terrified passengers he had heard a different sound— the unmistakable wailing of a baby from the hold. He asked the captain, James Wilson, to bring the little one and its mother to the deck. It was the captain's baby, born at sea. Wilson looked into the faces of the frightened men and women. Tears stood in the women's eyes as they held their shawls over their mouths. After a long moment, Wilson turned and went below. Soon, Elizabeth Wilson emerged on the sunlit deck. She stood tall and erect, holding her baby in trembling arms. Don Pedro looked down into the tiny trusting face. He sheathed his sword. Although he was a notorious murderer, he was also superstitious. If he killed this child he would suffer bad luck all the days of his life.

He ordered one of his men to go back to the ship. When the pirate returned he handed his captain a package. Stepping closer to Mrs. Wilson, Don Pedro held forth a bolt of beautiful sea-green brocaded silk.

"Please, ma'am, if you will name your daughter Mary, after my dear mother, and if you will accept this roll of silk to be made into her wedding dress, I will spare the lives of all aboard."

Elizabeth Wilson, tears in her eyes, nodded her consent.

The pirates returned to their ship and Captain James Wilson brought the *Wolf* safely into Portsmouth harbor several days later.

Mary Wilson grew into a tall Irish beauty with flaming red hair and green eyes set in a cameo face. On an August day in 1742 she married Thomas Wallace, her childhood sweetheart. She was twenty-two years old. Her mother had made her daughter's wedding dress of the sea-green silk, and guests remarked that no bride had ever looked more radiant.

But Mary's happiness was short-lived. In 1760 her husband died, leaving her with four sons to raise.

About this time, Don Pedro gave up piracy. The work was strenuous and he felt too old for it. He acquired six thousand acres of land in southern New Hampshire and, aided by his ship's carpenters and black slaves, built a Georgian Colonial mansion on a hilltop south of Henniker. It was a handsome frame building with ten rooms and six fireplaces, one of which was said to be the largest in any home in the state. Then he sought out Ocean-Born Mary (she was never called by any other name) and invited her to come live with him. She was forty years old.

"The place is yours," he said. "You can take care of me in my old age."

But another version of the story states that Mary's son Robert built the house for his mother and younger brothers to live in.

In either case, it is true that as late as 1781, a Spaniard, thought to be Don Pedro, lived in the house with Mary. He showered her with fine clothing and jewels and an elegant black and gold carriage drawn by a handsome four-horse team. Mary was happy. She entertained townspeople and also a number of distinguished guests—General Lafayette commemorated his first visit by planting a tree in the front yard.

Ten years after Mary and her sons had moved into the house, Don Pedro returned late one night from a "business" trip to the coast. Mary heard the murmur of voices in the field behind the house. Peering out the corner of a rear window, she discerned the figures of the old pirate and a large, swarthy man. Between them they dragged a large chest. They set it down and began digging a hole, their spades clanking against the rocks. Finally, the chest was buried, the hole filled, and the earth tamped down.

Mary felt sick. She went to the door in her night clothes to greet Don Pedro, but he brushed past her, saying that he was very tired and needed to sleep. He went directly to his room. Mary didn't sleep. All night she thought she heard moans arising from behind the house. Or was it the wind whining in the trees?

More than a year after this incident, Mary returned one afternoon from a trip to town in her carriage. But no stable boy met her to tend the horses. Nor was any servant to be found anywhere in the house. Mary discovered the slaves huddled in a garden shed, too frightened to speak. Moments later, she found Don Pedro's body lying facedown in the orchard, a cutlass plunged between his shoulder blades pinning him to the ground.

In keeping with a request he had once made, Mary had her slaves bury the pirate beneath the mammoth hearth of the kitchen fireplace. Townspeople then learned the identity of the "fine Spanish gentleman" who lived in the mansion, and rumors circulated that he had buried a fortune in gold pieces somewhere on his land. From time to time gangs of men swarmed over the grounds, digging for the elusive treasure. Mary made no attempt to stop them, and interest gradually waned. Since Don Pedro had bequeathed the house to her she vowed to remain in it until her final breath. She kept her word. Her sons had gone off to fight in the American Revolution, then married and established their own homes, leaving their mother alone in the house on the hill. Here she died at age ninety-four.

For the next one hundred years the house remained in the possession of the Wallace family. It was rented out, at least part of the time, but no family ever stayed long. Nor did they explain their hasty departures.

By 1910 the house stood empty and dilapidated, with a leaking roof and broken windows, and the once-beautiful lawn a jungle of weeds. During this time people began reporting strange goings-on in the house. Passersby saw lights in the windows at midnight, and those brave enough to creep up to a first-floor window claimed to see a very tall woman coming down the staircase. Others thought they saw a coach-and-four clattering up the driveway in the light of a full moon, and more than one Henniker inhabitant was certain he'd heard frightening groans coming from somewhere behind the house.

In 1918, a Mrs. Flora Roy and her bachelor son, Louis M. A. Roy (popularly called Gus), from La Crosse, Wisconsin, arrived to occupy the house. Mrs. Roy had bought the property two years earlier and had hired workmen to restore the house to liveable condition.

After the Roys moved into their new home, there was still some tidying up to do. One day mother and son were cleaning out kitchen cupboards and a built-in dresser between the dining room and kitchen. Mrs. Roy had gotten a very hot fire going in the kitchen stove to burn the rubbish, and her son held up a paper bag he'd found in a corner of the dresser.

"Throw it on the fire!" called his mother.

But something stopped Gus. It was as if an invisible hand had drawn his hand away from the stove. He opened the bag and found several pounds of blasting powder!

In 1938 a hurricane devastated millions of acres of land on the Eastern Seaboard. Boardwalks of New Jersey beach resorts were ripped apart and carried out to sea, along with scores of summer homes. When the storm hit New England it turned inland, and few areas were spared its fury. The day before it hit Henniker it rained hard all day, and Gus thought he'd better check the condition of the road before taking the car to town. Below his driveway there was no road— only a sea of mud! Trees groaned and bent in half and the smaller ones snapped like sticks in the wind.

When Gus fought his way back up the driveway he noticed that the garage he had built was swaying. If it went down it would crush his new car. He quickly found a few long poles and propped up the little building as best he could. Cold and drenched to the skin, he hurried into the house. His mother met him at the door. "Who was that helping you shore up the garage?" she asked.

"Nobody," said Gus, climbing out of his boots. "Nobody was out there with me."

His mother looked him straight in the eye. "Gus, a tall lady in a long white gown was helping you. I saw her with my own eyes. But just as you started toward the house she vanished."

But soon the lady in the long white evening dress appeared indoors. Gus saw her first, floating down the staircase, her red hair flowing behind her as if in a breeze. He knew then that Ocean-Born Mary had never left her home, and he felt that her spirit was there to protect him and his mother. Besides, he thought, maybe she likes the way we're taking care of her house.

One summer afternoon a visitor appeared at the front door—a pleasant, well-dressed woman who said she had once lived in Henniker, but was now living in Massachusetts. She asked Mrs. Roy if she might see the rest of the house.

Mrs. Roy was perplexed. "What do you mean?"

The woman said that before she moved, she had gone to the house one day just to see the inside. Friends had remarked on its beauty.

"A lovely and elegantly dressed woman welcomed me," continued the visitor, "but she would only show me the foyer and this front parlor. She said the rest of the house was being redecorated and not ready for guests."

Could the visitor remember the approximate date that she had called at the house? Of course. Mrs. Roy smiled. No one had been living in the house at that time!

As stories of the haunting spread beyond the immediate community, newsmen from all over the country descended upon Ocean-Born Mary's house, and Mrs. Roy never tired of regaling them with her tales. Her life was filled suddenly with excitement such as she'd never imagined. She welcomed prospectors with metal detectors who searched for Don Pedro's treasure. Nothing of value was ever found; a child dug up a stove lid one day.

Gus charged admission to the house and grounds, and it is said that he took in a tidy sum to help support his mother and himself. Every Halloween cars were lined up bumper-to-bumper in front of the house because rumor had it that on that night each year the beautiful specter arrived in her coach-and-four, alighted, and entered her home. Even today carloads of young people park in front of the house on Halloween in hopes of catching a glimpse of Ocean-Born Mary.

From 1960 to 1978 the house was owned by David and Corinne Russell, and their occupancy raised some questions as to the validity of the ghost. Susy Smith, in her book *Prominent American Ghosts*, states that she visited the Russells, who assured her that the house was not haunted and had never *been* haunted. Mrs. Russell said that she had cared for Gus Roy in his final illness, and he told her then that he had invented the ghost story in order to get people to visit the house.

Ocean-Born Mary's house still stands, as magnificent as ever. The siding is stained a deep, rich brown, and multipaned windows reflect the soft sunlight. It is a private residence, partially obscured from view by large trees and a rock wall.

And does the ghost of the beautiful Mary Wallace remain in the home she loved? Only the present owners know, and they have declined to be interviewed.

The Jersey Devil

By 1735 Mrs. Jane Leeds of Estelville already had twelve children. She complained to friends and relatives, "May the devil take the next one." And he did. Her thirteenth child was a monster.

The baby boy, seemingly normal at birth, immediately took on a grotesque appearance. It grew a twenty-foot-long snakelike body with a horse's head, bat's wings, pig's feet, and a forked, leathery tail. After thrashing the horrified onlookers with its heavy body it flew up the chimney. Its raucous screams silenced the storm that raged outdoors.

The people of the Pine Barrens of south Jersey were a superstitious lot who lived in fear of the supposed creature set loose in their midst. Here, in vast forests of oak and pine and soil too sandy for extensive farming, the "pineys" eked out a living in such places as Hog Wallow, Bony's Hole, and Calico. A tough, resourceful people, they gathered moss and pine cones to burn for warmth, and picked cranberries and blueberries to sell. But soon even grown men rarely ventured forth alone at night. Rumors circulated that the beast carried off children, large dogs, geese, cats, and ducks. The children were never found, but animal remains were strewn across a broad area.

The devil also dried the cows' milk by breathing on them, and sometimes it blew its foul breath upon fish in cedar swamps until the fish died from the poison and threatened the health of an entire neighborhood.

In 1740, the frightened residents prevailed upon a minister to exorcise the devil. The successful exorcism was supposed to last for one hundred years, but the hideous creature may have returned before the century ended on at least two occasions.

Legend has it that the naval hero Commodore Stephen Decatur visited the Hanover Iron Works in the Barrens in 1800 to test the quality of the plant's cannonballs. Decatur, only twenty-one years old at the time, was distinguishing himself in fighting the Barbary Coast pirates. One day while on the firing range he noticed a strange creature flying overhead. Taking careful aim he sent a cannonball through its body. Observers saw the gaping hole and watched in amazement as the creature continued flying. They knew then that the devil had returned.

Another sighting was made early in the nineteenth century by Joseph Bona-
parte, former king of Spain and brother of Napoleon. Joseph leased a country
place near Bordentown from 1816 until 1839, and was said to have seen the
devil while hunting game one day in the Pine Barrens.

In 1840, just as the minister had predicted, the devil returned with a ven-
geance, snatching sheep from their pens and terrorizing children who lingered
outside their homes past sunset. Residents all across south Jersey learned to lock
their doors, draw window curtains, and hang a lantern outside for protection.
No one knew when the cackling creature would come calling.

A tradition soon grew up that each reappearance of the Jersey Devil was an
omen of disaster. A few months after William Bozarth saw the devil near Batsto,
the Italian-Ethiopian war broke out. In 1909 a massive earthquake shook Italy,
and cloven tracks were seen all over Gloucester, Camden, and Burlington counties.

The week of January 16, 1909, was phenomenal; thousands of people saw
either the devil or his footprints. Schools closed, and some people refused to go
outside during the daytime.

Patrolman James Sackville was walking his beat in Bristol when he heard dogs
howling. Turning around he saw a winged creature hopping birdlike in the middle of the street and emitting a terrible scream. Drawing his service revolver,
Sackville fired at the thing. It rose high in the air and vanished.

In their book, *The Jersey Devil*, James F. McCloy and Ray Miller Jr. report a
sighting by E. W. Minster, the postmaster of Bristol.

Minster said: "I awoke about two o'clock in the morning . . . and finding myself unable to sleep, I arose and wet my head with cold water as a cure for
insomnia.

"As I got up I heard an eerie, almost supernatural sound from the direction of the river . . . I looked out upon the Delaware and saw flying diagonally
across what appeared to be a large crane, but which was emitting a glow like
a fire-fly.

"Its head resembled that of a ram, with curled horns, and its long thick neck
was thrust forward in flight. It had long thin wings and short legs, the front legs
shorter than the hind. Again, it uttered its mournful and awful call—a combination of a squawk and a whistle, the beginning very high and piercing and
ending very low and hoarse. . . ."

On Tuesday, January 19, 1909, Mr. and Mrs. Nelson Evans, of 200 Mercer
Street, Gloucester, were awakened at two-thirty in the morning by the noise of
the devil leaping up and down on the roof of their shed. Reporting the sighting
to the Philadelphia *Evening Bulletin* and *The Philadelphia Inquirer*, Nelson said
the creature "was about three feet and a half high, with a head like a collie dog
and a face like a horse. It had a long neck, wings about two feet long, and its
back legs were like those of a crane and it had horse's hooves. It walked on its
back legs and held up two short front legs with paws on them. It didn't use the
front legs at all while we were watching. My wife and I were scared, I tell you,
but I managed to open the window and say, 'shoo!' and it turned around, barked
at me and flew away."

One afternoon during that same week, Mrs. J. H. White of south Philadelphia was taking clothes off her lines when she noticed a strange creature huddled in the corner of the yard. As she drew near it stood up. She said it was about six feet high, its body was covered with alligator skin, and it spewed flames from its mouth. The poor woman screamed, then fainted. Her husband rushed out the back door to find his wife unconscious on the ground with the devil close by, still spurting flames. Mr. White seized a clothes prop and chased the intruder, but it bounded over a fence and vanished in an alley.

For a short time it was thought that the Jersey Devil had expired. William Wasso, a track walker on the Clayton-Newfield railroad line, spotted the devil about three hundred feet ahead of him. As the creature sniffed the third rail its long, slimy tail touched it. A violent explosion occurred, melting the track for twenty feet in all directions. When the fire and smoke cleared, Wasso saw no sign of the devil and concluded it had died.

But the devil was far from dead.

Later that week the creature went on a rampage, attacking Mrs. Mary Sorbinski's dog in south Camden. It was seven o'clock at night and already dark. Hearing a heartrending cry from her pet, Mrs. Sorbinski grabbed a broom and dashed outside. She flailed the devil with the broom until it let go of the dog, but not before the poor animal had lost a chunk of flesh. Mrs. Sorbinski, screaming in panic and shock, carried the wounded dog into the house and called the police. By the time Patrolmen Thomas Cunningham and William Crouch arrived, a crowd of over a hundred persons was already gathered at the home, trying to console their neighbor. This was thought to be the only time that a human witnessed the devil's attack upon a living thing.

Piercing screams suddenly arose from Kaighn Hill. The officers rushed in that direction and emptied their revolvers at the devil, but it flew off into the eastern sky.

At the end of the week the devil made another attempt to mutilate a dog. But it picked the wrong one. The fierce and fearless bulldog belonging to Mrs. D. W. Brown of Salem snarled and drove the infamous creature from her backyard.

All week the press ran eyewitness accounts under such headlines as "WHAT IS IT VISITS ALL SOUTH JERSEY?" Of the cloven prints the *Philadelphia Press* reported, "So uncanny is the mystery that many persons who did not know the word superstition, after careful study of the marks, are willing to ascribe them to some supernatural cause...."

The Philadelphia zoo offered a $10,000 reward for the capture of the devil. Zoo superintendent Robert D. Carson said it would be of great educational significance and would draw enormous crowds. Nothing came of his offer.

As quickly as the Jersey Devil had appeared, it disappeared. For eighteen years there were few sightings, and the people of the Pine Barrens resumed their peaceful and orderly way of life. But not for long.

In 1927 a cab driver had a flat tire late at night while headed for Salem. He had just finished changing the tire when the car began to shake violently. The driver looked up to see a gigantic figure covered with hair pounding on the roof of the car. The driver, leaving his jack and flat tire behind, leaped into his cab and sped away. He told the Salem police that he'd met the Jersey Devil.

In August of 1930, berry pickers in Leeds Point and Mays Landing reported that the devil was back, devouring all the blueberries and cranberries before moving north two weeks later.

The devil made a brief appearance on December 7, 1941, the day the Japanese bombed Pearl Harbor. However, the "pineys" decided that with the arrival of the new Atomic Age the creature would never be seen again.

Alas, it was seen, on November 22, 1951, when a group of youngsters gathered for a party at the Duport Clubhouse in Gibbstown. One of the boys glanced out a window to see the "thing" staring at him with blood oozing out of its face. After the boys saw the devil, their chaperone called the police, but by the time officers arrived the creature was gone.

Nine years later, in 1960, bloodcurdling cries terrorized persons near Mays Landing. State officials tried to calm the residents but found no explanation for the weird night sounds. Policemen nailed posters to trees saying the Jersey Devil was a hoax, but curiosity seekers poured into the area. Harry Hunt, owner of the Hunt Brothers Circus in Florence, offered $100,000 for the capture of the beast, dead or alive. If the Abominable Snowman could be captured at the same time the double billing would quickly bring in a million dollars, Hunt said.

The Bicentennial celebration of 1975–76 spurred the devil to more widespread activities than ever. Campers everywhere in the Pine Barrens said they were kept awake by loud, unearthly screams, and one camper walking a woodland trail one afternoon claimed to have been seized by a large, hairy arm.

Today there are few, if any, sightings of the devil that harassed south Jersey for 241 years.

Is there an explanation for the phenomenon? Maybe.

The original English, Irish, and German settlers brought their legends of demons with them. Belief in a "real" devil made it easier for the poor and isolated "pineys" to accept crop failures and other incidents of bad luck.

A deformed child may have been born to a backwoods woman who hid it or did away with it, giving rise to stories of a monster in the area.

Or did simple boredom birth the devil? The people of the Barrens led lives of quiet desperation. With little for them to look forward to, manufactured excitement made life bearable.

Perhaps the legend of the Jersey Devil was a means of keeping children in line. Like the big bad wolf of fairy tales, a monstrous devil could swallow a naughty child in one gulp. Fear, while perhaps not the best way to control a child, sometimes works. "The bogey man will get you if you don't watch out!"

Yet how does one explain the sightings of the devil witnessed by highly reliable persons: businessmen, police officers, government officials? Their reports are not so easy to dismiss as baseless hearsay.

Paved roads, electricity, and television have ended the isolation of the "pineys," and most of today's residents view the story of the Jersey Devil as a fictional legend. Yet some do not.

Fred Brown told author John McPhee, "The Jersey Devil is real. That is no fake story. A woman named Leeds had twelve living children. She said if she ever had another one she hoped it would be the devil. She had her thirteenth child, and it growed, and one day it flew away. It's haunted the earth ever since. It's took pigs right out of pens. And little lambs. I believe it took a baby once, right down in Mathis town. The Leeds Devil is a crooked-faced thing, with wings. Believe what you want, I'm telling you the truth."

Is he?

The Lodge

Jerry Sanders is a native Californian who jokes that people from there either believe in everything or nothing. "So it's easy for me to believe in a ghost."

Even that willingness to suspend his disbelief in the paranormal didn't prepare him for his introduction to Rebecca, the ghost at The Lodge, an elegant hostelry in Cloudcroft, a rustic Sacramento Mountains community in southeast New Mexico.

Sanders became the owner of the historic resort hotel in the fall of 1982. He and his wife Carolyn were ready to move into a house in Cloudcroft when the lease fell through at the last minute. Since a moving van was in transit with their personal belongings, the couple decided to temporarily store their possessions in an empty basement storage room of The Lodge.

"It's been reconstructed quite a bit, but at that time it was just a large storage area," said Sanders, an enthusiastic former Hollywood advertising executive. With their furniture and clothing in the room were valuable furs and jewelry. The door was kept locked at all times. Jerry and Carolyn Sanders had the only keys.

But that wasn't enough to keep Rebecca at bay, the transplanted Californian discovered.

"One night about eleven o'clock we went down to get a change of clothing," Sanders said. "We had stacked all of our clothing in chests so we could get to it, and we'd built a little aisleway. We got to the room and unlocked it. There was a light on in the back of the room. That was the first thing we noticed."

At first Sanders thought the glow was coming through a basement window, as if "someone had left their car lights on" in the parking lot near the window. Sanders switched on the overhead light. The light in the back of the room was coming through an interior door. It was open. Sanders said *the door had been sealed shut* until that moment!

"One of the chests had actually been pushed out so that somebody could get back in there," he said. "I realized then that somebody was probably down there. They had broken in through a window, or in some way I had not been aware of, and they were in there."

Sanders cautiously headed toward the light streaming through the open doorway, not knowing what to expect. He wasn't armed, nor did he really know what he'd do if he confronted an intruder. He needn't have worried.

"All of a sudden I heard a pipe break, [and then] a tremendous rush of water. It sounded like a four-inch main had broken. I followed the sound, which corresponded with [the direction of] the light. It led into this old bathroom."

Inside were two sinks with twin faucets on each sink. Water was spewing from the spigots so hard that it threatened to overflow.

"I thought that someone at the hotel had turned on a valve, or one had popped somehow, and the water was suddenly allowed to escape through the faucets." Sanders was able to turn off the water without difficulty.

The perplexed couple found their change of clothing and locked up. Jerry was understandably disturbed by what had transpired. Before he left, a quick inspection told him nothing had been damaged, nor were any possessions obviously missing. The windows leading into the storeroom were secure and unbroken.

"I asked our maintenance man if there could have been a valve somewhere on the backside of that [bathroom] that suddenly broke," Sanders continues. "The faucets had been left open because there wasn't any water in there." He was told that that explanation was improbable, if not impossible.

It was another ten days before Sanders found a possible, albeit fantastic, explanation for the mysterious water explosion. That was on the day when he had a chance encounter with a hotel guest, a woman who had been a maid there in the 1930s.

"She asked if I'd seen Rebecca yet. I said no. She asked if I'd heard stories about her and I said yes. Well, this lady said Rebecca lives in the room right behind the [basement] bathroom. She took me down there and I told her my story as I went. . . . There is absolutely no explanation." Sanders believes the incident was Rebecca's way of welcoming him to "her" hotel.

A strange story, yes, but not at all unusual at the mountain resort called by some "the best-kept secret in New Mexico." Stories of Rebecca have been common since at least the 1930s, three decades after The Lodge was built in 1899 as a residential hotel for employees of the Alamogordo and Sacramento Railroad cutting timber in the Sacramento Mountains to make railroad crossties.

By 1906, the forty-seven-room hotel, 9,200 feet above sea level, was opened to the public by the railroad. Rebuilt in 1911 after a disastrous fire, The Lodge has operated nearly continuously since then.

Over the decades, it has welcomed personalities as diverse as Pancho Villa, Judy Garland, Clark Gable, and every New Mexico governor since Miguel Ortero in 1901. Garland carved her name under a diminutive rainbow on a stairwell wall leading to the observatory tower, where on a clear day you can see for nearly two hundred miles.

Conrad Hilton owned the hotel in the 1930s and lived in what is now called the Governor's Suite.

The dazzling hotel has been refurbished and modernized inside and outside. Rebecca hasn't seemed to mind.

From the outside, the building would seem more at home in the Black Forest than in the American Southwest, surrounded as it is by towering pines and spectacular mountain scenery. With its cheery burgundy-and-gray shade, stained glass windows, lookout tower, and covered entryway, The Lodge has the appearance of a quaint European inn. The circular driveway skirts a serene pond with its own miniature waterfall. Nearby are the highest golf course in the nation and the southernmost ski area in the United States.

The guest rooms are decorated in what one travel magazine termed "a French-country look, with antique furniture, matched bed and drapery fabrics, high ceilings, clicking steam radiators, down comforters and French eyelet linens." Yet each room has an individual identity; no two rooms are alike.

In the spacious, two-story lobby, leather armchairs and sofas are drawn close to a copper-sheathed fireplace where a blaze can be found even in mid-summer. Fresh flowers grace the mahogany end tables, while a stuffed bear, its mouth agape in silent anger, rears on its hind legs near a doorway. Refined dining is offered at Rebecca's Restaurant, or on an outdoor dining patio overlooking the swimming pool, spa, and gardens. On weekends, the Red Dog Saloon in the hotel's lower level features live entertainment.

Jerry Sanders takes a particularly benign view of the idea that The Lodge is haunted.

"Usually you think of a ghost as something that's going to be a negative for a hotel. In fact for many years no one ever talked about Rebecca. I had heard the stories from a front desk clerk when I first came here looking at the hotel . . . I started asking questions. A lot of people said, 'Oh yeah, but we don't talk about Rebecca. We don't want to frighten any of our guests.' "

Sanders was "amused" by the stories, especially some descriptions of Rebecca as a beautiful redhead with distinctive blue eyes. That, he knew, was far different from the wailing, chain-rattling demon of fiction.

"Many people had also seen her in the Red Dog Saloon, which I thought was appropriate since spirits do tend to fly in saloons," he says, chuckling.

Before his experience in the basement storeroom, however, Sanders was not sure he fully believed any of the secondhand stories. Early on, he persuaded his wife that at least the house restaurant should be named after their ghost.

The precise origin of the ghost's name isn't known. It seems to be the sobriquet people associated with the hotel have always called their otherworldly visitor over the years. "Rebecca is a great name for a Victorian-style hotel, particularly when you think of her as being a beautiful ghost. It has a kind of character to it. We had some initial fears that the first time we served the food the tables would tip over or pictures would come flying off the walls. You really don't know what to expect," Sanders said.

The tables remained upright and not a picture so much as tilted, but Rebecca has definitely made her presence known in the dining room, especially for diners who may dispute her "existence."

Take the couple who came in for dinner one night, for instance; the nice middle-aged man and his wife were looking for nothing more than a quiet meal in a fine restaurant. But the husband, whom we shall call James, had read about Rebecca and wanted to make it clear in as loud a voice as possible that he thought the story was stuff and nonsense, certainly that part about her flaming red hair and porcelain white skin. The attentive wait staff said he didn't have to believe in anything if he didn't want to and left it at that.

The couple got through their soup and salad and had been served their main course without incident when Rebecca decided to make an issue out of James's cynicism—an empty wineglass on the couple's table suddenly exploded into hundreds of pieces, sending shards of glass onto the couple and several nearby tables.

James jumped up from the table, screaming that the hotel somehow "did that on purpose." Just how they could have concocted such a trick he didn't say. The innkeeper, maître d', and numerous waiters and waitresses apologized profusely, but adamantly turned away accusations that they had anything to do with the disintegrating wineglass. Indeed, the restaurant (*Rebecca's* restaurant, after all) had to replace the food at several tables at a cost to the hotel of about five hundred dollars.

As the couple left the restaurant, several witnesses contend that the lights inexplicably blinked twice. Rebecca saying good-bye?

On another occasion, a waiter carrying a tray full of empty wineglasses couldn't believe his eyes when a goblet in the middle of the tray burst. No one in the dining room could offer a reasonable explanation for that incident, either.

The hotel readily capitalizes on the presence of their beautiful eidolon. And Jerry Sanders doesn't apologize for that. "You have to realize that after we flirted with this and after we heard the stories we actually experienced some things that told us there *was* a real Rebecca. I kid about her and exploit her . . . but I really do believe there is a ghost in the hotel. In fact, two parapsychologists who have visited . . . agree. There is a spirit in the hotel."

But if Sanders, his employees, and various guests affirm that a ghost haunts The Lodge, they've had less luck in pinning an identity on her.

The story told most often of her origin is that Rebecca, or the woman who became Rebecca in her afterlife, was a hotel chambermaid in the 1920s or 1930s. At that time, some hotel workers lived in rooms in the basement quite near where Sanders and his wife had stored their possessions. Some people claim that Rebecca moonlighted as a prostitute and was killed by her jealous boyfriend, a beefy lumberjack who found her entwined in the arms of another man. Legend has it that he buried her body somewhere in the hotel basement.

If Rebecca *was* a lady of the evening, curious events in Room 101, commonly termed the Governor's Suite, may be linked to liaisons she might have had in that luxurious chamber. Although her ghost has been active in various parts of the hotel—the basement in particular—the scarlet-maned phantasm has a particular fondness for pranks in Room 101.

That set of rooms got its name because it was favored by visiting celebrities, including New Mexican governors. There's no direct evidence that any of them favored the "services" of Rebecca, or any other hotel employee.

As a front desk manager at The Lodge, Mrs. Johnnie Adams was privy to many "Rebecca stories," especially those originating in Room 101.

"The telephone rings and there's nobody on the line," Mrs. Adams said. "It'll drive guests crazy. You'll pick up the phone and there's a dial tone. I just laugh and say, 'Rebecca got you!' "

Sometimes the call comes *from* the Governor's Suite—although no one is registered there. A switchboard at the front desk indicates what extension a call is coming from. The extension in 101 rings the desk. A front desk clerk answers—the opportunity to hear a ghost should never go unheeded—and waits for Rebecca to register her comments. So far, she hasn't taken advantage of the opportunity.

Jerry Sanders believes there is a definite connection between the Governor's Suite and Rebecca.

"That's where she plied her trade [as a prostitute]. The interesting thing about . . . 101 is that the phone system has been changed three times . . . getting more modern. It's all computerized now. But 101 still has an antique phone. On all of the three systems the phone had the same problem. It will dial the front desk and there'll be no one on it. You pick it up and it says 101 on our computer register. Or [a guest] will be in 101 and the phone will ring there and there'll be nobody [on the line]. It's a phenomenon that always intrigued us because there's no reason for it to happen with that new phone system. It's just like that incident down at the water faucets."

Sometimes it's not only the phone in Room 101 that acts up.

"We've had funny things happen to our electricity," Sanders notes. "It was an old system and we've had all that replaced. There are the corridor lights in the hall that leads down to Room 101. For some reason we continually have problems with the light in front of 101. It's a big, old bulb light with a fan on it. That light will go on and off without anybody touching it whatsoever. If somebody is walking by, that light will go on. And when they walk away it will go off. It's the only one in the hotel that does that."

Members of the housekeeping staff have reported small annoyances, including ones in Room 101, over the years—escapades they often attribute to their resident ghost.

A former head of housekeeping told coworkers that after she had made a bed she would later find a distinct indentation on it as if someone had sat or lain on the blanket. She had guests' shoes mysteriously disappear from a room, only to show up in another guest room several doors away. At other times, the strip of paper placed over a freshly cleaned toilet seat would vanish. It wasn't torn or put in the trash. It would just be gone. Sometimes a maid would later find it on the floor outside the room.

New employees or ones who scoff at Rebecca seem to be particularly susceptible to the ghostly pranks.

"But she's not malicious," Mrs. Adams insists. "She's playful. I don't think she would hurt anyone. If she walked by . . . I would probably be scared out of my wits, but I wouldn't be surprised."

Mrs. Adams has never seen Rebecca, but she's had some close encounters. "When I go downstairs by myself late at night to make copies or get supplies . . . I say 'It's just me, Rebecca. I'm not going to hurt you.'

"[One] night I was down there about eleven-thirty by myself. Now, I'm not a 'fraidy cat . . . [but] the hair on my neck stood up. There were some weird sounds down there. What sounded like doors closing in the new office area. Now, it may be that it's just an old building, but I was thinking about Rebecca. I hadn't talked to her. . . . "

Innkeeper Judy Montoya had a similar experience in the basement offices. While working late one night, she slipped downstairs to look for some business documents. She couldn't find what she was looking for. She had just relocked the office door when she remembered where she had put the paperwork. She unlocked the door and turned on the lights. The photocopier had somehow been turned on and was spitting out blank pages. Minutes earlier, of course, the machine had been off.

Montoya had actually been "introduced" to Rebecca some time earlier.

Before Montoya took the position of innkeeper, she and her husband, Alex, sometimes visited The Lodge on weekends. Once they were there with his sister and brother-in-law in one of the larger family rooms. Alex had fallen asleep but abruptly woke up when he felt fingernails digging into his back. He was angry at the rudeness of his wife or sister . . . or whomever.

The problem was the three others were on the other side of the room quietly playing cards. Judy Montoya told her husband he was imagining things and should go back to sleep. He insisted that the sharp pain in his back was not a product of his imagination and asked his wife to look at his back. She lifted his shirt. Several scratch marks were clearly visible.

One new employee who quickly became acquainted with Rebecca is Lisa Thomassie, the hotel's marketing director in the late 1980s. She formerly worked at another hotel Sanders owned before she transferred to Cloudcroft in 1987.

"I lived in a hotel room [here] for about two months," Thomassie said. "One morning I was getting ready to come downstairs to go to work. I was at the vanity looking in the mirror when . . . the toilet handle went straight up and it completely flushed. It really terrified me. I got out of the room and came right downstairs. I told [the bartender] I had just seen Rebecca in my room and I didn't like it at all. Later I thought she was just welcoming me to The Lodge. I appreciated it, but she could have been a little more discreet."

Other guests and employees say Rebecca doesn't limit herself to the occasional telephone prank or mischievous activities most often associated with poltergeists, who can be quite noisy but rarely seen. She has been seen *and* felt on several occasions.

An unsuspecting male guest was startled one evening to find a vaporous female reclining in his bathtub. He quickly left the room, stationing himself in a lounge armchair until he collected his wits. "He was completely sincere," desk clerk Johnnie Adams said. "He'd seen something, whatever it was."

A woman vacationing in Cloudcroft in the mid-1980s recalled her experience with Rebecca in a letter she sent to the hotel:

> My husband, sister and I were staying in one of the family rooms. After a great dinner we returned to our room and went to sleep. At about midnight I woke up because I was too hot. After adjusting my covers I lay awake listening to my sister's breathing as she slept. I was laying on my left side. Suddenly I felt a hand on my right shoulder. Then a deep male voice singing "Won't You Be My True Love?" There were other words, but I can't recall them all. The tune seemed somewhat familiar to me because I remember [recognizing] the tune. Needless to say I was quite shocked. I shook my husband and asked him if he had heard the man singing. He said no. One more bit I should offer. When I turned to look I felt a "whooshing" kind of movement. No one was there. I lay awake most of the rest of the night. I don't think I was afraid as much as I was shocked. What I mean is I felt no harm. This is interesting to me as all day yesterday I had said how much I wanted to see Rebecca."

The letter writer had been staying in Room 104, just down the hallway from the Governor's Suite. The fact that the visitor claimed to have heard a *male* voice presents the distinct possibility that Rebecca *and* her lumberjack boyfriend haunt the hotel.

Another guest wasn't sure if he saw Rebecca, but he was puzzled anyway by something that happened to him at a late hour. As he was dozing off, the man heard a scraping sound in the hallway. He was curious as to who might be messing about at night. He opened his door a crack and peered out. A woman with long, red hair wearing a floor-length nightgown was rearranging a floral bouquet on an antique hallway chest.

The next day he asked the staff if the woman might have been someone who worked at the hotel. Not possible, they affirmed. Owner Jerry Sanders was "never quite sure" if the man was sincere or "pulling our leg."

A hotelkeeper tries to stay in tune with the needs of his guests, according to Sanders, especially if a ghost becomes involved in the equation. He recalls the guest who asked the front desk clerk if he could change rooms. Sanders was walking by at the time and paused to ask about the problem.

The guest said there was really nothing wrong with the room *itself*, but that he'd had a rather unnerving experience the night before. He had awakened sometime after midnight and glanced at the nightstand. His wristwatch resting there suddenly rose straight up in the air and glided to the top of a chest of drawers.

"He felt real uncomfortable in that room," Sanders said. "Understandably."

There is the tendency sometimes to blame a ghost for all matter of mischief, including that which could simply be mechanical failure of one sort or another. Then again, there are those things that go wrong in The Lodge for no reason whatsoever.

There were the two Santa Fe artists who made the spectacular quilt with a centerpiece "portrait" of Rebecca that hangs in the hotel lobby. In order to render a realistic version of Rebecca, the couple visited the hotel to take photographs of a painting based on descriptions of the ethereal woman that is used on various hotel souvenirs. They took the painting outside for better light. For some reason the artists cannot explain, the face did not appear in their photographs. The picture frame, Rebecca's dress, indeed all the details were present in the photograph—but the face of Rebecca itself was so over-exposed as to be featureless.

Again, Jerry Sanders puzzles over this additional mysterious incident: "I've taken pictures of [the painting] and had no problems. We thought it might have been the glare of the glass, but they took pictures from different angles. They were real cautious. It was really strange."

Sanders has one possible explanation: "Rebecca was in fact teasing somebody."

Some visitors have their own "relationships" with Rebecca. Desk clerk Johnnie Adams remembers the three ladies who always had to have one special room at The Lodge. One of the women explained that "Becky came" to visit them in that room.

Or there was the distinguished-looking gentleman who had "dinner" with Rebecca. On Halloween night, the tuxedoed man reserved a table in the hotel dining room and ordered dinner for two. He was alone. Everybody kept an eye on him, remembers one witness, because all during the meal he seemed to be talking to someone.

At the end of his ninety-minute dinner, waiters found *both* plates empty and *each* wineglass drained.

Waiters swear they saw him eat only his own dinner!

Hotel employees are careful about whom they discuss their stories of Rebecca with lest they scare away tremulous visitors. It doesn't happen often, they acknowledge, that potential guests react the way a family did several Christmases ago. A young couple, their son, and an elderly relative had reservations for several nights during the holiday season. Since they had never been to The Lodge, the family decided to check out the hotel during Sunday brunch several weeks beforehand. After the meal, the parents asked about Rebecca.

"If I know the child is scared or small, many times I won't say anything," said Mrs. Adams, the desk clerk. "But they kept asking questions and I answered as truthfully as I knew how. They told me they couldn't keep the reservations [because] their son was so scared. The little boy came up to me and said that he figured by the time he got to college he'd be brave enough to come."

The Red Dog Saloon has been a fixture at The Lodge since the 1930s. Situated in the basement of the hotel, the Red Dog is reminiscent of an Old West saloon with its rough-hewn walls, plank floor, and southwestern fixtures. Weekend entertainment keeps guests occupied until the wee hours of the morning.

As Jerry Sanders learned early on in his tenure at The Lodge, Rebecca seems to like the saloon almost as much as hotel guests. That may be because it occupies space once taken up with shower rooms used by hotel employees earlier in this century.

"We've had lots of stories about lights going on and off [in the Red Dog]," Jerry Sanders said. Workers cleaning up late at night see motion on the dance floor as if from a solitary, ethereal dancer.

Bartender Nosi Crosby grew accustomed to Rebecca's fondness for the saloon.

"When we give the last call, there's a pretty, red-haired woman who doesn't want to leave. You see her reflection in the mirror. When you turn around, she disappears. Whenever you have a tab left in the bar, you know Rebecca has been there. She looks more like the picture on the quilt. In a . . . long dress. A very pretty outfit."

Lisa Thomassie was startled one Friday afternoon to hear music coming from the empty Red Dog Saloon. When Thomassie asked the person she was with what was causing the music, her companion smiled and replied nonchalantly: "Oh, it's just Rebecca."

It's not unusual for the front desk to receive phone calls late at night from guests upset about loud music coming from the saloon. Night clerks patiently explain that it's not possible since the Red Dog isn't open. Employee Dick Adams has sometimes checked out the complaints, but has never seen or heard anything from the nightspot. How to explain the music? "Rebecca really enjoys dancing in the Red Dog," he says with a shrug.

During Prohibition, gambling was a favorite pastime for bar patrons. A number of years ago, a bartender closing up for the night was surprised to find a pile of old poker chips on the floor.

Lisa Thomassie: "We don't have any of those chips anywhere in The Lodge; we don't have any stored. The Red Dog has been renovated so many times, it's not like they could have sat there for twenty-five years without anyone seeing them."

Again Rebecca received the blame when it was proposed that she was merely playing a trick on an unsuspecting barkeep.

Perhaps the most bizarre incident attributed to Rebecca's peculiar, and some-times coarse, sense of humor involved the bartender Nosi Crosby.

"I usually don't get a chance to use the bathroom a lot," explained Crosby, noting that on some nights she is on duty by herself. "I usually run to the one upstairs, but one night I went to the bathroom downstairs by the Red Dog Saloon. I tried to turn the lights on, but they wouldn't [work]. It wasn't too dark and I thought no big deal. I went to one of the stalls and closed the door. When I was ready to use the toilet paper, I found there wasn't any. I said, 'Oh, s———!' "

At that precise instant, a hand holding a role of toilet paper appeared from under the partition. Crosby was alone.

"I didn't wait. I ran all the way upstairs without even my pants all the way up. I didn't want to think or to look and see if anybody was there or not. I was so scared I said I was never going to use that bathroom again. I'll tell you, if I ever run out of bathroom tissue again, I'll never say any bad words!"

*   *   *

The legend that is Rebecca of The Lodge continues to grow. While some guests may exaggerate her appearances and employees may give her credit for even minor annoyances, enough evidence has accumulated to convince most people that a ghost does indeed prowl the old hotel.

"The truth of the matter is," Jerry Sanders emphasizes, "that there's a basis for these stories. There is something here. I've never felt any maliciousness. Many of us have felt a strange energy, [but] it's not like you're scared when you feel it. If someone calls me crazy, I'm perfectly comfortable with myself."

So far no one who has spent any amount of time at The Lodge has called Jerry Sanders anything of the sort. Rebecca simply wouldn't stand for it.

Ordinary People

James M. Herrmann and his wife, Lucille, were a hardworking couple with two youngsters. In 1958, they lived in a well-kept green ranch home in Seaford, Long Island, with their two children—twelve-year-old Jimmy and a thirteen-year-old daughter, also named Lucille.

Mr. Herrmann, an Air France employee, commuted the thirty-five miles daily to his work in New York City. His wife, a registered nurse, stayed home to care for the family. Pleasant, kindly folks. But you wouldn't have wanted to visit them. Not in Seaford. Not in the late winter of 1958 when frightening, inexplicable events bedeviled the Herrmanns for five weeks—events that neither the police nor the country's most prestigious parapsychologists were able to explain.

The disturbances began on the afternoon of February 3, 1958. Mrs. Herrmann and the children were home alone when they heard the unmistakable sound of bottles popping their caps. The sounds came from all over the house. In the cellar a gallon bottle of bleach and a can of paint thinner were found uncapped, the contents spilling across the cement floor.

Up in the kitchen, they found that a bottle of starch under the sink was on its side, its cap off and the sticky, blue liquid dribbling onto the linoleum. In the master bedroom, Mrs. Herrmann discovered a small bottle of holy water tipped over. The cap was unscrewed and the water ran across the dresser top. Mrs. Herrmann, a devout Catholic, was greatly upset.

Next to the master bedroom, in Jimmy's room, legs were broken off a ceramic doll and pieces had been chipped from a plastic ship model.

When James Herrmann arrived home, he didn't know what to make of his family's incredible stories. But he warned each of them to say nothing to anyone.

On Sunday morning, February 9, the whole family was gathered in the dining room when the popping noises occurred again. James rushed from room to room. Holy water, toilet water, starch, bleach, paint thinners—the same bottles of liquid opened again by some force. In the bathroom a bottle of shampoo and a bottle of medicine had somehow dumped their contents into the sink.

James called the police. Patrolman J. Hughes was dispatched to the house. While he and the family sat in the living room the popping noises began again in the bathroom. Officer Hughes hurried into the empty room. The shampoo and medicine bottles were again upset. The officer would write later in his report that no appliances were running at the time, the house was quiet, and there were no obvious vibrations or outside noises.

After Officer Hughes made his preliminary findings, Detective Joseph Tozzi was assigned full-time to the case. He ordered a number of tests. An oscillograph used for measuring the slightest vibration was put in the basement. One bleach bottle spilled, but no vibrations in the floor were associated with the incident. The liquid was analyzed at the police laboratory; no foreign matter or signs of manipulation were found.

The Long Island Lighting Company checked all the wiring, fuse boxes, and ground wires in the house and found them in good working order. Maps of the terrain beneath the house showed no underground springs, and inspectors from the Town of Hempstead Building Department pronounced the house structurally sound, with only hairline cracks in the basement floor, probably caused by settling.

The Seaford Fire Department inspected a well in front of the house to see if any change in water level could have caused tremors felt inside the house. They determined that the water level had been stable for the previous five years.

Thinking that high-frequency radio waves might be causing the damage, Detective Tozzi interviewed a neighbor who had a radio transmitter. But the man said he hadn't used his set for a number of years.

Mitchell Airfield was contacted for a list of planes leaving on a runway near the Herrmann house on the theory that airplanes taking off *might* correlate with disturbances within the house. There was no correlation.

A layperson suggested capping the chimney to prevent downdrafts. This was done. It solved nothing.

A Roman Catholic priest also came, on request, to bless the house. But the bottles kept popping with such regularity that the media, by this time, were headlining the story. Press, radio, and television coverage was extensive. And letters from crackpots and publicity-seekers from all over the world deluged the mystified family with advice. The little town of Seaford had never experienced such notoriety.

But now, with the apparent elimination of natural causes for the disturbances, how could one interpret them? People said pranksters were at work, and some attention was focused on twelve-year-old Jimmy Herrmann.

The boy was a bright, brown-eyed honor student at the Seaford Junior-Senior High School who did exceptionally well in English and math. His hobbies were airplane and railroad lore, about which he was unusually knowledgeable. He also read science-fiction books, collected stamps, and enjoyed drawing pictures of rockets.

An obviously gifted child, he was clearly a joy to his parents, and well liked by teachers, friends, and neighbors. A not atypical preteen. Although the boy was not always in the room when the various destructive acts took place, he was usually somewhere in the house.

On Saturday, February 15, 1958, Miss Marie Murtha, a middle-aged cousin of James Herrmann, arrived for a visit. At one point during the day she sat on a chair in the living room while Jimmy sat across from her in the middle of the couch with his arms folded. His sister, at the far end of the room, was the only other person present.

Suddenly a porcelain figurine flew off the end table at one end of the couch and fell to the living room rug, but did not break. Miss Murtha couldn't explain the incident, but she told investigators later that she didn't think anything "supernatural" was involved.

On February 20 the mysterious forces struck with renewed vigor. Twice the porcelain figurine was thrown ten feet across the living room, the last time smashing it. A bottle of ink from a writing desk hurtled through the air, splattering the living room rug and wall. And a sugar bowl danced on the dinette table, then fell to the floor.

James Herrmann was devastated. His was a close-knit, affectionate family. He was certain his children were *not* playing tricks, that some agent he could not understand was accountable for wreaking havoc upon his lovely home.

The next day, James moved his family to the home of friends for a few days. Their sleep was blissful, uninterrupted. And when they returned to their own home, peace also prevailed. No bottles lost their caps and no objects levitated and crashed into the walls. Everything seemed normal. For a while.

On the night of February 25, a ten-pound portable phonograph in the basement reportedly flew several feet through the air and crashed against a shelf. An eighteen-inch statue of the Virgin Mary sailed from a dresser top and hit a mirror on the opposite wall. Oddly, neither one broke. And a moment later, a radio fell from a table and skittered across the floor.

Two nights later, *Newsday* reporter Dave Kahn visited the house. He was there to observe and write about a "typical" night in the Herrmann home. His most amazing moments came as he sat reading in the living room. By glancing up, he could keep his eyes on a direct line with Jimmy's open bedroom door. Without warning, a ten-inch world globe, kept on the top of a steel bookcase in the boy's room, soared through the doorway, crossed the hallway, and landed on the living room floor close to Kahn's feet. The reporter rushed into the bedroom and found Jimmy sitting up in bed rubbing sleep from his eyes. Blankets covered his legs. The tall bookcase had toppled over and was wedged between one corner of the bed and a radiator. Jimmy said the noises had awakened him.

Kahn wrote that it was "possible but improbable" that the boy had thrown the globe.

Others would witness equally puzzling events.

A week after Kahn's visit, John Gold, New York correspondent for the *London Evening News*, visited the Herrmanns. He claimed to have seen a flashbulb rise slowly from a table in the living room and strike a wall some four yards away.

In the late afternoon of that same day, four sharp knocks came from the kitchen wall.

And in the dining room a heavy glass centerpiece flew from the table and hit a cupboard, chipping a piece of molding from the cupboard before falling to the floor. Mrs. Lucille Herrmann told Gold that it was the second time that the centerpiece had moved by itself.

Mrs. Herrmann also found an expensive new coffee table flipped over. Such force had been exerted that the table was damaged. She asked Detective Tozzi and an associate, Sergeant Reddy, to come over and emotionally told them that the destruction in her home had to stop, even if it meant calling in a psychic or spiritualist medium. However, Mrs. Herrmann insisted the events were *not* supernatural in origin.

She didn't have to resort to that. In early March, the Herrmanns received a letter from Dr. J. B. Rhine, then director of Duke University's famous Parapsychology Laboratory in Durham, North Carolina. He and his colleagues had been studying the press accounts of the case and believed it merited their attention. The laboratory was investigating such phenomena as telepathy, clairvoyance, precognition, and psychokinesis. Because of the presence of youngsters in the family, Dr. Rhine gave some consideration to the possibility of a poltergeist at work. That phenomenon is usually found in homes where young children or teenagers are present. Although it's never been proven, the theory is that when sexual energies build up in teenagers those energies *may* be transferred into a sort of "vibration" that leaves the body like a radio impulse and plays havoc wherever it hits. Dr. Rhine asked permission for his colleague, Dr. J. Gaither Pratt, to visit the family.

Dr. Pratt was welcomed. He told the Herrmanns that, although reports of incidents similar to those they were experiencing were fairly common, none had been authenticated to the satisfaction of scientists.

Shortly after Dr. Pratt arrived in Seaford, he summoned a research colleague, William G. Roll, to join him. Both investigators interviewed family members individually and were convinced that none of them was perpetrating any prank.

"The family was much too shaken for it to be a colossal hoax," Dr. Pratt told a United Press reporter. Mrs. Herrmann also lived in constant fear that a flying object might injure someone.

On the night of March 10, 1958, at 8:14 P.M., while Mrs. Herrmann, Jimmy, and Lucille were preparing for bed (James Herrmann was away), the parapsychologists heard a popping noise in the cellar. Dr. Pratt hurried downstairs. A bleach bottle in a cardboard box had lost its cap. The bottle rested against one side of the box, with its cap behind the box.

Both investigators wanted to discover if this particular phenomenon could be achieved by known physical forces, and they began to experiment.

Roll detailed their findings in his book, *The Poltergeist:*

On the theory that someone in the home had surreptitiously placed a chemical in the bottles that would generate pressure, or that pressure had arisen in some other way, we bought some pieces of dry ice, that is, carbon dioxide in its solid state, and placed these in containers with screw caps, such as those in the Herrmann household. We found that when the top was loosely screwed on, the pressure easily escaped with a low, hissing noise without affecting the cap. When we screwed the cap on as tightly as we could by hand, the pressure increased until the gas forced its way out around the threads of the cap but without perceptibly loosening it. Of course, thousands of housewives every year do pressure canning in glass jars utilizing this principle—without complaining of "bottle poppings." Pressure escapes from the tightly closed lids without causing them to unscrew. When Gaither and I tightened the cover mechanically, we succeeded in exploding a bottle of relatively thin glass, but the cap remained on the broken neck. This had never been observed in connection with the bottles that lost their caps in the Herrmann household. When we used a bleach bottle of the type which had lost its cap when we were in the house, and when we tightened the cover mechanically, the buildup of pressure inside the bottle produced neither explosion nor unscrewing of the cap. In general, it became clear that pressure does not cause these types of caps to unscrew and come completely off. Either the gas escapes around the threads or the bottle explodes, the cap remaining in place. We found it made no difference if we oiled the threads of the glass.

For inexplicable reasons, this March 10 bottle popping was the last act of the Seaford "poltergeist," if, indeed, that is what it was. There had been a total of sixty-seven recorded disturbances between February 3 and March 10, a period of just thirty-five days. Incredibly, the Herrmanns had been visited by detectives, building inspectors, electricians, firemen, plumbers, parapsychologists, and various other "experts." None had offered a satisfactory explanation of what had happened.

Weeks after the house returned to normal, the family was still receiving requests from persons eager to "study" the house and interpret the "phenomena."

One physicist even charted "fields" that he believed were caused by water under the house. This, he said, was caused by a recharge basin, or sump, a mile away. The sump had been recently coated by thick ice. He thought that powerful vibrations caused by airplanes overhead might have jolted the ice so that shock waves were transmitted by underground water faults in such a fashion as to strike beneath the Herrmann house.

But the family no longer cared for any more investigations. James Herrmann said it didn't matter to him what moved the furniture and caused bottles to pop their tops in his home. And, as late as August 1958, the Duke parapsychologists were at a loss to explain the strange goings-on.

Mrs. Herrmann seemed to accept the events with amazing equanimity. She told Associated Press writer Joy Miller, "I don't think there is any definite solution. It was just one of those things with no rhyme or reason to it. But there was a definite physical force behind it."

Ordinary people. Extraordinary events. Pray they don't happen to you.

Three Men and a Ghost

Owen Jackson, Raymond Beck, and Sam Townsend are all employees at the North Carolina State Capitol, Raleigh. Jackson is a night watchman, Beck is a historical specialist at the Capitol, and Townsend oversees operations of the Capitol and Visitors Center.

Although their jobs are vastly different and they rarely see one another outside their workplace, they do have one thing in common—they all know the ghosts in the Old North State's Capitol.

Because he is most often in the building at night, Owen Jackson hears the ghost's nocturnal ramblings as he walks his rounds or sits at the reception desk near the visitors' entrance in the east corridor of the main floor. It was at that desk one night that . . .

A woman screamed.

Jackson remained at his post. "If she'd needed me, she woulda screamed again," he reasons. Jackson has no idea who cried out, nor did the thought of phantom screeches seem all that unusual to him given the myriad, peculiar noises associated with the Capitol.

Jackson, a silver-haired man well over six feet tall, has never *seen* a Capitol ghost, but he does hear them—loud and clear because of the superior acoustics in the 1840 Greek Revival building. A retired farmer, he has heard the unexplainable sounds since he first started to work at the Capitol more than fifteen years ago.

Jackson hears books fall to the floor, but never finds any missing from the shelves. Sometimes a door slams behind him, but when he turns to look the door is locked, just as he'd left it a moment earlier. No one is in sight. Nor should there be. The building is locked.

And the manually operated elevator often lumbers from floor to floor by itself, stopping to open its doors as if to let out some ethereal passenger.

The old building is one of the smallest and best preserved of the nation's state capitols. The granite halls and many of the furnishings look much the way they did upon completion 150 years ago. Outside, ancient oaks and elms shade the statues of such illustrious native sons as former presidents Andrew Jackson, James Knox Polk, and Andrew Johnson.

The Capitol building, however, is no longer the seat of government. In 1961 the legislature moved into a new state governmental complex two blocks away. Only the governor and the secretary of state maintain offices in the Capitol. The second and third floors are administered as a historic site by the State Division of Archives and History.

Jackson is aware that a few officials may stop in to finish work at night, but he knows who they are and the hours they keep.

One night the watchman heard a window break on the second floor. He grabbed a broom and hurried upstairs to sweep up the pile of glass. He needn't have bothered. Nothing was disturbed.

On another evening, Jackson was at his usual post, seated at the reception desk on the first floor. He had an unobstructed view of the small rotunda, highlighted in the center by a statue of George Washington. He could also keep an eye on the east entrance. A stairway to Jackson's right was partially concealed from his view. Suddenly, he felt the pressure of a hand on his shoulder. He swung around in his seat. No one stood behind him.

Then there was the night when a fierce wind seemed to roar through the building. Jackson said he heard the wind outside too and thought the branches would be torn from the century-old trees. When he looked, however, not a leaf or branch was stirring. Thirty seconds later, a strange calm descended. "If you'd been stone deaf, it couldn't have got no quieter," he said. "I knew it was a haint."

Although Jackson says he's never afraid at work, he admits, "It don't make you feel good if you hear something and can't make it out."

The tales go on and on. A daytime guard says the ghost never comes around when other people are present. He also knows that *he* has nothing to fear. "I'm a musician," he said, "and ghosts never bother musicians." He doesn't elaborate on this most peculiar assertion.

Raymond Beck, the curator of the Capitol and a history museum specialist with the North Carolina Division of Archives and History, used to kid with Jackson about the strange noises in the building. The joking stopped, though, in the early spring of 1981 when Beck decided to work late. He wanted to catch up on some restoration work he was doing in the state library on the third floor. He told Jackson to be sure to let him know if anything was headed up the stairs to "get him." Jackson grinned. So did Beck—but not for long.

The lights were on and a radio played softly as Beck bent over the papers on his desk. Sometime between ten o'clock and midnight, he got up to replace some books on the shelves. And stood stock-still.

"It was the feeling of someone looking over my shoulder and not saying anything," he remembered. Beck closed up shop and left. He says it's the only time he has ever felt uncomfortable in the building.

Five months later while Beck was talking to his superior, Sam P. Townsend Sr., the latter remarked that he'd had a very strange experience in the library the previous night.

"He told me basically the same experience that I had had up there," Beck said. "Totally independent corroboration of what I'd experienced." Neither man knew what to make of the incident. But Sam Townsend didn't need much convincing that something odd was going on. He already had three puzzling experiences.

Townsend is a large, imposing man with a friendly face and outgoing manner. He has lived in the Raleigh area for fifty years. Trained as an engineer, he always seeks scientific explanations for everything. His official title is Administrator, State Capitol and Capital Area Visitors Center. He defines his job as "restoring, preserving, and interpreting the Capitol." To this end, he and eleven assistants organize a variety of educational events and prepare audio-visual programs relating to the Capitol and its history.

His job description does not include hobnobbing with ghosts. But at eight o'clock on a June night in 1976, Townsend began to wonder if he should not revise his list of duties. He was completing paperwork preparatory to the reopening of the Capitol building. It had been closed for a year for renovations.

The administrator was working in Gov. James E. Holshouser's office just inside and to the left of the south entrance. Suddenly, he heard keys rattling in the lock of the north door and he assumed that Secretary of State Thad Eure was coming in. Eure's office was by the north door, diagonally across from the governor's suite. It was not unusual for the secretary to return to his office of an evening.

Townsend heard the heavy door swing open and footsteps cross the stone floor. Looking forward to a brief visit with Eure, Townsend left the governor's office and crossed the rotunda to the secretary's door. He swung it open. Eure was not there.

As Townsend stood there, he heard keys rattling behind him at the south door. He turned around, but the door did not open. He went outside and conducted a fruitless search. Townsend said that all the doors except the north door were locked and bolted that night.

A year later, Townsend had his second encounter with unexplained phenomena in the North Carolina Capitol.

His permanent office is on the second floor of the building in the northeast corner of the old Senate Chamber. It was formerly the office of the Clerk of the Senate and still bears the black letters CLERK on the door. In the southwest corner is another door labeled COMMITTEE leading to a room that was basically unused in 1977. Townsend works in his office three nights a week because he says he can accomplish more during those hours without the ringing telephones and other interruptions of the daytime.

The Senate Chamber is an inviting place, radiating warmth and dignity. The mahogany desks and chairs, made by William Thompson of Raleigh in 1839 and 1840, are positioned on a sea of antique red carpeting decorated with gold stars, while overhead hangs a century-old chandelier.

While at work in his office one night in 1977, Townsend heard footsteps coming from the committee room and approaching his office door, which he'd left ajar. He thought Raymond Beck was coming over, got up to greet him and threw open the door. Neither Beck nor anyone else was in the hallway.

Townsend would hear the pacing several nights each week, always at about eight-thirty, over the next two or three years. But after a copying machine was moved into the committee room, the footsteps ceased. They were never heard again, even after the machine was removed from the room.

The burly administrator dismisses the idea that the steps were caused by heating or cooling systems, temperature changes or the age of the building. He said the footsteps were unmistakable. He lives in an old house himself, and thus is familiar with the creaks and groans of aged structures.

Townsend believes he may have glimpsed an actual ghost just once. He had just arrived one evening and started into the Senate Chamber to head for his office when he jumped back. Someone stood inside the door. A moment later, the figure vanished.

Townsend does not know who or what it was. He allows that the phenomenon could have been caused by outside floodlights shining through the windows, perhaps creating unusual reflections. Also, a black marble fireplace inside the doorway could have reproduced light in a pattern that resembled a person. Townsend isn't willing to give a definitive answer.

Of his four experiences, Sam Townsend says he is "most impressed and most perplexed by the rattling of the keys in the first-floor doors." He can find absolutely no explanation for the sound. He says he is definitely not a believer in the supernatural, but is "intrigued by unexplained phenomena."

Murders and suicides often precipitate the appearance of ghosts, but historian Raymond Beck can't account for any that have occurred in the Capitol. However, he did discover a letter from a state legislator, written in the late 1860s, referring to a murder that took place immediately *outside* the building.

Beck says there are also rumors of shots fired during an altercation between two nineteenth-century legislators. Further research could verify or lay to rest that particular legend.

Owen Jackson, meanwhile, has always believed that the ghosts are the spirits of politicians—Republicans checking up on Democrats and vice versa, with or without a shooting match!

Jackson's workday ends shortly after midnight. Although no watchman replaces him for the remainder of the night, he leaves the building in good hands. Passing the statue of President Washington on his way out the door, he says, "Let George do it."

Legends of the Plains

The State Historical Society of North Dakota is housed in the modern North Dakota Heritage Center on the capitol grounds in Bismarck. Before the Society moved there in 1981, it occupied the Liberty Memorial Building, also on the Capitol grounds.

The Liberty Memorial Building is of 1920s vintage, designed to house several state offices, including the supreme court and the state library as well as the historical society. According to former employees, however, more than books and artifacts dwelt in the old building. They say a mysterious, ghostly presence, nicknamed the "Stack Monster," also stalked its hallways.

If appearances count for anything, the historical society's former quarters certainly fostered ghostly legends. Museum exhibits spilled over several floors, while hundreds of items acquired since the nineteenth century gathered dust in maze-like, subbasement rooms. Prehistoric skeletal remains, pioneer memorabilia, bound newspapers, and even some state records were stored in the cramped quarters. The entire place was eerie. The only light came from bare light bulbs hanging from cobwebbed beams.

A former superintendent of the historical society, James Sperry, spent a considerable amount of time in the Liberty Memorial Building. Enough hours to wonder about two strange incidents he experienced during his years with the Society.

On a day in July 1972 Sperry was working late in his office on the second floor. It was about nine o'clock. A steady rain fell outside his windows. His collie/Lab mix dog, Shadow, snoozed at his feet.

Sperry got up to stretch his legs and wandered out of his office. He strolled down to the first floor where he found Frank Vyzralek, a society archivist, also working late. As they chatted, Shadow started to growl. Suddenly, she ran down the hall barking, then bounced down the steps leading to the basement storerooms. Within seconds she bolted back up the steps with her tail between her legs. Sperry and Vyzralek had no idea what Shadow saw or heard, or what scared her. They were quite sure they were alone in the building. But perhaps Shadow had seen or sensed something unsettling in the darkened basement.

On another occasion, Sperry alighted from the elevator in the basement. He saw a man in a white shirt walk back into a storage room. Though the light was dim, he thought it was a staff member and followed to find out who was down there. Sperry reached the room and turned on the light. He looked around. There was only the one doorway going into the room. It was impossible for anyone to have slipped past him. Yet the mysterious intruder had vanished.

Another witness to the Liberty Building's peculiarities was the archivist Frank Vyzralek. His experience that night with James Sperry was not the only time he worked late at night; he even came into the office on some holidays.

So it was that Vyzralek was in the old building late on New Year's Eve 1969. At about midnight, just before the turn of the new year, he was overwhelmed with the sensation that he should leave the building. "It was time to get out," he recalled thinking at the time. Though nothing untoward happened, he quickly shut off the lights and left.

Vyzralek's predecessor as archivist, Liess Vantine, swore he couldn't explain an incident in 1967. Vantine was working after regular hours with another employee, Craig Gannon. The other workers had left for the day. Liess was in the subbasement when he heard a voice he thought was Craig's: "Come here, Liess." Vantine wandered through the stacks and was surprised not to find his colleague nearby. Eventually, Vantine located Gannon several floors above, where he had been for over an hour. He had never called Vantine's name.

Walter Bailey, a historic preservation planner for the society, had an experience similar to Vyzralek's when he worked in the old building from 1973 until the move in 1981. On several occasions he would be overwhelmed with a sense that he should get out of the building. It was always at night and always when he was alone. Bailey described it as an urgent feeling, making him want to leave immediately, not ten minutes later. Nothing overt ever occurred; it was simply an understanding that he didn't belong in the building anymore—never any hostile force or a belief that he was actually in any physical danger. That he could see, anyway. And, Bailey said, the dread had nothing to do with the lateness of the hour (it usually transpired around midnight) or that he was usually alone. Bailey said he could be fully engrossed in a project when it happened. It was "like a bell going off in my head," he emphasized.

Bailey also heard occasional footfalls at night. Nothing similar occurred during the daytime because, as he recalled, the floors did not lend themselves to creaking or otherwise producing noises when they were walked upon by the crowd of daytime workers. When the footsteps were particularly distinctive at night, so that it seemed someone was in the building, Bailey always looked around for the interloper.

Without knowing it, Bailey may have produced a candidate for a nocturnal visitor. He said they seemed to come most often from the main floor, near the former society superintendent's office.

Russell Reid had been the Historical Society director for many years. As a bachelor, Reid devoted his personal and professional life to the Society. He often slept in his office. Could the spirit of such a committed civil servant have been responsible for the hauntings?

Or could it have been the former superintendent who startled Ron Warner late one night?

Warner, an administrative officer, returned to his office around eleven-forty-five after traveling out-of-town on Society business. As he entered the empty building, he heard someone cough. He stopped and listened and called out, "Who's there?" When no one answered, Warner looked around but all the office doors were locked and the lights turned off. He finally left, though he was always certain of what he had heard.

The so-called Stack Monster has not been heard from in the new Heritage Center. Maybe that's because Gloria Engel thinks the ghost left in the week before the move out of the old Liberty Memorial Building.

An administrative assistant, Engel was at her desk in the soon-to-be-vacated building. From her vantage point, she had a clear view of the large, heavy outside doors on the south side of the building. She was looking at the door when it very slowly opened, and then closed as if someone were going out. She saw no one near the door. Engel thought the Stack Monster left that day.

If the ghost, or whatever it is, decides to visit the new Heritage Center, it may encounter some difficulties. It will have to pass through a security system boasting the latest electronic equipment. All visitors and employees who enter the building must clear a security entrance and show special photo ID cards.

Fortunately, historians don't want to lose any part of the past, including historic monsters or ghosts. So, to make the move to the Heritage Center complete, the Stack Monster was reportedly issued its very own security badge. However, where the picture should be, there is only a gray background. Staff members want to make sure that the ghost feels welcome should it desire to check into some newer quarters.

The Writing Rock

On a high, windswept hill in the northwestern corner of North Dakota, a field-stone shelter protects two gray granite boulders whose chiseled patterns have defied translation and interpretation. This is the Writing Rock Historic Site, established in 1936 by the State Historical Society to preserve these ancient and mysterious stones.

The larger rock, a ten-ton slab, is five feet high and four feet thick, and covered with hieroglyphs. Such pictographic writing is common to peoples throughout the world who do not have a written language.

The writing, filling the top and two sides of the rock, consists of lines, dots, circles containing dots, and the mythological figure of the thunderbird. The inscriptions are believed to have been carved at different periods, and many hypotheses have been put forth to explain their origin. At various times the pictographs have been ascribed to travelers from lost continents, wandering Norsemen, or Asian explorers. But anthropologists and historians think that the prevalence of the thunderbird may indicate that the markings were made by the Late Prehistoric Plains Indians.

Many years ago excavations of graves in the area yielded hammers and hatchets, seashells, arrowheads, elk teeth, and beads of various shapes and colors. In one grave beads were found that measured fifty-two feet when strung.

The Writing Rock site has always held supernatural significance for many of the Assiniboine, Sioux, and Plains Chippewa. Of the numerous Indian legends associated with the rock, the one heard most often was that told by Joe Lagweise and Tawiyaka, of the Qu'Appelle Agency in Saskatchewan, Canada. When these two Sioux were young men, in the 1870s, they visited Writing Rock and heard the story from an old man camped there.

In the days of the ancients, the old man said, eight warriors stopped for the night near the rock. Just as they were drifting into sleep they heard someone calling in the distance. Fearful of an enemy attack, they got up and searched, but found nothing wrong. They settled down again and the air was calm and the night peaceful.

In the morning they heard the voice again. It was clear and light, a woman's voice. No one could be seen. But, in their search, the Indians found the large rock. To their amazement, their own likenesses were pictured on the granite slab. All eight of them were shown with their packs spread on the ground. The warriors, unable to understand this phenomenon, continued on their way.

On their return they passed the rock again and saw that the picture had changed. It now appeared to show a scene from the future. The men hurried home and told their people. Then the entire village packed up and moved closer to the rock. Upon their arrival, the Indians saw that the picture had changed again—now it showed the village with its tipis.

From that time on the rock was believed to foretell the future. But that power was lost after white settlers moved the smaller rock to a spring about a mile from its original resting place. Later, this boulder was taken to the University of North Dakota for study. In 1956 the shelter over the large boulder was erected, and in 1965 the smaller rock was returned.

Crazy Loon

Buttes reach skyward, casting long shadows toward evening on the rolling plateaus near Amidon in southwestern North Dakota. South of that village, on the west side of U.S. Highway 85, is Black Butte, eight miles in circumference, with rock cliffs near the summit rising a hundred feet above the grassy slopes. At the base lie huge boulders, torn from the sides of the mesa by the action of wind, ice, and snow. Berries grow on the north side of the butte, while on the south side a cave holds the winter's snows until midsummer. From the top of the butte a splendid view unfolds for those sturdy enough for the climb.

During the latter years of the nineteenth century, Black Butte was called H.T. Butte because it was part of the H.T. Ranch, the largest horse ranch in the state. In those days the surrounding countryside was devoted to the ranging of cattle, sheep, and horses. It was only after the homesteaders arrived and began cultivating the land that ranching was curtailed.

At any rate, the H.T. Ranch required a large number of expert cowhands. Among those employed was a wrangler named Bob Pierce who, because of his merciless riding, was nicknamed "Crazy Loon." He rode his mounts everywhere at breathless speeds. It was hard for his boss to keep him in horses.

On one occasion, Pierce was teamed on the circuit with old Colonel Sullers.

As the two set forth, the talkative colonel launched into a political discussion and pretended not to notice that his companion was spurring his horse to breakneck speeds. Sullers kept abreast, however, delivering what amounted to a monologue until his horse stepped into a hole and sent him flying.

Fortunately the old man's injuries were not serious. Cut and bruised, he limped to a nearby stream where he washed the dirt and blood from his head and face. Pierce turned back to join him.

The unhappy Colonel Sullers blamed Pierce for his injuries. "When you're dead," he said, shaking his finger at his younger companion, "your ghost will ride the top of the hills and howl like a gray wolf."

Bob Pierce subsequently died, killed perhaps on one of his wild rides. After his death a horseman was often seen on dark nights, galloping up the steep sides of Black Butte. Sometimes to the chilling howl of the gray wolf.

Holy Hills

Some three miles southwest of Cannon Ball, a small village south of Bismarck on the Missouri River, is a landmark known by the interesting name of Holy Hill. Just when or how the place was given its name is not known, but it was a place of spiritual significance to Native Americans.

A Sioux man named Joe Huff told one of the stories about Holy Hill:

In 1913, Huff was in Cannon Ball ready to return home when an elderly Sioux, Eagle Staff, asked Huff to go with him to his house for an overnight visit. Huff agreed and climbed in the wagon next to Eagle Staff for the journey to his log home.

Once arrived, they talked until late in the night. At last, Eagle Staff said, "Have you ever heard the spirits working on Holy Hill?"

"No," Huff replied.

"This is the month for the spirits to work," Eagle Staff explained, "but as they do not work every night I do not know if they will work tonight; if they do I will knock on your window and you can get up to hear them."

Huff went to bed and fell asleep. Soon, however, a knock at his window awakened him. Eagle Staff was there.

"Listen, the spirits are working," he said to Huff, who had dressed and gone outside.

Holy Hill was nearly a mile to the southwest, but Huff heard a clicking as if two rocks were being struck together. *Click, click, click, click*. And then a few seconds of silence until it would start up again.

Huff wanted to ride over to Holy Hill to investigate, but Eagle Staff said it would be useless.

"The spirits will leave as soon as you arrive. But if you have a good ear, get down on the ground and listen," Eagle Staff said.

Huff did as he was bidden. The clicks were even more clear when Huff placed his ear to the ground. It was like that for two miles around, Eagle Staff said. At ground level the clicks seemed to come from directly beneath, but when Huff stood again they drifted through the air from the direction of Holy Hill.

Eagle Staff had heard the mysterious noises since at least 1907. The clicks stopped in about 1923. Eagle Staff thought the spirits of Holy Hill were frightened away by the white people and their radios. What other explanation could there be?

The Deadly Wedding Gown

Could it be true that a North Dakota woman died because her sister's vengeful spirit returned on the woman's wedding day? Or, as the attending physician speculated, was embalming fluid the deadly agent? Either way, the story is extraordinary because it details a set of real events for an oft-told legend—a wedding gown that causes death for its owner.

There are two young women in this story, Lorna Mae Eberle and her sister, Carol. They lived in a small North Dakota town in the 1930s.

Lorna Mae was the younger of the two, with a cheerful disposition and extraordinary physical strength, a good prospect for one of the young farmers in the neighborhood. She was worth any two hired men, it was said, and certainly proved that on her family farm, which she ran virtually single-handed.

The older sister, Carol, was quite the opposite. Although prettier than Lorna Mae, she was sullen in her outlook on life and lazy around the house. The sisters shared the home with their father, an elderly farmer who usually gave in to Carol's petty demands. Mr. Eberle's wife, the girls' mother, had died in a tragic fire.

Carol Eberle may have lacked a pleasing personality, but she made up for that in being extremely strong-willed. What she demanded, she usually received.

But that did not extend to the man she most desired to marry.

His name was Ben Berg, a widower with three small children on a farm not far from the Eberles. Ben asked Lorna Mae to be his wife, as much for her ability to work side by side with him on the farm as anything else.

Carol was livid. She was far prettier than Lorna Mae, she told anyone who would listen, and so what if she wasn't a draft horse like her sister? Ben ought to be satisfied with marrying the loveliest girl in the entire county, she insisted.

Shortly before the wedding was to take place, however, Lorna Mae developed serious abdominal pains. Sister Carol was sent to fetch the doctor. Gossip had it that she dawdled in town before returning to the farm without the physician. She made vague comments about not being able to find the doctor. Lorna Mae was near death when Carol finally bundled her into a buckboard wagon and set off for the doctor's office. Lorna Mae Eberle died of a ruptured appendix soon after reaching town.

Carol saw the events as almost providential. She set about to make Ben Berg her husband, and to hell with common decency. At Lorna Mae's funeral, before the open casket bearing her dead sister in the wedding gown she had planned to marry in, Carol pleaded with Ben to marry her.

He was as aghast as the Eberle relatives who overheard the insensitive remarks. He put her off as best he could, saying it was far too early for him to think of a future without Lorna Mae.

The funeral services had ended and family and friends made their way out of the small church when Carol made her next move. She told the undertaker to remove Lorna Mae's wedding gown. Despite her father's outrage, she got her way.

"She won't have use for it in the earth," Carol sniffed. "A shroud will do as well."

And so it was that Lorna Mae Eberle went to her grave wrapped not in her beloved wedding dress but in a simple pauper's shroud.

A month later Ben Berg gave in to Carol's persistent courting and agreed to marry her.

The wedding day was scheduled for a Sunday in mid-July. Guests sweltered in the one-hundred-degree heat, shifting uncomfortably in their wool suits. The soon-to-be Mrs. Carol Eberle Berg looked radiant in Lorna Mae's wedding dress. But suddenly she started to waver, clutching at her throat and gasping for air. She collapsed and died in Ben's arms, her tongue protruding from her mouth.

An autopsy failed to provide a cause for death. Heatstroke was ruled out, as was any other natural cause. What the doctor did offer as the reason for Carol's death, however, was hard for most of the townspeople to accept. He said that the high-necked wedding gown had absorbed some of the embalming fluid used for Lorna! The gown had been on Lorna Mae's body for three days before Carol removed it. Somehow, the doctor said, Carol's profuse sweating during the wedding ceremony had caused her pores to open too far and the deadly fluid to enter her body.

What most people believed, though, was that Lorna Mae's spirit had returned to strike down her evil sister. A ghost's revenge can be swift . . . and deadly.

The Return of President Garfield

The three-story Greek Revival house straddles a hill overlooking Garfield Road at the edge of Hiram, Ohio. Its narrow clapboards are painted a subdued red, and the large, old-fashioned windows are framed by wide white shutters. A handsome vine wreath on the door welcomes visitors. It's the kind of place you'd like to come home to.

That's what Bruno and Dorothy Mallone thought when they bought the house in 1961 and moved it to its present location. For 125 years it had stood on the campus of Hiram College, but was scheduled to be torn down to make room for a new dormitory. Now, on a lot filled with flowering shrubs and trees and a low, rock-walled terrace, the house looks as if it had always been there.

Although they didn't know it at the time, the Mallones had bought a house haunted by the ghosts of earlier residents, including President James Garfield, who go about their tasks unmindful of the living occupants.

Pam Mallone, the couple's daughter, who lives with her parents, began researching the history of the house. She found some fascinating information.

The house was built in 1836 and turned into a boardinghouse that same year for faculty members of the college, which was known, until 1867, as Western Reserve Eclectic Institute.

James Garfield was the twentieth president of the United States and in his first year of office when he became the second president to be assassinated. He studied at the institute from 1851 to 1854. Two years later, with a degree from Williams College, he returned to Hiram as a teacher and principal. He moved into the boardinghouse at that time and the following year was named president of the school.

In 1856, Garfield married Lucretia, whom he called Crete. She was a frail, religious woman, and the marriage was not a happy one. The couple lived in the house until 1861, when Garfield went off to fight in the Civil War. His wife returned to her parents' home.

The house had several owners until 1907, when Marcia Henry, a professor of English, Latin, and Greek, bought it. Her father, Charles, had been a close friend of the Garfields, and the two families established warm ties that lasted until

Garfield's assassination on September 19, 1881, two months short of his fiftieth birthday.

When Marcia Henry died in 1958, she willed the house to Hiram College with the stipulation that her nephew, Charles A. Henry, could live in it. He chose not to and turned it over to the college. Old-timers still refer to the house as the "Henry Place."

Right after the Mallones moved in, Dorothy's relatives came to visit. On the first evening, they all gathered in the living room, and the conversation turned to the history of the old house. Dorothy had mentioned earlier that President Garfield had once lived there.

Someone asked if the house was haunted.

"Of course it is," Dorothy joked. "Every once in a while James walks around."

At that moment, the light in an adjoining room blinked on.

That was just the beginning of the Mallones' personal journey into the unknown.

For the first three or four years, it was only the dining room light that perplexed the family. It came on by itself, often when they were leaving the house. If someone returned to turn the light off, it would be on again before the car cleared the driveway. Although the house had been rewired when the Mallones moved in, Bruno called an electrician to check the light. He found nothing wrong.

The problem was solved one night after Dorothy's bridge club met at the house. She was cleaning up in the kitchen when the light came on. She went into the room and turned it off. When she got back to the kitchen the light flipped on again. After the fourth time, Dorothy had had it.

"That's just about enough of that!" she yelled. Whatever it was got the hint. The dining room light works perfectly now.

Unfortunately, the living room light next took on a mind of its own. Since then every light in the house, with the exception of the dining room lamp, may be found on. The Mallones never know how their house will be lit up day or night.

A young man from Dorothy's church youth group experienced the lighting phenomenon. He had come over to talk about a program they were planning. The two of them sat on a sofa when suddenly the light above them went off. Dorothy apologized, saying it must be a loose bulb or loose switch.

"No," the young man said uneasily. "I can feel a presence here."

At that time no one outside the family knew of the manifestations in the house.

Only once was Dorothy frightened by the erratic behavior of the lights. At three-twenty one morning, one of the lamps on the dresser in the master bedroom came on. It wasn't plugged in! The bright light awakened the couple. Bruno took it in stride.

"Just go back to sleep," he yawned as he glanced at the bedside clock.

Bruno did. Dorothy did not.

The next night the other dresser-top lamp turned on at precisely the same hour.

While the family ate breakfast one morning, the overhead light snapped on. Dorothy glanced at the wall clock. It had stopped at precisely three-twenty. So had her watch.

Pam Mallone's historical research had failed to uncover anything significant that might have occurred in the house at that time of day. She did learn, however, that the Garfields' first child had died there, but the time was not known.

When the Mallones' dogs slept in the kitchen they'd bark sometimes early in the morning. Whenever Dorothy went downstairs she'd find them growling at the back door. After a while they would quiet down and go back to sleep.

The family's problems with utilities soon included the water system. Faucets would be found running.

"It would be the faucet maybe in the downstairs bathroom," Dorothy notes. "We'd turn it off. We'd be downstairs and hear water running upstairs and have to go up and turn that one off."

Then there is the sudden cooling of the house.

Dorothy remembers a particularly hot summer day with the thermometer hovering near 95 degrees. The Mallones came home to a freezing kitchen and dining room. Tippy, their dog, refused to go in either room. Eventually the rooms warmed, but not before Bruno and Dorothy wondered if what psychics said was true, that a cold room is often a harbinger of a ghost.

The Mallones have also had some encounters with poltergeist-type activities—objects moving with no one near them. The family once watched a candlestick fly off the mantel. The candle landed in the middle of the living room floor and then leaped onto the love seat.

Burning candles have sometimes exploded, spattering hot wax on the wallpaper, curtains, and windows.

After an area newspaper published an account of the apparent haunting, two young couples came to visit. Before leaving, someone complained, "Isn't anything going to happen?"

"Do you want to contact us?" Pam Mallone asked aloud.

Suddenly the candle snuffer leaped from the mantel and flew halfway across the room. The guests fled.

A young fellow visiting the Mallones brought a cigar and put it behind candlesticks to see if anything would happen. Nothing did. Eighteen months later the family was sitting in the dining room when they heard the rattle of cellophane. They found the cigar completely unwrapped and lying a third of the way across the living room floor.

Garfield was fond of smoking cigars. Pam has often smelled the odor of cigar smoke so strong that her eyes watered and she coughed. None of the Mallones smokes.

Soon after a repairman replaced the pump on the family's automatic washer, Dorothy discovered that it wasn't working properly. The repairman returned and tipped the machine. The screws he had soldered to hold the pump in place were all standing upright on the floor. He told the Mallones that in twenty-five years of repairing washing machines he had never seen such a thing. On another occasion they found the washer moved partway across the basement floor.

Bruno Mallone, a schoolteacher, was skeptical of these phenomena until he had a few experiences of his own.

One afternoon he was alone in the house watching a Sunday afternoon football game on the living room television set. He had set a glass of ginger ale on the sewing machine beside his chair. When he turned to pick up the glass, it scooted several inches. He reached again, but the glass skipped across the surface and fell to the floor. He hadn't touched it.

While grading papers of an evening, he heard music coming from the living room—the family's melodeon, to be precise. But everyone else was out of the house. He got up, checked the room but saw no one. He recalls that there was a slight wind that night, but not strong enough to cause any peculiar sounds. He is certain of the music he heard.

Perhaps the strangest incident relates to a crossword puzzle that Bruno had started at school. Since he hadn't had time to finish it, he bought another copy of the newspaper on his way home as he left the original at work. He was too busy that night to complete the puzzle. In the morning, when he opened the paper, the puzzle had been completed! And it was not in Bruno's handwriting.

Neither his wife nor his daughter claimed to have touched the paper. Bruno took it back to the drugstore where he had bought it, but none of the clerks could explain the mystery.

As the Mallones studied the crossword, they saw that each of the e's resembled a backward 3. Pam recalled that she had once seen President Garfield's diary. His e's were identical to those on the completed puzzle.

The number of visitors to the house increased after television crews filmed the house and interviewed the family. Guests have varied reactions—some are anxious and ill at ease while others are comfortable, if curious. At a party of young people one night, a young lady paled and began shaking. She screamed that something was standing behind her.

"Well, if there's something here," Dorothy began, "why don't we try the Ouija board?" The girl and a friend sat in front of the fireplace, knees touching and the board between them on their laps. Neither girl knew anything about Garfield.

Dorothy asked if they knew the name of Garfield's wife. They didn't and neither did Pam at that time. "It just happened so fast," Dorothy explains. "It spelled C-R-E-T-E and that's what Garfield always called her." The guests were astonished.

In 1979 Connecticut psychics Lorraine and Ed Warren lectured at nearby Hiram College. They later toured the Mallone home.

The Warrens knew nothing of its history, yet found the place filled with good ghosts.

Mrs. Warren, going into a light trance, saw a fragile woman in a long, flowing dress. She had respiratory problems and moved slowly through the house. She felt that the woman and her husband were somewhat withdrawn from each other. In the living room she sensed an empty cradle near the fireplace.

In the master bedroom Mrs. Warren felt a strong, domineering woman with a "masculine face."

The Mallones revealed that the house had been lived in by James Garfield and his wife and that their first child had died in the house. Pam Mallone had already seen some of the first lady's clothes in a museum and knew that she was a tiny woman. She had also read that Mrs. Garfield had had a serious breathing problem that may have accounted for her aloofness and her refusal to attend college functions.

Dorothy concluded, therefore, that the strong, domineering woman had to be Almeda Booth, a student and later professor at the college. Almeda lived in the boardinghouse when Garfield was first there.

She may have been in love with the future president, although there is no evidence that he returned her affection. Curiously, after James and Lucretia were married, Almeda and the Garfields were often seen together.

The Warrens suggested that the family try to communicate with the spirits by periodically tape-recording activities in the house. They did, and sometimes when they play back the tapes they hear chimes and the pinging of glass, sounds that weren't apparent as the family went about its business.

And voices.

When the house was filled with visitors and a tape was running, Pam noticed that one of the dogs was agitated. The animal was in heat and Pam feared it might urinate on the carpeting. She shook her finger and said, "No, no, no." The dog lay down. When they played back the tape, there was a lot of pounding and knocking followed by a man's deep voice commanding "No, no, no."

Dorothy also heard the male voice just as her daughter entered a room. "Did you hear that, Pam?"

Pam said, "Yes, what did he say?"

The man's voice echoed, "Yes, what did he say?"

When the Mallones' son, John, came home from the marines, he, like his father, was skeptical of the incidents. Once when the tape was running in a roomful of people, the young man said he wasn't going to sit there and ask silly questions. Everyone kept silent while the tape ran. When they played it back, they heard the voices of a man and a woman speaking gibberish. Or perhaps, Dorothy said, it was a foreign language they didn't understand.

Pam said she took the tape to the language laboratory at the college. One professor started listening, then called in his colleagues. According to Pam, the linguists determined that there was a mixture of languages on the tape; some words were spoken in Spanish; others in Hungarian and Russian.

Another time the Mallones recorded the voices of a man and a woman in a language they'd never heard. Bruno took the tape to the college and learned that the couple spoke Greek and were discussing where and how to hang a picture. Garfield was fluent in Greek.

Dozens of people have heard these tapes, the Mallones say. But, they claim the voices faded for some reason after about a year.

Pam's room seems to be the center of a lot of activity. This is the same room

Garfield and his wife had lived in. Once when Pam tried to nap the light above her bed went on and the floor register rattled as it always does when someone walks over it. She heard footsteps but could see no one, although, she says, she felt a man's presence. Then the light went off.

The young woman found all the pictures taken off a wall of her room and placed on the floor. A broken cuckoo clock started running.

Pam has actually seen only one apparition. In the middle of the night she awoke shivering. A woman suddenly appeared and tucked a blanket that had been at the bottom of the bed around her. Pam said "thank you" and the figure left. Not quite sure if she had been dreaming or if perhaps her mother had been in her room, Pam asked Dorothy about the incident. Her mother said she had been sleeping. Later, Pam found an old photograph album containing faculty pictures. She recognized a picture of Marcia Henry, the previous owner of the house, as her benefactor that night.

Dorothy Mallone has also seen a ghost in the house—a tall man who entered the master bedroom early one morning. Dorothy saw him in the gloom as he came through the doorway and thought he was Bruno. He walked to the window and stood gazing out.

"Well, are you going to get back in bed or aren't you?" Dorothy asked. She got up but quickly realized that her husband had left for school. The figure at the window was gone.

Dorothy and Pam Mallone were not frightened by the ghosts.

Psychic Leta Berecek visited the house and experimented with automatic writing in an effort to learn something about the ghosts. Holding a pen in one hand and shutting her eyes, she let the pen move by itself. A woman's small, neat handwriting appeared first. She wrote about "Andrew," a sickly child who used to come and visit. He liked to work jigsaw puzzles, but after they were completed he was afraid to take them apart. He always wore a scarf in the house because he was so cold.

The handwriting quickly changed.

"I am Andrew," the words said. He represented a large group of spirits who knew they were dead, but enjoyed the house nevertheless. He promised they'd leave if the Mallones didn't want them around. He wished the family would light more candles and that Pam would string popcorn and cranberries on the Christmas tree. He liked that. Leta never learned Andrew's last name, nor precisely who he was.

Years after Andrew wrote his messages, Pam made garlands for the first time. As she worked, a string of lights blinked on the tree. When she hung the last string of popcorn around the bottom of the trees the lights stopped blinking. Now Pam decorates the tree every year with popcorn and berries, and the lights always glow steadily.

Leta Berecek held several sessions at the house. A candle once flared when she was writing. The flame widened to several inches in diameter and shot a foot or more into the air.

Leta then switched the pen to her left hand.

"I am James Garfield," came the words on the paper. "If you need proof, look at the candle. I am unhappy because so-called friends had me murdered." He didn't elaborate on his accusations. Garfield was left-handed. Leta Berecek is not.

A schoolteacher friend of Bruno's visited near Christmas one year and brought a woman psychic with her. As the psychic sat by the tree, the angel on top began spinning. She also said a young boy and girl had just run past her into the hall.

Do the ghosts of James and Lucretia Garfield, Marcia Henry and "Andrew" haunt this lovely home? Before she died, Mrs. Henry promised her nephew that she'd come back.

Are there other, unknown entities enjoying eternity with the Mallones?

Bruno, Dorothy, and Pam Mallone know only that something comes and goes at will. The front door opens by itself, and the family has always wondered how it does that since the doorknob doesn't work and the door can only be opened by a Yale lock. Sometimes neighbors have found it opened when the Mallones are gone.

Then one night in May 1986 the three were all in the front room. The door was locked. They heard a click, glanced toward the door and watched wide-eyed as it swung open.

"I don't know that night if 'they' came in or went out," Dorothy says matter-of-factly. "We just sort of joke with them and don't think too much about it."

The ghosts in this Ohio home have a very understanding and sympathetic family to call their own.

The Keeper of the House

Waynesville is a quiet village nestled on a hillside overlooking the Little Miami River valley. Platted in 1796 and incorporated in 1797, it is older than the state of Ohio. The 1,800 residents cherish their fine historic homes, perhaps none more than Doug and Pam Campbell.

In 1984 the Campbells bought the only brick Federal-style house in town. With its two stories and spacious grounds, their new home would be the perfect place for a growing family. The Campbells have two sons—Douglas Junior, then twelve, and Chad, who was six.

Douglas is an industrial designer with the United States Air Force at Gentile Air Force Station in Kettering, Ohio, and Pamela is a marketing communications manager for a company in Wilmington, sixteen miles east of Waynesville.

The family moved into their new home on August 4, 1984, a Saturday. Within a few days, they began wondering what was going on in their wonderful old home. Some examples:

- Pam's blue shoes disappeared. They turned up later in a guest bedroom, which she had cleaned in the interim.
- An alarm clock was found in the cookie jar.
- Pam discovered her colander balanced atop a canning jar which rested on top of a kitchen cupboard.

Little things. Funny things. At first, Pam and Doug blamed their sons for these pranks until it became evident that the boys were not at fault.

But those small annoyances were just the beginning.

On a hot summer afternoon the family decided to go swimming. However, one of the boys could not find his blue swimming trunks. Pam and Doug turned the boys' room upside down, removing drawers from chests, searching closets, going through all the clutter that youngsters accumulate in an amazingly short time. Finally, they all gave up and left the house. When they returned, the swim trunks were in plain sight, stretched out flat on top of a chest in the boys' room.

On an evening not long after, the Campbells went shopping for plants and garden tools. While at the store, Pam bought a beautiful outdoor lamp to replace an old one mounted on the side of the house. Later that evening Doug removed the old lamp and installed the new one. However, in the basement Doug discovered that the old lamp had been connected to a piece of frayed, cracked, and cloth-coated wire that went up through the insulation in the walls of the house. All of this old wiring was supposed to have been replaced, but this piece had somehow been overlooked.

"It was only a matter of time before we would have had a fire." Pam said.

Despite these minor irritations, the Campbells noticed that they were becoming comfortable and secure in the house. Pam said that this sense of belonging was one they'd never felt in previous houses they'd lived in.

"It's like someone is telling us how to take care of the house, how to fix it, how to make everything right," Doug added. "We feel protected."

In American small towns, acquaintances are made readily and friendships may bloom. It wasn't long before the Campbells met town historian Dennis "Denny" Dalton and questioned him about the house.

He told them their house was built in 1860 by industrious Quaker farmers, Emmor and Mary Satterthwaite Baily. The house soon became a popular overnight stop for drivers freighting goods on the stagecoach road that ran past their house, the main route between Cincinnati and Columbus. Fresh horses were available, and the drivers slept in an unheated room above the kitchen.

The energetic Mary Baily served rib-sticking meals to the wagoners, but she didn't limit herself to the teamsters. She soon became a prominent hostess in Waynesville society and was often assisted in her party-giving by her widowed mother, Elizabeth Linton Satterthwaite. In 1864, Mrs. Satterthwaite moved in with her daughter and son-in-law, leaving her son Abel and his wife to operate the Satterthwaite homestead nearby. Mrs. Satterthwaite found her daughter's home more beautiful than her own, and came to think of it as hers.

The Campbells were fascinated by this story, and Dennis Dalton later gave them a book detailing much more of the history of the house.

Meanwhile, the oddities inside the house continued.

One of the most peculiar incidents involved a set of soccer cards. Doug coaches a club team and, in order to play, each child must have a card with his picture and age on it. The cards are kept by the coach and are presented to the officials at each game. Without the cards the game can't be played.

One April day while Pam was out of town on a business trip, Douglas went to the bedroom to get the set of cards from the pegboard where he kept them. They weren't there. His sons said they didn't know what had happened to them.

Doug called his wife, but Pam wasn't of any more help.

"He . . . just tore the house apart looking for them," Pam recalled. "It was Thursday and that's garbage day. But he wouldn't even put out the garbage. He sorted through it all looking for those cards. I tried to reassure him over the phone that anything that's missing always turns up somewhere. It's just a matter of time."

But Doug didn't have the time.

On Sunday he called his wife again. "I found the cards," he cried. "They were under the mattress of our bed!"

And why had he thought to look there?

"Well, the whole time Pam was gone I didn't make the bed. I was getting to the point where I was pulling drawers out, dumping stuff out, like you have to do when anything is missing," Doug explained. "You dump the drawers, fold everything neatly, and put it back in. It's spring housecleaning every month for us. So, the beds were the last thing. I just started lifting mattresses. And there they were."

At about the same time as the soccer cards incident, a flashlight seemed to sprout legs.

Pam bought Doug a very large flashlight after he had some late-night difficulties priming the water softener in the basement. It's hard to see into all the dark corners down there. The couple decided to keep the flashlight on a hook on the basement door where it would always be handy.

The very next night the flashlight appeared on the stovetop with the light on, pointing at the side door. Pam just shakes her head thinking about the roving light.

Then the disturbances began. Disembodied voices broke the stillness of the night. Doors opened and closed by themselves. And footsteps crossed the bare, polished floors.

"One night at about eleven-thirty when we were in bed," Pam began, "Doug turned to me and said he heard noises." She turned his concern aside and replied, jokingly, "Yes, I know. There's a meeting going on in the dining room. Don't worry about it. Just go to sleep."

During the 1950s, owners John K. and Helen Preston christened their home "Far Hills Party House," opening it up to meetings of various area organizations. Mrs. Preston also catered wedding receptions, and hired local cooks to help. Groups moved constantly in and out of the house.

Recalling this early history, Pam said, "So many people have passed through this house over the years you start to wonder if some stayed on."

There are other sounds after dark. Pam has heard a baby cry in the guest bedroom. In talking to relatives of Emmor Baily, she learned that it was the birthing room, and was also used as a sickroom because it could be kept warm; it's the only bedroom with a working fireplace. It was also Elizabeth Satterthwaite's room. She died there on December 25, 1871, at the age of eighty-five.

The Campbells did not speak to anyone about the strangeness of the house. They would soon learn that they were not alone in believing that there was something wrong with it.

In the summer of 1985, while the family was vacationing, historian Denny Dalton house-sat for them. He will never forget his introduction to the house's keeper.

"That first day," Dalton began, "I went upstairs to the guest bedroom with my clothes and things I'd need for two weeks. The bedspread was turned down. I thought that was a little extra touch of hospitality, which certainly endeared me to the family. I hadn't known them well at the time."

Dalton unpacked and later went to supper with his mother. He watched a little television and read until shortly after midnight.

"I went upstairs to go to bed. When I turned on the light, I saw that the bed had been remade! There was nobody in that house but me. I had the only key other than the one the Campbells carried."

Pam later told Dalton that turning the bed down was a little quirk of hers, something she liked to do to make people feel comfortable. But when he told her the bedcovers had been pulled up tight a few hours later, she shared his astonishment.

Such a "spooky" house should attract trick-or-treaters on Halloween, at least the braver ones, but children shun it. "It's really disappointing," Pam said. "No one will come here."

Her own sons have a hard time persuading their friends to come for visits. "They'll come inside," Doug said, "but they don't want to stay."

At one time young Chad didn't want to stay either. On a bitterly cold winter day in 1987 when he was nine years old, he went into his parents' upstairs studio, looking for a pencil. The room was unheated.

Suddenly, a voice came out of nowhere.

"Don't you want to get warm?" it asked.

Chad flew down the stairs.

By 1988 rumors had spread beyond Waynesville about the Baily-Campbell house. On October 24, 1988, Denny Dalton called Pam at work. Would she and Doug allow WKRC-TV, Channel 12, to come up from Cincinnati to interview them?

Pam agreed.

Dalton called back to say that they were bringing a forensic psychic along, a woman who worked with the Cincinnati police. Pam started to have doubts, fearing in part her husband's reaction to a psychic.

That night Pam and Denny Dalton told Doug about the plans.

"I got a funny feeling," Doug said. "I didn't want this to be a carnival side-show . . . and I got very defensive. I did not want this psychic telling me there's an evil presence in my house, because there's not."

Doug finally agreed, partly because curiosity got the better of him.

"I thought more about the feeling we've always had that something is watching over us, telling us how to take care of the house. I just *had* to know what was here."

Two days later, on October 26, 1988, George Ciccarone and a crew from the television station arrived. They were accompanied by professional psychic Judy Schleutker.

Mrs. Schleutker found a lot of "activity" in both the dining room and the den. She said that as soon as she walked into the house she caught a psychic glimpse of "a small, elderly lady." The Campbells showed her various old pictures. When they found a photograph of Elizabeth Satterthwaite, Mrs. Schleutker sat at the dining room table to study it. Finally, she looked up. "This is the woman who haunts your house." She said the picture matched the figure she'd "seen" earlier.

The Cincinnati psychic went on to say that Mrs. Satterthwaite believed the house was still her home and that people have invaded it without paying attention to her. She hated being ignored, Mrs. Schleutker pronounced.

The psychic determined that Mrs. Satterthwaite was a good spirit, friendly and full of concern. She was a "people" person who loved to entertain, but on her own terms. And unlike most Quaker ladies of her time, she enjoyed fancy things, such as lace and flowers. Pam was impressed by that remark because she had decorated the guest bedroom in Victorian style with lots of lace and floral-patterned fabrics before she ever heard of Elizabeth Satterthwaite.

Judy Schleutker then moved into the central hall on the first floor. She sat on the stairway steps and beckoned sixteen-year-old Doug Junior to her side.

"Your little brother is afraid in his bedroom at night," Mrs. Schleutker announced. "But you should *not* fear Mrs. Satterthwaite. She stays in your bedroom to watch over you boys because she wants to protect you. She thinks you are her grandsons."

While WKRC filmed the conversation, she also said it had been Mrs. Satterthwaite who had spoken to Chad in the studio. The boy tried his best to feel relieved.

Mrs. Schleutker urged the boys to speak to the spirit. It would help the ghost materialize, she said. "She wants to be seen."

Eerily, the psychic also correctly noted that the spirit was in great physical pain. It is a historical fact that Mrs. Satterthwaite suffered from severe rheumatoid arthritis.

The television crew spent several hours in the house. The film was scheduled to be shown on Friday night, October 28. That was also the night of Denny Dalton's "Toast Your Ghost" walk.

Because there are a number of homes in the village alleged to be haunted, Dalton conducts an annual after-dark tour past these homes, telling their tales as he goes. It's always held near Halloween and is a fun event for the community. This year the ghost hunters would finish the evening with cookies and hot cider at the Campbells' and watch the television special.

Pam described the evening:

"We were having a nice party . . . gathered around the big dining room table. Suddenly, one of our guests screamed and rushed in from the den. She'd been in there warming up by the wood stove.

"The woman had reached up to the mantel to pick up one of the Shaker boxes I keep there. Her brother makes those types of boxes as a hobby. She wanted to see who had made mine. I had five boxes arranged in a row from smallest to largest. She put the box back on the mantel and looked away. In the next instant she looked back and the boxes were all mixed up.

"Everyone started laughing and telling me how clever I was to arrange such a really neat trick. I said it was *not* part of the entertainment. We crowded into the den to see how fast we could rearrange the boxes. It takes longer than forty-five seconds and it also makes too much noise.

"At eleven-twenty we watched the segment about our house. There was lots of excitement, then after it was over people started to leave. About a dozen of us women remained at the dining room table. All of a sudden, a woman yelled and pointed to the stairway. I swung around. A smoky gray triangular-shaped figure was moving slowly up the stairs. I knew *that* was our ghost. Mrs. Satterthwaite loved to entertain, but when the party was over she expected her guests to leave!"

Again her guests thought it was some sort of legerdemain. It definitely was not.

Pam felt vindicated when a guest said upon leaving, "I don't know how to explain this now. I know what I saw and I saw something go up those stairs."

The Baily-Campbell house was quiet, psychically speaking, throughout the holidays and the remainder of that year.

Then on the night of January 10, 1989, Doug and Pam were awakened by a bloodcurdling scream from eleven-year-old Chad. They rushed to his room. He had had a nightmare, but had calmed down and wasn't scared anymore. He told them Mrs. Satterthwaite was there. He didn't see her, but he did see a blue vest at the foot of his bed and knew a man was standing there. He sensed the presence of two other ghosts. Something had also pulled up the bedclothes and tucked him in.

A week later, sixteen-year-old Doug Junior came pounding into his parents' bedroom. He was determined not to sleep in his room ever again.

"I had just slammed my dresser drawer and *she* came up behind me and said *shhhh*. She's in there all the time, watching me and looking over my shoulder when I'm trying to do my homework," the teenager told his mother.

That said, the boys pulled an extra mattress into the master bedroom and slept on the floor. Their parents wanted them out. They weren't budging.

In desperation Doug and Pam decided to try an impromptu exorcism in their sons' bedroom. Feeling both foolish and hopeful, the couple walked around the room, speaking to Mrs. Satterthwaite as to a living person.

They told her that they realized she loved the boys, but that she was frightening them.

Would she please leave?

The boys were impressed. They moved back into their room and nothing more happened—not there or anywhere else for five months.

But it was not to be the end.

In June 1989, a dinner guest glanced out the window into the garden and giggled nervously. "I just saw a lady in a long, gray dress and bonnet go past your window," she told Pam and Doug.

Mrs. Satterthwaite was still around, busying herself outdoors now that the weather was warm. The psychic had told the Campbells of the old woman's love for peach pies, especially with fruit taken from the orchard that once graced the land next door.

Maybe there was something more to the sighting. A house had been built the previous year in the orchard. It still stood vacant and unsold. Perhaps Mrs. Satterthwaite occupied her time keeping people away from *her* orchard.

A year passed.

No funny tricks.

No surprises.

Then it all began again.

On a Sunday morning in the summer of 1990 Pam and Doug Campbell heard a knock at the kitchen door. Doug opened it. No one was there.

Several weeks later, Pam arrived home from work. In her bedroom she found one blind pulled all the way up. She always left all four blinds down.

"Okay, Mrs. Satterthwaite," Pam declared to no one in particular, "if you're really playing your games again you better let me know you're really here. Do something different."

Pam got home the next afternoon. In her bedroom she found the blind at the opposite window pulled up and the others left down. Pam stood smiling in the center of the room.

The keeper of their house had returned. This time for good.

Katie James

Susan Woolf really didn't know what to expect on that hot Oklahoma summer night a quarter century ago. A senior history major at what was then Southwestern State College at Weatherford, Woolf was especially interested in the lore and legends of her native state. The last thing she suspected was that the evening marked the beginning of her efforts to solve a ninety-year-old murder mystery and in the process confront her own skepticism about the existence of ghosts and haunted places.

Several weeks earlier, a classmate had told Woolf that there was a site not far from Weatherford where "you could see a ghost." Although she didn't pay close attention to the details in the young man's tale, except something about a "dead woman," her curiosity was aroused. Woolf was a self-described "smart aleck" at that time in her life. She hardly expected a "real" ghost to show up. But she agreed to go anyway.

The weather was still hot and sticky even at nine o'clock that night. Woolf asked her friend to drive. He knew the way and, though she never admitted to it, she didn't know how stalwart a "ghost hunter" she would turn out to be.

Woolf climbed into the passenger seat and set off with her friend for an area about six miles northeast of Weatherford, near a bridge over Big Deer Creek.

"We drove to a portion of a farm field that abutted a creekbed," Woolf remembered. "The field was cleared, and we drove in and turned to the right, parking the car facing the creekbed, a deep cutout; sort of a small canyon. Both sides were heavily overgrown with trees and brush.

"The theory was that one drove in, parked facing the creekbed, and waited for the 'ghost' to appear. I recall being told that if you were brave enough to await the ghost's approach to some close proximity, then the car's ignition, radio, and electrical system would fail.

"We turned in and parked and waited for not very long, around ten or fifteen minutes. . . ."

Woolf's skepticism was unfounded. Something did show up: a luminous blue light of "no particular shape or description, rising from out of the creekbed and slowly coming toward us."

The light was clearly visible—and rolling directly at them across the farm field. That was enough. Woolf told her friend to start the car and leave. Fortunately the ignition worked and they sped away.

While that one experience with a mystery light might have been enough for most people, Woolf's innate curiosity was stronger than any fear of what might lurk in the old creekbed.

"We returned the next afternoon," Woolf said. "I wanted to try to find out what had caused the light. We checked the trees and other vegetation in the streambed. We could find no obvious source."

There were no electric wires anywhere near where the light danced toward them, nor anything else that might have produced what is commonly known as a will-o'-the-wisp, or marsh gas. They didn't notice any great quantities of rotting vegetation, sometimes said to be responsible for the strange gaseous vapors.

During their search, however, they did find something interesting. A small, weathered plaque was attached to the old bridge. On it were the words:

DEAD WOMAN'S CROSSING, 1905

So her friend had been correct. A "dead woman" had something to do with this isolated section of Big Deer Creek.

Susan Woolf found the mystery deepening: Who was this anonymous woman? How did she die? Could it have been *her* "ghost" that haunted this otherwise pastoral scene?

The answers to those questions came slowly. During a lengthy, personal investigation, Woolf uncovered the woman's identity and the circumstances of her death in one of the old Oklahoma Territory's grisliest unsolved murders.

Woolf never returned to the bridge to see if the ghost would reappear. Not out of fear, she emphasized, but because her compulsion to solve an old murder took up most of her free time over the following weeks and months.

"The fact is we were becoming absorbed in what we were finding out about the woman who had given the crossing its name. And, too, I think it was because the more we learned about what had happened in that field, the more disinclined we were to trifle with whatever might have been there."

If ever a ghost had the right to haunt the living, the spirit of Katie James, the woman for whom the bridge is named, should wander the banks of Big Deer Creek forever. She was twenty-nine in 1905 and the mother of an infant child when she was brutally murdered, her decapitated body dumped near Dead Woman's Crossing.

From a distance of nearly nine decades, the facts in the case are not easy to ascertain. Even in 1905, many pieces of the puzzle were missing. What Susan Woolf found out, however, and later published in an issue of the *Chronicles of Oklahoma*, was the compelling story of a woman slain for unknown reasons . . . and the origin of what is known as Dead Woman's Crossing:

Katie DeWitt James was not a happy woman on July 7, 1905, when she and her fourteen-month-old toddler, Lulu Belle, boarded the train at Custer City,

Oklahoma. Although she was a homesteader, a former schoolteacher, and a respected member of the community, her marriage was crumbling. The day before she had filed for divorce from her husband of four years, Martin L. James. The reasons for the divorce are not known, but they must have been serious enough to cause Mrs. James to want to leave Custer City for an extended period of time. She bought a one-way ticket to Ripley, in north central Oklahoma, to spend some time with the family of her cousin, Wellington Knight.

Not much is known about the life of Martin James before his marriage in 1903 to Katie DeWitt. He was not at the station on the morning of July 7 to see his wife off. His absence would fuel speculation about his involvement in the events that were to follow. It had been Katie's father, Henry DeWitt, who had traveled the thirty miles from his farm near Taloga to bid farewell to his daughter and granddaughter—the last time he saw his daughter alive.

Mother and daughter never made it to her cousin's home in Ripley. Their disappearance, however, wasn't reported until her father became concerned. It was Katie's habit to write to her father nearly every day whenever she traveled. Several weeks passed and DeWitt had not received a single letter. Strangely, Martin James evidently never questioned the lack of communications, even though his only child had gone away with her mother. James remained on the farm that Katie had homesteaded before her marriage—and which would have reverted to her in the event of a divorce.

The record doesn't show that DeWitt ever contacted his son-in-law about his concerns. Instead, Katie's father went to the state capital, Oklahoma City, to ask Sheriff Garrison for help in finding a detective who might assist him in finding his daughter and grandchild.

Garrison recommended a man named Sam Bartell. He and DeWitt decided to begin the search in Clinton, the first town of any size Katie James would have passed through on the train to Ripley. But no one remembered a woman with a baby getting off the train there on July 7.

While Henry DeWitt had to return to his ranch, Bartell went on to Weatherford, next on the train's scheduled stops. He got there on July 28, 1905. A wide-open city of fifteen-thousand at the turn of the century, Weatherford boasted eighteen saloons and seventeen gambling casinos. In this raucous milieu almost any activity—legal or otherwise—was usually tolerated, if not actively promoted.

Bartell met with his first success. He was able to piece together the final movements of Katie James.

Witnesses told Bartell they'd seen a woman answering Katie James's description in the company of one Mrs. Fannie Norton, a sullen woman of dubious virtue. Katie, little Lulu Belle, and Mrs. Norton had spent the night with Mrs. Norton's brother-in-law, William Moore. The following morning, Mrs. Norton, with Katie and the child, had left the Moore home in a buggy heading in a generally northeast direction. That was the last time anyone saw Katie James alive. Mrs. Norton returned to Weatherford alone, returned the rig to the livery and took the next train back to Clinton, her hometown.

Katie had evidently met Fannie Norton on the train from Custer City. Mrs. Norton probably boarded the train in Clinton. For unknown reasons, Katie had

gotten off the train in Weatherford with Mrs. Norton and agreed to spend the
night with her at Moore's house outside town.

Little is known about Fannie Norton. During Susan Woolf's modern-day
investigation, she found evidence that Mrs. Norton was more than likely a
prostitute. That only deepens the mystery as to why a woman of Katie's fine
reputation would strike up an acquaintanceship with someone like Fannie
Norton.

Detective Bartell followed the route the women had taken when they left
William Moore's house. Near Big Deer Creek he found a rancher who had seen
Mrs. Norton's buggy in a field near the creek. Later, according to Bartell's written
account of the investigation, Mrs. Norton stopped at the farm home of Peter
Birscheid and left a baby with them, assuring the Birscheids she would pick up
the child when "she returned from a trip." Katie James was not with her. The
child was Lulu Belle. Her clothing and blanket were stained with blood when
she was left with the Birscheids. Bartell returned to town and examined the
buggy Mrs. Norton rented. He found bloodstains on one wheel.

Bartell telegraphed Henry DeWitt of his findings and the baby's location—
she was still with the Birscheids—and returned to Oklahoma City. He had determined that after a brief stop in Clinton to gather up her four children, Mrs.
Norton had gone to Guthrie, where she enrolled her children in a private school.
She also told acquaintances that no one was to be told of her visit, nor of her
eventual destination of Shawnee, some twenty-five miles east of Oklahoma City.

Henry DeWitt took Lulu Belle back to his ranch. He then rendezvoused with
Bartell in Oklahoma City. Together the men went on to Shawnee, where they
reported their case to the police. Mrs. Norton was located and promptly arrested.

The woman was not unknown to territorial authorities. She had been tried on
charges of shooting a Weatherford bartender in the back, but had been acquitted
by a sympathetic jury.

Mrs. Norton, a small woman dressed in worn clothing, was visibly nervous
during police questioning. She admitted knowing Katie James, but told a "rambling story" about the events of early July 1905. She adamantly denied murdering
Mrs. James, claiming instead that Katie had gone off with a man in a covered
wagon when they reached Big Deer Creek. Bartell was convinced otherwise,
based on the evidence he had collected.

He would never have the chance to prove his case.

As she sat unguarded in a jail corridor after questioning by police, Fannie
Norton started vomiting and quickly lost consciousness. Several doctors called
in to examine her concluded she had swallowed poison, likely morphine, cocaine,
or strychnine, according to their inconclusive analysis. Less than an hour after
her collapse, the only real suspect in the case was dead. No one claimed her
body. She was buried in a pauper's grave.

But Katie James was still missing. A murder had apparently been committed
but still there was no hard evidence of the crime. And the prime suspect was
dead.

Rewards were offered for information leading to the "arrest of the person or
persons who murdered Mrs. Katie James." Even the Oklahoma territorial governor contributed three hundred dollars to the reward fund.

Two large, and ultimately unsuccessful, searches were mounted along both branches of Big Deer Creek near where Fannie Norton was last seen with Mrs. James and her daughter. Then on August 31, 1905, nearly two months after her disappearance, the remains of a female thought to be Mrs. James were found near where she had last been seen.

The discovery was purely by chance. A lawyer named G. W. Cornell had taken his boys fishing at the creek and stumbled across the skeleton when he got out of the buggy. The remains were in plain sight near a well-used wagon crossing. The skull, with a bullet hole behind the right ear, was several feet away from the rest of the body. A .38 caliber bullet was still lodged in the skull, and the revolver itself was found nearby. Buggy tracks were visible near the body. It looked like Katie James had been shot while she rode in the buggy and her body pushed out.

Lawyer Cornell's son remembered the event decades later both because of its inherent drama . . . and because his father used the reward money to buy him a pony.

Henry DeWitt identified his daughter's body through the tattered but recognizable clothing, her hat, a comb in her hair, her shoes, and a gold wedding band upon her left hand. She was buried in Lot 1, Block 35, of the Weatherford Cemetery.

The circumstances of her brutal murder, however, were not so easy to discover. A coroner's inquest concluded on September 2, 1905, that Katie James died "by means of a gunshot wound fired from a .38 caliber pistol in the hands of Mrs. Fannie Norton . . . on or about the 8th day of July 1905." Robbery was the motive, the coroner found. The most damning evidence against Mrs. Norton came from the lawyer who represented her in the shooting of the Weatherford bartender—the gun found beside Katie's body was the one Mrs. Norton used in that incident. No other suspects were named at the inquest, but there were many unanswered questions and plenty of speculation about the mysterious murder.

The most perplexing problem was why the body wasn't found during the two earlier organized searches and the many attempts by individuals to collect the reward through their own surveys near Big Deer Creek. The body was in the open, without any attempt at concealment.

This suggests that Fannie Norton had one or more accomplices. The most likely candidate, investigators suspected, was Martin James. Newspaper accounts say he didn't take part in any of the searches and showed little remorse when his wife's body was found. However, he had an airtight alibi for the time of his wife's murder and was never charged with the crime.

A court eventually awarded him half of Katie's estate, the other half going to little Lulu Belle. In March 1907 Martin James married a seventeen-year-old girl, was given custody of Lulu Belle, and soon thereafter sold the farm and left the territory. He was never heard from again.

The rest of the questions are nearly as puzzling as the first.

Why did Katie James get off the train at Weatherford with Fannie Norton in the first place? The women were apparent strangers to one another. Perhaps they were drawn together on the train ride when Katie told her about her marital problems. Was Mrs. Norton in league with Martin James? Maybe she deliberately struck up an acquaintanceship with the young mother in order to lure her to her death. But Katie was hardly a naive girl. She had homesteaded in a hostile, male-dominated environment, was educated enough to have been a school-teacher, and was a well-liked member of her community. At the age of twenty-nine, with a young daughter to care for, it is odd that she would change her plans so dramatically and go off with a woman she had known for less than a day. Yet that is what the evidence suggests.

Was robbery really the motive, as the coroner concluded? Witnesses suggested that Mrs. Norton had seen Katie open her purse and thus might have spied the twenty-three dollars she was carrying, a substantial sum of money in those days, especially for a woman who led a precarious existence. There is no indication whether any money was found in Katie's purse lying near her body. And the gold ring was still on Katie's finger.

As the brutal murderess she was portrayed to be, Fannie Norton behaved oddly. When she was arrested in Shawnee, she was apprehensive and gave con-flicting stories of her relationship with Katie James.

And why take her own life? A month had passed since the murder and no body had been found. The trail was growing colder by the day. She was certainly not afraid to resort to violence, as her involvement in the bartender's shooting attested. She had four children to support in a private school. The suicide only makes sense, the speculation was, if she had an accomplice, someone she was so afraid of that she took her own life rather than being faced with a trial, prison, and perhaps an attempt on the part of her accomplice(s) to keep her quiet.

Did Martin James know Fannie Norton? Was he the mastermind behind the murder? He had a strong alibi, but that would certainly not exonerate him if Mrs. Norton had committed the actual murder. He most assuredly had a lot to lose with the divorce. The farm would have reverted to his wife, Lulu Belle would have gone with her mother, and he would have been left penniless. A possibility exists that he entered into a conspiracy with Mrs. Norton and, perhaps, another unidentified person to kill his wife. Virtually nothing is known about James's personal life or his personal acquaintances before (or during) his marriage. It's conceivable that he became acquainted with Mrs. Norton and together they hatched a plan to murder his wife.

The likelihood of a second accomplice is strengthened by the fact that the field near Big Deer Creek had been gone over at least twice by organized posses searching for Katie's remains, plus many freelance searchers. A candidate for the role of the unnamed accomplice is certainly Mrs. Norton's brother-in-law, Wil-liam Moore. He could have concealed the body and later, after Mrs. Norton's suicide, returned it to where the killing took place and where it was eventually discovered.

Susan Woolf's original intention was to find out why a bridge over a rural Oklahoma creek was called "Dead Woman's Crossing." In the process, Woolf thinks far more was accomplished:

"I do not know if the ghost still appears at the crossing, although I think it does not. I think there was a ghost, and that it is no more. I had the very strong feeling that we were researching something that was intended to let the woman rest. It was because of that feeling that we worked so hard to try to solve the murder. I honestly believe that the ghost ceased its appearance, at least during that time, because something was being done to let it rest."

But there was another incident that caused Woolf to wonder whether the ghost of Katie James was not somehow closer to her than she suspected:

"I was spending one weekend at my parents' during that summer when we spent almost all of our time tracking down the mystery of Katie James. I got up in the middle of the night and happened to glance into the mirror that was on my dresser. I have the distinct recollection of having seen a woman's face (and head) in the mirror. I recall looking at the whatever-it-was for a minute or so, and then calmly going back to bed.

"For me to have . . . looked at a disembodied head in a mirror and then gone back to sleep is incredible, as I suspect it would be for most people. I must admit that I have a great deal of difficulty in admitting to such, or to my belief in such an experience. But, were I under oath on a witness stand, I would have to swear that I definitely recall seeing something in that mirror and being absolutely unafraid."

Woolf doesn't know if the image was that of Katie James. She does know that she saw *something* that night. But, she hastens to add, "I have never, ever seen such a thing since."

A dancing blue light that frightened two college students, an unsolved murder at the turn of the century, and a ghostly face in a mirror. All mysterious events that may show how a restless ghost found peace at last—through the tireless efforts of a sympathetic historian named Susan Woolf.

Mr. and Mrs. G.

MURDER/SUICIDE
ORPHANS
FIVE CHILDREN

by
Bruce Trachtenberg
Oregonian Staff Writer

A Portland mother of five died of gunshot wounds early Sunday in an apparent murder/suicide in a north Portland home where she had sought refuge.

Her former husband turned the gun on himself after first shooting her, according to the Multnomah County Medical Examiner's Office.

Dead are Marles H., 36, and Billy H., 42.

Mrs. H. and the children had been living at the home of Mary L. Bellanger . . . where the shooting occurred.

"She came here in hopes of finding some protection," Mrs. Bellanger said. "We had known each other for about four and one-half years. We used to live next door to each other."

The Medical Examiner's Office said Mrs. H. was beaten and killed about 2:50 A.M. Sunday after she let her former husband in the house. (Billy) H. also died of a gunshot wound.

Arrangements for the five H—— children await action by the Multnomah County Juvenile Court and the Portland Police Bureau of Youth Division.

Mrs. Bellanger said she hopes the children can spend Christmas with her family.

"I hope the Court is good enough to let the kids stay here for Christmas. We want to try to make this the best Christmas that we can make for them. We don't want to upset them anymore than possible."

The Police Youth Division said later Sunday the children would be allowed to spend Christmas at the Bellangers' home.

—Portland *Oregonian*, Dec. 24, 1973

The murdered woman didn't have a chance. She died just inside the front door, on a couch near a built-in cabinet with glass doors. The gunshots blew the glass doors to pieces. Blood was everywhere.

The five children and the Bellanger family escaped harm.

In 1973, *domestic violence* wasn't a term that most people had even heard of, let alone read about on the front page of their newspaper. Twenty years later it's impossible to determine what led a desperate man to murder his estranged wife two days before Christmas and then turn the gun on himself, to understand what horror raced through his frenzied mind that would move him to blow away a person he must have once loved.

But that unspeakable act reverberates still in the house where two lives ended.

The dead couple may haunt the Portland home in which their lives came to such a tragic end.

The three story Victorian house looks much the same today as it did in 1973. It's in a north Portland neighborhood filled with turn-of-the-century homes built for managers and employees of a meat processing plant. They are well kept, although most are smaller than the one in which the couple died. Old sidewalks make an evening stroll inviting. Embedded in the curbs are the iron rings where suitors once tied their horses while calling on their sweethearts.

In the early 1980s, the house was put up for sale. Michael and Carolyn Brown were looking for a large, older home to buy and the place seemed perfect.

The Browns had first looked at the house when it was listed at $58,000, but didn't pursue the matter. When the price dropped even lower, the couple couldn't pass it up.

Carolyn Brown explained:

"Michael was with his mother and sister in Europe. Our other house was just a block away, so my mother and I decided to go through the house. I liked it. Michael and I had seen it before the original owner had moved out. When Michael called from Ireland I asked him to think about the house and when he came back we went through it again. We bought it."

The Browns offered $42,000, an amazingly low price considering the condition of the house and the generally high housing costs in the United States. Their offer was readily accepted.

The house was in good shape. The outside had been freshly painted, as had the interior. Beautiful fir floors had been well maintained.

New storm windows and carpeting to protect the floors were the only additions the Browns had to make. A previous owner had taken great pains to remodel the home. Even the heating system was in good shape.

Michael and Carolyn—with daughters Gennie and Cassie—moved in during November 1985. Their lives haven't been the same since.

Perhaps they should have paid closer attention to subtle indications that the house was . . . different.

"For a year and a half before we came, the house was vacant," Michael recalled. "Of course, the neighborhood kind of joked about the house being haunted, just because it was an old house, and it was vacant for [so long]."

The Browns didn't know anything about the murder/suicide twelve years earlier until the last owner stopped by while he was visiting the city.

"He came by to see the house," Carolyn said. "As he was leaving he just said, 'Oh, by the way, did you know there was a murder/suicide here?' We talked to the neighbors and they said there was a lady who had left her husband and came to this house with her kids. The husband came here real irate and killed her and . . . himself."

When she was a little girl, Carolyn imagined it might be exciting to live in a "haunted" house. She had no way of knowing her childhood fantasy might really come true.

"What was really strange," Michael added, "is that we both had a strange feeling about the house. We didn't really discuss it between us, but we both felt that something was here."

The visiting former owner and neighbors confirmed their suspicions. "We both said bingo, that's it," Michael said. "There *was* something that happened here."

The first inkling that their "new" old house was *haunted* didn't occur until a year and a half after they moved in. At first, Carolyn thought her concerns came because of her self-described "active imagination."

"I just ignored it [feelings about the house]," she said. "I didn't mention anything to Michael, but I always had an idea, nothing specific, that there was something that we couldn't figure out about our home."

Six months later, Carolyn discovered that Michael, too, had the same wariness. She knew that it wasn't likely her husband imagined events. As a law enforcement officer for a Portland municipal agency, Michael is well trained as an objective fact-gatherer and observer. When the couple started comparing notes, however, they discovered a mutual inclination to believe that some things they attributed to chance or the natural creakings of an old house might be something more.

And when they found out about the murder/suicide, confirming the circumstances by reading the original news clipping, the Browns started wondering if there wasn't something to stories of murder victims haunting the houses in which they died.

A propensity to disbelieve the midnight frights of a small child eventually led to the first of nearly two-dozen separate encounters the Browns had with what they believe to be the ghosts of Marles and Billy.

"Cassie was the first one to see them," Carolyn said matter-of-factly. "She was nearly three years old. She would tell me that a lady was tucking her in bed at night.

"She said she was a very nice lady, and there would be a man off to the side. The man scared her. He would never smile, just watch. He never did anything mean, just watched. Something about him just scared her. The lady would pull the blankets up and tuck her in, and she'd go back to sleep," Carolyn recalled.

Because of her young age, Cassie had a hard time describing the night visitor. She knew, however, that the woman wasn't her mother. She said the woman had long hair. Carolyn's hair is short and usually permed.

Carolyn told Cassie it was a dream in order not to frighten the child, but she knew something else was going on.

"I have a bad habit of not tucking blankets under the mattress," she confessed. "I just pull them up so the kids can get out of bed if they need to."

When she checked on her daughter before going to bed, the blankets were usually tucked under the mattress and pulled tightly up to the child's chin. She assumed Michael had done it when he kissed his daughter good-bye before going off to his night shift. The mystery deepened during their later conversations—neither one had tucked the blankets under Cassie's mattress.

"Cassie wasn't afraid at all," Carolyn said. "She was just curious about why the lady was tucking her in. Of course, I kept telling her it was a dream." Carolyn knew her daughter wanted to believe that it was *only* a dream, yet at the same time saw that Cassie doubted her explanation.

The man lingering in the background was worrisome.

"He was a little behind the woman," Carolyn said of her daughter's description. "He wouldn't smile, just stand there. She didn't really want to concentrate on him because he made her nervous. 'I was a little scared of him,' she said. But the lady was nice."

The woman didn't make a sound except to whisper "shhhh!" as if quieting an unsettled child. Or stopping a little girl from crying out in fright at the sight of her ghost nanny.

Early in the fall of 1987, another incident involving the Brown children mystified Carolyn:

"Both girls were sleeping in Gennie's bed. Because we have a large house, heating can get expensive so we used an electric heater in the girls' room. Well, one night it was warm when we went to bed, but I woke up at about four-thirty in the morning, freezing. It was cold. I was worried about the kids so I went to their bedroom to turn on the electric heater. It was already plugged in and turned on. The room was warm."

The following morning, Carolyn asked her elder daughter if she had plugged it in.

"Oh no, Mom," Gennie answered. "I'm not allowed to do that."

"At least the kids were warm," Carolyn sighed, not wanting to linger too long on the unanswered question of just *who* plugged in the heater.

A second seemingly impossible event a few days later also dealt with appliances with minds of their own.

Some explanation is necessary. In the Browns' first-floor living room, one particular electrical outlet has a large adapter that will hold six separate plugs. In that adapter they have plugged in a television set, two VCRs, a lamp, and a cordless telephone. The latter has a particularly heavy plug-in, so large in fact that if it is accidentally knocked, the entire outlet adapter will fall out. If, for instance, Michael wants to unplug the lamp, he has to hold the wall adapter in place to do so.

Early one evening, Carolyn and the girls were out of the house and Michael was sleeping until his midnight shift started. Before he went to bed, he had set one of the VCRs to record a program from seven to eight o'clock.

Carolyn picked up the story:

"I got back home at nine P.M. Michael asked me why I unplugged the VCR. I told him I just got home. He said the VCR was unplugged, but his show was recorded. Nothing else was unplugged, just the one machine. It just couldn't have fallen out. No animals were in the house, in fact no one else was in the house and Michael was sleeping. There was no way that machine could have come unplugged at eight o'clock when no one else was home."

Michael, too, was stumped. "That was really tangible," he said. "That was when it was really confirmed [to me]. Prior to that, I thought there must be some logical explanation. But that VCR incident couldn't be explained because there was nothing that could have done that. I couldn't believe it."

Carolyn echoed her husband's sentiment. "We weren't sure how to react. There was a part of me that was a little excited that my childhood wish kind of came true, and yet I was nervous because of the kids."

The hauntings grew progressively more pronounced.

"There was one period when there was so much activity, footsteps and that sort of thing," Michael said, "that we wouldn't even go and look at one point. I remember us watching TV and we'd hear footsteps and not even bother to check."

Sometimes the incidents seemed prankish, such as the occasion during February 1988 when both the television set and radio came on by themselves.

"One night the kids spent the night over at Michael's mother's house," Carolyn remembered. "He was at work and I was upstairs sleeping. All of a sudden I heard this man's voice downstairs, booming. I grabbed Michael's gun and I went downstairs and the TV was on. Scared the wits out of me. I turned off the TV and I slept on the couch. I put Mike's gun under the couch. Then the radio upstairs turned on. I stayed on the couch."

Carolyn refused to go back upstairs. She said she wanted to be close to an outside door.

Within a few months, Carolyn seemed to arrive at an uneasy truce with the ghosts in her house, especially when they disturbed an otherwise peaceful night's sleep.

"During the summer—like that summer of 1988—when it's real hot, I let the kids sleep downstairs where it's cooler. Now one time I was sleeping on the couch, the kids were on the floor, and our husky/shepherd dog was sleeping with us. Sometime around one or two in the morning, I heard walking upstairs. From my bedroom to the girls' room, back and forth among the three bedrooms. My first reaction was that Cassie was looking for me. So I yelled up to her that I was downstairs. I still heard the walking. I got up and Cassie's sleeping on the floor with Gennie.

"The next logical thing was that Fairfax, our dog, was upstairs. I called to him and his head popped up next to me. At this point I was still hearing footsteps and I thought, well, Michael's at work and all of us are down here, so it must be Mr. and Mrs. G." Those were the nicknames she had given to the ghosts.

Carolyn wasn't about to let two ghosts keep her up all night.

"I went up to the landing and asked 'them' to stop walking around because they were going to wake up the kids."

"They" stopped.

When mysterious noises became too loud in the house, or the aimless walking disturbed her sleep, Carolyn again asked the ghosts to quiet down. Usually it worked, although she admitted feeling foolish for carrying on conversations with invisible people.

The ghosts were particularly noisy on another late night in 1988. Carolyn explained:

"I had just bought some furniture to go in Cassie's bedroom and there was no room for her to sleep in there, so Cassie slept with Gennie in her room. I heard knocking at maybe midnight or one o'clock in the morning. It sounded like it was at my door, but I wasn't sure. I said, 'Come in, Cassie!' But no one came in. The knocking stopped for a minute and then it came again, only louder.

"Fairfax, who was in my room, was scared. He wouldn't go to the hallway when I opened the door, thinking it was one of the kids who wanted me but wasn't coming in. There was nobody out there. I checked on the kids; they were both asleep."

At first, Carolyn thought her girls were playing a trick on their mother, a late-night game of "Let's scare Mommy!" She went back to bed, leaving her door slightly ajar so that she could see down the hallway. She expected to see one or both of the girls tiptoeing toward her bedroom. Instead, Carolyn found the phantom knocking had moved to another room.

"It was coming from Cassie's room," Carolyn said, which was unoccupied that night. "I wasn't sure, but it sounded like maybe the furniture or something in the wall. It kept getting louder the more I ignored it."

Once again, Carolyn got upset enough to scold the ghosts.

"It was like they wanted attention. So I said 'Okay, you got my attention, now knock it off! You're too loud, we're trying to get some sleep!!' The noise did stop. That seemed to work."

The Browns' large husky/shepherd dog, Fairfax, gave some clear indications to Carolyn that he, too, was wary of all the strange noises. "He'll do different things. He would always check on the kids in their bedrooms at night, always. He would hardly sleep, just go back and forth between their rooms. But when things were happening, like the knocking, he wouldn't leave me, in fact he would not even leave my bedroom."

When the family left the house for some reason, Fairfax went berserk. He chewed the blinds in the front room, and when they locked him in a pantry, gnawed on the doorframe trying to get out. For a period of time they had Michael's sister look after him in her home. He was fine there.

A new dog the Browns purchased, named Tuffy, seemed to settle Fairfax a bit. Now the family puts both dogs in the backyard whenever they leave. But Fairfax intensely dislikes the third floor and insists on sleeping in the master bedroom each night. According to Carolyn, Tuffy doesn't exhibit any odd behavior in any section of the house.

An air of protectiveness was also evident in the frequency and intensity of the hauntings. Billy and Marles, if indeed they are the ghosts as Carolyn and Michael Brown suspect, didn't take kindly to visitors. On several occasions, the ghosts announced their visits in most unsettling ways.

Carolyn's nephew, Jonah, got more than he bargained for when he stayed over one night. "He heard arguing upstairs and just assumed it was Mike and me," Carolyn remembered. "Well, I was sleeping at the time and Mike hadn't even come home. Jonah didn't know that because he was sleeping on the couch. He heard the arguing and tried to ignore it and then the voices moved to the living room, around where the doorway is."

The doorway to which Carolyn was referring was the one that once led to the kitchen from the entryway. It had been blocked off some years ago. It was also the exact place where Billy murdered his wife and then turned the gun on himself.

Jonah had pulled the blankets up over his head, but decided to peek after a few moments.

"He saw a woman and a man there arguing. They stopped and looked at him and it scared the wits out of Jonah. He covered his face and told her to go away."

After a few seconds of silence he looked again. They were gone. For a very long time, Jonah would not visit his aunt and uncle, and after that only if there was a large family gathering.

"He's feeling better, more secure," Carolyn said. "But that was something that scared the poor guy."

A next-door neighbor, a woman named Nina, had two strange experiences in the Browns' home. She often helped Carolyn clean the three-story house. Once when she was on the third floor working, while the Browns were gone, she heard a scream come from somewhere in the house. Nina knew no one else was with her. She quickly gathered her cleaning supplies and left for the day.

On another occasion, while dusting the second-floor landing, Nina heard the front door latch open. Someone walked across the floor downstairs. She called out that she was cleaning the staircase. She supposed Michael had come home early. Everyone else was gone. There was no answer to Nina's shout. Footsteps again crossed the first floor, the front door unlatched and then closed.

"She didn't work for us for very long," Carolyn said. "After that experience she said no thanks!"

Shortly after the Browns moved in, Carolyn's brother and his girlfriend came for a brief visit. They stayed on the third floor. A few nights after their arrival, the young woman was in the basement laundry room late washing clothes when a voice called out, "Hello down there!" She ran upstairs in the belief that someone had come into the house and was looking for a family member. No one was on the first floor. Carolyn and her daughters were asleep in the master bedroom.

"This was around the time that we did not believe things were happening," Carolyn said. The direct confrontations with their live-in ghosts were yet to come.

Carolyn was told about the incident the next day. "I just said it might have been the kids yelling down the laundry chute, but I was pretty sure that the kids were sleeping since they were in my bed. She didn't completely accept my answer and she didn't do the laundry after that."

The children—Gennie and her little sister Cassie—told their parents of numerous incidents in which they saw or heard the ghosts. One encounter even involved another well-known ghost story.

The girls had just seen a television adaptation of Oscar Wilde's "The Canterville Ghost." Cassie especially loved the story of Sir Simon's attempt to scare away an intrusive American family that inherits a haunted English castle.

Carolyn Brown picked up the story from there, on a night when Cassie wandered into her parents' bedroom:

"One morning around three o'clock, I heard Cassie calling, 'Sir Simon! Sir

Simon! Please come back, I want to talk to you.' I leaned over and told her to go to sleep, but I kept hearing her calling to him. It was in November 1989."

When her daughter wouldn't settle down, Carolyn realized something odd was going on.

"Who are you calling, honey?" Carolyn asked.

"Well, I saw Sir Simon, Mom," Cassie replied firmly.

"You saw Sir Simon what?"

"The ghost, Mom, the ghost!" Cassie declared.

Carolyn asked her to explain what she meant. She was half-asleep and not fully cognizant of what the little girl was trying to say.

"Well, Mom," Cassie started, "I came in here to climb into bed with you and he was standing there looking at you. Then he saw me and disappeared. But he didn't look like the guy on TV at all. He had kind of short hair like Dad and he wore clothes like Dad. He was kind of gray."

"Well, that's very interesting, Cassie," Carolyn said. "But why are you calling him to come back?"

"I want to invite him to my birthday party," Cassie replied, thinking that Sir Simon would be the perfect guest of honor at her upcoming birthday.

"Honey," Carolyn said carefully, "I don't think your friends would appreciate a ghost coming to your birthday party."

The Browns told their daughters early on that in all probability ghosts inhabited their house. "We had to be honest with them," Carolyn said. "How else could we explain all this stuff to them?"

Cassie talked about Sir Simon for days after. Her mother patiently told her that *their* ghosts were not the scary kind at all. They were good ghosts who plugged in heaters when the girls were cold or tucked them in bed. She explained the nice things they did. But to the girls, living in a haunted house was quite exciting. Gennie often told the stories to her friends at school.

Carolyn cautioned them about spreading too many tales.

"I told them not to tell their friends too much because they'd be too scared to come over. You have to be careful. And I've told them that some people don't believe in ghosts, so they know that."

Nevertheless, Carolyn laughed, "They think it's funny that their mom tells the ghosts to knock off the noise."

A month later, in December 1989 on the eve of Christmas, Gennie caught a glimpse of someone lingering around the Christmas tree. It wasn't Santa Claus.

"She had come downstairs and saw a man looking at the tree," Carolyn noted. Gennie apparently wanted an early glimpse of the presents she would be opening later that morning. "His back was to her. She got excited because she thought that maybe it was Santa Claus or her dad. Anyway, he turned around and disappeared."

At that, the child got scared and quickly returned to her bedroom. She didn't tell her parents about it until later.

What frightened Gennie was the sudden knowledge that the man next to the tree definitely wasn't her father and wasn't wearing a suit like Santa Claus. She later described him for her mother in ways similar to Cassie's description of her Sir Simon.

"I told her that it was Mr. G," Carolyn said. She said he was probably looking at the beautiful decorations the girls put on the tree and their fine presents.

Apparitions and disembodied voices became the norm for all the family members. Carolyn heard and saw unexplainable phenomena many times. "We'll see a white thing out of the corner of our eyes; it disappears when we turn around. Michael recently asked me if I ever saw a white apparition. I told him I thought I was the only one. I also hear a man's voice every once in a while. I'll be in the kitchen and I'll hear a man in the dining room. I'd think it was Mike and I'll come out and no one is there."

She said the words were indistinct, as if someone might be talking on the telephone or carrying on a hushed conversation.

At one point, Carolyn was in the living room when she heard a woman crying in the kitchen. At first she thought it might be Gennie or Cassie in some trouble. But when she called out for the girls, she discovered they were upstairs and had been there for quite some time.

The sudden, separate appearances of two ghosts frightened the Browns more than any other occurrence during their tenancy. Both times the ghosts decided to present themselves in the night.

"Mike was at work, the kids were sleeping, and I had my door cracked open," Carolyn said. "The hallway light is always left on. I woke up and I saw a man walking toward me. My first impression was that Mike had come home early, but then I realized he was still at work. We have a ceiling light that has a pull chain. I'm looking at him and scrambling for the light, swinging my arms back and forth looking for the chain. By the time I got the light on he had gone away.

"The light was coming in from the hallway so I couldn't see him too good, but it was more than a shadow. I could see his face a bit, not clearly, but I could see him. I slept with the light on after that."

The apparition's casual stroll toward her was so natural that Carolyn felt certain it was Michael. There was no anger or menace in his walk, only a slow deliberate pace that ended in the brilliance of the overhead light.

A dream vividly rendered? The power of suggestion arising from living in a haunted house? A trick of light? Carolyn doesn't think so. The man she saw was a solid, three-dimensional figure that looked for all the world like a human being. Only it wasn't.

Michael Brown's encounter with the ghost was so distressing that it stayed with him for days and weeks to come.

"I was on the early day shift so I had gone to bed earlier than the rest of the family," Michael recited. "I left the door slightly ajar and the hall light was on. I had just gone to sleep when some noise woke me up. I looked up and a lady was approaching me. I thought it was my wife in some kind of a gown or negligee. I seemed to lose track of time, except I could see she was more slender than my wife, her face was more slender and she had a different hairstyle. It was more of a straight hair style that went down to her shoulders. I actually thought it was my wife up until the time I put my arms up and the lady got really close. I realized it wasn't and that's when I let out a yell."

Carolyn came racing into the room. Her husband was sitting up in bed, the overhead light on. She asked him what had happened. He insisted everything was all right, he'd had a bad dream, that was all. He just wanted to go back to sleep. The next day, though, Michael told his wife that he'd almost embraced a ghost.

"That was the most tangible thing that's ever happened to me," Michael said. "That made a believer out of me."

Over the years Michael and Carolyn have grown accustomed to frequent reminders of their ghostly tenants. Not all of them are nearly as confrontational as the couple's nighttime visits from Billy and Marles.

Some incidents were merely annoying, while one seems to defy the laws of gravity:

- "Once Michael came downstairs," Carolyn said. "He'd been sleeping and the kids were in bed. He asked me if we'd been on the third floor. I said no. He told me there was someone walking up there. The kids were sleeping and the dog was downstairs with me. I told him he should go ask them to stop. He wouldn't. He said he would just stay downstairs with me for a while."

  Carolyn later performed her by now usual vocal exorcism. "When we went to bed, I asked them to please stop the noise, the walking around, because we were going to bed. It stopped."
- Strange things often happen on the house's third floor. The family uses it for storage and as a playroom for their daughters. It's well lighted, with a door that opens onto a sundeck. Sometimes it's too well lighted.

  Michael said: "I was across the street talking to a neighbor and I saw the lights on, which I thought was strange. I was walking back across the street to come home and the light went off."

  When he came in the door, Michael found his wife and children downstairs. No one had been on the third floor for some time.

  "The third-floor lights are always going on and off," Carolyn said. "I'd have to ask the kids if they'd forgotten to turn them off. It's really hard to tell when the kids forget to turn them off or when the lights are doing it by themselves."

  It happens often. The family leaves for a few hours in the evening, leaving the house in darkness, and when they return home lights are ablaze in various rooms. Gennie's bedroom lights are often popping on. With the exception of the bathrooms, all the ceiling lights on the second floor are operated by pulling on chains that hang down from them.
- A window in Gennie's bedroom has a peculiar habit of opening by itself. "During one period," Michael said, "I would find the window open, the inside window. The storm would still be closed. I'd shut the window and lock it and tell Gennie please not to open it. She said she wasn't doing it. I don't know how long it went on for, but it was almost a daily occurrence. I would shut the window again, and lock it, and then I'd find it open."
- Michael's paycheck stubs from work were the subject of one peculiar episode.

"We keep them in a folder in the filing cabinet," Carolyn said. "I found them out by the kitchen telephone. Of course, Michael thought I took them out and I thought he had taken them out. They stayed there for about two months before he asked if I was done with them so he could put them away. I looked at him and said I didn't take them out. He said he hadn't. I asked the kids, too. Why would they be taken out? Why would they be there? They were just left in the kitchen. That was a strange thing." Perhaps ghosts, too, are interested in the financial affairs of the living.

Despite the puzzling episodes with lights, windows, relatives, knockings, footsteps, and even mysterious figures in the night, none seemed particularly violent. If the Browns didn't precisely "accept" the presence of ghosts in their fine old Victorian home, neither were they especially frightened by anything that happened. It never entered their minds to give up the house.

The closest Carolyn Brown came to feeling that the ghost couple could cause some harm came on Christmas Eve 1990. It involved, of all things, mixed nuts.

The Browns had the family Christmas celebration at their house as usual because it could accommodate everyone. Carolyn's sister-in-law had brought a plastic tray filled with a variety of fresh nuts. All of their relatives had left and Carolyn was cleaning up in the kitchen. Michael had gone to bed. The children were sleeping.

"I was putting some stuff away and noticed that the tray with the nuts was halfway off the table," Carolyn recalled. "I pushed it back on the table and then I started putting things away again. And then the tray just flipped backward. It was like someone had taken his hand underneath and flipped it up. The tray hit the wall and nuts scattered everywhere."

Carolyn turned off the lights and ran upstairs.

She didn't tell her husband why she suddenly appeared in the bedroom. The next morning, Michael discovered the mess in the kitchen and cleaned it up. He asked her what had happened. "I asked him if he remembered me coming upstairs so suddenly? I told him what had happened. I didn't feel like cleaning up the nuts at that point."

In early August 1992, a new twist was added to the Brown family haunting.

Carolyn was making plans to paint the ceilings in several rooms. She had carefully surveyed the ceilings to determine how much paint would be required. But one morning her plans were put on hold. As she looked over the living room ceiling, she noticed four brown-colored streaks extending only a few inches in one area.

"It looked like someone had taken his thumb and three fingers, rubbed them in dirt and then dragged them across the ceiling," Carolyn said. The marks were not there the day before, she emphasizes, because she had examined that section of the ceiling.

The high ceilings cannot be reached even with the tallest stepstool in the house. No workmen had been in the house. There seemed to be no logical explanation for how they got up there. The mysterious smudges remained there for months afterward.

To add to this new mystery, only a few days before the discovery of the ceiling marks, one of the ghosts made an audible appearance.

Michael was working the overnight shift and therefore Carolyn wasn't surprised when she heard the bedroom door open shortly after daybreak. Dozing lightly she heard her husband walk toward her. But the footfalls quickly retreated from the room, and down the hallway. The next thing she knew the front door opened and slammed shut, causing a wind chime hanging on the doorknob to tinkle.

A bit upset by what she considered her husband's bizarre behavior, Carolyn came downstairs to investigate. Michael was coming in the back door. He had been taking out the garbage and had not been anywhere near their bedroom. He, too, had heard the front door slam shut and wondered who was up at such an early hour. The couple looked at each other and knew immediately that it was another piece added to their ghostly puzzle.

Michael and Carolyn Brown haven't seriously considered moving from their home, especially since the entities never seem to upset the children or want to harm them. If there had been the slightest indication that the entities were evil or malicious, Carolyn said they would have moved away. Their experience has been characterized more by a peaceful coexistence. The ghosts don't seem to dislike the Browns, they just want to impress upon them their indelible presence.

"We've basically accepted them," Carolyn said. "We do get scared and would like it if they go. But the kids were concerned that the ghosts might be going away. They don't want them to. The kids want them to stay. It's exciting to them."

As to why their house is haunted, Carolyn has had a lot of time to think about that:

"He [Billy] made a mistake. Is he sorry for what he did? Is he trying to make amends? I try to come up with my own interpretation. And I feel honestly that the lady likes being close to the kids, tucking them in. She misses her kids and wants to look after ours. Nothing negative has ever happened really, I mean besides getting scared once in a while. But nothing truly threatening."

Michael and Carolyn think that the murder/suicide was an act of passion involving only the former occupants. Their ghosts don't harbor any ill will toward the living.

"I feel relieved that nothing negative has happened. We can make this whole ghostly situation a positive thing as much as possible. We can't afford to move and we don't really want to move yet. I really like the house. There's a lot we can do, especially when the kids reach their teens," Carolyn noted.

The couple have plans for remodeling the third floor into a master bedroom with a sitting room and art studio. The girls would have the second floor, while the couple's present bedroom would become the family room.

In the meantime, Michael plans to research the history of the house and find out as much as he can about the circumstances surrounding the deaths of Billy and Marles. He wants to know the personalities of the couple who linger long after death in the house where they died.

"The ghosts are pretty respectful of us," Carolyn summarized. "I think part of it is that we try not to react too much. I just tell them to stop what they're doing. Of course, they do give us a start now and then."

When necessary, however, Carolyn is stern with their supernatural guests. "I told them not to show themselves in front of the kids. I will not have them scaring my children!"

Even the most pertinacious phantom is no match for a mother protecting her children.

NOTE: Certain names in this story were altered to protect the privacy of some individuals, living and dead.

Diary of a Haunting

The place: A beautifully restored eighteenth-century farmhouse on the outskirts of Allentown.

The time: April 2, 1983, 4:00 A.M.

Billy Micklos was asleep on a chaise lounge on the first floor. He'd had a long, hard workday and, being too exhausted to take a shower, decided not to join his wife, Linda, in bed. He'd clean up in the morning.

He was awakened by a noise like the crackling and popping of wood. When the noise intensified, Billy decided it sounded more like a dog coming down a staircase, its toenails clicking on bare wood. But the family's two large dogs were asleep in the cellar.

"And then before I can even turn my head my whole body was frozen and I couldn't breathe," Billy began. "The only thing I could do was see and think . . . It was like that for quite a few seconds, then it went away, so I figured it was my nerves. Then I heard the noise of toenails again. It went away, but by this time I was a little bit afraid to get up or do anything."

Billy would experience two more similar episodes within the next few minutes. "The last time I tried with all my strength to pick up my arm. I could move my arm maybe an inch. It was just frozen and that was the end of that."

His normal functions returned near daybreak. Billy has no idea what happened to him. His wife likened it to a possession. They agreed it was the most unnerving of all the unexplained incidents that have occurred in their house since they moved in during 1977. Whatever it was that "visited" Billy would manifest itself in different ways to frighten Linda and their two young children—Billy Junior and Nicole.

So many "weird" things happened, from the beginning, that Linda began keeping a diary. She discovered that a lot of the mysterious activity occurs at Christmas and in April. Most of the noises are heard about three o'clock in the morning. Linda said, "You're in a deep sleep and whatever happens it wakes you up and it's just enough to get you . . . you're waiting to hear more, and they don't do it."

Here, then, are some of the incidents from her diary:

- A galloping horse circled the house, keeping Linda and Billy awake for several nights after they'd first moved in. They heard it kicking up gravel, but there is no gravel and there was no horse! Each night the couple would peer out the window to see only moonlight filtering through the trees. The house is isolated, set in deep woods, and far from the nearest neighbor. What had they heard? They have no idea.
- More ominous was the man with a handlebar mustache and red eyes. Linda said she saw him clearly, peering into a window of the room that would become little Billy's bedroom. She was glad her son hadn't seen him.
- Soon Linda began hearing tiny voices crying, "Mommy! Mommy!" And little Billy started seeing a small girl walking close to his mother. Linda felt that the house was filled with grief and sadness. It *was*—two hundred years earlier! Linda researched the history of the house through its Pennsylvania Dutch owners to George Schubert, a Revolutionary War soldier and the original settler. The cabin Schubert built on the site burned to the ground, and, after he had built the present farmhouse, five of his children died of smallpox within a week.
- Christmas Eve, 1981. Eight-year-old Billy and his sister, Nicole, were both sleeping in little Billy's bedroom with the door open. Nicole was restless and woke up suddenly. She grabbed her brother and pointed. A large, glowing figure stood beside the open doorway of their parents' room. Then it vanished as quickly as it had come.

In the morning little Billy told his parents that they'd seen "a shiny Jesus figure," and that later a black-haired man had come to the side of his bed. He was very frightened because he said he didn't want to see anything else. The man wore a white shirt and resembled the child's grandfather. But later, when Billy was shown a picture of a man who had once lived in the house, he said that was the man who had been in his bedroom.

Little Billy's cousin, Scott, has also seen the man. The white-shirted specter walked from Billy's dresser into the closet, and vanished.

During another Christmas season, the Mickloses invited their good friend Larry to join them for the holiday. Larry was a Vietnam War veteran whose marriage had broken up. The Mickloses had cut their tree a couple of days before Christmas and asked Larry to decorate it. He enjoyed doing that kind of thing, and Linda thought it would help to take his mind off his grief.

The weather was unseasonably warm, too hot for Christmas, but Linda wanted a fire in the fireplace to create a holiday atmosphere. While her husband carried in the wood, Larry worked on the tree.

When the men were finished they sat down to relax. The room was warm and cozy. Soft firelight lit the cathedral ceiling and flames reflected on the tall French windows. The pungent odor of fresh pine filled the air. Suddenly, the tree started shaking and all the balls fell off and rolled across the floor. At first Billy thought the cat had jumped into the tree. It hadn't. Billy said, "Somebody grabbed that tree and it shook so bad you couldn't believe it."

Then the room became icy cold and the men started to shiver. Linda ran upstairs and brought down flannel shirts for them. A popular belief is that the temperature drops just before the appearance of a ghost. Billy decided to find out. Over the fireplace, his wife had arranged a sleigh filled with colored balls packed tightly together. "Listen," he began, "if anybody is really here knock the balls out of the sleigh." He said that ten minutes later a ball rose from the sleigh and dropped onto the mantel.

December 23, 1983. Billy was sick in bed, too ill to sit up. He had lit a kerosene heater in a small building on the property to prevent its pipes from freezing. The building had been the groom's quarters when the land was a horse farm. Larry lived for a time in this building before he moved away and later committed suicide. By Christmas Billy was feeling much better and went to check the kerosene heater. It would run only twenty-four hours on one fill. "That should've been bone dry and out," he said, "and when I got down there it was full and burning." To this day Billy can't explain how the heater was filled, but he suspects that somehow Larry had returned to do his friend a favor.

On a Friday night during another Christmas season, Angie, a relative from Ohio, was a houseguest of the Mickloses. She was sleeping in the loft. Sometime between 1:30 and 2:00 A.M. Angie was awakened by a loud scratching noise. It started at the top of the stairway and grew fainter as if a heavy dog were going down the stairs, then pausing at the bottom. About twenty minutes later, Angie heard a sound in the kitchen like a metal plate or bread tray falling off the counter. She would learn, in the morning, that no one had been in the kitchen at that time. Angie wrote, "A few minutes later there was a presence sitting on the ladderback chair in the upstairs loft. It felt like a friendly presence, as though the ghost just wanted to join in our conversation, or just listen. . . . Also a candle that was blown out became re-lit, just the wick glowed and it went out about fifteen minutes after we felt the presence in the loft."

Wednesday night, December 18, 1985. At eleven o'clock, Linda was in the bedroom reading while her husband was showering in the basement. Suddenly piano music filled the house. Linda heard it clearly. Billy, with shaving lotion on his face, raced upstairs and into the bedroom. "Tell me you were just playing the piano, Linda." She shook her head. "You know, you hear a lot of stories about pianos playing, but ours never played," he said. "But this night it played . . . and we know it wasn't a cat walking on it unless he was going forward and backward." The piano never played again.

Everyone who stays in the house hears footsteps in the attic and the clicks of old-fashioned thumb latches as doors open and close by themselves.

April 9, 1981. At 1:30 A.M. Linda heard "something" climbing the stairs. The children were asleep and the dogs in the cellar. The steps stopped outside the bedroom door. Then the latch rattled. Linda thought that was odd because their bedroom door opens easily. She said she wasn't frightened, but she woke up Billy and they both watched the door. The latch continued to rattle and the door vibrated. Finally they both got up and threw open the door. Nothing was there.

Later that morning Linda went upstairs to make the beds. Inside little Billy's empty room she heard deep breathing, as if someone were asleep. She paused only long enough to glance under the bed, then flew down the stairs, screaming for her husband.

Billy was out in the barn, but ran immediately to the house. They went up to the bedroom and stood in the doorway. The breathing was heavy and coming from near the bed. Billy walked over to the bed, looked under it, checked behind the dresser and the other pieces of furniture in the room. Just as he put out his hand to touch the bed, the breathing stopped. Linda never again went upstairs when she was alone in the house.

April 25, 1984. Shortly after midnight Linda was again reading in bed. Suddenly, her childhood music box stored beneath the bed started playing its tune, "Stranger in Paradise." She ran downstairs to tell Billy. It was a night of strange disturbances, she recalled, because earlier as she had walked past a round piecrust table the lamp on top of it turned itself on.

The doorbell too seemed to have a mind of its own. On Saturday, October 29, 1983, at 5:00 P.M., when the family was all home, the doorbell rang continuously for three minutes. No one was at the door. On Sunday, November 6, 1983, at 5:00 P.M. the bell rang again for three minutes. No one was anywhere to be seen. Billy took the doorbell apart, including the button.

"Outside, eleven-thirty that night right while we were going to bed, the bell started ringing again," Linda said. "He had the whole bell dismantled on our dining room table."

November 10, 1983. At 4:00 A.M., the doorbell again rang nonstop. Linda and Billy went downstairs and this time Billy removed the wires. He installed bolts and cowbells on all the exterior doors.

But one night when the family was upstairs, Billy heard a horse walking outside and a door open. The cowbells rang and a woman shouted, "Oh, no!" Billy heard the door shut and the horse trot away. He didn't go downstairs to see if anyone had gotten into the house because he knew no one could have come through the bolted door. In the morning Billy tried to make the cowbells ring with the door shut. He shook his head. "There's no way."

Not all the incidents are major ones. Linda says many are "cute and fun" and she doesn't write them all down. Old houses have few, if any, closets, so Linda stores out-of-season clothes in heavy blanket trunks. More than once she has discovered the trunks turned completely around.

One morning she was alone and was soaking clothes in the washer downstairs. Meanwhile, she decided to clean the kitchen sink and brought the bleach bottle halfway up the stairs before remembering that she'd left the lid downstairs. No matter. She poured the bleach into the sink, set the bottle down and went into the sunporch for a moment. When she returned to the kitchen, she found the lid screwed tightly on the bottle!

Billy received a belt buckle as a gift from his brother. He put it away in the sock drawer of the dresser. Shortly after they'd moved into the house, the belt buckle he was wearing broke and he went to get the new one. It was gone. No one knew where it was.

"I emptied that drawer out on the bed about five times looking for this thing," Billy said, "and I kept going back to that drawer. You know, the tenth or eleventh time that buckle was in that drawer, and I thought to myself, well maybe it's like being in the forest and you can't find a tree. Maybe it was there all the time and I didn't see it, but I sure would've heard it when I emptied the drawer."

One Thanksgiving Billy went to bed at nine o'clock. He didn't feel well and thought he'd eaten too much. As he lay in bed he heard a booming sound coming out of one of the walls. At first he thought it was music playing in another part of the house and reverberating through the wall. No. It was a steady *boom, boom, boom,* unlike music. Then he realized that the sounds were synchronized with his own heartbeat. He said the incident lasted "a good five minutes." He called it "weird."

Apparitions appear throughout the house, especially a man in black who walks out of the powder room and into the living room. Billy has seen him many times. Linda suspects that former residents, long deceased, return somehow to "see" what the new owners have done to the house. She only wishes that the ghosts would not frighten the children.

May 6, 1982. Little Nicole was in the bathtub while her mother was putting away laundry in the second-floor bedrooms. Suddenly, Linda heard her daughter screaming. She dashed into the bathroom to find Nicole climbing out of the tub and pointing at the attic door, which is inside the bathroom. The child was just learning to talk and cried, "Someone knocking at door."

Linda grabbed Nicole in her arms, ran downstairs and yelled for Billy. He was in the yard. The three of them returned to the bathroom because Linda wanted to shampoo Nicole's hair. "Billy waited to open the [attic] door," Linda said, "because he was scared. My whole head became numb . . . I couldn't stop shaking." That night Nicole slept in the living room.

May 7, 1982. At 3:30 A.M., little Billy called his mother. He had heard cabinet doors closing and drawers being shut in the kitchen. It wasn't the first time he'd described these noises. But now he was so frightened that Linda let him sleep with her and Billy. When he got up he told his parents that he had seen a man hunched over his father's side of the bed. The man had a mustache and stood sideways. Could it have been the red-eyed man who had looked in the child's bedroom window when the Mickloses had first moved in?

Less than a year after his sister's frightening experience in the bathtub, little Billy would have his own.

February 28, 1983. At 7:00 P.M. the child was taking a bath. Suddenly, he ran, dripping wet, down the stairs, yelling that something was walking down the attic steps.

Linda was home alone with her son. She comforted him but would not go up. Neither would he.

A lot of activity is generated in the children's rooms.

On a cold January night in 1980, a guest named Kathy was sleeping in little Billy's room when she was awakened by a lot of banging and thumping. It seemed to come from inside the closet and also from the exterior of the house near the windows. Normal sounds were magnified. The hum of the refrigerator was so loud that Kathy thought it was in her room. Then she felt someone breathing upon her. She dived under the covers.

February 15, 1981. Angie was visiting again and was sleeping in little Billy's room. Early in the morning she was jolted out of bed by three terrifying screams. Someone ran from the direction of the kitchen. Ten minutes later Angie heard the noise of vomiting near the upstairs bathroom. She did not investigate. She would learn later that no one in the family had been up!

Linda's mother has had several experiences in the children's rooms. March 3,

1982, at 3:00 A.M., while sleeping in Nicole's bedroom, she awakened to see a thin woman with gray, unkempt hair standing sideways in front of the light switch by the door. The ghost was transparent; Linda's mother could see the light switch through the figure. From the neck down, however, the apparition appeared smoky. The mother put on her glasses to see the "visitor" better!

February 15, 1986. Linda's mother again visited, sleeping this time in little Billy's room. In the middle of the night, she heard noises overhead as if someone were struggling with window screens. Then came the tread of heavy footsteps. She was not frightened. It was five years to the day since Angie had slept in that room and heard screams.

Billy has more visual experiences than other members of his family. "I do the hearing," Linda says. "He sees stuff." One night he awakened to see a man and a woman standing together in the open doorway of the bedroom. They were small people, their heads and faces clearly visible even in the dark. But, curiously, each had only what Billy described as a "heat wave body." He felt as if he were watching heat coming off a street; the waves were vertical and shaped somewhat like a human torso. No feet were visible. Billy thought he watched the couple for at least a minute. Then little Billy started talking in his sleep and the figures vanished.

But Billy's experiences are not limited to the house. In his workshop, tools vanish and then reappear when his back is turned. He bought a lot of screwdrivers and now when one disappears, even briefly, he has another one at hand.

The barn is a center of frightening activity. One of Billy's first jobs after the family moved in was to clean out the twenty-four horse stalls. He said the manure was three to four feet deep and he had to rent a front-end loader to remove it.

One summer night about ten o'clock he was working in the bottom of a stall, shoveling out the last of the manure. "I'm shoveling this stuff out in the open, in the middle [stall] and I heard somebody working in the stall next door, so I walk over, I look and there's nothing."

Billy returned to his work and again heard shoveling. He checked a second time. Nothing. Then he heard a horse walking outside. The Mickloses' horses were in the upper barn, but Billy thought one of them had gotten out. He walked outside and looked all around, but saw nothing. Had the phantom horse returned?

One nice evening Billy decided to ride one of his horses. Halfway down the driveway the animal stopped, turned around and raced back to the barn. She had evidently seen something that Billy couldn't see.

Another night, as Billy was locking the barn, he heard a human growl behind the door. "It was one of the scariest things that ever happened to me," he said. He didn't stop to investigate. He has also felt a tug on the back of his shirt while locking up. And the odor of pipe smoke fills the barn. Billy does not smoke.

At five o'clock one morning Billy went out to the chicken coop. As he raised the barn door, Murphy, the Irish setter, barked wildly and Billy yelled at him to settle down. He let the barn door down and had just started walking toward the coop when "this thing is hanging there with a red and blue uniform on with no head. Then right before I got to it, it disappeared . . . I walked right through and got the eggs."

By the time Billy got back outside it was daylight. Was he frightened? "No," he said, "you don't get scared in the daytime like you do at night. It bothered me, but I didn't really get scared because I really saw something."

A couple of years later, Billy saw the figure again hanging from the rafters. Linda learned from her research that a man who had lived there after the Schuberts committed suicide in the barn.

In spite of Billy's sightings he doesn't believe in ghosts. "Until one of them actually comes up and grabs me by the throat in the daytime, then I think I'll believe it." Yet he retains a sense of caution about things unknown and perhaps unknowable.

One day Emil, a house painter, arrived to paint the front doorway. This was shortly after the Mickloses had had a fire in the attic caused by a short circuit in the old wiring.

Referring to the fire, Emil said, "What's Linda doing, burning up the ghosts? Wasn't the ghost in your barn helping to put out the fire?" Billy warned Emil to watch his words because he'd be going up on a ladder. The painter didn't respond.

When Emil was up on the stepladder Billy talked to him while he worked. Suddenly, Emil plunged to the ground, landing on his back in a clump of bushes. When Billy asked him if he was all right, he said, "Somebody pushed me."

"Right off the back of the ladder," Billy explained. "He just went. I mean he couldn't even have time to grab the ladder." The ladder remained in its upright position.

Emil was a professional painter with forty years of experience and had *never* fallen from a ladder. He injured a leg in the accident and was unable to return to work for a month.

The phenomena were still occurring in the 1990s, but with less frequency. "As soon as it seemed that we could laugh about it and not fear it, it didn't come on as strong," Linda said. She recalled feeling especially calm after seeing a "whitish-gray cloud" hover above her stove while preparing a Thanksgiving dinner. Billy often sees that oval-shaped cloud in the basement. The Mickloses have no idea what it means. "You know, your imagination could run away with you," Linda said. She paused and looked around. "But there's definitely something here."

The Lady in Black

Doña Mercedes Wedderburn wanted to go home. A recluse in her husband's house in Narragansett, she spent all her days pacing the upstairs hallway while sobbing and pointing out to sea through the long, narrow windows. Since no one in the seaside village had ever met her or seen her in the streets and shops, no one missed her after they heard she was gone.

Her husband, Captain Japhet Wedderburn, was amassing a fortune in the China trade and was away at sea for months, and sometimes years, at a time. Doña Mercedes's only companion was the house servant, Huldy Craddock.

One day the captain returned without notice and said that since his wife was so unhappy in Narragansett he would be taking her back to Barbados to visit her people.

On a dark, sleety night, Wedderburn's ship sailed out of the harbor. Two years later, the captain returned alone. Where was his wife? She wanted to stay a little longer, he said. He'd pick her up on his next trip.

But the next trip was the last for Captain Wedderburn. While at the helm of a clipper ship called the *Black Arrow*, he died of a heart attack off Cape Hatteras, North Carolina.

The story of the sad and lonely Spanish lady is one of the most poignant in Rhode Island lore. And no one knew it better than Huldy Craddock, who had spent so many years in the captain's employ.

Here was the tale as Huldy told it:

"Japhat Wedderburn built a right nice house—four stories high and all sided with white clapboards and green shutters at the windows. It was a big, four-square house like all wealthy sea captains built in the 1800s. It wasn't as fancy as some houses inside because almost no one saw it but me. Yet the doorway made a lot of people stop and stare. It had columns on either side and on top of them something I think they called a broken pediment. Anyway in the center of it was the most beautiful carved wooden pineapple anybody ever saw. It looked almost real enough to eat. Sometimes I wanted to reach up just to touch it, but of course it was too high. The pineapple was supposed to be a sign of welcome, but with the captain gone so much there wasn't many visitors.

"Well, after I'd been doing for the master for a number of years, I sensed his restlessness. He was real fidgety like, always pacing the floors when he was home. I knew he didn't need no more years at sea. He had more money than he could ever spend and he should be settling down. He needed a wife. But it weren't up to me to say so. A lot of people said he had a woman in every port, but I never did believe that.

"I used to picture him with a lovely lady on his arm here at Wedderburn and all the other rich captains and their wives arriving for the holiday parties. I'd make the balsam wreath for the door and decorate the house just so with white candles in the silver candelabra on the table and a garland of greenery climbing the staircase. I'd be busy for days ahead of time baking, decorating, polishing the silver and laying the table for a holiday feast.

"And then it happened. My wish came true. Captain Wedderburn brought a woman home. He introduced her as his wife—Doña Mercedes Wedderburn from a wealthy family in Barbados. She was tiny and fragile as a doll, all dressed in black. The high tortoise shell comb and the black lace mantilla she wore made her seem taller. I bowed and when I lifted my head her dark eyes met mine and she smiled real sweet. I knew we would get along good.

"I can't remember now exactly how long the captain stayed after bringing his wife to the house, but I do recall that five weeks was about the longest he ever spent at one time. I left them alone and hummed a happy tune as I went about my work.

"The day after the captain left I went upstairs to clean. I was sure I heard someone crying so I went on up to the third floor. Mrs. Wedderburn had her hands over her face and was pacing back and forth in the long corridor. When she saw me she stopped and gazed through one of the long windows that gave a view of the sea. Then she began talking and sobbing at the same time. But I couldn't understand a single word she said. She turned around and said, 'No habla Usted el español?'

"Was that Spanish for something? I shook my head no. When she kept on crying I put a hand on her shoulder to try to comfort her and I said I'd make a pot of tea. But she stared at me real funny. I knew then she couldn't understand English! Oh, the sadness of it all—just the two of us in the big house unable to talk to each other. The captain spoke several languages real good, but I never saw a single book about them in the house.

"I took Mrs. Wedderburn by the hand and led her downstairs where I made the tea and set out biscuits on a silver tray. I thought maybe I should leave her alone, her being the mistress of the house and all and me being the servant, but she motioned me to sit down in the other chair.

"I don't rightly recall now who started the sign language, but she and me got along pretty well, at least part of the time. I found a book that had maps in it and showed her where we lived. She started crying again and I was wanting to hold her close and wipe away the tears. You know she was just like a little, lost child.

"One day I drew a picture of the Wedderburn house and the village shops with a big black arrow between them, pointing to the stores. It was market day and I wanted her to go with me to pick out the food she wanted me to cook. A lot of the rich captains' wives went along with their servants. It was a chance for them to gossip, and gossip never hurt a soul.

"Well, as soon as I got Mrs. Wedderburn's shawl she shook her head no. I reached for her hand and she put it behind her back. I could figure it out though. Her not speaking English made it so she couldn't talk to anybody. I just thought the sights and the smells and the crowd of people would make her feel better. Sometimes a little getting out like that lifts a body's spirits. Anyways, I went on alone as I did every market day.

"Then a thought struck me as I was walking back. Even though I didn't get much schooling maybe I could teach Mrs. Wedderburn English. I'm not a person that's real bright when it comes to books so I knew I could never learn Spanish. I found a big tablet of plain white paper and drew pictures of tables, chairs, houses—just ordinary things you know and I printed the English words beside them in big black letters. It was the worst mistake I ever made! She banged a tiny fist on the table and ran upstairs.

"After that she was doing nothing at all but walking all day long in the upper hallway and crying and pointing to the sea. Somehow I had the queerness that she wasn't waiting for her husband. She was waiting for a ship to take her home. One day when I was cleaning her room I saw a valise open on the bed. It was full of clothes and jewels. Then I knew for sure. It gave me a real chill. What if the master returned and she was gone? I couldn't watch her every minute with me needing to clean the house and shop and cook and all. And how could I stop her if she wanted to leave? That weren't my business.

"There was days when Mrs. Wedderburn never came downstairs, not even to eat. I was telling Madie, the day servant next door, about the mistress not eating. I was afraid she'd get sick. Madie said to fix the meals on a pretty tray and take them up to her. I tried, but it was no use. She just walked and cried and wrung her hands day after day waiting for a rescue ship that never came.

"But finally Captain Wedderburn got home and just at that time I took sick, and couldn't work. I had such terrible stomach pains I never got out of bed most days. Couldn't keep food down either. I never been sick a day in my whole life. The captain always said I was big and strong as an ox and could do the work of two or three servants.

"There was just me and my sister, Lettie, living in the little house our parents left us when they died. I begged Lettie to go to Wedderburns to work in my place, but she wouldn't leave me. She did go tell the captain she'd try to find a new servant but he said no, he and his wife would be leaving real soon. She wanted to visit her folks.

"It must've been nearly two years before the captain returned alone! There was sure a lot of gossip about that. But he said his wife wanted to stay on with her folks for a while. I was feeling better by then, but not so as I could do the work in a big house. I went to tell Captain Wedderburn that I couldn't work for him anymore, but he said he didn't need me. The next thing I heard was that he died of a heart attack on the way to get his wife. It was real sad, about the saddest thing that ever happened in our village. I liked the captain and he was always good to me."

* * *

Several months later Huldy Craddock died. The villagers said she had worked herself to death. They all contributed toward the expense of a nice funeral. The church altar was banked with flowers, the mourners sang "Rock of Ages," and Rev. Ephraim Purdy preached a fine sermon. Lettie was comforted.

The house was then sold to Josiah Squires, son of Jacob Squires, a prominent attorney. Josiah and his wife Priscilla and their three children were delighted to move into such a large place. The children needed space for themselves and their friends, and their parents did a lot of entertaining.

A month after the family had moved in, little Sarah, the five-year-old, came running downstairs. "Mommy! Mommy! Come quick!" She tugged at her mother's dress. "There's a lady upstairs and she's crying." Priscilla Squires was busy in the kitchen. "Whatever in the world are you talking about, Sarah? This is *our* house. No one else lives here."

Sarah squeezed back her tears. "Honest, Mommy."

To calm her daughter's fears, Mrs. Squires followed her up to the third-floor gallery. Sunlight poured in the long windows that gave such a splendid view of the sea. It was a pleasant, restful place. "You see, Sarah, there is no one here."

"She was standing right where you are, Mommy. She was all dressed in black."

At that moment Sarah's older sister, Hortense, came into the hallway. "Mother," she began, "I have seen the lady too. She walks back and forth and sometimes just stands real close to the window looking out to sea." She paused. "John saw her once too. He said she had some kind of a big comb in her hair and a veil over it, but I didn't notice that. It was the night you had that party. He thought she was one of the guests."

Priscilla Squires felt uneasy. Surely all three of her children had not imagined something that was not there. While Sarah was busy playing with her friends and the other children were in school, Mrs. Squires took to spending time in the hallway. She never saw a thing. She never heard a sound. And she never told her husband about the mysterious woman that the children said they'd seen.

When Josiah's work took him elsewhere, the family sold the house. Over the years a succession of families occupied the place, and at least some of them claimed that at sunset they saw a woman in black pointing through the windows and crying. But whenever someone approached her, she dissolved in the shadows.

In 1925 a charitable organization bought the property to use as a summer retreat for poor children from nearby cities. The house had not been kept up and needed major repairs. In the library workmen found that the hearthstone of the fireplace was badly cracked and should be replaced. But the owners decided that the entire fireplace wall should be torn out. The workmen, with their crowbar, pried up the stone. There, in a hole beneath the stone, was a small, rude coffin.

When the coffin was opened, the workmen staggered back in horror. A magnificent tortoiseshell comb rested on the top of a human skull, and the skeleton itself was wrapped in rags of black lace.

Ghosts of the Grand Strand

Sixty miles of wide, white beaches, known as the Grand Strand, frame the Atlantic Ocean off the coast of South Carolina. Warmed by the Gulf Stream, the area has become a popular tourist mecca visited by fishermen, golfers, sunseekers, and those who wish to do nothing more than enjoy the beauty of this land.

Here, a visitor might see, beyond a grove of magnolias, the ruins of a nineteenth-century rice plantation, or glimpse a figure sweeping through a shadowed alley of live oak trees hung with moss. Was the figure real? Maybe. Maybe not. The ghostly legends of the Low Country are numerous. They've been handed down through many generations, and the natives are usually pleased to share them.

Here are two of the most popular stories:

The Warning

Pawleys Island is a sliver of beach joined to the South Carolina mainland by two short causeways. It's an unpretentious kind of place with no high-rise hotels, no condominiums, no golf courses or fast-food restaurants. No neon, either. Southern gentry live simply in weatherbeaten cypress cottages built by their ancestors. In the summer they enjoy trapping crabs in the tidal creek separating the island from the mainland, lazing in a hammock, or strolling the sands while watching the gulls wheel overhead and the surf roll in.

That's what island residents Jack and Clara Moore were doing on the evening of September 19, 1989—walking the beach and enjoying the beauty of the fading day. Suddenly, a man appeared and walked past them. As they turned to speak to him, he seemed to vanish. The couple didn't think there was time for him to duck into a house or behind a breakwater.

Who had they seen? Clara Moore thinks it could have been the Gray Man of Pawleys Island, the legendary specter who appears before each hurricane to warn residents to leave. Though the man they saw didn't say anything, the Moores didn't need a warning. They were already packed.

At midnight on Thursday, September 21, 1989, Hurricane Hugo boiled up out of the east and crossed the South Carolina coast. The screaming 135-mile-per-hour winds spun buildings, boats, and trees through the air, cutting electrical power and plunging the barrier islands into terrifying darkness. The eye of the storm, arriving at high tide as it did, hauled a tower of water seventeen feet above ocean level. Pawleys Island was devastated. Fourteen houses were destroyed and dozens more were damaged. Some were blown across to the mainland. An inlet was cut at the southern end of the island and into the inlet a house was dropped, its pink shutters still intact. Not since Hurricane Hazel, in 1954, had a storm wiped out the South Carolina coastline.

Automobile dealer Bill Collins would never forget Hazel. He and his bride were honeymooning in a Pawleys Island cottage in October of that year. Early one morning someone knocked at the door. Collins thought he was dreaming and rolled over to go back to sleep. He couldn't. The knocking persisted. Cracking one eye open, Collins noted the time on his bedside clock—5:00 A.M. Who comes calling at that hour? No one except a neighbor in distress. Yet the island was almost deserted on that October day in 1954.

Collins crawled out of bed and padded barefoot to the door. On the porch stood an old man in rumpled gray pants, gray shirt, and a gray cap pulled so low on his forehead that the features of his face were shadowed. Collins had never seen him before.

"The Red Cross sent me to warn everyone to get off the island," the stranger began. "Big storm blowing in."

Collins smelled the brine on the man's clothes. Suddenly he was gone.

"He just vanished," Collins told his bride, who was now awake. Only the urgency in the old man's voice persuaded the couple to get out. Within an hour they were back on the mainland, in nearby Georgetown, and a short time later Hurricane Hazel hit Pawleys Island. It was one of the most devastating storms of this century.

When the Collinses returned to the island, they found that most of the cottages had washed out to sea and dunes thirty feet high had disappeared. Yet their house was untouched by the storm's wrath. Towels that Mrs. Collins had hung on the porch to dry were still there, as was the TV antenna on the roof.

Collins had met the ghost of the Gray Man—that benevolent specter who looks out for the residents of the island. Legend says that no harm will come to those who see him.

The Gray Man first materialized before the storm of 1822. Even though the rice planters who settled the island knew they'd built in the path of hurricanes roaring up the coast from the Caribbean, the likelihood of savage storms striking the island seemed remote.

The daughter of one planter was spending a summer on the island, awaiting the arrival of her fiancé, who had been abroad for several years. He returned safely to Pawleys, but, in taking a shortcut through a bog, his horse stumbled and fell. Quicksand devoured man and beast.

The grief-stricken girl walked the beach day and night. One windy day she saw a man in gray coming toward her. Recognizing her dead lover, she ran to him with arms outstretched. But before she reached him he was swept into the sea. Her father, upon learning of the incident, was convinced his daughter was suffering a mental breakdown and rushed her to a Charleston hospital. She was pronounced in excellent health.

The next day a hurricane hit the island and raged for two days. Stunned survivors mourned the dead, then cleaned up the litter and rebuilt their homes. In time the island of oleander and oak trees became again an oasis of peace and beauty.

So the island remained for seventy-one years. And during all that time the story of the mysterious man on the beach was told and retold. A legend had been born. The Gray Man, it is said, would always come to warn the islanders of an approaching storm.

One day in 1893, an odd-looking man appeared at the door of a French family named Lachicotte. The visitor was dressed in gray from head to foot. He said nothing, but shuffled his feet, then turned away. The Lachicottes fled their home immediately. Others were less fortunate.

The day that had begun as sunny and pleasant, with a breeze stirring the curtains at open windows, turned sullen. The sky darkened while at the same time the sea appeared to be on fire. The tide never ran out; it came thundering up over the sands until the entire beach had vanished. Trees snapped, their limbs exploding like firecrackers. Birds beat their wings helplessly, seeking sanctuary from the roar of winds and water.

Whole families died, perhaps none more pathetically than members of the Flagg family, who were vacationing at their summer homes on Magnolia Beach, now Huntington Beach State Park north of Pawleys Island.

When the sea washed under the doors of the cottages, young Dr. J. Ward Flagg and his parents climbed as high as they could into a beach cedar tree. The surf churned over them. Old Mrs. Flagg was the first to go, on a wave forty feet high. Her husband, seeing her vanish, let go his grip and went after her.

When the storm abated, the sea turned back and the sun came out. Rescuers reaching young Dr. Flagg, or "Wardie," as they called him, had to pry loose every one of his fingers from a bough of the tree. A small niece and a servant escaped death with him, but the doctor's brother, the brother's wife, and five children all lost their lives.

A baby's shoe and undergarment swung from a barren treetop; a woman's shoe, unbuttoned to the last button, stuck up in the sand like a hideous marker; clothing, splintered furniture, and shards of glass that had once been cottage windows littered the beach.

Day and night survivors searched for bodies. A wagon loaded with empty coffins rumbled across the strand, and whenever a body was found it was placed in a coffin and taken to the porch of a neighboring church. Ministers were kept busy praying for the dying and conducting funerals for the dead.

The water, rising a foot higher than Hazel, was the result of what is said to be the worst storm in South Carolina history.

Dr. Flagg never fully recovered from the tragedy. He locked himself inside the house on land that is now part of Brookgreen Gardens, and the seasons passed without his knowledge. With window shades lowered, he saw neither sunshine nor rain. Friends tried to encourage him to leave the cottage, but he refused. Dr. Flagg's loyal servant, Tom Duncan, who survived the storm with him, kept house for him.

Finally, the doctor did leave his house. There was no one else to tend to the sick of the area. He also served as postmaster, but whenever he could he paced the beach, gazing out to sea and stooping to pick up articles washed in on the tide. He told Tom that as he walked the sands his mother, father, and the rest of his relatives spoke to him. Their voices brought him solace.

It is said that even today those persons keen of eye and ear may see the misty forms of the Flaggs and hear their pitiful cries.

And, although the Coast Guard now alerts residents of in-coming storms, the Gray Man of Pawleys Island still makes his rounds, shuffling from cottage to cottage to deliver his warning. Is he the lover who was killed? Or just a nameless shipwrecked sailor? Does it really matter?

NOTE: Dr. J. Ward Flagg was a nephew of Alice and Allard Flagg (see following story).

The Lovely Lady of the Hermitage

ALICE. A single name on a flat marble tombstone. A child of sixteen dead of typhoid fever. And today, nearly 150 years after her death, her ghost walks, searching for a ring.

The story begins in 1848 when Alice Belin Flagg, her brother, Dr. Allard Flagg, and their widowed mother moved into the Hermitage at Murrells Inlet. Alice loved the plantation house with its imposing white pillars, wide brick steps, and large rooms, which were light and airy. The building, of imperishable pitch pine, had taken slaves four years to build.

But Alice's happiness would be short-lived. She fell in love with a turpentine dealer.

The news devastated Mrs. Flagg. Ever conscious of the family's place in South Carolina aristocracy, she warned her daughter, "Child, he is beneath our station. He will disgrace our family name and bring you nothing but unhappiness." Her voice was hard and sharp.

Alice turned to her brother. "You heard her," said Dr. Allard, as everyone called him. "He's nothing but a common laborer." He lit his pipe and stared at his sister above the flame of the match. The muscles of his face tightened. "Mother and I forbid you to see him."

But Alice did see him—many times, in a grove of oak trees far from the house. It became their secret trysting place.

One afternoon Alice told her lover to come to the house the next day. She'd be home alone. Her mother would be in Charleston and her brother would be attending several critically ill patients. He came—a tall, slim man with erect bearing and a kindly, reassuring face. From his pocket he brought forth a tiny box, took out the diamond ring and slipped it on her finger. The gem caught the light, reflecting it in long silver rays. Alice and her lover embraced. At that moment Dr. Allard walked into the room. "Get out!" he roared.

Alice watched her lover stride from the room, but made no attempt to follow him. Her brother drew near and stood silently before his sister. Then he pulled the ring from her finger. "Alice," he said in a voice now calm and composed, "you will break your mother's heart and mine too if you marry that man." He paused and turned the ring in his fingers. "But he has given you this ring. It is not mine to dispose of. If you'll wear it on a ribbon concealed in the neck of your dress, mother will never know."

Alice nodded and fought back the tears.

Early one morning two weeks later, Mrs. Flagg discovered the ring on the chest in her daughter's bedroom. She shook Alice awake and demanded an explanation. When none was forthcoming she screamed invectives at both Alice and the absent lover. Alice pulled the bedclothes high up under her chin. She felt sick.

Then the door banged open and Dr. Allard entered the room. He noticed the ring on the chest. "Mother, you've had a restless night," he began. "Come along now and let me give you a sedative." She went willingly, supported by her son's strong arms. As their footsteps receded down the hallway, Alice knew that she could no longer remain in the house. She would be sent away to a boarding school in Charleston. Her mother and her brother had discussed that possibility at one time. Alice buried her face in her pillow and wept.

Dr. Allard drove his sister to Charleston, the carriage jouncing over broken sections of roadway and the steamer trunk rattling in the rear. The trip, a distance of about eighty miles, took four days.

At first Alice was excited by the sights and sounds of the city. King Street and Meeting Street were filled with the bustle and banter of shoppers and the clatter of horses' hooves on the paving. Shade trees of every variety lined the streets, and after dark the gaslights shone softly on the leaves.

But the novelty of these distractions soon paled. Alice could not concentrate on her schoolwork. Although she tried to complete the daily assignments, her heart was elsewhere. She overslept her classes. Her new friends, noting her listlessness, tried to help her. Unsuccessfully.

But by the time spring came Alice's spirits soared. The school term would soon end and she could return home to her beloved. At the May Ball, Alice, resplendent in a white gown, glided across the floor with one young man after another from Charleston's aristocracy. Her eyes shone brilliantly and a high color came into her cheeks. But she would not remember this night.

Early the next morning Dr. Flagg was notified to come and take his sister home. She had become critically ill.

Allard Flagg set out immediately. At the school he wrapped his sister in blankets and placed her in the carriage. A friend had packed the gown.

Upon reaching the Hermitage, Alice was put to bed immediately. Typhoid fever had struck, as it did every spring in the Low Country. The physician could only try to keep his sister as comfortable as possible during her remaining hours.

Alice soon realized that her ring was not on her finger and cried out for it. Legend has it that her brother had thrown it into a creek on the way home. A sympathetic cousin soon appeared with a ring, but Alice, even in her delirium, knew it wasn't hers and threw it on the floor. Two days later she lapsed into a coma and died.

Alice's mother was not with her dying daughter. Like many other residents of the swampy coastal area, she spent the months of May through September in the mountains to escape the deadly fevers so prevalent during the warm weather. Unwilling to call his mother home, Dr. Allard had his sister dressed in her ball gown and the coffin lowered into a temporary grave on the plantation. Later, in the presence of the grief-stricken family, the body was permanently buried in the Flagg family plot in All Saints Waccamaw Episcopal cemetery, three miles west of Pawleys Island.

But Alice does not rest easily. When the moon is full and a mist rises over the fields of the Low Country, she returns to the home she loved. Some say she still searches for her lost engagement ring. So many have reported seeing Alice that she may be the most authenticated ghost of the Grand Strand. She always appears in her beautiful ball gown.

Since 1910 the Willcox family has owned the antebellum home. Clarke Willcox and his wife, Lillian, both now deceased, never saw Alice, but one member of the family saw the lovely apparition many years ago.

During Clarke Willcox's childhood his mother's sister, "Aunt Lolly," often visited her only sister's family. Early one morning Aunt Lolly was seated at the vanity brushing her hair. Suddenly, in the mirror, she saw the bedroom door open and a young girl enter the room. When the girl did not speak Aunt Lolly swung around. No one was there. Hairbrush in hand and screaming, the woman flew down the stairs. She never slept in that room again.

Through the years a number of superstitions have arisen about Alice. Young people say that if you walk thirteen times backward around the grave you can commune with her spirit. It's said that once a young woman walking in the opposite direction saw her own ring fly off her finger. Friends spent most of the day trying to find it.

Red roses or camellias often appear on Alice's tombstone. No one knows who brings the flowers, but some believe that the ghost of her lover has something to do with it.

NOTE: The water surge from Hurricane Hugo in 1989 reached the front porch of the Hermitage, but did not enter the house, which suffered relatively minor damage from fallen trees.

Watchers on the Stairs

Marlene Akhtar did not expect to have so many encounters with the supernatural in her historic Hot Springs home. Nor does she know precisely who the ghosts she saw might have been—in life. What she is certain of, quite positive about, in point of fact, is that the dreadful, unearthly scenes she saw played out are as vividly detailed in her mind's eye today as when they occurred nearly two decades ago.

A witty, vivacious woman with long, flowing hair the color of midnight, Akhtar made her home for nearly eleven years in a rambling house perched on a hillside promontory commanding a breathtaking view of downtown Hot Springs and the southern edge of the Black Hills.

The house has twenty rooms, seven outside doors, and hardwood floors throughout its five thousand square feet of living space. A unique octagonal living room in the center of the house is set off by an intricately stenciled oak ceiling two and one-half stories above the floor. A narrow, winding staircase hugs the living room wall, ending at a trapdoor cut into the edge of the ceiling. Opening the door reveals a round "hidden" room, or lookout, actually the inside of the house's cupola. Nearly continuous windows provide dramatic vistas of the red rock canyon walls that rise above the city.

Developer Fred T. Evans built the house in 1891 as a "guest house" retreat for wealthy Iowa businessmen visiting the curative hot springs that gave the city its name. Legend has it that gambling, carousing, and frolics with frontier whores were common entertainments within its walls. Two small bedchambers situated off the living room staircase are reputedly where the ladies of the evening plied their trade.

Evans's guest house was eventually purchased in 1925 by Chicago developer F. O. Butler. Earlier, he had bought the nearby Spanish-style mansion known as Villa Theresa, built in 1916 by Ernest DeMoulin, another Chicagoan. DeMoulin had named it after Evans's widow. She had sold all the Evans Height property, upon which the guest house was located, to DeMoulin after her husband's death. The exotic manse that was Villa Theresa seemed out of place with its roof garden, tennis courts, billiard room, and landscaped terraces.

The scion of the family that began Butler Paper Company, F. O. Butler was a prominent summer resident of Hot Springs until his death in 1955. He owned the Seven-Bar-Eleven Ranch, a thousand-acre spread outside town, on which he bred horses for his Oak Brook, Illinois polo club. His holdings in Hot Springs eventually included the entire mountaintop upon which the Villa Theresa, and its guest house, Marlene Akhtar's former home, are located.

The Akhtars—Marlene, her physician husband, and their five children— bought the old guest house in 1974. The family lived in the house until the mid 1980s.

"You can't get the feeling of a haunted house now because it's so beautiful," Marlene concedes. Extensive renovation by the most recent owners has transformed her former home into a gracious bed-and-breakfast establishment, called appropriately enough the Villa Theresa Guest House.

"But this much I can tell you, I saw the ghosts. I did not expect to see them. I really did not want these things to happen, but I don't make things up. So whatever it was and why I happened to be the one that saw them, well, maybe some day it will have to be solved. I am curious," she said.

Not long after Marlene and her family moved in, the first in the series of strange events took place. Though they lived in the house for over a decade, virtually all of the ghost sightings took place within the first two years of their residency there.

"I was on the couch right here," Marlene gestured, pointing toward a corner of the octagonal living room, across from the foot of the staircase. "I saw a lady walking down the stairs. She was absolutely beautiful, very regal, in a long dress with beige lace. Probably from the 1890s. I thought she was either a prostitute or the wife of one of the gamblers who had come. This was a private gambling house in that era."

Marlene was struck with the elegance of the woman, noticing especially that her shimmering brunette hair was worn swept back and tied in a bun. The bodice of her dress had a kind of thin, lacy ruffle and looked to Marlene like an evening gown popular at the turn of the century.

"She was coming down the stairs, her hand on the rail. She wasn't looking down, just straight ahead. I saw her just long enough for her to take a few steps and then she disappeared," Marlene said.

The popularity of the house with guests of Fred T. Evans, and its rowdy reputation in the days when thousands of visitors flooded Hot Springs to bathe in the tepid "health" waters, make it virtually impossible to trace the identity of the ghost. It may even have been Theresa Evans herself.

The suddenness of the woman's appearance on the staircase startled Marlene, particularly the fact that the ghost appeared as a flesh-and-blood figure. Marlene wasn't particularly alarmed. However, her composure in the presence of beings she thought must have come from the spirit world would not last long.

"He was sitting up there," Marlene said with a shudder, recalling her encounter with the next ghost, a glowering man sitting on a step at the same spot where the woman had appeared earlier. Marlene was again resting on the couch, but this time her son, John Davis, was beside her. He noticed his mother staring at something about halfway up the staircase. He asked her what was wrong, but she was too startled by what was on the staircase to reply.

"The ghost was watching me. I was frightened by the way he was studying me so intently. When I looked at him and made eye contact, I was scared. He hadn't been there a few minutes before, and then suddenly I saw him staring at me. It happened so fast, and then he disappeared in just seconds," Marlene said. He spoke not a word to her. Marlene's son also saw him.

The figure Marlene locked eyes with was crouching behind a railing on a step outside one of the small bedchambers. His hands were curled around the banister, his head pressed against the railings as he peered down at Marlene and her son. He didn't appear as "real" as the woman, Marlene recalls. She said that looking at him was like viewing a faded photograph.

Marlene and her family had a difficult time coping with the notion that their house was haunted. On the one hand, they weren't afraid of the occasional ghost sightings, yet they never felt entirely comfortable in their home.

"Whatever I did in this house just went disastrously," Marlene remembers. "It was like the house just did not like us. It didn't want us. The house was angry, because no matter what we did it would be undone." She didn't have the slightest clue as to what the house was upset with, or why the man on the staircase seemed so upset with her.

She tried her best to ignore the supernatural goings-on.

"I knew they [the ghosts] couldn't hurt me so I didn't concern myself with them. I never felt they were after me, except for the man sitting up there on the landing. It was the way he was staring" that made her nervous, Marlene said.

Not even a third encounter with the house's resident spirits could entice Marlene to move away, an episode involving a much more frightening scene—the ghostly reenactment of what may have been a murder!

"I . . . saw a man standing with this woman. She only came up to his chin," Marlene said. Again the apparition took place on the living room staircase, on a landing about halfway up to the "lookout" room above. This time the figures were much more contemporary in appearance. "She was wearing a full skirt, like a poodle skirt, with white, rolled-down socks. And the two of them were fighting just violently. My recollection is that the energy coming from him was evil, just full of malice and hate. On her part it seemed like a lovers' quarrel, jealousy maybe. And then she reached up and grabbed his hair and pulled it. He threw her over the banister. Before she hit the floor, they both disappeared."

The entire episode lasted less than a minute, but Marlene was able to register the details. The man appeared to be in his early forties, with thick, wavy hair, dressed in slacks and a long-sleeved shirt. The woman had very dark hair, and may have been Hispanic. Marlene said the woman was definitely not the same one she had seen earlier, but the man may have been the same one as before.

Was there ever a murder in the Villa Theresa's guest house? The records are not entirely clear, but it appears there were no documented homicides in the house. If not that, then what did Marlene see?

"My husband, who is Pakistani, wrote to a friend in Pakistan who is psychic," Marlene said. "He didn't mention anything about these events, only that we had bought a house. He didn't even describe the house. Well, his friend wrote back two weeks later and said a woman had been killed here and her body put in the river. It was called a suicide. The river is very small here, so it would be pretty hard to drown unless she was drunk. We hadn't even said there was a river in town." It's also possible that a person unconscious, or dead, from a fall over a railing could be placed facedown in a shallow stream and have the death look like suicide or an accident.

Marlene's theory is that the young woman may have been a maid in the house during the 1950s. According to some sources, a domestic who worked at the house "vanished" one day without a trace. Who was the man Marlene saw push the young woman over the banister? She thinks it may have been a former owner, a man known for his violent temper, who may have been having an affair with the woman. But the evidence is scant for any final pronouncement, and Marlene never saw either ghost again for as long as she lived in the house.

"It left me with a bad feeling for a long, long time because the fight was so vicious. Yet, there was still a sense of excitement . . . an intriguing quality to all of it," Marlene added.

Most of the episodes involved Marlene, but at other times her children and even her dog, Gus, were involved in the events.

Marlene was tidying the living room when something puzzling happened to the little dog.

"He was standing up on the landing looking through the banister," Marlene said. "I was busy, but I kept glancing up at him because he was looking down at me. He was cute, his little ears were sticking through the banister. But all of a sudden I looked over and there he was standing on the floor, looking back up the stairs."

Marlene didn't hear Gus fall, nor would he have had time to scamper down the stairs. Did one of the ghosts somehow "float" him down? That seems preposterous, but any other explanation is equally as peculiar. The episode remains a mystery.

"All of our dogs acted oddly. They'd bark and run, but there'd be nothing around. They would watch something, or sometimes look over my head. My husband used to make the comment, 'What are they seeing?' I just didn't pay much attention to that after a while."

Marlene's son, John Davis, was involved in several other bizarre occurrences. A friend of his was spending the night in a guest bedroom in the basement when he noticed the doorknob on an outside door turn several times. He called out, believing John was playing a trick on him. When he didn't get an answer he grabbed the knob and threw open the door. No one was outside. Marlene recalls the boy rushing up the stairs, saying he would never again venture downstairs.

Hot Springs is the only town of significant size for miles in any direction. Students from outlying farms and ranches are bused long distances to the local high school, and it's not unusual for winter snowstorms to strand the youngsters in town. So it was that another of John's classmates spent the night in the Akhtar living room, his first—and last—overnight at the house.

"He saw a blue light moving around" near the ceiling of the living room, Marlene remembers. "He was petrified. He got up and couldn't go back to sleep. He said he didn't care what kind of a snowstorm there was, he'd never spend the night here again."

John Davis remembers that shortly before his friend watched the strange light bouncing around, they had both glimpsed a man dressed in a dark suit glide from the entryway into the front bedroom. There was no one meeting that description in the house that night.

Other incidents involved Marlene's husband's brothers.

"One stayed in the living room, sleeping on the couch, and he heard noises up in the dome [lookout room]. We had that little door to it pushed open, and he saw a red light moving around up there, and sounds like someone was moving around. He was so terrified he never came back to the house."

On another occasion, a second brother, a mechanical engineer by profession, had parked his Volkswagen camper in front of the house during a visit. He wanted to work on the engine.

"He basically knew the structure of the car, even though he didn't have a whole lot of hands-on experience," Marlene recalled. "But everything he did went wrong. Finally one day he was working on a part on the front porch when the car engine caught fire. We were somewhere else in town and heard the fire siren. You know how you always wonder if it's your house? Well, we came up the road and it was! He was so frightened he sold the car. He wouldn't touch it again."

Marlene's husband and his brothers, as Pakistanis, are familiar with a belief in their culture that spirits can inhabit objects. "He thought the car was jinxed or filled with a bad spirit," she said.

In 1990, the Villa Theresa guest house was purchased by Margaret and Dick Hunter, native South Dakotans who had spent the previous twenty years in suburban Minneapolis. Dick was raised on a ranch in central South Dakota, but gave up farming to return to college and pursue a law degree. He practiced tax law in the Twin Cities. Margaret Hunter has a degree in home economics, and put that education to work as an interior design consultant while raising their children.

The couple wanted to return to South Dakota. They were near retirement age, but much too active to settle into idleness. What they found instead was Marlene Akhtar's unique former home, the perfect blend of a home for them and plenty of room for one of their dreams, a bed-and-breakfast. After a year of renovations and improvements, the Villa Theresa Guest House again welcomed visitors to Hot Springs, just as it had done nearly a century before. The clientele of the 1990s, however, is of a much more genteel nature!

Under the watchful eye of Margaret Hunter, the house was transformed into an exquisitely furnished inn. Priceless antiques, including Bronze Age artifacts, pioneer quilts, and heirloom furniture throughout are but a few of Margaret's touches. She is a particular fan of noted South Dakota painter Harvey Thomas

Dunn, an artist known for his work in the *Saturday Evening Post*. His sentimental paintings of Dakota pioneer life grace many of the walls.

Three rooms on the main floor have been converted into bedroom suites, each named for wives of past owners. The Fanny Butler Room has stenciled floors and a bird's-eye maple bedroom set and is decorated in blues and burgundy; the Louise Schroth Room is furnished with a queen-size four-poster bed with a decor of laces, rose velvet, and soft green moire. And the Marlene Akhtar Bedroom has an ivory iron bed over which is spread an antique lavender quilt. All of the rooms have separate baths, but are linked to a common sitting room with a sink, ironing board, and comfortable chairs for browsing through the Hunters' many books and magazines about South Dakota. A massive oak rolltop desk takes up one corner of the room.

Downstairs, a separate apartment, which the Hunters have called the Margaret Room, has been fashioned to accommodate one or two families. It features an outside entrance, living room, and fully equipped kitchen.

Breakfast is served each morning in the large main dining room at a table that could seat twenty in comfort. Margaret cooks hearty egg dishes, country ham, and baked bread, served with a selection of fresh fruit.

The Hunters take a cautious approach to any suggestion that their B&B is haunted. Lanky Dick Hunter looks the part of a western rancher, but with a preciseness of speech and manner that reveals his legal training. He neither accepts nor rejects Marlene Akhtar's ghost sightings.

Margaret Hunter maintains a steady good humor and interest in the supernatural history of her guest house. Two personal incidents in the realm of the unexplained bolster her curiosity about the house.

On the first night the couple spent in their Hot Springs home, their bedroom furniture had not been unpacked, so they slept on a mattress on the floor. Sometime during the night, Margaret awoke to see the flash of a disembodied face hovering over her. She didn't recognize the man, and wasn't even really sure of what she had seen. A few days later, however, while browsing through a history of Hot Springs, her eyes fell upon a photograph of the house's former owner, Chicago developer F. O. Butler—a near-perfect likeness of the face floating above her that night!

Margaret and Dick's grown son visited several weeks after the couple opened for business to help with some final remodeling. He told his parents that he had a hard time sleeping in one of the small rooms off the staircase—the old brothel rooms. He felt he was being watched by someone all night.

Margaret also jokes that even the local children don't come around on Halloween. And at an open house the Hunters held in mid-1990, several local residents inquired as to whether they had "seen anything yet." Such is the responsibility of owning one of South Dakota's premier haunted homes.

The Villa Theresa Guest House has been relatively free of specters on the staircase, or anywhere else for that matter, for some time now. Perhaps the extensive remodeling and agreeable atmosphere engendered by Margaret and Dick Hunter have something to do with it. The ghosts may have gone back to wherever ghosts go when they're finished with their earthly business.

And yet Marlene Akhtar is not entirely convinced the hauntings are over.

"It's like the house is waiting. Waiting to express itself," she says.

She doesn't want to be around the next time the ghosts decide to reveal their continuing interest in this haunted B&B.

Clara and Lizzie

Thirteen-year-old Clara Robertson was alone practicing the piano when it happened. Someone walked down the long hallway of the boarding school and entered the music room where she sat engrossed in her lesson. It would be a classmate, she thought. It wasn't. Clara looked up into the skeletal face of a little girl. The specter wore a tattered pink dress streaked with green mold; tangled locks of black hair hung to her shoulders. Rotted teeth protruded from a fleshless mouth.

Clara screamed, fled into a nearby bedroom and leaped into bed with another girl who was stricken with the flu. The ghost followed and, gliding silently to their bedside, began to tug at Clara's hair. Unable to speak, Clara buried her face in a pillow and waved her arms to chase the hideous thing away. Moments later, the two frightened children rushed downstairs to report what had happened.

Fellow students snickered. There was no such thing as a ghost, they said. Not in the prestigious albeit curiously named Brinkley Female College, an academy for small girls. Not in Memphis, Tennessee. Certainly not in 1871.

Of course, tales of a haunting *had* surfaced from time to time at the boarding school, but they revolved around the founder, old Mr. Brinkley. He'd gone bankrupt, then insane. A few people thought that his restless spirit roamed the rooms of the gloomy antebellum mansion on DeSoto Street (now South Fifth Street). But a ghost child in a pink dress? Never.

Only Clara had seen the supposed ghost. Her sick chum couldn't verify any of the report. Humiliated and fearful, Clara did not sleep that night. The next afternoon she practiced the piano. No ghost appeared.

But on the third day the specter was back. Two students were with Clara in the music room when they were bewildered by a strange sound, as if someone were splashing water onto the floor. In the next moment, all three girls saw the hideous, grinning girl in the mildewed clothing. The pungent smell of damp earth filled the room.

The girls ran shrieking down the staircase and, in their haste, bumped into a startled Jackie Boone, a young instructor. She calmed them down, then agreed to return to the music room with them.

The little spirit was still there. Or so the girls said. The teacher saw only an indistinct shadow in the far corner of the room. She told Clara to ask the ghost what it wanted.

"Do not fear me," the girl ghost told Clara. "My name is Lizzie. I was the last to die in my family. Treasure lies buried five feet deep under the old stump behind this house. Please dig it up, Clara. I want you to have it." With those words the ghost faded away.

Miss Boone said she hadn't heard any of the speech, only an odd rumbling noise.

Within the week the story got out. Memphis newspaper headlines screamed the salient facts:

BRINKLEY FEMALE COLLEGE HAUNTED AND IN AN UPROAR OF TERROR AND CONFUSION.

THE GHOST MAKES A 'KENO'

FURTHER SUPERNATURAL AND STARTLING REVELATIONS FROM BRINKLEY COLLEGE

Fear gripped the city. Frightened mothers kept lanterns burning through the night, children cried if left alone, and men who had to be out at night fortified themselves with a "Ghost Cocktail" concocted by some enterprising Memphis bartender.

Dr. Meredith, principal of the school, ordered a thorough investigation. *Pranksters*, he grumbled to himself.

Meanwhile, Clara's father, J. R. Robertson, a Memphis attorney and civic leader, hired a spiritualist medium named Mrs. Nourse. The medium gave Clara pencil and paper and explained that messages from the spirit world would be given to her and she must write them down exactly as they were given. It would be Clara's first experience with automatic writing.

The medium put Clara into a trance. After she had lapsed into glassy-eyed slumber, neighbors who'd been invited to the séance asked their questions.

Who *was* the ghost, they wanted to know. In an unfamiliar hand, Clara wrote, "Lizzie Davidson." Old-timers recalled that the mansion had been built before the Civil War by a Colonel Davidson, and that the family's eight-year-old daughter, Lizzie, had died there in 1861. They remembered that the child had been buried in a pink dress rather than the customary white.

Other spectral messages arrived unbidden: The Brinkley family had no legal claim to the property, one claimed. Davidson's deed to the land was inside a large glass jar, along with coins and jewelry. The jar, buried beneath a stump, must be found by Clara Robertson herself. Or so the messages asserted.

Mr. Robertson became uneasy during the séance. He wanted to believe his daughter's stories about the little ghost girl, but his keen analytical mind couldn't accept this venture into a world far removed from reason. At the same time, he was fascinated by the writing penned by Clara, writing that she would never recall composing. After much deliberation, Mr. Robertson decided to schedule more séances in his house. After they yielded corroborative evidence, he thought it was his duty to help Clara locate the jar. He discussed his plans with Dr. Meredith. The principal agreed the "treasure" should be found.

Beneath a pale moon on a frosty February night, several men with shovels dug deep trenches around the old stump. The sound of picks striking rocks sang in the night air. After several hours of fruitless digging, the workmen were dismissed until daybreak. A few broken bricks were their only discoveries.

When the pick-and-shovel gang returned at dawn, Clara and her father were among the first arrivals to watch the work. The stump was finally pulled free, and as Clara gazed down into the deep hole, the spirit appeared to her. No one else saw it. The ghost chided her for not seeking the treasure herself. Clara slithered down into the hole, lifted a heavy pick, but couldn't swing it. She fainted. Her father then took over the job. Ten minutes later, he'd unearthed a five-gallon Mason jar! It was tightly sealed, and although partially covered with mold, bags and packets could be seen inside. Also a large yellow envelope. The missing deed? Then, in the strangest of all of the episodes, Clara said the spirit's voice warned that since Clara herself hadn't uncovered the jar, it must not be opened for sixty days.

Mr. Robertson took the jar home with him, but soon had to summon the police to protect his house from mobs of people, all demanding to see the mysterious container.

Then he announced his new plan. Clara and her father would open the jar on the stage of the old Greenlaw Opera House, at the southwest corner of Union and Second, on the morning precisely sixty days from the moment their find had been unearthed. Admission would be one dollar, half of the money to be given to Clara in partial compensation for the "terror and suffering" she had endured, and the other half to benefit the city's orphans.

But, one night just before "Opening Day," J. R. Robertson heard a noise in his backyard and went to investigate. When he did not return promptly, servants went looking for him. They found the attorney lying unconscious in a pool of his own blood. His head had been slashed and red marks on his throat seemed to indicate that he'd been choked.

He was able to tell this story: As he'd stepped out the back door, three men jumped him. One pistol-whipped him about the face, another seized him around the throat. A third attempted to scalp him with a long knife. They demanded that he turn over the jar. Robertson told them it was suspended by a rope *beneath the seat in the outhouse!* Repugnant though the hiding place was, the ruffians found the jar and fled with it.

Though it was never seen again, the jar's contents were allegedly revealed to Clara in another séance. A newspaper account said that the jar contained two thousand dollars in gold, a diamond necklace, gold jewelry, and some "important papers."

Was Clara a serious young spiritualist or only a bored adolescent bent upon creating a little excitement? Did her father stage the "jar robbery" to avoid splitting the find with others? No one knows. But her story has passed into legend and is still considered Memphis's most fascinating ghost story.

At the end of her schooling, Clara Robertson married a fellow spiritualist and, although she conducted many séances, the sad little ghost in the torn pink dress never appeared again.

Brinkley Female College itself faced a series of financial crises and eventually closed. The building then became a tenement for railroad workers. As surrounding houses were razed, the great gray mansion stood alone, its paint peeling, its massive front pillars crumbling—a fading specter itself of another time.

In 1972 the house was demolished. The ghost girl was gone forever.

Never-Never Land

The year was 1921. A child was killed in some sort of fall along Beale Street in Memphis. Her name was Mary. Too young to die, the little girl's ghost eventually sought refuge in the Orpheum Theatre, not far from the scene of her death. At least, that's the legend.

The original Orpheum Theatre, built in 1890, burned in 1923. The current theater was completed in 1928. No one is certain *exactly* when Mary first appeared, but for sixty-odd years the little ghost has been reported romping throughout the Orpheum, almost since the reconstructed legitimate theater/movie palace opened. Doors open and close by themselves, a quiet voice giggles, and then soft-stockinged feet patter up and down aisles. And the majestic pipe organ plays random notes by itself—when it isn't even turned on!

When the curtain rises on a stage production, Mary sometimes occupies her favorite seat—C-5. Her vacant stare and odd appearance cause patrons seated nearby to whisper about the odd little child in the quaint dress.

Although Mary has never been known to create a disturbance during a performance, casts of visiting companies often feel uneasy in the house. Actors are, by nature, superstitious, and members of the New York company that performed *Fiddler on the Roof* in 1977 were no exception. They were so convinced that the place was haunted that they demanded a séance be held on a balcony following the opening-night performance. Afterward, some actors claimed to have seen Mary in her school uniform of white middy blouse and pleated skirt, her long, dark braids cascading down her back.

Theater personnel believe that Mary was either twelve or thirteen years old when she died and that her spirit may be searching for playmates in the cavernous building. The Orpheum is a fairyland of opulence, just the place to delight a youngster born long before the "magic" of Walt Disney World. Sunlight pours through a huge rotunda gilding the ornate one-ton chandeliers hanging from the ceiling. Thick maroon carpeting and heavy drapes insulate the building from outside noises. And tiered balconies and innumerable dressing rooms and storage areas provide endless hiding places for ghostly games of hide-and-seek.

If Mary can be called a blithe spirit, she was also a helpmate, at least on two reported occasions. Nearly thirty years ago, Harlan Judkins, an organ restorer, was hired to do some work on the theater's mighty organ. He, his brother, and a friend worked together, and almost always at night when there'd be no interruptions. But one night they encountered a mystifying problem that they couldn't fix. The trio took a coffee break in a nearby café, and when they returned to the theater found the organ was "fixed."

On another night Judkins was working alone on the organ. He had just coded and bundled a set of wires and needed his screwdriver, which was out of his immediate reach. If he put the wires down to go get the tool he'd have to rebundle the wires before installing them in the organ. Suddenly, he looked down and there, at his feet, lay the screwdriver. Judkins told a reporter, "I don't understand this and I don't want to understand it. Thanks a lot, but this is a little bit beyond me."

Judkins never again worked in the Orpheum at night.

However, another man did work on the organ at night. He had a screwdriver, a wrench, and a pair of pliers. But before he could begin to tackle the job, his tools vanished. He never found them. He called the atmosphere in the Orpheum "weird."

Night maintenance men agreed with that assessment. One said he saw a small girl dash down an aisle. While trying to escape the building after that incident, he broke his key in the door.

On another night, a volunteer electrician working alone in the theater heard a female soprano voice. Whenever he investigated, the singing stopped. He left, and on the way to his car he said he heard the singing begin again.

The assistant project director for the Memphis Development Foundation, which owns and operates the theater, once admitted having "eerie feelings" in the basement and in the projection booth. Like many others, he has heard unearthly footsteps and seen fleeting shadows late at night when the building is dark and empty.

Although many people have heard Mary and witnessed the results of her pranks, relatively few have *seen* her. Those who have never forget the experience. The person is suddenly overcome by bone-chilling cold deep within his body, a coldness incomparable to anything he has ever felt before. Then comes the uncomfortable feeling of being watched by someone.

Teresa Spoone saw Mary on a warm April night in 1979 when she and friends stayed late in the theater to listen to an organ concert by Vincent Astor, an Orpheum staff member.

Spoone recalls that when Astor played "Never-Never Land" from the musical *Peter Pan*, the theater turned bitterly cold. Suddenly, two women in the group noticed a faint light dart into the theater from the lobby and vanish behind the last rows of seats. All three women looked back toward the lobby and saw "a little girl with brownish hair dancing in the distance." Spoone got up and started toward the child, but halfway up the aisle she stopped in her tracks.

"It was like she was calling me," Spoone told a reporter at the time. "That really scared me because I felt like if I went near her I'd never come back the same."

Two of Teresa Spoone's friends, however, did reach the lobby, but by that time the apparition had vanished. Deep rumblings came from inside an adjacent broom closet, and the frightened women hurried back to their seats.

Writer David Dawson can empathize with Spoone and her friends. For one night in the 1980s he and a dozen others, including artists and reporters, turned ghost hunters. By the light of a full moon they entered the Orpheum Theatre. Each went his separate way to explore the empty dressing rooms, storage areas, catwalks, the basement with its noisy air conditioners and elevator motors.

Dawson recalled visiting the auditorium and taking a seat in the shadows at one side of the stage. Again, Vincent Astor played the organ. When he began a version of "Never-Never Land," the theater seemed to grow hotter. Hot. Not cold. Or so Dawson thought.

Five minutes later, Dawson forgot about the heat when "suddenly, without reason, I felt like a stranger, shaky, a long way from home," he wrote in *Memphis Magazine*. He turned to speak to the person he thought had been sitting next to him. The seat was empty.

Dawson stood up and made his way back to the lobby, where the rest of the group had reassembled. An hour and a half had passed since they'd entered the theater.

No one had heard unearthly footsteps, nor singing in the night. No one had seen a ghost. Yet no one was quite the same. They agreed that something mysterious, something indefinable lurked within the walls of that historic building.

"It [the Orpheum] remains an ideal world for a shy and lonely little girl," Dawson wrote, "waiting for a crowd to come and play make-believe with her in her own never-never land."

A theater is illusion and perhaps an illusion should never be disturbed. Especially when it's a ghost.

The Marfa Lights

One night in 1973, Samuel Whatley was driving home from his job as a computer operator. On a lightly traveled road east of Marfa, Texas, he saw lights coming toward him. Strange, he thought, because he seldom met a car at this predawn hour. Perhaps it was a tourist traveling all night to avoid the heat of the day. Whatley rolled down the window of his pickup truck to wave a greeting.

Suddenly, a reddish-orange light the size of a melon appeared outside the truck window. The lights ahead of Whatley had vanished. There was no other vehicle on the road. He floored the accelerator, but the light moved along beside the truck. If Whatley slowed, the light slowed. His hands were damp on the wheel.

"Hell, I was scared!" Whatley told a reporter from *The Wall Street Journal*. "I was crawling out of my skin." He estimated the light had stayed with him for two miles before vanishing.

That same year, geologists John P. Kenney and Elwood Wright were prospecting for uranium in the area. They saw the light on several occasions and became so fascinated by it that they kept a journal of their sightings.

On March 19 the men were sitting in their car ten miles east of Marfa. About 10:00 P.M. horses in a nearby field whinnied and bolted. Then a ball of light floated in from the southwest, with another one behind it. Kennedy and Wright estimated that each ball was about half the size of a basketball. The lights bobbed up and down a few hundred feet away, hovered over a clump of bushes, then disappeared.

What had the three men seen? They don't know. There is no evidence that Whatley knew anything about the sightings made by Kenney and Wright, and they had never heard of him.

For more than one hundred years the lights have been seen in the Mitchell Flat area between Alpine and Marfa. They vary in intensity, sometimes appearing as stars sparkling over a mountaintop in the Chinati Range and at other times as one huge globe shining so brightly that it can be seen for fifty miles. Motorists driving the thirty-five-mile stretch of U.S. Highway 90 between Alpine and Marfa frequently see the lights.

Robert Ellison is credited as being the first white man to witness the appearance of the lights. In 1883 he went out to west Texas and saw what he thought was an Apache campfire. After scouring the countryside on horseback, he realized the lights were not those of a campfire or a homestead. On his many cattle drives from Alpine west to Marfa, Ellison saw the strange lights. But he never feared them, nor did his son-in-law, Lee Plumbley, who first saw the lights in 1921.

Plumbley explained to Nancy Roberts, author of *Ghosts of the Wild West,* "To me, it has always been a friendly light. When you are out at night in this country, the towns and houses are far apart. When you've ridden for miles your first view of the light becomes a friendly thing, like coming upon a homestead and seeing a lighted window. It's a welcome, familiar sight."

Early settlers would have understood Plumbley's feelings. They called the lights "ghost lights," and superstitions needed no explanation. Some believed the Indians' story that the lights were the spirit of a Chisos Apache warrior who was sealed into a cave to guard stolen gold. Later, white men thought the lights were Pancho Villa and his men moving supplies across the Rio Grande after dark.

But modern man "knows" that there is a rational explanation for the origin of the lights, and that science will provide it—of course.

During World War I the beacons were thought to be guidelights to detect enemy invasion from the south. Except no invasion ever took place.

The same notion fired the imagination of a Major Davidson who, during World War II, sent up pilots from a nearby air base to investigate the lights. When the pilots buzzed the lights, the mysterious orbs floated into Mexico, then winked out. Finally, the pilots were ordered to "bomb" the lights with bags of flour to serve as source markers. In the morning nothing was found except white powder covering the land.

Endless investigations were conducted by the army and the air force, while reporters from every major Southwest news medium jostled one another in their haste to scoop the story. There was no story, save the Pentagon's final directive—leave the lights alone.

Could the lights come from phosphorescent minerals? No such minerals have been found here.

Rotting vegetation sometimes bursts into flame, giving off vapors known as swamp gas. But in this arid rangeland of West Texas, no swamps exist. The nearest river, the Rio Grande, is sixty miles south.

John Derr, a geophysicist, thinks that what are seen may be "earthquake lights"—electrical atmospheric charges generated by the shifting and grinding of rocks deep below the earth's crust. Although such lights are frequently associated with earthquakes, their presence does not necessarily predict quakes. Marfa has had no earthquakes.

Some area residents believe that odd atmospheric effects have something to do with the lights. Mirages are common. More than one person has reported seeing false mountains shining in the distance. Because Marfa is in a basin between mountain ranges it does have a lot of unusual weather.

The automobile headlight explanation is advanced for every case of mystery lights in the country. In this instance, the lights are said to be coming from cars approaching a hill on U.S. Highway 90. But the lights glow steadily, unlike a car's headlights which flash by in seconds. And of course no automobiles existed in the nineteenth century.

The most recent speculation comes from astronomers at McDonald Observatory. They think that the lights may be caused by the Novaya Zemlya effect, in which light beams are bent by adjacent layers of air at different temperatures and carried over long distances. The source is unknown, although UFO enthusiasts say it's the reading light from a flying saucer!

Gary Cartwright doesn't believe in flying saucers, but he says, "I promise you, *something's* out there."

In August 1983, Cartwright and a group of writers gathered on the highway halfway between Marfa and Alpine, looking south across an abandoned air base toward the Chinati Mountains. All of the persons were hard-boiled skeptics, but at least one would be less so after the night's experience.

Cartwright wrote in the *Texas Monthly* of November 1984, "When the first point of light appeared where there had been only darkness, there were some nervous giggles and a fluttering of rationalizations, and when a second came dancing above and to the right of the first, I swear something ice-cold moved across my skin. The points of light appeared one or two or sometimes three at a time, moving diagonally and sometimes horizontally for ten to fifteen seconds. They would vanish and then reappear in some new location. They could have been a mile away, or twenty or thirty. . . . No one spoke for a long while. Somewhere out there an animal wailed. San Antonio poet Naomi Nye told me later that she thought the experience changed her life. She said she had dreams in which the whole energy of the dream was directed at trying to figure out how to 'get to the lights.' "

One man *did* get to the lights, and his experience remains the most bizarre of the many legends. Years ago a rancher living near Shafter, in the Chinatis, often had to climb high to reach strayed stock. Late one day as he was climbing, a blizzard caught him. Snow pelted down and the wind knifed through him as darkness fell. He knew there was no chance of making it safely back to his cabin. But if he stopped walking he'd freeze to death. On a bend in the trail a huge outcrop blocked his way. He was lost.

Suddenly, flashing lights confronted him and seemed to speak, although the rancher could never explain how. He understood that he was far off his route and close to a precipice. He must follow the lights or die.

The lights led the rancher to a tiny cave, and as he crawled into it, glad to be out of the cutting wind and blinding snow, a large light followed him and remained close enough to warm him by its heat. A smaller light accompanied the large one.

The lights somehow made the man understand that they were spirits from an ancient time who had come to save him. The man slept, and when he awoke the lights were gone and the sun was shining. The precipice was just beyond the outcrop where the lights had confronted him.

That's the story that the rancher's daughter, Mrs. W. T. Giddens of Sundown, told Texas author Ed Syers. She accepted it as fact, and added, "The lights came down in our pasture all the time . . . They're friendly."

*   *   *

In July 1989, an investigation sponsored by the NBC Television series "Unsolved Mysteries" sought to solve, once and for all, the Marfa lights enigma. A trio of scientists—an astronomer, a geologist, and a chemist—set up a series of infrared video and film cameras to record the lights' appearance. Precise steps were taken to avoid mistaking car lights on a highway in the Chinati Mountains with the ghost lights. Powerful marker beams were placed at either end of the highway so that any light appearing between them could be accounted for. A radio beacon tower visible in the mountains was also duly noted.

At 11:59 P.M., the century-old lights became visible—far outside the path of the highway, in an area known to be uninhabited. The images were recorded on video and film as slightly greenish orbs that seemed to pulsate, expand slightly and then vanish, reappearing a few minutes later.

The scientists agreed that the lights were something of natural origin, but were unable to offer a unified opinion. It may have been refracted starlight, or possibly luminous gases released through thin cracks in the earth during earth tremors so slight they are undetected by scientific instrumentation.

Whatever the cause of the Marfa mystery, area residents say they like their "friendly" lights. Quite a few say they hope the puzzle is never solved, keeping the ghost lights the town's unique claim to international notoriety.

The Three Nephites

To appreciate the stories of the Three Nephites, it is necessary to know that the doctrine of the Church of Jesus Christ of Latter-day Saints (the Mormons) holds that after Jesus' ascension from the Holy Sepulchre, he appeared in South America to persons known as the Nephites. Jesus taught them that they had been chosen by God to know the true gospel and to teach it to the nonbelievers. This was the beginning of His ministry in the New World.

Then, as proof of His Godhead, Jesus raised a man from the dead and performed other miracles similar to those he had performed earlier in Judea. Before His ascension into Heaven, Jesus appointed twelve new apostles from among the Nephites and asked them what they desired. Nine asked to be raised up when their earthly work was finished, and three asked to remain on earth forever, doing His work.

And so it was that when the Mormons first settled the land that would become the state of Utah, these three wandering patriarchs appeared, bringing hope and courage to those early pioneers who struggled to clear the land, to fight the great plagues of locusts and grasshoppers, and to survive the periodic droughts in the harsh environment of the great American West.

For 150 years these holy men, the devout believe, have roamed the towns, villages, and isolated settlements of this intermountain state; there is scarcely a locale that has not been touched in some way by the Three Nephites with their bone-white feet, their long, flowing white hair and beards.

They travel singly by most accounts, arriving unseen, unbidden, often seeking a meal or simply a place to stay the night. They come on foot, usually, less often by a rickety cart pulled by an ancient nag. They cure the sick, bring prosperity to the poor. The host who shelters a Nephite never learns his true identity until after he has left. After the stranger vanishes, leaving no earthly trace whatsoever, the Mormon family believes they have been touched by the hand of God.

The Nephites remain on earth voluntarily. Although the earliest reports of their encounters with faithful Mormons came from Utah, later stories started coming in from all over the world as the Nephites supposedly followed Mormon missionaries who sought converts in every part of the globe.

Eminent folklorists such as E. F. Fife, Richard M. Dorson, Hector Lee, and Jan Harold Brunvand have spent years collecting stories of the Three Nephites, and their files contain hundreds, if not thousands, of sightings. The Three Nephites evidently appear to persons in all strata of society, and have for the past century and a half. They have not gone away, even with more sophisticated methods of transportation and a generally skeptical population. Encounters are reported even today.

Whether rooted in theology or folklore, fact or fiction, or somewhere in between, individual experiences are worth the telling.

One spring day in 1852 an old man knocked at the door of a family living in Salt Lake City and asked if he might eat with them. The Mormons had settled the area only five years earlier, and hardships were evident everywhere. The woman of the house hesitated only momentarily, then invited the wayfarer to share the family's humble meal of water, bread, and onions.

He ate quickly, then asked what he owed her. When she refused his money, he left, saying, "May God bless you. Peace be with you."

The woman ran to the door, but the man was gone. When she turned to clear the table she noticed that his food was still there, uneaten!

During years of drought when this woman's neighbors were starving, her larder was always full. She *knew* it had something to do with the stranger's visit.

One summer evening, two young women on horseback were trapped on a mountainside when their horses panicked before a crevice filled with sliding shale. The animals refused to move forward or backward. One of the women, a devout Mormon, dismounted and scrambled to the mountaintop, hoping to find a hiker or perhaps a prospector. But the area was deserted. Picking up a willow switch, she returned to her companion. They took turns flailing the horses, but nothing could get them to move.

Suddenly, a voice called out from somewhere above them. "Sister, how did you come here?"

Incredibly the women found themselves and their horses in the next instant on top of the mountain. They had no recollection of how they got there. A bearded man in clean blue overalls helped them ride safely away from the dangerous cliff edge.

The young Mormon rider turned to thank their benefactor, but of course he was not in sight.

She nodded to her friend. "That was one of the Nephites."

Niels Nielson was finishing up chores when the wagoner drew up to the barn. "I was wondering if you could put up me and my team for the night," said the tall driver from the narrow wagon seat. "Come purty far. I'd guess about eighty mile."

Nielson cast a jaundiced eye on the man. No one could have traveled that far in the dilapidated rig drawn by bony horses. But country folk the world over seldom turn away one in need, and it was virtually unknown on the Utah frontier.

"I think the neighbor up the road could pasture your horses," Nielson offered. "I'll go with you."

When the men returned to the house, Mrs. Nielson was ready to serve supper. Nielson looked at his wife, then back to the traveler. "We ain't got much, but if you'd like to share . . ."

The man interrupted. "It warms the heart to find such hospitality." Drawing a chair up to the table, he ate and talked at the same time. "I stopped at several places in town, but not a single family was willing to take us in. One day they'll be . . . sorry."

Mrs. Nielson looked uneasily at her husband. Unaccustomed to having strangers in her house, she became nervous. She did not like the man's talk, although she couldn't exactly say why.

After supper, the visitor became more voluble. He spoke of places he'd been all over the world, exotic names such as New York, London, Vienna—places the Nielsons recalled dimly from their geography lessons at country school many years before.

Mrs. Nielson finally decided the man was a liar. She would test him.

"You ever been to Kansas?" she demanded. "I'm from Atchison."

A smile crossed the man's face. "Know it real well. Did you know the Birrells who lived around the corner from the bank? Such a kind family. Had two lovely daughters."

Of course, Mrs. Nielson knew them. Atchison was still a small town. "How . . . how long since you've been there?" she stammered.

"A year and a half," he replied. "You ever know the Walter James family?"

"Their daughter Sue and I were best childhood friends." Mrs. Nielson nodded. "But that was years ago. I lost contact with her."

The man stretched his legs to the fire. "She married Bill Brewer. They got four nice children."

Mrs. Nielson was astounded. Bill Brewer was a mean squirt of a kid, always teasing or mocking someone.

The visitor read her thoughts. "Brewer's a prosperous family man now, real successful. Well liked by everyone."

Suddenly, Mrs. Nielson seemed to lose her breath, bent over and left the room. Her husband explained that the doctors thought she had cancer.

With that the talk ceased, and when Mr. Nielson excused himself the visitor bedded down by the fire. In the morning he did not want breakfast. He seemed somehow chastened, preoccupied. Mrs. Nielson packed him a lunch, and he did agree to take it with him.

"May God bless you always," he said, stepping to the door.

The Nielsons watched him start off down the road. A few minutes later relatives came up that same road, and Mrs. Nielson asked them if they'd met the wagoner with the scrawny team. They said they'd seen no one on the road. There was no other way to go.

In years to come, those families who'd turned their backs on the prophet suffered bad luck while the Nielsons' prosperity increased. But the greatest blessing was the curing of Mrs. Nielson's "cancer." She never endured another pain. And she never did figure out how their visitor knew so much about her hometown. She suspected he'd never been there at all, but how else could he have gained his knowledge of the place?

One day as Mrs. Nielson and her husband talked about the stranger, she exclaimed, "Of course, that's it! He must have been one of *them!*"

Her husband smiled and allowed that he agreed.

John and Isabella Price and their baby son lived in a one-room home in Salt Lake City. John's parents lived with them. When the baby was but a few months old, he became very ill. No remedies seemed to help. Neither did prayers.

Then, late one evening, a stranger knocked at the door and asked for shelter. The man appeared well groomed and wore a gray suit.

Grandpa Price explained that they had no extra beds, but the caller said it didn't matter. He was very weary, he said, and would welcome the opportunity to simply doze by the fire, its heat keeping him warm for the night and the cabin roof sheltering him from the elements.

Grandpa agreed to that. He put another log on the fire, then, from his own pallet in a dark corner, kept an eye on the sleeping figure. He was determined not to fall asleep lest some harm befall the young family.

Sometime during the night, Grandma Price awakened and saw the stranger sitting at the table. It was covered with a white tablecloth that the family did not own. It was so dazzling white that it hurt her eyes just to look at it. Mesmerized, she watched the man eat bread that seemed to be of the same dazzling white. The Prices never ate white bread.

In the morning, the family offered the visitor breakfast, but he politely declined. Grandpa Price walked him a short ways from the house.

When the old man got back home, he found his grandson cooing and laughing in his crib. He was perfectly fine.

The Prices always believed a Nephite had been sent in answer to their prayers.

On a day in 1944, a man and his wife were traveling by truck across a desolate stretch of highway when they picked up an old man who stood by the roadside. Although he seemed to be somewhat vague about his destination, he was most knowledgeable about current events. He knew a lot about the ongoing World War II and the couple was fascinated by his stories. Then, all of a sudden the man asked to be let out.

"Surely not here," the driver said. "Why, there's no house or building in sight."

The wind was picking up and blowing sand and tumbleweeds across the hood of the truck.

"This is the place," insisted the odd passenger.

Since he couldn't be persuaded to ride on to the next town, the driver let him out.

The old man thanked the couple, then wagged a finger at them.

"On your way back you'll be hauling a dead man. And the war will end in August," he prophesied before disappearing from sight.

The couple soon came upon an automobile accident in which a young man was killed. They hauled the body back to the nearest town. Even though World War II did not end until August of 1945, the man and his wife said the rider had been a Nephite.

In some cases a Nephite happens upon a scene when a life hangs in the balance, as in this case from years ago.

A child not yet in his teens had carried a sack lunch to his father, who owned a flour mill. Once delivered of his obligation, the youngster got to fooling around with the machinery and his hand became caught in a cogwheel. The child's mighty screams brought his father running just at the instant his son pulled his hand loose. The flesh hung in torn and bloody ribbons.

At that moment, a withered, white-bearded man appeared. He grabbed the youngster's wrist and placed a thumb on a vein to stanch the flow of blood. With his other hand, he reached into the flour bin behind him and clapped big handfuls of flour over the injured hand to soak up the blood. Then he turned to the father and instructed him to tear a flour sack into long strips. Working with great skill and care, the old man bound the child's hand with the narrow bands of cloth.

"Don't touch that hand for three weeks," the man instructed before taking his leave.

The boy and his dad went to the mill door, but saw no one in any direction.

The father put his arm around his son. The Good Samaritan had been a Nephite.

The boy's hand was completed healed . . . in three weeks.

A man named Rencher was driving his wagon down a country road when he met an old gentleman. Rencher offered the fellow a ride, and as the two sat together on the high spring seat they talked of the weather and the crops. Eventually, they got to talking about the Book of Mormon. Like many of his neighbors, Rencher attended church, but was not well versed in church doctrine.

The hitchhiker, however, seemed to have a fount of information. He spoke at length about scripture, testimonies, and revelations. Rencher, entranced by the man's knowledge, failed to stop at the neighboring farmhouses as he usually did. He only waved a hand and passed on by.

After some miles, the man asked to be let off; he declined Rencher's invitation to stay overnight at his home. As the man climbed down from the wagon, the skittish horses reared up and, in trying to control them, Rencher lost sight of his companion. He was gone.

Rencher's curiosity was aroused. On his next trip he stopped to ask people along the way if they knew who the man might have been.

"But Brother Rencher," they all pointed out, "there wasn't anyone with you on the wagon seat."

Are the stories of the Nephites truth or myth? In the end it scarcely matters. The Gentile, or non-Mormon, may doubt their authenticity, but to the devout they offer proof of God's intervention in the affairs of men.

In 1972, distinguished folklorist Jan Harold Brunvand wrote, ". . . even now, supernaturalism *is* alive and well in Salt Lake City, as elsewhere in Mormon country."

It's likely to remain so for a very long time to come.

Emily's Bridge

To well-heeled sports enthusiasts Stowe, Vermont, is the Aspen of the East. They come to ski the powdered slopes of Mount Mansfield, to wine and dine in distinctive hostelries, and, in the gentler seasons, to golf and ride horseback in these scenic valleys of the Green Mountains.

An occasional visitor, wandering beyond the limits of the village, may come upon a covered bridge—an unpainted, weathered relic of a bygone era, its boards dilapidated, its metal roof overhung by dead and dying leaves of brush and trees grown wild for more than a century. This is the oldest and last remaining covered bridge in the Stowe area. If the visitor has camera in hand, he will snap a picture of the bridge and call it "Picturesque New England." Another photo for his album.

The stranger will not know that this is Emily's Bridge, and that the name of the stream is Gold Brook, where the discovery of small amounts of gold in the water sparked the belief that a mother lode lay waiting to be discovered. (It never was.) If only a few local historians know about this failed bonanza, nearly everyone knows the legend of Emily—for her ghost tarries at the bridge for the lover who never comes. But how she came to be there, or even if she *is* there, is the subject of some dispute.

Emily was a young bride jilted at the altar in the 1800s, so one story goes. Stomping out of the church in her wedding finery, she mounted her horse and galloped toward the groom's house on Hollow Road. As she started over the bridge, her horse bolted and threw her to her death on the rocks below. In that era, the bridge did not have a roof.

Another version of the tale has Emily chasing after the bridegroom in a buggy. She failed to negotiate a turn onto the bridge and the buggy overturned, sending the horse and Emily plunging fatally over the embankment.

As recently as 1968, another story surfaced as to how the bridge came to be haunted. Emily was thirty-six years old, fat, unattractive, and in love with a young man named Donald. Although he didn't return her love, he did get her pregnant. Her father insisted that the couple marry. Donald refused and committed suicide by jumping off the bridge.

A month later, Emily gave premature birth to twins who lived only a short time. Inconsolable over the deaths of her lover and their offspring, she jumped off the High Bridge, a nearby covered bridge that no longer exists. When they found her body, she was wearing a bright red wedding dress. According to the story, this all took place in 1925.

Is there any truth to these stories? One source attributes them to the work of a high school student who, finding nothing of a supernatural nature in and around Emily's bridge and required to turn in a paper for speech class, embroidered the old legend with the aid of a Ouija board.

The stories nevertheless prevail, and some have found their way into print over the years. The first version is ubiquitous among young people of the region. They say that late on a quiet night you can see a white-clothed woman trying to cross the bridge, then hear her dying screams as she plunges toward the water. Vengeful even in death, Emily is said to chase young men but leave women alone.

A young Stowe resident named Vaughn said that once he and a carload of young men were sitting at the approach to the bridge when the ghost of a woman dressed in a wedding gown appeared. She stared at the car, then circled around it slowly, peering in the windows. Suddenly, she took hold of a door handle and pulled it so hard that the car swayed. Unable to figure out how to get inside, she stepped back, regarded the vehicle once more, turned and left.

Another young man from the village drove up to the top of Luce Hill late one night to watch a thunderstorm roll in. Bolts of lightning skipped from one mountaintop to the next, and thunder roared in the man's ears. Rains came on a high wind and, as the drops pelted the car, the fellow started the engine and headed toward town. He stopped in the covered bridge for shelter. Suddenly, he heard voices and saw lights at each approach to the bridge. He rolled down the car windows. There was only silence, and no lights visible save for those of his car. Emily keeping her vigil? He wondered.

Hazel Carlson, a retired nurse and native of Stowe, once worked in the infirmary at Johnson State College, north of Stowe. She told a news reporter that patients came to the infirmary with scratches and bruises on their arms and legs that they said were caused by "invisible attackers" inside Emily's covered bridge. Carlson, however, was not impressed. She'd heard that some students were holding nocturnal séances at the bridge and that one young woman became so upset that her friends took her to a priest for counseling.

One group of visitors found the "spirits" in a particularly playful mood. A bed sheet spattered with ketchup had been hung from the rafters of the bridge!

Emily's ghost may simply be a case of teenage pranksters "haunting" one another. That's the belief of Dick Sweterlitsch, an assistant professor of folklore at the University of Vermont. He wrote the authors, in part: "Several students of mine from time to time have interviewed people living near the bridge, and there is no factual material to back up the haunting. More than anything, the story is a teen-age parking spot legend. Ironically, there was a teen-age killing within three or four miles of the bridge, but that has not become linked with the bridge."

Yet, according to residents interviewed by a reporter in 1969, people who had begun to build houses near the bridge were frightened away by the apparition of a young woman. Others, hearing the story, abandoned plans to build in the area.

Old-timers, maybe with a wink of the eye, know that Emily will not tolerate a housing development near her bridge.

Emily is persistent.

In Olde Williamsburg

Williamsburg. The restored capital of eighteenth-century Virginia. A day-to-day world of men and women long since passed from the scene. Today's visitors come to learn of the people, events, and characteristics that gave the lovingly restored city prominence in our nation's history. They tour the beautiful Georgian mansions, or perhaps the old Capitol, where concepts like self-government and individual liberty were first enunciated, or they might ride in the horse-drawn carriages down tree-shaded Gloucester Street, and *perhaps*—if they're lucky—catch a glimpse of a ghost or two along the way.

The George Wythe House

The best-known ghost tale of historic Williamsburg is connected with the George Wythe House built during the mid-1700s. Wythe was a patriot, the teacher of Thomas Jefferson, and America's first law professor. The origins of the legend date to the 1770s when Sir Peyton and Lady Ann Skipwith visited here for an extended period. Ann Miller Skipwith was a young Scottish woman with a fiery temper that flared unpredictably. Born about 1741 near Petersburg, Virginia, young Ann had married Sir Peyton and taken up the comfortable life of a planter's wife in Mecklenberg County. The couple frequently visited the Colonial capital—often for weeks at a time. One evening, while attending a gala ball at the Governor's Palace, the couple had an altercation and Lady Ann fled angrily into the night.

Hurrying across the damp Palace Green toward the Wythe House, Lady Ann lost one of her slippers, a red shoe with diamond incrustations. But she didn't stop to retrieve it. She rushed through the front door and dashed up the stairs just as the clock was striking twelve. One shoe off and one shoe on made a peculiar clicking rhythm all the way up the staircase in the dark and empty house. Years later, other occupants reported hearing this same rhythmic noise at midnight. Rather like that of a person with a peg leg, one witness said.

Even today, strange incidents occur. Recently, a hostess at the Wythe House felt someone tap her on the shoulder, but when she turned around no one was there. Another hostess heard the scraping of furniture being moved when the house was empty. Still others say spectral gentlemen sit in wingback chairs by the unlit fireplace in the study.

However, employees at Colonial Williamsburg talk guardedly about the alleged ghosts in the Wythe House, and indeed throughout the village, preferring to emphasize, instead, the historic role of the buildings.

But one official, Peter Logan, granted an interview to reporter Bill McLaughlin of the *Richmond Times-Herald.* Logan said that although he'd never heard or seen anything unusual in the Wythe House, he couldn't completely discount the stories he'd heard from colleagues:

- A custodian working upstairs one night heard a man and a woman talking in the parlor—after the building had been closed for the day. As he walked downstairs to investigate, the voices became louder. He threw open the parlor door, but the voices stopped. The room, of course, was quite empty.
- On another evening, after hours, a different custodian saw a woman in colonial dress standing at the top of the staircase. For a quick moment he thought she was one of the historical interpreters in period costume employed by Colonial Williamsburg. But as he approached her, she vanished.
- On several occasions, all at night, witnesses have reported seeing a colonial woman seated at a dressing table, combing her hair. The figure always fades away. It's the same bedroom once occupied by George Washington.
- A hostess climbing the same staircase as above felt pushed back by an invisible "force" at the landing, where the air is often frightfully cold. After a short time the pressure eased.

Does the spirit of Lady Ann Skipwith haunt the Wythe House? The line between myth and reality is finely drawn here, but in this case reality seems to contravene the legend.

The legend is that Lady Ann fled the Palace ball because she believed that her husband was consorting with her sister, Jean. Some tales have her committing suicide over her husband's alleged infidelities. Actually, Lady Ann Skipwith died in childbirth in 1779. Sir Peyton did marry Jean—but not until eight or nine years after Ann's death.

Of greater significance is the fact that Sir Peyton and Lady Ann never lived in the Wythe House, but apparently did pay extended visits. George Wythe himself was living in his home before and after Ann's death. Although Wythe's name is little recognized today, he was a prominent colonist and mentor of Thomas Jefferson.

However, Wythe met a demise horrible enough itself to have given rise to any number of tales. He was allegedly poisoned by a grandnephew who had anticipated a substantial inheritance. Wythe clung to life long enough to exact his revenge and write his murderous kinsman out of his will. The new colonial capital had moved to Richmond in 1780, and it was there that George Wythe died in 1806. Because he hadn't died in his Williamsburg home, it is improbable that it is his ghost that haunts the house.

Other candidates for the ghosts of Wythe House are Sir Peyton Skipwith's brother, Henry, and his wife, Elizabeth, who occupied the house at the end of the 1700s. Elizabeth may be the one running up the staircase, but not because she was coming from a dance at the Palace. It had burned down earlier. Elizabeth Skipwith died in 1819 and is buried in Burton Churchyard.

Of course, it's still possible that Lady Ann does, indeed, haunt the house. She was probably a guest at the Wythe House the night she fled the Governor's Ball. Who's to say 240 years later?

Reporters regularly visit the George Wythe House, but none admits to seeing or hearing anything that can't be explained. The haunting of this ancient house does not happen on cue.

The Peyton Randolph House

A young female tourist asks, "Is this house haunted? I have a very uneasy feeling on the stairs and in some of the rooms."

A husband and wife stroll through the exquisitely restored rooms. "Do you feel it?" he questions her at various places. "Yes, here . . . and here . . . and . . ." she replies at several junctures.

Several historical interpreters, guides employed by Colonial Williamsburg, won't work at the house. One won't go upstairs even during the day unless someone is with her. Why?

At the foot of an oak bed in an upstairs bedroom, a vaporous female figure wrings her hands in worry and despair.

Do the tragedies of bygone days linger in certain old houses, the events permanently "recorded" in wood and stone like some psychic videotape to be replayed at the most unexpected moments? It may seem so in the beautiful Peyton Randolph House, along with the George Wythe House one of only five original structures at Williamsburg. For two hundred years, residents and their guests have heard the shattering of a mirror and the heavy tramping of boots across a polished floor. But there is never any broken mirror, and no one marches through the house—not anywhere. And there is the sad lady in the bedroom who warns others away from this house of grief.

The house itself was built about 1715. Its first owner, Sir John Randolph, served as clerk of the House of Burgesses in 1728. He died in 1737, and his widow continued living in the house until her death. Then it passed to John's second son, Peyton, who followed in the footsteps of his eminent father, serving a nine-year term as speaker of the House of Burgesses, and then as president of the First Continental Congress in Philadelphia in 1774.

Peyton died a year later at the age of fifty-four. His widow, Betty Harrison Randolph, stayed on in the house until the conclusion of the American Revolutionary War. Eventually, the house was sold out of the Randolph family.

In 1824, a Mrs. Mary Monroe Peachy was owner of record, and although historical facts are sketchy, it's believed that the house gained notoriety as a place of sadness at about this time.

And it's no wonder: One of Mrs. Peachy's children died in a fall from a tree, and siblings died of various illnesses. A man in the family committed suicide in the drawing room. Much later, after the Civil War, a young orphaned soldier boarded with the Peachy family while attending the College of William and Mary. But he soon contracted tuberculosis and suffered a protracted and agonizing death in the house.

Servants felt that the house was jinxed and feared to speak of what they saw or heard, even to one another.

Because so many families have lived in the Peyton Randolph House, it is impossible to identify the spirits of those who remain. A little two-year-old girl was sleeping in one of the upstairs bedrooms when suddenly, in the middle of the night, she began screaming. Her mother rushed to her side, but the child could only sob, "Man . . . man . . . all white." She pointed to a corner of the room. There was nothing there, but the mother remained with her daughter until she fell back asleep.

Years later, a man sleeping in that same room awoke to see the white, translucent shape of a man standing in a far corner. He had never heard the child's story, nor was there any way to identify who the figure might have been.

Historical interpreters at Colonial Williamsburg have reported seeing a young man in a blue colonial outfit. He's sometimes mistaken for a fellow employee— until he vanishes in front of their eyes!

One interpreter had such a frightening experience several years ago that she rarely speaks of it. She was alone in the house and standing at the top of the staircase on the second floor. Suddenly, she felt something trying to push her down the stairs. She held tightly to the banister and did not fall. She described the sensation as an "evil presence," and has never forgotten the terror of that moment. Could this be the same "staircase ghost" that haunts the Wythe House?

But the strangest, and certainly the most permanent, incorporeal resident of the house "lives" in the small, oak-paneled rear bedroom on the second floor. The room itself is beautifully appointed with a corner fireplace and two narrow windows facing north. A low-post bed is positioned next to one of the windows.

Overnight guests, who were often assigned to that room, appreciated its warmth and coziness.

Until midnight.

Then all hell broke loose.

With the tolling of the great hall clock, the figure of a woman appeared at the foot of the bed and called the sleeping guests by name. Some guests dived under the covers; the more courageous sat bolt upright in bed to face an elderly woman in a flowing gown and wearing a lace-trimmed nightcap on her gaunt head.

To the guests' horror, moonlight shone through the figure and polished the bones of her skeletal face. One brave guest went back to sleep and told her hosts in the morning that she felt the ghost had come to warn her of impending tragedy in her own life.

Others were not so sanguine.

One couple, awakened by the voice of the ghost in the bedroom, fled the house in their pajamas in the middle of the night!

Pedro Jones can understand that fear.

In the 1970s Jones worked as a security guard at the Peyton Randolph House. He was preparing to leave one night when he heard moans and groans coming from the basement. When he went down to investigate, the door slammed shut and locked behind him. He tried to move, but couldn't. He can't recall how many minutes passed before his boss knocked at the *front* door. At that moment, Jones was no longer paralyzed. The basement door unlocked by itself and Jones fled forthwith.

Jones later left Colonial Williamsburg for a different, and presumably less ghost-ridden, job at the College of William and Mary Police Department.

To this day, no one has been able to explain the crashing glass, the heavy footsteps, or the grieving old lady who lives upstairs. But those who have experienced the phenomena over two centuries *know* what they've heard and seen. And they've been as real as any *other* artifacts at Colonial Williamsburg.

The Clocks

The ghosts of Williamsburg are not limited to the restored colonial-era houses in the old city. The apparition that Russell T. Simons encountered on Lafayette Street was of a far more recent vintage.

Simons, an air traffic controller now living in Oklahoma, had moved to Williamsburg in 1977 to look for employment. He had vacationed there as a child and thought it would be an interesting city in which to live and work. What he didn't have in mind was a most unexpected encounter with the supernatural. It took place on Lafayette Street in a boardinghouse owned by a man we will call Mr. Alexander.

This is Russell Simons's story:

"I have no recollection of how I was awakened that night. The fact that I was awake at all is in itself noteworthy; I was a very sound sleeper, and it was extremely unusual for me to wake up before morning. Sometime during the night I came to be awake. I was lying in bed looking at an apparition about ten feet away from me, by a window in the corner of the room. It was a woman of slight proportion with dark hair and a kindly face. She seemed to be looking at me, but was in no way malevolent. The corner of the bed obstructed my view of the floor beneath her, but I had the distinct impression that she was floating a few inches above it.

"The apparition was monochromatic, and was illuminated by a pale light about the color of moonlight. It did not emit light; everything around it was still in darkness. The figure was transparent enough that I could still distinguish the window frame and curtains through it.

"I felt very calm and safe, as though she wanted me to know that she meant no harm. In fact I went back to sleep after a few minutes. That was the most unusual aspect of the experience. The specter seemed to control my emotions.

That's the only explanation I can find for my calm reaction. Had I been asked prior to this event how I would react under these same circumstances, I would have predicted that I would flee from the house, never to return!

"The following morning I discovered my alarm clock had stopped running during the night. Nothing I did would make it run again. I never considered that it was in any way related to the apparition.

"I had already decided not to mention what I had seen to Mr. Alexander. However, I met him on my way out and we started a short conversation. I mentioned that I needed a new clock because mine had broken. 'Don't waste your money,' he said, almost in amusement.

"He told me that he was at his wife's side when she passed away at the hospital. When he returned home he found every clock in the house stopped at the exact time of her death, with the exception of one clock. He purchased new clocks, but after a week or so they, too, would stop at the same time as all the others. He led me to a room and opened a drawer in his desk. It contained at least ten clocks. All of them that I could see had stopped at the same moment as mine. Mr. Alexander said it was the same moment as his wife's passing.

"Also in his room I also saw an old photograph of a woman. He said it was his late wife. It was the same woman whose apparition I had seen in my room.

"He then took me to his living room and pointed out a very old clock hanging over the mantel. It had been his wife's most cherished possession, over 150 years old, and handed down within her family for many years. Mr. Alexander said it was the only clock which would work in his house. At the time I saw it, it was running and showed the correct time.

"The room I was staying in had been Mr. Alexander and his wife's room. After she died, he had decided to move into one of the smaller rooms and rent the larger one to tourists.

"I stayed there for about another week and had no other unusual experiences. When I did leave, the first thing I did on arriving at my new quarters was to plug in my alarm clock. It ran perfectly."

Do not be fooled into thinking ghosts can materialize only in ancient buildings. Even the most innocent-appearing dwelling may conceal sights better left unseen.

Burnley

To the casual passerby, the seventy-one-year-old building at Broadway and Pine, in Seattle's Capital Hill district, looks like a typical old office building. But inside, it's far from typical; it harbors a ghost named Burnley, never seen (at least not yet), but often heard.

The South Annex of Seattle Central Community College occupies the building that was, until recently, the home of the Burnley School of Professional Art (renamed the American Institute of Art and now relocated on Elliott Avenue). For over forty years Burnley students and their teachers coexisted, if somewhat uneasily, with an unseen prankster who opened locked doors, rearranged desks, and tramped up and down the rickety wooden stairs. And after the artists moved out, he stayed on in the place he knew as home.

Isbel Trejo-Connor, manager of the college's microcomputer lab on the second floor, says Burnley has a real fondness for women, and never seems to bother the male staff members.

One day in September 1987, Isbel was sitting in the middle of the storage room taking inventory. Suddenly, she was hit on the head by computer disks falling from a shelf. No accident. The shelf was off in a far corner of the room. And she was alone. Several days later, the same thing occurred. Isbel, annoyed, told Burnley to cut it out, that she had work to do. She told a reporter that he hasn't bothered her since.

And who *is* Burnley? Legend has it that he's the spirit of an eighteen-year-old Broadway High School student who was killed during a fight after a basketball game in the one-time gym on the third floor. He either fell or was thrown down a back flight of stairs. No records exist, however, to support the story.

Just why the ghost is named Burnley isn't clear. There doesn't appear to be a connection between the ghost and the art school's founders, Edwin and Elsie Burnley, who taught their first classes there in 1946. From the beginning, students working alone or late at night reported noises in adjacent rooms. Yet whenever they investigated, they could discover no explanation for the noises.

The Burnleys' daughter, Maralyn Blume, assisted them as a receptionist while attending college, and she often found doors, locked at night, mysteriously unlocked the following morning. She could never account for it.

In 1960, Jess Cauthorn, a freelance commercial artist, bought the school from the Burnleys and, unknowingly, inherited the ghost. Cauthorn, a large, amiable man, refused to tell a reporter whether he believes in ghosts, but his daughter, Nan Cooper, says that her father was always frustrated by the inexplicable incidents—lights burning after they'd been turned off, chairs rearranged, and desks overturned—and tended to blame the mischief on the students. Nan said that the students were more willing to risk facing a ghost than the wrath of her father.

Nan, a student at the school from 1973 to 1975 and later a teacher there, is well acquainted with the strange goings-on in the building.

"In the middle of the afternoon you'd be sitting there," she began, "and it was like someone was in the other room doing some paperwork, then walking around. It wasn't that scary ghost stuff; it just seemed like someone was there. And I'd always make sure the front door was locked because sometimes you get weird people off the street, just wanting to go to the bathroom."

Nan learned to shrug off the footsteps, but on one occasion she was badly frightened. Hearing distinct, measured footfalls, "heel, toe, heel, toe" coming close, she said, "I just grabbed my purse, flipped off the lights, and went tearing down the stairs three at a time."

Mary Renick, a former student and part-time office employee, understood that feeling. She was taking down an art display late one night when she heard someone walking down the second-floor hallway. She looked out and the footsteps went right past her! She flew down the stairs and out the building. From then on she wore a cross on her necklace.

The footsteps were not limited to one part of the building, Nan Cooper emphasized. But "there was just always somebody there, just one person, not a crowd." Trash cans were sometimes dumped out, desk drawers thrown open, and sheets of neatly stacked papers found scrunched into balls. Oddly, nothing was ever missing. The incidents happened year-round, but would come in spurts.

No one, except possibly a student named Anita, ever actually saw these things happening. Anita was at her desk one day and saw her X-Acto knife and markers roll across the desktop.

According to Ms. Cooper, almost every janitor who ever worked at the school has at least one story to tell. Her favorite concerns a former janitor and student at the school, who is now an art director in California.

She remembers one incident in particular:

"He'd come in early on a dark winter morning just to sweep up a bit. In order to get the light on you have to go into this real tiny room on the top floor and flip the main switch before you go to the individual rooms. He had gone up there one morning and walked into a dark classroom just to drop his stuff off. As he was going back to turn on the lights he heard this crash and he looked back into the room and saw that three or four desks in the middle row had just flipped over, all askew, chairs overturned. . . ." Nan said the fellow swore the crash had come from inside the room.

Another student-janitor named Mike was working late one night in 1981. As he walked down the hallway to put his bucket and mop away in a storage area inside the men's room, he noticed that the door to that bathroom was just closing. No one was supposed to be in the building. Mike cautiously went into the bathroom and pushed open the doors of the stalls with the mop handle. No one was there. He told the story in the morning to the rest of the staff. Nan Cooper recalled that "it kind of freaked him out." She said the ladies' room too was a place where "the vibes were strong."

And it wasn't only the students and staff who felt that there was something wrong with the building. Visitors often complained of uneasiness or a sudden coldness.

Always there was the unexpressed fear that someone, at some time, might be in danger, but only one incident of physical contact was reported to school officials.

A woman telephoned Jess Cauthorn one night to say that she'd been standing in front of a window on the top floor when she felt something push her from behind. The low windowsill was at the level of her knees. She wheeled around, but saw no one.

The incident that no one has ever forgotten has been dubbed "The Night the Platform Moved."

A five-foot platform on which models posed was always kept in a corner of an upstairs room. One weekend night, the student who had just finished repainting it was downstairs relaxing and eating a hamburger in the locked and empty building. Suddenly, he heard a tremendous crash right over his head. He dashed upstairs and found the big model stand in the opposite corner of the room. How had it gotten there? To this day it remains a mystery.

Jess Cauthorn was a logical man who tried to find answers to the puzzling phenomena in his building. He thought someone *must* be gaining access to the school, and he had the locks changed. It made no difference.

Next, he installed a silent alarm system that alerted a private protection agency should a door or window be opened, or any disturbance trigger the electronic eyes. The system was something of a fiasco. Every alarm turned out to be a false one. The company made no charge for the first false alarm, but each succeeding call cost the school forty-five dollars if security guards were sent out to check.

The alarms kept coming in. Cauthorn finally decided to investigate the school himself whenever the security company called him to say the alarm had gone off. The system was costing him far more than he'd ever anticipated. But he soon tired of being awakened at 2:00 A.M., getting dressed, and driving the thirty miles from his home to the school. He suggested that his daughter be called instead. Nan Cooper lived in an apartment only a few blocks from the school and had a set of keys.

The calls continued—at eleven-thirty, at two, and at four in the morning. Nan always took her boyfriend with her on these middle-of-the-night forays. "We'd take my number-three-iron golf club," she said, "open the door and deactivate the alarm. No one was ever in the place. All the circuits were connected and the doors were locked. We just couldn't figure out what triggered the alarm." Neither could the company that installed the system. They rechecked the wiring and found all connections were in place. Everything, in other words, was in perfect working order.

Sometimes two months would pass without a false alarm, then the phone would ring early in the morning. "At that time of night I knew who it was," she said. "I got to know the guy who worked nights for the company. It became a real joke and he'd start laughing and say 'Okay, what do you want us to do?' and I'd say to just forget it. Nobody ever broke in."

The art school moved out in 1986 and the building was gutted and remodeled. When Nan Cooper heard that supernatural activities were still going on, she was somewhat surprised. "Now there's tinted glass, miniblinds, elevators, and nothing to rattle. You know it'd be a real boring place for a ghost."

Apparently Burnley doesn't agree.

The Package

The year was 1937. The depths of the Depression. Dick Owens was a young man who saw that his future probably lay elsewhere, away from the small Wisconsin town where he grew up. On an early September day of that year he prepared to depart for the West . . . where he would encounter a most insistent visitor.

As he pulled together what personal belongings he would need, Owens was interrupted by a visit from Earl Mayhew, one of his closest friends. The two spoke for a few minutes and then shook hands warmly. If all went well, Owens told Mayhew, he would try to return home for a visit the following summer.

A few hours later, Owens and another friend hopped a freight train heading west. The men eventually traveled through five states, landing in Everett, Washington, at midnight about a week later.

Owens had an uncle living on a farm near Kent, Washington. The pair had it in mind to make it to his place the following day, if they could hold out that long. Their last solid food had been peanut butter sandwiches somewhere in Idaho several days before. Sleep in the bouncing freight cars had come in fits and starts.

Owens and his friend walked from Everett to Kent, a distance of nearly fifty miles, "on empty stomachs and no sleep," Owens recalled. A milk truck driver gave the young men a lift the last few miles and let them out a half-mile from their destination.

Dick Owens, who now lives in Renton, Washington, remembers how events unfolded next:

On his uncle's farm was a guest house with two bedrooms, a living room, kitchen, and bathroom. The men ate their first full meal in a week, took baths and headed for separate bedrooms—and blessed privacy from each other.

Sometime during the night, Owens awoke because someone was shaking his shoulders. Earl Mayhew was sitting on the bed. His Wisconsin friend had a package in his hands all tied up with red, white, and blue twine, holding it out as if offering it to his friend.

Owens shook his head and said, rather angrily, "Get out of here, Earl. I'm too tired to talk." He fell back asleep.

In the morning, Owens attributed his "hallucination" to being overly tired. The men arose, dressed, and had a very late breakfast. They felt somewhat refreshed, but that didn't last long. They headed for their bedrooms for naps.

Shortly afterward, Owens woke with a start. Earl Mayhew was back tugging at his sleeve. Again he held out that package tied with twine. Owens was annoyed.

"Earl," Owens snapped. "Can't you take a hint? Get the hell out of here and take that package with you. I'm bushed—so *please* don't bother me again."

At breakfast the next day, Owens's aunt handed him a letter from his mother. It had come the day before, but she had decided to wait until he had recovered and felt rested.

Owens could hardly believe the words: Earl Mayhew had been killed while riding his motorcycle to the Minnesota State Fair the day after Owens left for the West.

Almost a year later, Owens did return home to Wisconsin. One morning as he was passing the Mayhew place someone called his name. He looked up and saw Earl's mother running toward him. She hugged him and cried in great sobbing gasps.

Finally, she asked him to wait right there. She had something to give him.

A few moments later, she came out of the house with a package in her hands.

"Here," she said, "this is for you. Just before he left for the fair, Earl asked me to make sure you got this. It's that brown herringbone suit you always admired on him. He bought a new powder-blue suit to replace it."

He recognized the package, even down to the red, white, and blue twine and brown wrapping paper. It was the same package Earl's ghost had tried to give him on his uncle's farm.

Owens didn't refuse the package this time.

The Wizard's Clip

Both fear and curiosity drove people to the home of Adam Livingston, a Middleway planter, to see the demons perform. They were not disappointed. Dishes tumbled out of cupboards and smashed on the floor, lanterns were blown out with no one near them, and money vanished. Horses galloped around the house at night, except the beasts were never seen. Heads of chickens and turkeys dropped off, sometimes in front of startled onlookers. Livingston's barn burned and his cattle died. Bells rang and shrieks rent the night air.

One afternoon Livingston saw a man in a wagon stopped before the house. He walked down to the road to offer assistance, if needed.

"Get your damn rope out of the way!" screamed the wagoneer. "I want to pass."

"But there is no rope. Your imagination is playing tricks on you," Livingston said. Surely the wagoneer was drunk.

The driver, red-faced with anger, climbed down from his seat, drew a knife from his belt and slashed at the rope. The knife passed through the air, cutting nothing.

At that moment, another wagon driver came along and asked why the rope was stretched across the road. Swearing at Livingston, he leaped down and he too slashed empty air with his knife.

Livingston, humoring the men, said that if they proceeded slowly, with great caution, they could continue, unimpeded, on their way.

The horses never hesitated, and soon the wagons were out of sight.

But then came a new development, more frightening than those that had gone before. Day and night the family heard the sound of shears. Sheets, blankets, bedspreads, towels, and clothing were cut into crescents and other peculiar shapes. For months the invisible scissors-wielder worked, even going into a shed to cut Livingston's boots, saddles, and harnesses into spiral shapes.

One elderly woman visitor removed her good silk cap and wrapped it in her handkerchief to guard it from being clipped before entering the house. When she left the house she unwrapped the cap. It was cut into ribbons!

A German tailor in Middleway scorned such tales and promised to expose the true source of the wizard clipping. One day he walked past Livingston's house, carrying a package under his arm. It contained a suit he'd just finished making for a nearby planter. All of a sudden he heard the sound of shears above his head, but saw nothing. When he reached his destination he discovered that the suit had been cut into shreds.

Livingston tried to find a reason for these cursed manifestations. He had always been a devout Lutheran and God-fearing man, married, if uneasily, to a Catholic woman. But then he recalled that stormy night in 1794 when a mysterious stranger had appeared at the door. The man, middle-aged and neatly dressed, asked for shelter until the weather cleared. Livingston's wife prepared a modest supper and the seven children, unaccustomed to travelers, hovered like frightened birds in the corners of the kitchen.

In the middle of the night, Livingston awoke to sounds of wheezing and gasping. He got up, knocked on the stranger's door and asked if he was all right. The man coughed violently. Livingston opened the door and rushed to the bedside. The stranger, barely able to speak, said he was dying. Could his host summon a priest?

Livingston consulted his wife. She said she didn't know of any nearby priest, nor any who would come out on such a night of wind and rain. Her husband was relieved. Years ago he had sworn that no Catholic priest would ever set foot upon his property.

The stranger died unshriven, his name unknown. Neighbor men helped Livingston bury the body in a corner of the property. Later a small stone cross was erected on the grave.

Hours after the burial the phenomena began; they would continue for years.

The distressed family soon became unable to sleep and Livingston could not perform his chores. Finally he implored his pastor to perform an exorcism to rid the house of its evil spirits. But the clergyman refused, saying that the power to exorcise existed only in the early church.

An Episcopalian vicar failed to cast out the spirits, as did three Methodist ministers. Then one night Livingston saw, in a dream, a beautiful church on a mountaintop; a man in splendid robes stood at the entrance. He heard a voice say, "This is the man who will help you." Friends in Shepherdstown helped Livingston locate the man—Father Dennis Cahill, a Catholic priest. Cahill went to the home, said prayers, and blessed the house with holy water. As he turned to leave, a leather satchel of money that had been missing for weeks dropped onto the doorsill.

The manifestations stopped, and the grateful family was now able to sleep at night. But not for long. The supernatural forces returned. By this time the story of the spirits in the Livingston house had spread from coast to coast, and the Diocese of Baltimore sent the Reverend Dmitri Gallitzin to investigate the phenomena. After living in the house for three months, Gallitzin recommended an exorcism. Father Cahill joined Father Gallitzin, and as family members kneeled, the priest commanded the evil spirits to leave the house. They did.

Livingston was so grateful to the priest that he converted to Catholicism and, in 1802, deeded 40 acres of his 350-acre estate to the church. In 1978 a religious retreat called Priest Field Pastoral Center was built on the land. It is a peaceful place at the edge of a virgin cedar forest.

Yet modern times have not prevented visitations by supernatural forces. On one occasion a Baltimore priest, escorting a tour group, was walking near Priest Field's chapel when the shank of his steel-rimmed glasses was sheared in two.

A woman visitor had her slip cut and the straps of her handbag severed. And a man focusing a camera watched it come apart in his hands. Many persons who use the retreat complain of uneasiness.

Is it God's way of making people pay more attention to the world of the spirit? Some think so.

Something Evil on Larabee Street

The haunted house of legend must look the part. A Victorian pile is ideal, one replete with gables and turrets, and windows heavily curtained to ward off prying eyes. A grotesquery of gargoyles crouching along the sagging roof line adds a certain sinister ambience, as does a weed-choked lawn encircled by a black, wrought-iron fence topped with elaborate scrollwork and spikes. The ancient garden gate must swing on rusted hinges.

The haunt hunter should not be fooled by this portrait painted by fictionists. It is more accurate to say that even the most quiet village neighborhoods can present scenes of inexplicable terror for the innocent or unwary.

The rural enclave of Horicon, Wisconsin presents such an attitude of peaceful tranquillity. Peaceful, that is, until one family found their lives shattered by menacing apparitions and psychological horror.

Here the vistas Norman Rockwell might have depicted are deceptive. In a ranch-style bungalow along South Larabee Street, amid the clutter of bicycles and skateboards, lawnmowers and lawn ornaments, there played out a haunting so bizarre and shocking in its effect that the entire community had an unwilling role in the story that eventually captured the attention of media around the world. It's a tale of a menacing, elusive, evil phantasm that chose an ordinary family for persecution so brutal they fled their home in the middle of an icy January night, literally escaping for their very lives.

Allen and Deborah Tallmann moved their young family into the three-bedroom home in the spring of 1986. The house was one of ten built in the neighborhood two years earlier through the Self-Help Housing Project of Dodge County. The original owners of the house had moved out in less than eighteen months. The Tallmanns didn't ask why. Perhaps they should have.

The couple had two children, a boy aged seven and a daughter not quite a year old. We will call them Kenny and Maryann. Deborah was pregnant and would give birth to another daughter, Sarah, in November 1986.

In every way the Tallmanns were typical of any family in the town. Allen went deer hunting each fall with friends. He worked hard at his job and wanted nothing more than to live in peace with his young family. Deborah devoted her attention to the children and took pride in her well-kept home.

"When we bought the house we were real excited and happy because it was ours and we owned something for once in our lives," Deborah Tallmann said. "It was a great opportunity. At the time."

Allen qualified for a low-interest Farmers Home Administration (FmHA) loan. Mortgage payments were small. The family figured they would have the house paid for well before his retirement.

It was not to be. Their joy in buying a piece of the American dream turned into a nightmare of vaporous figures, guttural voices threatening death, phantom flames, frightened children, and finally, a penetrating fear that left the family on the verge of madness.

South Larabee Street is a short roadway, extending only a few blocks at the south edge of town. Until houses were built there, it was a small marsh best known as a hangout for teenagers and their occasional beer parties. The old Catholic cemetery, St. Malachy's, is two blocks away. The houses in the development look much the same, primarily one-story ramblers with attached garages. The dominant house color is white. There are no sidewalks. Children scamper across lawns or whiz up and down the street on bicycles while parents still visit across backyard fences. It is a safe and secure neighborhood that nearly typifies the ideal of small-town American life.

The Tallmanns seemed to fit right in. Deborah was thirty years old; Allen was thirty-two.

The first few months in their new home were uneventful. The couple spent their time painting and decorating and getting to know their neighbors. But, within a short time, Deborah and Allen began to notice changes in their home and family so subtle that only much later were they able to understand their significance.

Deborah remembered: "It was after a couple of months. We didn't see anything and nothing unusual happened, but it seemed like our health started going downhill. I had my kids in the doctor's office at least once a week and sometimes three times. They had everything. Allen was sick, too, and my Maryann was in the hospital twice, once for chicken pox and once for a cold and ear infection. Allen had back problems. We were just sick all the time."

At first they thought the illnesses could be traced to building materials used in the house. But a check with building inspectors found that was not the case. Neither asbestos nor other toxic substances were present in the house.

Allen's personality, too, began to change. He was easily irritated. When night fell he became "itchy," in his words, and got "real jittery, short-tempered." He often argued with Deborah over trivial matters. When their second daughter was born in November 1986, he threatened to leave the family and went on a drinking binge. It was uncharacteristic behavior for him. Looking back on the episodes, he can only attribute his mean disposition to their life in the house on South Larabee Street.

The house also seemed to have alarming effects on visitors, particularly Deborah's mother and sister. According to Deborah, "We have real close family relationships, and when we moved in our families would come and visit us all the time. We had a brand-new home and they liked coming here. But it seemed that after a couple of months the visits from our family . . . well, they just didn't want to go there."

During her pregnancy, Deborah was diagnosed as having placenta previa, the mislocation of the placenta in an abnormally low position in the uterus. Deborah was confined to her home; doctors cautioned her not to perform housework or other heavy chores. Her mother came over almost every day from August 1986 until the baby was born three months later.

Deborah eventually found out just how much her mother disliked their "dream home."

"She told me after I had the baby that she couldn't wait to leave the house. And the farther she got away, the more relaxed she became because she was so tense in the house. She would tell me it's a beautiful house, but she just didn't like it."

Deborah's mother said the house was "suffocating" the family, causing a kind of "vacuum" that seemed to be sucking the life out of them.

At about the same time, during the summer and early fall of 1986, Deborah's sister also stopped visiting. The reasons were the same, a smothering sensation whenever she stepped through the door. "She told me she would love to come over," Deborah said, "but she got headaches whenever she was in our house and actually got sick to her stomach."

The Tallmanns bought a kitten they named Cat soon after they moved in. Within a few weeks, "Cat went absolutely berserk," Deborah said. "She would actually climb the walls. Sometimes she would come flying across the living room and climb right up a door." Once she even crashed into the wall. Cat's rude behavior seemed particularly prevalent after sunset.

Allen started putting Cat in the bathroom at night, even though it would howl. One night, however, he decided to leave Cat on the living room couch. That was a mistake.

"A couple of hours later," Allen Tallmann recalled, "Cat came running across the bed. Deborah had a chest of drawers and a TV set on top with a cable box on it. The cat jumped straight up to the cable TV box."

The cat then sprang for the wall. "It was hanging right on the plaster walls, just like an owl." Allen shook his head at the remembrance of the episode.

The couple found a new home for Cat within a few days.

Not long after Cat's antics, another, more perplexing incident still left the couple unconvinced that the strange behavior by those who visited—or lived in—the house on South Larabee Street was anything out of the ordinary.

Deborah and Allen wanted a night out before their next baby was born. Even more than they wanted to admit, the sickness of their two children, the attitudes of in-laws, Allen's changing conduct, and the problems with Cat were beginning to weigh upon the couple. They just wanted to get away from everything for a few hours.

They hired a baby-sitter, a girl of sixteen who had babysat for them before, and made plans to dine at a favorite restaurant in nearby Beaver Dam. The evening was pleasant and relaxing, a welcome respite from the growing tension of the past few months.

Their serene evening ended abruptly when they returned home and opened their front door. The baby-sitter rushed to meet them. She blurted out a fantastic story that left Allen and Deborah dumbfounded, yet understandably skeptical. While the baby-sitter and seven-year-old Kenny played a board game in the kitchen, a chair at the table started rocking back and forth. It bounced around and then suddenly stopped. The girl was shaken by the incident, yet neither Deborah nor her husband really knew how to respond.

"I just looked at Allen. We didn't want to say she was lying, so we just kind of brushed it off as, well, maybe it did and maybe it didn't," Deborah said. The girl was from a good family and had never said anything even remotely as amazing as the tale she reported that night. Young Kenny Tallmann corroborated the girl's story when his parents questioned him the next morning. He was as upset as the baby-sitter at the incident.

The household returned to a semblance of normalcy over the next six months. Deborah gave birth to Sarah in November, Allen went deer hunting with friends, and both tried to adjust to the pattern of life with a new baby. The children made new friends in the neighborhood. Kenny was in school most of the day, so little Maryann tried to help Mom as best she could with the new baby.

In mid-1987 the parents decided seven-month-old Sarah could begin sharing a room with her big sister. Kenny had been sleeping in the larger of the two children's bedrooms. He moved into the smaller room, and the girls were given bunk beds in Kenny's old bedroom.

For whatever reason, the room switch by the children triggered a new round of increasingly violent incidents.

"On the same day we moved Kenny into the room where Maryann had been sleeping, we had put a clock radio in there, one with a sleeper alarm," Deborah Tallmann remembered. "He had gone to bed with the radio on so it would go off when he went to sleep. He came out after a while and said the radio had switched stations. We thought maybe the radio had picked up static, or another station had come in, something on that order. We didn't make too much of it."

Deborah took Kenny by the hand and led him back into the room. She tucked him in, tuned in a radio station, checked the sleep timer and left the room. Kenny came running back out a few minutes later. The radio had again changed stations, only this time Kenny said he saw the knob turn and the tuning indicator spin across the dial. Deborah and Allen had no way of verifying what Kenny said, but they saw he was very frightened. They believed him. He was usually a pretty reliable little boy. To placate her son, Deborah removed the radio from his room and put it in the front closet.

Deborah feared this would add to Kenny's growing irritability. He frequently refused to go to his room alone at bedtime, and rarely slept through the night. He heard "noises," he said, like someone was banging on the water pipes in the basement. Maybe, his mother reasoned, the pressures of a new school, new neighborhood, and a new sister were causing him to feel some resentment. Deborah had given birth to Kenny before she met and married Allen. Although the boy spent some time with his natural father, the two weren't particularly close. "We thought maybe this was his way of getting more attention," Deborah said.

A second episode involving a small suitcase stowed under Kenny's bed did nothing to dispel his mother's belief that perhaps he *was* making up stories to get attention.

Kenny had again fought going to his room that night. After the by-now-usual kicking and screaming, Kenny had calmed down enough for his parents to turn off the lights and go back into the living room. A few minutes later, Kenny came running out crying that the suitcase had slid out from underneath his bed. It had zoomed across the floor and then scooted back.

Deborah refused to believe him. That just couldn't possibly have happened, she scolded him. She thought he just wanted to stay up late and watch television. Kenny insisted that he had seen the suitcase move. Deborah put him back in bed. When, in a short time, he ran out repeating the same story, Allen grabbed the suitcase, which was under the bed, and tossed it in the same closet where the radio had been secreted.

All three children had disturbing nighttime experiences during the summer and early fall of 1987.

"Our kids rarely slept straight through the night from the day we moved into that house," Deborah said. "We were up all the time with them; it almost seemed that whatever was in that house would wake the kids up. We could go in and check them and they'd be sound asleep and all of a sudden they'd be crying or fussing. It always seemed to happen about the time we'd crawl into bed. We'd no more than get into bed and the kids would be awake, and they'd stay awake for a long time."

Sometimes her parents heard Maryann, who was now nearly two and one-half years old, talking to someone. Deborah said, "We'd wake up in the middle of the night [to] hear her giggling and talking ... We never really thought that much about it. We believed she was talking to the doll or her teddy bear." She and Allen joked that their daughter seemed to be having her own little "tea party."

Any lightheartedness they felt at Maryann's nocturnal ramblings soon ended, however. The girl's odd conversations soon gave way to nightmares that sent her running to her parents' room.

"She would get to our room and talk about the noises she heard," Deborah said. "She'd say 'Don't you hear it?' And we didn't know what it was. She would make the sound 'Shhh ... shhh ... shhh.' Like it was a voice." A voice trying to quiet a frightened child?

Oddly, all three children were rarely awake at the same time. When one woke up with a nightmare, the other two remained asleep. While Maryann babbled away, Sarah, in the same room, would not be disturbed. Kenny's separate room kept his own nighttime problems from affecting the girls, and vice versa.

Until September 1987, the peculiar episodes came in irregular patterns. For several days in a row, the children would have restless nights or Allen and Deborah would fight over minor incidents. Then the household returned to normal for a week or so before a new trauma struck the family.

Deborah never heard voices, but there were other peculiar occurrences. "I heard the garage door open and close. I thought maybe somebody had come in over the fence and went in the back door because we had a freezer full of meat [in the garage]. I called up the neighbor next door and said I thought somebody was in the garage and asked her to hang on to the phone while I went to look. There was nobody out there, but the garage door had opened and shut. I heard it."

Violent nightmares also became a problem for Deborah. Like most people, she occasionally had dreams vivid enough to wake her up, but after her move to South Larabee Street her nightmares became so violent they made her think she was going mad.

"I had them all the time in the house, one right after another. Horrible nightmares. I'd wake up in the night crying, and I'd ask Allen if I was going to have nightmares like this all my life. They would be terrible, ungodly. I would dream my kids were dying, that Allen was dying, my father would die. People would come up from the basement and line us up along the wall and just shoot us all down. Or, people would kidnap my kids, or they would fall in the river and drown. Over and over again . . . people were going to hurt us."

Deborah can't explain or understand what caused this onslaught of terror-filled dreams, only that they seemed to worsen the longer she lived in the house.

The long nights of soothing their frightened children frazzled the couple's already taut nerves. Only Allen seemed capable of bringing comfort to the children. He would lie on the floor of the girls' room until they settled down, then go into Kenny's room until he fell asleep.

"I heard the banging when I was in there," Allen said, referring to the noises Kenny had earlier complained about. "I told the kids it was the water heater . . . I went down to the basement a lot of times with running hot water upstairs to get the water heater to kick in. You could hear a couple of little plinks and hear the humming from the burner, but the noises I heard the nights I spent in Kenny's room, well it was like mice or rats or something crawling around. . . ."

But investigate as they might, the couple never found evidence of rodents. According to the couple, the house was extremely well insulated. Allen looked through the low attic, checked around the foundation and in the floorboards for any signs that animals had somehow gotten inside. Eventually, he dismissed the idea.

For all of the problems the family was facing, Deborah rarely discussed the situation with her husband. "We never talked about the fact that maybe something was going on."

"I fought it," Allen said. "I fought it all the time. Deborah thought there was something in our house. I didn't go for that at first. We used to have some bad arguments."

"But we never really sat down and talked about it," Deborah added. "I mean, just sat down and said this is happening, now what are we going to do about it. Never did we talk about it until . . ."

Until the vague feelings of uneasiness, increasingly cranky children, and family tensions gave way to a number of events with one thing in common—they could not be attributed to the imagination.

When the weather started getting cooler, late in September 1987, Allen Tallmann started painting the concrete walls in the basement. It is a finished basement, but only used by Deborah for her washer and dryer and as a playroom for the children. The couple had plans to partition the area into a couple of extra rooms.

By now it had become routine for Allen to stay in the girls' room, stretched out on the floor reading stories until their steady breathing told him they were asleep.

One night in the early fall, Deborah asked him to come upstairs, Allen recalled, so he could get the children to sleep. "I took the paintbrush and I laid it right across the paint tray. I was upstairs probably a half-hour, forty-five minutes at the most. I told Deb I was going to go back down and paint just a little bit more. It was about nine-thirty. Now, up until this point I wasn't scared in the house. Nothing bothered me. Well, I went downstairs and my paintbrush had been pulled out of the pan and was jammed upside down in a can of paint."

Allen was dumbstruck. The brush was propped absolutely upright, the wooden handle completely immersed in the epoxy paint, like a prankster had placed it there. He hadn't left it that way, but that was the only thing he knew for certain.

"I didn't say anything. I asked Deb to throw down some towels. I told her I must have knocked the paintbrush into the can, but I knew I didn't. I cleaned the paintbrush off and painted a little while longer."

A few minutes later he glimpsed a shadow flitting across the basement. He thought it might have been a passing car's lights throwing silhouettes across the walls and furnace (a basement window faced the street), but he wrapped up for the night and headed upstairs.

"A kind of chill went through my spine. That was enough painting for one night." He decided against telling Deborah what had happened.

Another odd incident in the basement almost made the couple believe that it *was* a prankster and not the supernatural out to harm them. Allen found one of the basement windows removed and propped against the wall one morning.

Deborah said: "The window was just like it had slid down. Almost like someone had gone into the basement and set it there and crawled back out. We thought somebody had broken into our house. If someone had kicked it in, it would have fallen and crashed. We were home the night before so we would have heard it." Allen had a valuable collection of hunting rifles, power tools, and a chain saw in the basement, but nothing appeared to have been taken. They didn't call the police.

"What we couldn't figure out," Deborah said, "is if somebody broke in, how did they get from that high up down to the floor, because they would have had to scoot through the window and jump down. That's okay, I guess, but in order to get back out they would have to climb on a chair or something. It was real puzzling, but we just put the window back and let it go."

Deborah admits that after the window incident a certain paranoia took hold, an almost palpable sense that the family was being watched. She rarely went to the basement alone.

"It would be very warm outside, but we would close all the windows and lock them. We just wouldn't leave them open because we were afraid somebody was going to come in."

The family bought a dog to help foster a sense of security. It was a young shepherd/Labrador mix that they were mistakenly told had been housebroken. That wasn't the only problem they had with him.

Deborah said: "The dog barked all night and it messed in the house. The first night we had him there, I had to send it outside to the fenced-in yard. The dog barked at the house, especially when it was night. All day long it would be in the kennel but as soon as the sun started to set, the dog would pace back and forth barking. It just wouldn't shut up. We tried to discipline it. We would bring it in the house, but it just went crazy, scratching at the door wanting to go out. But if you left it outside it would start barking again. We couldn't keep it in and we couldn't keep it out."

Unlike the cat, the dog stayed with the family. The barking problem subsided somewhat with training, although he remained edgy in the house after dark. The Tallmanns found out later that other neighborhood dogs often barked at their house for no apparent reason.

In October 1987, Allen Tallmann was promoted to foreman on the night shift at the manufacturing plant where he worked. Deborah wasn't looking forward to the prospect of being alone with the children until Allen returned at one or two in the morning.

Later in October, Allen became sick with a severe sinus infection and cold. He took medicine, but nothing seemed to improve his condition. The frequent trips with their sick children to the doctor over the past months had been expensive, even with the family's insurance covering part of the cost. Allen was reluctant to seek medical treatment for himself.

One night at about ten o'clock, however, his condition worsened. "I had taken a shower and crawled in bed," Allen remembered. "I was sleeping when I started coughing and then threw up. I got real short of breath."

Deborah called Allen's mother in a panic. She came right over and said she would watch the children while Deborah took Allen to the hospital. He was worse by this time; he had a difficult time catching his breath. Deborah was concerned over her husband's deteriorating condition and called an ambulance.

Hospital personnel stabilized Allen's condition, gave him medication, and sent him home with Deborah a few hours later.

Allen's mother met the couple at the door, purse and car keys in hand and ready to leave. After a perfunctory inquiry into her son's health, she hurried out. The couple was startled at her rather brusque manner, but they thought she was simply tired from a long day.

However, a telephone conversation sometime later between Allen and his mother indicated another reason entirely for her rudeness. "I asked her if she got a funny feeling when she was at our house because it didn't seem like she wanted to visit us anymore," Allen said. His mother hesitated momentarily and then admitted that, yes, she didn't enjoy coming over at all and, in fact, couldn't wait to leave whenever she was there. She had been especially upset the night Allen went to the hospital.

"That night she was lying on the couch after the kids had gotten settled down and had dozed off," Allen said. "It then seemed like somebody woke her up. She said there were red eyes looking in the window. She blinked and couldn't believe it. She looked again and they were still there." The couch Mrs. Tallmann napped on was directly beneath the living room's wide front window. When she sat up, the staring eyes vanished. Mrs. Tallmann thought someone was looking in through the window, according to her son.

"The only thing that crossed my mind," Deborah Tallmann offered, "is that a car might have driven in the driveway directly across from us. But then she had gone to the window and looked out and she didn't see anybody. You'd think she would have seen them [neighbors] getting out of their car."

Whatever it was, Allen's mother had been very happy to see her son and daughter-in-law return home that night.

Mrs. Tallmann's description of the red, glowing eyes turned out to be prophetic. That devilish image was to return on several occasions over the next few months.

The most frustrating aspect of the couple's twenty months on South Larabee Street was their inability to identify any *specific* pattern of activity, of something, anything, that would point to a cause for all their problems. They desperately wanted to believe that perhaps it was a prankster that was responsible. The acts were too random, certainly, to connect them with the supernatural. Were the nervous animals simply misbehaving? Did Allen's mother really see taillights? Was Allen confused about where he had left the paintbrush? Maybe the children were just being cranky, as children often are.

Or perhaps it was something more, a slowly developing pattern of harassment by some sort of entity that for whatever reason had found a haven in the Tallmann home.

On Friday, November 19, 1987, Allen, along with his father and brother, left on their annual weekend deer hunting trip to an area near Wisconsin Rapids, a city in central Wisconsin. Deborah didn't want to stay alone with the children. Her sister volunteered to stay with her at the house. Both Allen and Deborah weren't entirely convinced that someone wasn't harassing them and went so far as to put a lock on the door that opened onto the basement stairs. Allen still wondered about that mysterious incident with the basement window.

But the house was quiet during Allen's absence, and for the next week. On the following Saturday, November 27, however, an accidentally watched scene from a television show started a new wave of anxiety in the family.

"My mom was baby-sitting for the kids," Deborah said. "Maryann and Kenny were watching television. My mom was flipping through the channels when she turned on a show that had a big bonfire, and out of this fire came running a man wearing a pig's head. It must have been a horror movie of some kind. My mother changed the channel, but not before Maryann noticed what was going on."

When Deborah put her to bed later that night, the explicit television scene remained with the little girl. She told her mother that there was a fire in her room and somebody was watching her. She wouldn't settle down. Deborah had to sit with her until she finally fell asleep.

The images of fires and men wearing animal heads plagued Maryann for days afterward. She cried about fires on the door, in the windows, and that "something" was hiding behind the door ready to pounce when the lights were turned off. A nightly ritual began whereby Maryann took a pitcher from the kitchen cupboard to her bedroom, put all the "monsters" inside and then snapped the lid on the container. She then dumped the "monsters" in the garbage can. Deborah assured her daughter that they were all gone after that.

The problems Allen and Deborah had with Maryann were never discussed with Kenny. "He was fearful enough," Deborah said. "We didn't need to add to that."

Once Maryann awoke so quickly in her lower bunk bed, she hit her head on the bunk above her. She cried about "a fire on the door" and came charging down the hallway and jumped into her parents' bed.

Did the television images contribute to Maryann's nightmares? Her mother thinks that was only part of the problem. Deborah continued to hear her daughter "laughing and giggling," saying something like "hi there" while the rest of the house was silent and dark. When the child became overtly frightened and joined her parents in bed, she would say "It's coming" and then state matter-of-factly, "It's here . . . it's here." When her parents asked who, or what, was coming, Maryann got upset and wondered why her parents couldn't hear or see "it."

On the Sunday before Christmas 1987, a new chapter was added to the family's woes, one that would presage their final flight.

Eight-year-old Kenny had an encounter with a mysterious figure, a three-foot-tall, hideous-looking, wrinkled old woman.

"Kenny came into our room and said that he woke up to see this lady standing by his door," Deborah said. "When I went with him to his room I didn't see anything. He said she was very old, very ugly, and had a glow around her . . . like a fire. She had long black hair . . . I tried to tell him it was his imagination and he should go back to sleep. About five minutes later he called to me that she was standing there again."

Deborah sat up with her son for the rest of the night. She couldn't convince him that it was either his imagination or, as she suggested, an "angel" come to visit him.

"She's too homely to be an angel," Kenny shot back.

When Kenny left for school in the morning, Allen and Deborah had their first long conversation about the similarities between Maryann's nightmares and Kenny's glowing woman. They also started comparing notes on all the bizarre occurrences over the past eighteen months.

"I told him about Kenny and the little old lady and how she glowed like fire," Deborah said. "We never mentioned anything to Kenny about what was happening to Maryann. The stories were just too similar, too coincidental to ignore. I started talking about how pale Kenny was and how my mom [didn't like] being in the house. . . ."

The couple realized their lives were slowly coming unraveled, their children increasingly disturbed. Yet they were at a loss as to what steps should be taken. They considered selling the house, but thought better of it after they calculated the money they might lose in the transaction.

Deborah decided that she would call their pastor, Rev. Wayne Dobratz. "If we had a ghost, the person you would call is a minister," Deborah said. Pastor Dobratz couldn't come over right away, but promised he would stop by as soon as possible.

Other problems surfaced during the couple's discussion that morning at the kitchen table. Allen confided to his wife that he had a growing uneasiness whenever he came into the house. He had the impression "something" was waiting in the garage for him, watching his every movement. When he pulled down the garage door, Allen said it was like "shutting himself in a tomb."

One night as he walked from the garage into the house, he felt a tugging on the lunch pail he held under his arm, as if an unseen arm was trying to pull it away from him. So intense was his dread of entering the house that sometimes he was reluctant to even turn into his driveway.

Deborah remained relatively untouched by the malevolence, but her biggest fear was seeing what was happening to her husband and children. They seemed to be the primary targets of the hostility.

Pastor Dobratz's first visit to the house did not assuage the Tallmanns' fears.

"We told him what was going on," Deborah said. "We asked him if he had ever dealt with anything like this before. It was the devil, he said. Well that upset us even more. We were already scared enough, but to think that the devil was in our house . . . !"

The pastor wanted to know if anyone in the family had been playing with a Ouija board, or had held a séance. The Tallmanns hardly knew what to say. They didn't dabble in either activity.

"He convinced us that we had a spirit in our house. It more than likely was not *the* devil, but it was *of* the devil and our house was cursed," Deborah recalled. "He thought maybe somebody had gotten into our house, someone that had something against us, and put a 'spell' on the house."

Pastor Dobratz told Deborah and Allen to start attending church each Sunday. The family was nominally religious, but their attendance hadn't been on a weekly basis. "It seemed like every time Sunday came around, our children were sick or I'd have been up all night and I was exhausted," Deborah said, but the family did start attending church regularly. The minister also suggested that the family recite prayers and read passages from the Bible to rid the house of the evil. They followed his advice.

Allen and Deborah didn't believe the devil, or his minions, were responsible for what was happening to their family. Allen said he "couldn't believe in my heart that the Lord would do something of this nature to me. We might not go to church all the time, and I use a little foul language once in a while, but never have I done any bodily harm to anybody or ever threatened anyone. For my pastor to say we've got the devil in our house . . ."

But, at the family's request, their pastor returned to South Larabee Street and blessed the house. All was quiet until a few days before Christmas.

"Kenny had been allowed to sleep on the couch in our living room because he was so frightened to go to his room at night," Deborah said. "We always left a light on, and when he slept he faced our Christmas tree. I could see him from our bedroom. We had all gone to bed as usual when about three-thirty in the morning Kenny called out to me that the ghost was in the living room. I got up to look but didn't see anything. He said she had been right where I was standing. I went back to bed, but no more than five minutes later he said she was back again. She had gotten bigger."

Again, Deborah ran into the living room. Kenny said the figure vanished just as his mother reached him. When it happened a third time, Deborah, frustrated and not a little frightened, remained in her bedroom.

"Kenny said she was looking at him," Deborah said. "She was standing by the Christmas tree. When he asked her what she wanted, she just stared at him harder. I heard him say, 'Why don't you just go away and leave us alone!' That's when I came back out into the living room. He was so scared, it was like he was paralyzed."

Deborah fully believed her little boy. He was wide awake, she had heard him shouting at something. His fear was too real. But who this phantom woman was, and why she had menaced Kenny, was a mystery. Perhaps it was the same diminutive figure he had seen some months before, his mother surmised.

Deborah said: "There was little doubt in our minds after Kenny saw that little lady. I didn't want to put up with any more of it. I had about all that I could take. The kids were paranoid, they wouldn't let me go to the bathroom, they wouldn't go to the bedrooms themselves. I had to constantly take them almost everywhere I went. They always got frightened. After a point you can't explain these things to children anymore. I couldn't tell them not to be afraid, because I was scared myself. The minute it got dark out, the house was in chaos. The girls were screaming, Kenny was yelling. I couldn't put Maryann and Sarah to bed because Kenny wouldn't stay in the living room by himself."

The more Allen thought about what Pastor Dobratz said, the angrier he became, barely able to concentrate at work. He decided to go after the evil himself, if indeed that was the cause of his family's turmoil.

"I came home and at the top of my lungs I yelled for whatever it was in my house to leave my children alone. I said if it wanted to fight, it could fight with me."

That was not the right approach. Everything just got worse.

"I went to work the next day, but that night I had a dream about a child near a line fence. I didn't know the child, but it was at somebody's farm in the country. As I was driving my car down the road, I stopped to watch him playing around by a barn. I looked across the fields and it was lightning and thundering, so I thought I'd better watch this child because there was no house around.

"I looked up into the sky and saw a funnel cloud come down and start racing across the field. The wind was howling and whistling. I ran to grab the child and got him in the car, but he got back out. He wasn't going with me. About a mile up the road was our house. I couldn't worry about him anymore because he didn't want to come with me. So I drove quickly to my house to get my own children. But when I got there they were gone; there was nobody there. There were no curtains in the window. I kept looking back and the tornado was coming, but there was nothing left in our house."

Allen awakened from the nightmare in a cold sweat, nervous and frightened by the vivid details. What, if anything, did it mean? he asked himself. An innocent child? Howling tornadoes bearing down upon Allen and the little boy? A house deserted? Dreams could foretell the future, he once heard. Could this nightmare so real be connected in some way to the mysterious events plaguing his family?

Allen arrived home from work just before one o'clock a few days later on Thursday, January 7, 1988. The house was dark, save for a night-light in the kitchen. As he put his key in the front door lock, a faint whistling followed by a gust of wind came from the direction of the garage door. The breeze became stronger as he turned the door handle to go inside. He thought immediately of his earlier dream.

From somewhere a voice called out, "Come here!"

Allen jumped off the porch and ran to the side of the garage. He thought someone was hiding there trying to scare him. He didn't see anyone near the house. The street was empty at this hour. He strained his ears to catch the sound of running feet but nothing disturbed the cold, bleak night.

"I stood out there maybe five or ten minutes," Allen said. "My wife and children were in the house, but I had to find out where this voice came from. I just couldn't find anything, so I started back up the sidewalk to the porch when it started in again—a howling noise. I started to put my key into the lock when that voice said, 'Come here!' Only it was real loud this time."

Allen quickly looked back over his shoulder.

"I saw this glowing coming from the garage. It got brighter and brighter. I backed off the porch, but it seemed to draw me nearer to it. Flames were coming out of my garage and then the eyes appeared in the overhead door."

Shimmering green eyes punctuated with bloodred pupils seemed to float in the wide door. Eyes that matched the description of those seen by his mother several months before.

"I really don't know how I got the door open so fast, but once I did I ran inside and slammed the door," Allen recalls.

For several seconds, Allen leaned trembling against the doorframe, listening to see if the commotion had awakened anyone in the house. It hadn't. But then a horrifying thought occurred to him.

"I said, 'Oh, my God, my garage is on fire.' I opened the door and ran back out."

There was no wind, no phantom voice beckoning Allen to move closer. The garage was dark. He walked slowly down the sidewalk toward the attached garage. He really couldn't quite believe what he was seeing: nothing out of place, all things quiet and peaceful.

He peered through the garage window but could see only the dim outlines of bicycles, tools, and outdoor furniture stored along the walls. He turned and ran back into the house, bolting the door after him.

"My lunch pail was sitting on the floor by the front door. I picked it up and started walking toward the kitchen when it seemed that something, somebody, came up from behind and slammed against me. My lunch pail went flying across the room, hit the table leg and opened. My Thermos bottle rolled out across the floor."

Allen quickly picked up the spilled contents and ran into the bedroom, sensing all the while that "this thing" was right behind him.

Deborah had finally awakened at the racket coming from the living room.

"He came flying into the bedroom, threw his keys on the dresser, jumped in bed and just lay there," she said. Allen stared at the yawning doorway as if in anticipation that his tormentor would soon appear.

Suddenly Allen sat up straight. "Can you hear it? Can't you hear that howling?"

Deborah shook her head. She was truly frightened, for herself, for her family, and especially for her husband, who seemed on the verge of collapse. She grabbed him by the arm and demanded to know what it was he heard.

"It sounded like it was growling at me," Allen said later. "But I think it was more the sound of that wind, it was just howling, a whistling noise. It would be real high and then go very low. It was right there in the bedroom. I didn't see anything, but I could hear it, all the time."

Allen got out of bed and turned on every light in the house. The couple stayed awake until dawn. They were scared. None of the children awoke, even though Allen wandered through the house for hours, telling "it" to leave him and his family in peace.

"It seemed like this thing was zeroing in on one person," Allen said. "It would tune everybody else out and keep them sleeping." On this night, Allen was the target.

Remembering that traumatic night, Deborah said: "Allen is not a person that scares very easily, and I'm not either, but he was absolutely terrified."

Allen fell exhausted into bed at daybreak. Deborah stayed up to get Kenny ready for school.

None of the children knew what had happened to their father, although Kenny sensed the next day that his mother was very upset. She refused to tell him what was wrong.

Allen contemplated drastic measures. "I can remember one night shortly after this incident at the garage door when I came home thinking that I was right on the edge of losing control. I was going to put shells in my deer rifle and wait for this thing. Blow it to hell. But Deb stopped me. She said it's not something you can shoot, you can't kill it."

After Allen's "challenge," he realized the evil force was focusing even more intently—on him.

"I'd feel this thing as soon as I got to the door. It was like somebody was trying to shove me back out. I wouldn't even go through the [attached] garage anymore. And once I did get inside, I couldn't sleep, or if I did get to sleep, it would wake me right back up. I'd walk through the house and it seemed like it was always there, but I never could see anything. And that was really working on my mind. I'd be at work and think about it constantly, hour after hour. Everybody was at home and there I was . . . I'd get off work and be fine, but then I'd get down to that street and this thing was there to meet me every night, as soon as I pulled in the driveway. It would never show itself to me, but it was there."

Each night the couple latched all the windows, locked and barricaded the doors going into the basement and garage so they wouldn't rattle in the middle of the night, another regular occurrence that they tried to ignore.

Deborah said: "Allen was going to buy metal bars to put on the basement windows. I told him that whatever was happening, it was not coming from outside our house. Barring the windows wasn't going to keep it away. Locking the doors wasn't going to keep it away. By pushing the chair up against it, the door wasn't going to rattle, but something else was going to happen. It was going to continue to be there, no matter what."

The family had turned from keeping a single light on at night while they watched television to having every lamp in the house ablaze from dusk until dawn. With Allen at work each night, Deborah was dealing with three terrified children who followed her every movement around the house.

Deborah tried to persuade Allen they should move away right after Kenny's encounter with the strange woman. Allen resisted leaving. He thought that somehow they could figure out what was going on.

"I told Allen that he went to work and was safe," Deborah said. "He didn't have this happening, this constant pressure."

Allen's attitude toward the events always fluctuated from day to day. When there was a period without odd events, he would settle down and be encouraged that his family could somehow "survive" South Larabee Street. When the sun shone and the world seemed a bright and cheerful place, the Tallmanns breathed easier.

Neither did they ever question their own sanity. "We knew that we were all right," Deborah said. "Something was happening to us."

The Tallmanns just didn't know what it was. A human agent was still very much a possibility to them. They believed someone might have had a grudge against them and was using "black magic" or "witchcraft" or trickery to get even. Pastor Dobratz said it was a "possibility."

However, neither Allen nor Deborah could think of *anyone* who would want to harm them. Especially disturbing was the idea that someone would want to hurt or frighten their children. Though the couple were natives of the region, they were newcomers to Horicon itself and didn't know that many people. With three small children and a modest income they rarely socialized, except at family gatherings and a rare dinner out.

The family's final days in the house were filled with strange and intense events that became, in the end, the breaking point.

On Friday night, January 8, 1988, Jonathan, a sixteen-year-old relative of Allen's, spent the night at the house so the two could get up early the following morning to go ice fishing. At about midnight, the teenager walked into the kitchen to look for a snack. The refrigerator door was standing open. That may not seem extraordinary until one realizes that the floor-levelers at the back of the refrigerator were broken, so the unit actually leans *backward*. Thus the door always swings shut when it is opened. Or it *did*, anyway.

That wasn't the only strange incident during the teen's visit. Late Saturday afternoon, January 9, after a morning of ice fishing, Jonathan loaded his suitcase in the Tallmanns' car parked in the driveway so Allen could drive him home. As the boy headed back into the house, he noticed a floating red light through the garage door window. It seemed to hover near the ceiling of the garage. When he got back inside he asked Allen if he kept a light on in the garage. Puzzled,

Allen walked out to the garage to have a look around, but found nothing to account for the light.

By the end of this day, odd lights would be the least of the Tallmann's troubles.

After Allen returned from taking the boy home that evening, Deborah, as usual, asked him for help in putting the girls to bed. She was very upset about what had happened to Allen's young relative.

Deborah said: "I wouldn't go back there by myself to put them in bed. So Allen and I both went. I was praying to let whatever was happening be gone. The girls were almost sleeping. Kenny was in the living room and he kept calling, 'Are you coming out?' So I went out there to do some housework and Allen stayed in the room."

The next few minutes were a turning point for the family, according to Allen: "On normal nights when we'd put the girls to bed they would put up a fuss for an hour or so. They would stay awake, or they'd raise their heads up. They'd look to see if we were still there. They didn't want to go to sleep until they got to the point where they just couldn't hold their eyes open anymore.

"Well, for some reason that night the girls were relaxed and they went right to sleep. I was lying on the floor about ready to get up when I heard this high-pitched sound just like I heard the night in the garage . . . kind of like a vacuum cleaner. I sat right up and looked but it died back down. I lay back down and it came back. I thought it was something in the furnace pipe."

What Allen heard had nothing to do with furnace pipes or anything else of a mechanical nature. For the first time Allen saw the face of the evil on Larabee Street.

Rising from the carpeted floor came a fog. At first less than a foot in height, the misty substance grew until it reached nearly to the ceiling.

Allen shrank against the wall as the vapor took on form, a human figure shimmering in the center of the room. A head took shape, with two penetrating red eyes and sickly green pupils fixed intently on Allen.

A translucent arm rose from the body and pointed as the wraith moved inexorably toward him.

A voice as if from the grave issued from the thing:

"You're dead!"

As it seemed about to envelop him, the figure dissipated in a burst of light.

Allen staggered out of the bedroom. His wife thought he was having a heart attack. He looked stunned, almost paralytic in his movements.

"He was completely white and his lips were purple," Deborah said of her husband. "He stumbled into the wall, ran into the birdcage and he just looked at me, tears coming down his face. He wouldn't tell me what happened. He just kept saying, 'Leave me alone, leave me alone!' "

Deborah quickly telephoned Pastor Dobratz and begged him to come over. She choked back tears as she described Allen's behavior. Something must have happened to Allen in the bedroom, she told her pastor, but he wouldn't tell her.

Reverend Dobratz said he would be right over.

Deborah returned to her husband, who by now had collapsed in a chair at the kitchen table, his head buried in his hands. Again she asked him what was wrong. He told her the incredible story.

Within a few minutes their pastor had arrived. The household was in chaos. The children had been awakened by their father's cries and were sobbing. Neither of the girls had awakened during their father's actual ordeal in their bedroom.

Pastor Dobratz urged the couple to leave the house immediately and not to return until after church the next day, Sunday, January 10. They needed no more persuasion. Suitcases were quickly packed and the family left for a relative's home. Deborah glanced at the garage as their car pulled out of the driveway. At the top of the garage door glowed a small, intense flame. She blinked and looked back. The image was gone. She still isn't sure whether what she saw was in any way real, or merely a by-product of that chaotic night.

The Tallmanns awoke Sunday morning planning to attend church services with Allen's family. However, a half-hour before church Allen discovered he couldn't start the car, even after repeated attempts.

"We called the church and told Pastor Dobratz. He said that didn't surprise him," Allen said.

The pastor suggested the couple wait until after the church service started at ten-thirty and then try their car again. At ten-forty-five Allen climbed in the car and turned the key. The engine roared to life. The Tallmanns believe the entity pursuing them simply did not want them to go to church.

The family tried to outwit their unknown adversary.

"We thought that if whatever it was didn't want us to go to church and have communion, we would have the pastor come to our house on Sunday night and give us communion . . . and bless our house."

Pastor Dobratz came Sunday night, administered communion, and led the family in prayers. He also advised them to play religious music all night and handed them a stack of cassette tapes. They followed his advice and, according to Allen, "it was one of the most peaceful nights we had since we moved into the house. The children didn't wake up. I got up a couple of times to check on them and never once did I feel anything was there. It seemed like whatever was there just could not tolerate that church music and just didn't want to come around."

Monday, January 11, dawned bright and very cold. It almost seemed that the prayers and recorded church hymns had worked in ridding the house of its evil presence.

Kenny went off to school, Deborah puttered around the house, and Allen took care of some chores. Jonathan had volunteered to stay with Deborah and the children until Allen got home from his late shift. He came over after high school that afternoon. The night had passed quietly, but Deborah wasn't ready to face the darkness by herself.

This would be the last day the Tallmanns spent on South Larabee Street.

Allen left for work at two o'clock. Twilight cast the street in deep shadows by four-thirty. The sun set at a few minutes before five o'clock in the afternoon.

At six o'clock, Allen called home from work. He asked if the house was quiet. It was. He made Deborah promise to leave the church music playing. She agreed.

Jonathan had taken the children to play in the basement rumpus room. They were having a good time, Deborah told her husband over the phone. For once Allen thought his children were at ease. He knew Jonathan liked the kids and they in turn enjoyed having a "big brother" to play with.

An hour and a half later, at about seven-thirty, Allen called back. Deborah told him the children had just come upstairs to get ready for bedtime. Jonathan promised them he would read and stay in the room until they fell asleep, just like their daddy did.

Everything was calm—almost too calm, Deborah remembered later. She assured her husband in that seven-thirty call that there had been no unusual events. Even Kenny seemed to have settled down.

Allen hung up promising that he would telephone again an hour later. He never got the chance. Within forty-five minutes Deborah, Allen's nephew, and the three children were in the car sitting outside Allen's workplace.

Deborah Tallmann relives those final hours:

"I had a habit of getting the kids ready for bed about eight o'clock. But with what happened to Allen Saturday night, I didn't want to go to the room with the kids. [Jonathan] went back there. I was going to do some housework. God, that had to be the most horrible night of my life! I was doing the dishes and all of a sudden he started screaming, 'Debbie, Debbie, come quick, please come back here!'"

Deborah couldn't move. The teenager was screaming at the top of his lungs from the bedroom, and the little girls were crying. That much Deborah knew, but she just couldn't face whatever had happened in that bedroom a few yards away.

"I just stood there. I didn't know what to do, but I ran to the phone to try to call the pastor and he wasn't there. I could hear him crying out 'Debbie, come here quick, oh my God! Oh my God!' I didn't know what was going on."

Kenny had run into the living room. Deborah told him to go back and see what was wrong.

"I can't, I can't," Kenny cried back. Deborah screamed at him to go to the bedroom and come back and tell her what he saw.

"Mom, it's there. I can see it!" Kenny said breathlessly as he ran back into the living room.

Maryann quickly followed Kenny out of the bedroom. "It's Baby Jesus, and he loves you! Don't be afraid!" the child assured her mother, between sobs. Deborah had tried to tell the children that any strange figure appearing in their room was Jesus, hoping the statement would calm them.

This time it didn't work.

"I was running around the house saying, 'No, that's not Baby Jesus!' Finally Jonathan came out of the room. I asked him what happened and he said it was in there. I asked him where Sarah was and he said she was still in the bedroom. I told him to get Sarah, that's it, we're leaving. We were not staying there anymore. I got our coats. The kids were just hysterical. I said we were going to Daddy's work. I turned off all the lights except for the one in Kenny's room. I wouldn't go back there. And one in the living room. I got them [all] in the car. And when I pulled out of the driveway and as I went past the house Kenny said 'Mom! Mom! It's looking out of the window at us!'"

Deborah dared not turn her head. She took her son's word that something stared after them as they sped down South Larabee Street that frigid January night.

The little band of refugees arrived at the factory where Allen worked a few minutes later. Jonathan and the children were crying. They begged Deborah not to leave them alone in the car, but she told them to lock the doors while she went inside to find Allen.

"He came around the corner and I looked at him and said I wasn't going to take it anymore. I didn't care what happened, we were not going back there. I told him he had to come out to the car to talk to the kids," Deborah said. His nephew was still too upset to describe what had taken place in the bedroom.

Deborah called Pastor Dobratz, and he told them to meet him at the church. Allen took his nephew in the car he had at work, and Deborah followed with the children in their other car. As he drove to the church, Allen found out what had taken place:

Maryann and Sarah had been tucked in bed. A night-light cast a faint glow about the room. Jonathan was stretched out on the floor gazing at the ceiling, a glass of lemonade at his elbow. In the kitchen he could hear Deborah washing dishes, while soft church hymns coming from a cassette player drifted down the short hallway from the living room.

Jonathan yawned and turned over onto his stomach, his face toward the partially open bedroom door. He, too, was getting sleepy, listening to the little girls' even breathing and restful music.

Suddenly Sarah jumped up in bed.

"Hi there!" she called out.

Jonathan thought that he must have fallen asleep and that Deborah had slipped into the room. He rolled over onto his back and looked across the room. It wasn't Deborah he saw.

Hovering near Sarah's bed was a human figure, too indistinct for Jonathan to determine its sex, but nearly identical to the one Allen Tallmann had witnessed a few days before.

It moved toward Jonathan and, as it did, spoke to him: "Now, you're involved!" But as it moved forward it melted away and was gone before it reached him.

Jonathan started crying and calling out for Deborah. Both girls were now wide awake. At the same time, Jonathan felt as if he were frozen to the floor, unable to move out of the path of the hideous entity. Kenny had been awakened. He caught a brief glimpse of the figure after Deborah asked him to go back into the bedroom.

Jonathan was able to pry himself from the floor and stumble into the living room, upsetting his glass of lemonade in the process. Maryann got out of bed to follow after him, leaving little Sarah alone and frightened. Within minutes, Jonathan had gone back for her and, with Deborah and the other children, fled the house.

After Allen heard the entire story, he realized that this had been their last night on Larabee Street. After the family conferred with Pastor Dobratz at the church, they decided to go to Allen's mother's home. But not before Allen insisted on driving by the house.

Deborah refused to accompany him, still distraught and feeling somewhat guilty over her inability to cope with the trauma of the last few hours.

"I felt helpless. There my kids are screaming. It could have been hurting the kids, but I didn't have any idea. I figured Kenny had seen it before so he at least had some idea what it looked like. But you can't go back there [to the bedroom] and shoot it, you can't hit it over the head. Later I felt real bad but someone [later] said I did the right thing because if I had seen it and something happened to me, what would happen to the kids, you know.

"After we left the church we got to the cars and Allen said he had to go down past the house. I said he was crazy. He said that everything we own was in that house and if it was on fire or something, he had to know. Allen had his car and I had my car and he had Jonathan with him. I wasn't going past it, so I waited at the end of the block.

"He went down the block toward the house and I sat at the end of the street in my car with the kids. I watched him go by the house. He turned around and came back down to where I was parked.

"He said you're not going to believe this, but every single light was on in that house, every light in the basement, the garage light, all the yard lights were on, bathroom lights, the bedroom lights, the kids' room, everything. He said the house was lit up like a Christmas tree. I didn't leave those lights on."

The family spent the night with Allen's mother. Once there, they again called Pastor Dobratz to tell him every light in their house seemed to be on. Allen wanted to go back and turn them off.

"Pastor Dobratz said the house was lit up, but it's not costing you a dime, there is no energy there," Allen said. "It's this thing that's giving the house energy to show that there's lights on in the house. No one else can see it from outside. He said if I went back in that house I'd never come back."

Allen decided to wait until daylight to return to Larabee Street.

Early the next morning, Tuesday, January 12, Deborah called the pastor to tell him they had to return to the house to get some belongings. It was their intention to leave, permanently, and stay with relatives until they could figure out what to do. And get their lives back in order.

Pastor Dobratz told them to be prepared for anything when they returned to their home. What they did find surprised them, but not in any way they expected.

"We walked in and every light in the house was turned off except for the living room light, which I had left on. But the bedroom light that I left on in Kenny's room was switched off," Deborah said.

Allen continues: "I checked every window in the house. I looked down in the basement. To me this whole thing could not be possible, even though I'd seen this thing. It was still mind-boggling. This can't be happening to us, you know, it can't be true. Things can't make my house light up, like the pastor said, and yet have no energy going through the light bulbs."

Allen couldn't find any problem that would account for the glowing lights he saw in and around their house the night before. All the lights seemed to work fine when they were switched on.

The Tallmanns took clothes, small pieces of furniture, some children's toys, and Allen also gathered up his valuable gun collection. Other than that, they left their other possessions for another day. Neither one sensed anything odd or unusual in the house that morning, but that didn't surprise them. "It seemed during the day it was like any other house," Deborah emphasized. A few days later, Allen, with the help of several church members, packed the rest of the family's belongings. They timed their work so the job would be completed before sundown.

For several days, the Tallmanns wrestled with the question of where they would live and what was to be done with their house. His mother was willing to shelter them until they could find other accommodations.

But on Thursday night, January 21, the problems in the house on South Larabee Street became general knowledge, and the Tallmanns subjects of intense public and media scrutiny. On that night, Horicon Police Chief Douglas D. Glamann called Allen at work. He had heard rumors of a "ghost house" in Horicon, he told Allen, one that belonged to the Tallmanns. Was that true? he wanted to know. After a long pause, Allen admitted that he and his family had fled their house a week before, believing it was haunted.

Chief Glamann suggested that he meet with the family to determine if there was anything his department could do to help. He said there were already reports of cars driving by the house, and curious spectators wandering around the yard. There had even been some inquiries from the media, he said.

"Never did we realize that it would go to this length," Deborah said. "It just floored us completely. The police chief contacting us, people going past our house. At first we couldn't believe it. We had enough problems to deal with and then we had this other stuff going on too. But nobody knew how to help us. I mean, we didn't know where we were going, but we knew we couldn't go back [to Larabee Street]."

That was just the beginning of the intense skepticism voiced by Horicon residents toward the events, and the sensational media interest in the Tallmanns' experiences.

While the Tallmanns stayed with relatives, the Horicon rumor mills were passing along what allegedly had happened in the house: a driverless snowblower clearing the sidewalks and driveway, a ceiling that dripped blood, coffee cups floating through the air, and a fiery hole to Hell that opened in the house.

None of those events ever occurred, but their repetition, along with skimpy details of what had actually taken place, was enough to cause lines of cars to crowd South Larabee Street. The police eventually had to cordon off the street.

Doug Glamann is a handsome, dark-haired officer of the law, with a penetrating gaze and no-nonsense manner about him. He was just thirty-two, already a ten-year veteran of the police force, when he first met with the Tallmanns and helped them get through their ordeal.

According to Deborah Tallmann, "He was a lifesaver. He is the one that kept us floating through all this. Without him we would have sunk."

Chief Glamann, a Horicon native who had left a factory job because it was "too routine" to become a policeman, first heard about the Tallmanns on January 21.

Chief Glamann said: "One of my night-shift officers came in and asked me if I had heard that we have a haunted house in Horicon. I just laughed and carried on with what I was doing. But I bumped into him five minutes later and he said he was serious. It's all over town, he told me. That was early in the morning, and all throughout the day wherever I went people were asking me about this. I didn't even know where the house was located. I started hearing rumors there was a house with blood running out of the walls and . . . stuff."

Late that afternoon, the police department received an anonymous telephone call from someone in the Tallmanns' neighborhood. The caller wanted to know if the police knew about anything "going on" nearby. Chief Glamann eventually discovered that the house being discussed was owned by Allen and Deborah Tallmann. One neighbor admitted to the chief that the family had left the house, but refused to discuss the situation any further.

With some basic police work, Chief Glamann found that Allen was scheduled to work that night.

"I called him at work," the police chief said, "and told him who I was and that I had heard some stories and that I'd like to hear it from the fellow who should know best. His initial response was that he didn't want to talk about it. I asked him why and he said I'd probably lock him up, thinking he was crazy. I said, 'Listen, in this business I hear a lot of bizarre stories.' I said, 'Why don't you just tell me the story and we'll see what we can do for you.' "

After five or ten minutes of coaxing, Allen told Glamann the general outline of the family's experiences. The veteran officer listened and then suggested that Allen and his wife come down to police headquarters the following morning. After some hesitation, Allen agreed. Chief Glamann wanted the face-to-face meeting so he could "look him [Allen] in the eye and see if this [was] all on the up-and-up or not."

The couple arrived at police headquarters in the basement below the town library at about nine o'clock the next morning. Their behavior was the first indication for the chief that something was seriously wrong.

"Debbie was kind of high-strung and had a nervous laugh. Al hardly had any eye contact with me. He was always staring at his shoes. It seemed his emotions and his will to survive were just drawn right out of him."

Glamann said Allen looked to be near exhaustion.

"They informed me then that they were working with their pastor" on trying to understand the trauma they had gone through, Glamann said. "They were very strong that they wanted to keep it quiet. I said I can do it. If you tell me you don't want something out, we'll do that for you."

Glamann wasn't able to keep his promise. Throughout that Friday and into the weekend, word spread quickly around town about the "ghost house" on South Larabee Street. The crowd at a local high school basketball game Friday night was abuzz with rumors of what had transpired. Scores of cars drove down Larabee Street, dozens of people tried the doors and windows of the Tallmanns' house, all hoping to get a peek at what was inside.

Police had to erect barricades at either end of the street and made several arrests for disorderly conduct or public drunkenness. One man showed up with a Bible in hand, promising that he would exorcise the ghosts by shouting "Devil be gone!" He was arrested.

On Sunday night, January 24, WMTV-TV in Madison, Wisconsin, aired the first television report about the haunting. But as in the other television, radio, and newspaper stories for the first several days, the Tallmanns were not identified by name, nor did they personally speak with any reporter. They were adamant about not wanting publicity. The media seemed satisfied to report rumors of blood-spewing walls and runaway snow throwers without trying to verify any of the happenings.

Glamann tried to oblige requests for all the media interviews he could fit into his schedule. When the number of reporters grew too large, he held a press conference to try to squelch some of the more outrageous speculation.

"I stood up and said there's no blood coming out of the walls and there's no snowblower running around by itself; I'm not telling you the people's names, I'm not giving out the address, and I'm not telling you what we discussed [with the family]," Glamann recalled.

While he was trying to handle dozens of media inquiries, Glamann also wanted to do something to help the Tallmanns.

"We comforted the family as much as we could. We went into the home with the pastor from their church one evening at about nine o'clock," Glamann said of his personal inspection of the Tallmann home on Monday, January 25. Two police officers accompanied Pastor Dobratz. The minister "wanted to do something in there to see if he could get something stirred up, and they went along to be witnesses. I told them to look for any kind of projection devices, or any kind of recorder. They went through the whole house. Both [of the officers] were wearing voice-activated tape recorders through the whole ordeal and nothing unusual came on the tape."

Glamann's officers examined drapery rods to see if the dust that often accumulates there had been disturbed, thus indicating that some sort of "instrument" could have been hidden there to produce the ghostly images. The men didn't see anything unusual. The only unsettling incident occurred when the telephone rang several times, but on each occasion the line seemed dead. One officer disabled the receiver—or assumed he had—but the phone rang anyway, again with no one on the line.

Chief Glamann and Horicon's mayor, who wanted to see the inside of the house for himself, arrived an hour or two after the officers and Pastor Dobratz examined the house.

"I was in the house maybe half an hour," Glamann said. "A very warm, cozy little house. A nice house. I was really impressed. The furniture they had was nice, the decoration of the house just made you feel like home. I had some apprehension going in there. You're wondering if something is going to pop out of the wall."

What troubled Glamann the most was not finding any logical explanation for the events, of either natural or supernatural origin.

"That was the hard part. First of all, this is the type of complaint most police departments I found out later don't [investigate]. Secondly, we're trained to look for the physical things in life, that's part of our job. There's a reason for everything and when you run into something like this it was very frustrating for us. We're seeing their [the Tallmanns'] depression and their anxiety, yet we can't help them."

From the chief's first interview with Allen and Deborah, he fully believed that the family had gone through a wrenching, emotionally draining experience. He wasn't willing, however, to accept the notion of a haunting. But neither was he prone to dismiss their incredible story outright.

"I spent a good deal of time with them and the kids," Glamann said. "The way they looked, they went through some kind of ordeal. I can't tell you exactly what, [but] the way they looked, I can believe that they'd either been through it or something strange happened to them."

James B. Nelson of *The Milwaukee Sentinel* was the first reporter to personally interview the Tallmanns. He uncovered their names and where they were staying by using public records at the city clerk's office and at the Dodge County courthouse.

Nelson asked Chief Glamann to intercede with the family on his behalf. The reporter said he would honor the family's wishes not to be identified, at least as long as other media outlets did the same. Glamann believed a published interview with the family would put some of the more grisly rumors to rest.

Allen and Deborah Tallmann agreed and met with Nelson on Tuesday evening, January 26, to tell their story. On Wednesday morning, the first of Nelson's several articles about the Tallmanns appeared in the *Sentinel*.

While Nelson spoke with the parents, Chief Glamann talked with young Kenny Tallmann, hoping he could determine some reason that the family had "made up" the entire yarn. He didn't succeed.

"In talking with him [Kenny] . . . we could go through it and I could wait a week and run into him again and we'd go through it again, and it [Kenny's story] was identical. I was trying to trip him up because the pressure was on me to find out what was going on here. My first instinct was to look for something with the people."

Glamann also looked into Allen and Deborah's backgrounds.

"I can honestly tell you we didn't even know they were living here, so that indicates there were no problems. We never had a complaint against any one of their family members while they were here. They were just going about their business . . . just living their lives. I think Debbie was the one that summed it all up. When they got that house, that was their dream house. They spent all their time working on it, making it the way they liked it. They had planned on staying there for a very long time. It didn't work out that way."

The police chief also considered the Tallmanns' earlier notion that someone with a personal vendetta against the Tallmanns might have been to blame. A person with enough sophistication to make an entire family believe their house was possessed.

"That thought occurred to me. [Allen's] a foreman and maybe he got someone mad out there. I talked to his boss in a closed-door session for a good hour and a half. He said Allen had a super attitude, a very likable guy. Everybody liked him there, he's never been a problem with anybody." Glamann eventually dismissed the idea that the events had been the work of a prankster.

Allen's employer feared losing him, Glamann found out, especially after Allen suggested they might move to another state to avoid the unwanted publicity and initial community scorn. When the family decided to remain in the area, but not in Horicon, Allen returned to work and found his employer and co-workers very supportive.

Glamann also discovered that Allen Tallmann had passed a federal security screening because some of his work involved manufacturing instrumentation for the armed forces. The chief said the government usually does a very thorough job in security investigations and should have turned up any personal problems that might have accounted for the family's plight.

That section of Horicon upon which the Tallmann house was built also came under scrutiny. Glamann noted that Horicon had been a major Indian settlement centuries ago. However, a check with the local historical society turned up nothing unusual ever having been unearthed by archaeologists on the land that became South Larabee Street.

Ironically, Chief Glamann's father, Don Glamann, was the city's chief of public works in 1988. He told reporters that in his forty years of work in the city, he had never heard of Indian mounds or archaeological digs near the Tallmann home. Old St. Malachy's Catholic Cemetery, two blocks away from Tallmanns', is the nearest cemetery.

Several skulls, believed to have been Winnebago Indians, have been unearthed over the years at various construction sites in Horicon and now repose at the historical society. However, none apparently came from the Larabee Street vicinity.

Before houses were built on Larabee Street, Glamann said, the area was on the fringe of a marsh and devoid of structures. It was a popular hangout for teenagers, the chief said, noting that during summer nights the department usually received several phone calls about noisy parties there.

Attitudes of townspeople initially skeptical toward the idea of a "haunted house" in Horicon gradually changed in the days and weeks following the first media reports. At first, the entire episode had been the target of lighthearted banter on Milwaukee and Madison radio and television stations. James Nelson had been the only reporter to interview the Tallmanns, who were still being shielded by Chief Glamann.

The chief was harsh in his criticism of the media treatment of the story. "I made a comment something like when a person is on the ground and writhing in pain, are you [the reporters] the type to come up and give them another kick in the belly. . . ."

Reporter Nelson's accurate, straightforward, and sympathetic story in the January 27 *Milwaukee Sentinel*, the first to include comments from Allen and Deborah Tallmann, together with Chief Glamann's tough statement, seemed to turn community sentiment toward trying to understand the turmoil the family was going through. Nelson published several more stories over the following weeks, all based on interviews with the Tallmanns.

By the time media interest waned in late February, the Horicon story had been featured on radio and television talk shows around the world (Glamann was interviewed by both British and Australian radio networks) and written about in newspapers and magazines across the country. NBC Television re-created the haunting, with the family's permission, during a segment on the popular series "Unsolved Mysteries" in October 1988.

When Chief Glamann asked reporters why the intense interest in this story from tiny Horicon, Wisconsin, the answer was always the same: If what happened to the family was serious enough to drive them out of their home in the middle of winter, then it was a story warranting coverage.

Curiously, the local newspaper, the *Horicon Reporter*, didn't write about the events until well after other media had the story. And then its stories were mostly about the "mass hysteria" of the media. The co-owner of the newspaper told a magazine reporter that "it was a nonstory. There was no story here; it was a case of herd journalism. Unless something is significant news, we're not going to run a story about it."

Neither did the state's largest newspaper, *The Milwaukee Journal*, find the Tallmanns a legitimate subject for news coverage. That newspaper's science reporter, Paul Hayes, was quoted in a professional journalism magazine: " . . . ghosts are a little more preposterous than UFOs—at least there's a percentage of a chance that other forms of life exist out there in the universe . . . It's far easier to explain this as the imperfectibility of the human brain."

Meanwhile, the editor of the nearby *Beaver Dam Daily Citizen* said his newspaper initially treated the story as a joke, but quickly changed its focus to examine the effects on the family. Jeff Hovind thought the story certainly merited coverage: "It's probably the most newsworthy thing to come out of Horicon in as long as I've been here . . . For anyone to say it's a nonstory, when it's the big event in town—that's mind-boggling."

The *Sentinel*'s James Nelson wasn't particularly concerned with whether or not the Tallmanns had seen apparitions, or lived in a "ghost house." He noted that the family had avoided all contact with the media out of fear that they would be exploited, first living with relatives, then moving into a motel until they found temporary refuge in a house provided by a parishioner from their church.

"They knew I wasn't going to turn around and make fun of them. I mean, it's not our job to make fun of them," Nelson said. His articles concentrated on the Tallmanns' personal story, rather than an investigation of paranormal events. "I don't care whether they saw a ghost or not," Nelson emphasized.

A trio of psychic investigators was called in to examine the house by Chief Glamann after his own investigation failed to find a physical cause for the incidents the Tallmanns reported. Parapsychologist Carl Schuldt, psychologist Don Mueller, and author Walter Uphoff agreed that there was no evidence of trickery and that the appearances of supernatural beings claimed by the Tallmanns were probably genuine.

Uphoff, a retired professor and author of two books on the paranormal, told a reporter: "They were not lying. They are rational, sane people that [sic] would like to get rid of a problem. There is at work there a force that needs to be dealt with and asked to be on its way. If that does not happen, the family will continue to have problems. They did not leave because they were imagining things."

*   *   *

Police Chief Glamann concluded his investigation still unsure about what really happened on South Larabee Street. He was sympathetic to the family's plight, perhaps because he had seen several bizarre things during his police career. When he worked nights, Glamann said he saw mysterious lights in the sky on several occasions. Were they UFOs? He never officially reported them for fear other officers or community residents would think he was "crazy," even though he was with another policeman at the time who also saw the darting sky lights.

And what is Glamann's final analysis of the Tallmann haunting?

"I wish I knew, I wish I had someone come in and say this is exactly what we were up against here . . . I've learned a lot about all these things, parapsychology and things I never knew before. I believe what they told me they honestly believe to be true. Why would they leave, in the middle of the night, and why would they put themselves through all that . . . trouble and just keep running around? There probably are things out there that we cannot actually get a handle on right now, or describe in terms that make everybody happy, with a rational determination of it all."

A few months later, Glamann was commended by the International Association of Chiefs of Police for his compassionate and professional handling of "a difficult situation."

In early February 1988, Allen and Deborah Tallmann signed over the title on their "dream home" to the FmHA, which then had the home appraised and subsequently resold. The arrangement was unusual because the FmHA usually asks its borrowers to "test the market" before it assumes title to houses.

State FmHA rural housing director George Berger allowed the procedure because "these folks have been under a lot of stress."

Allen Tallmann said the family lost about three thousand dollars when the FmHA acquired the house for resale.

The family that bought the house said nothing unusual had taken place in the home.

After living for several months in the old house provided by friends from church, Allen and Deborah bought a small home in a another Wisconsin city—financed with a new FmHA loan. Their lives returned to normalcy, but the important question lingered: Why did all this happen to them?

"If there would be some way that we could know why it happened," Deborah said. "I've always said that everything in life happens for a purpose, and I keep feeling there must have been some purpose behind this. If I could figure out what the reason was . . . or if somebody could come to us and say this was it, we would have an answer. There is no answer, and that's the hard part. Everybody can speculate on what they think it was, but nobody can come right out and say *this* is it. . . ."

Allen and Deborah Tallmann, Kenny, Maryann, and Sarah now lead relatively quiet lives, although there are occasional reminders of their life in Horicon.

Deborah occasionally meets people who ask about their experiences. A few express outright disbelief, while others are sympathetic or simply curious. "The farther away it gets [in time], the better it is," Deborah said. She said she doesn't care if people don't believe what happened to them. She knows that some sort of supernatural event drove them away from Horicon, and if people have a hard time understanding that, well . . . so be it.

Allen "has a hard time with it," Deborah said. He still doesn't understand *what* happened to them or *why*, she said. Sometimes a loud noise will frighten him and make him realize he still hasn't let go, so he can get on with his life.

Kenny is a student who is occasionally reminded of his home in Horicon. Once a friend asked him if he'd ever been in a haunted house, referring to a carnival attraction at the upcoming Wisconsin State Fair. Kenny didn't understand and said, "Yes, but I don't want to go there again."

He usually sleeps with blankets over his head, Deborah said, even on hot summer days. He will not take a bath if he is the only person in the house.

Maryann sometimes remembers her mother's attempt to persuade her that any mysterious figures in her room were not to be feared. The child asks: "Why doesn't Jesus visit me anymore?"

Little things have changed with the family. Allen and Deborah almost always take the children with them. "I never feel comfortable leaving them with a baby-sitter. Maybe my sister will look after them occasionally, but that's it," Deborah said.

The family tries to avoid reliving the events, or talking about it unless someone brings it up. Even then Deborah is careful about what she says. She has refused numerous interviews, including a proffered appearance on the popular *Oprah Winfrey Show*.

"It's always there," Deborah said. "When it's dark outside is when it's the hardest. I don't know what it was, I guess we were in the wrong place at the wrong time. But I just can't believe that whatever was there came when we came and left when we left. Maybe the house was out to get us, or we were caught between some sort of opposing forces."

Deborah is content with their lives today.

"This [new house] is our real dream home. Our life has changed for the better, our kids are comfortable, and the house is perfect. This is our place in life."

NOTE: Some names in this story were changed at the request of the participants.

The Tower Ghost

The two Swedish stonemasons neither spoke nor understood English. But they understood their ancient craft well, and, as immigrants, were glad to have found well-paying work. St. Mark's Episcopal Church in Cheyenne would be the most beautiful structure they had ever built, with a magnificent round tower and steeple.

The original church, built in 1868, was the first in Wyoming. But now, in 1886, the congregation wanted a more imposing house of worship, a replica of the British church celebrated in Thomas Gray's poem "Elegy Written in a Country Churchyard."

The Swedes worked well together. From dawn to dusk one operated the horse-drawn hoist on the ground, lifting the precut stones to the other man, who cemented each stone in place. They had already sunk a foundation wall fifteen feet deep to support the massive weight of the bell tower. The walls of the tower would be four feet thick at the base, tapering gradually as the tower grew in height. The work was slow and painstaking, and the rector, Dr. George C. Rafter, asked his parishioners not to distract the men by watching them at work.

One day Dr. Rafter stopped by to see if his men needed anything, possibly more blocks or cement for that day. Only one man was on duty and he seemed highly agitated. Without looking up at the rector, he muttered that his partner had taken sick and been unable to report to work.

Dr. Rafter went on about his errands, only to learn the next day that neither workman had appeared. Their landlady said that one of the masons rushed into the house, gathered up the few belongings of both men and fled. Inquiries were made all over the city, but the Swedes had vanished.

Because American stonemasons lacked the skills at that time to complete the tower, workmen roofed over the uncompleted tower, thus making a study for Dr. Rafter.

In time Dr. Rafter moved on to another church, and his successor was delighted to inherit the quiet, private study. Except that it wasn't quiet. The new rector began hearing hammering sounds in the walls and muffled voices from the ceiling. The attic was checked, but no person or animal was ever found. In

1904, the uneasy clergyman resigned, and the study was permanently sealed off. Sometime later the room was opened up and a new pipe organ installed there.

The congregation, however, was displeased with the uncompleted church, and in 1927 workmen were summoned to finish the bell tower. Though plans for a soaring steeple were abandoned, the round tower rose another sixty feet. Eleven carillons, weighing twenty tons, were installed. But the work did not proceed smoothly. There were arguments and bitter feelings. Some men said the tower was haunted. They heard faint hammering beating against newly laid walls; others heard voices whose words they couldn't distinguish, and still others, hearing nothing unusual, called their fellow workers "crazy." Several times work ceased as angry workmen walked off the job.

When the foreman was no longer able to keep construction going, he appealed to Father Charles Bennett, rector of St. Mark's at that time. Father Bennett was a quiet, thoughtful man who never made a hasty decision.

He didn't believe in ghosts, but he believed in the sincerity of the foremen.

"You think the ghost is a friendly one?" he asked.

The foreman nodded. "The older men tell many strange tales, and sometimes I see the fear in their eyes." He paused. "You see, sir, they believe that the ghost would be happy having its own private room."

Father Bennett was incredulous, but tried not to show it. After a long moment, he said, "All right. Tell your men to proceed."

The private room then built in the tower would have suited the most discerning ghost. Light streaming through the Gothic windows warmed an inlaid wooden floor. A chandelier, hung from the hand-patted plaster ceiling, was often seen burning at night. The room could be reached by a spiral stairway accessible only from a private entrance in the basement. It led to no other room.

Of course after this the haunted tower was no longer a secret. Parishioners and townspeople alike knew the room had been built for a ghost. Churchgoers claimed to hear voices, and although the words were usually jumbled, one sentence came through clearly: "There's a body in the wall." Some members were so frightened that they transferred their memberships to other churches.

The mystery was finally solved in 1966 when the Reverend Eugene Todd, then rector of St. Mark's, was called to a nursing home in Denver where a very old man he had never met wanted to talk to him. The rector was extremely busy with church affairs, but the urgency of the message impelled him to go.

The old man was the surviving Swedish stonemason. He told an incredible story. When he was young, he said, he had worked with a fellow mason on the bell tower for St. Mark's church. The Swede said that one day his partner fell from the tower and was killed instantly when he struck the basement floor. Both men were illegal immigrants and the survivor, fearing deportation or possibly charges of murder, stuffed his partner's body in an unfinished section of the wall, bending it to conform to its curvature. He slathered a layer of cement over the corpse before setting the stones in place over the remains.

The old man sighed and leaned back against his pillows. "I left Cheyenne right off, and went to South America." But now his dying time had come, he said, and he wanted to go back to the United States "to set the record straight." He did not know why or how he had been taken to the Denver nursing home.

Much later, Brad Hamilton, a reporter for the *Wyoming State Tribune*, interviewed Father Todd. Did the minister believe in ghosts?

"No, I do not. But this one I do," he said.

"Why?" Hamilton asked.

"You just come down any evening, let me lock you in the bell tower, then tell me what you think the next morning."

The reporter declined the offer.

In 1979 the bell tower was opened for public tours, an expectedly popular Halloween event. Throngs of residents climbed the eighty-five-foot spiral stairway to the ghost's quarters, laughing and joking about the ghost "snatching" them. Only the hardiest continued their journey up another flight of stairs that led to the carillon room, from which the ghost was said to speak.

Several years later, a Cheyenne radio station invited Ms. Lou Wright, a popular Denver psychic, to spend Halloween night broadcasting from the tower. A deejay would accompany her. Lou figured the program was planned to boost the station's ratings, but no matter. It sounded like fun, and since her expenses would be paid, she agreed to do it. She could not have known the horror that awaited her.

Lou and the deejay met Father Todd at the church, and as the three ascended the stairway to the tower, Lou was overcome with dread. When she mentioned it to the rector he handed her an article about the stonemason buried in the wall. Lou had known nothing of the history of the church.

Soon she felt the presence of a second spirit, this one not nearly so frightening. Who was he? An elderly, white-haired man who walked with a cane, she said. Father Todd told writer Debra M. Munn that the psychic had described the former rector, George Rafter, "exactly as he was. That surprised me, since she had no way of knowing about him."

Lou and her companion settled into the tower room and Father Todd left, carefully locking all the church doors behind him—to prevent any corporeal entity from entering the building.

The deejay set up his equipment, turned on the transmitter apparatus and Lou, looking out a window, began to describe what she "saw": little balls of white light flitting among the gravestones of the church cemetery far below. She didn't know if they were supernatural or not. At any rate, this would be an interesting evening, Lou thought, and certainly a novel one. Never before had she spent a night in a church tower.

But then, her fear returned. Rows of tiny blue lights "climbed" the stairway to the tower, and in the room itself a slimy substance began oozing from the baseboards. Suddenly, the carillon bells began to ring. Above the din a man's rough voice shouted, "Get out while you still have your mind!"

The deejay broadcast an appeal for help and fortunately his request was not dismissed as a prank. Within fifteen minutes Father Todd and the manager of the radio station arrived and escorted the frightened pair from the church.

Twenty minutes later the bells rang again. Police searched the carillon room and found no evidence of human intervention. The floor was white with dust. Meanwhile, a newspaper reporter at the scene spotted a man sitting in a pew and went to question him. The man vanished. Father Rafter?

Although Lou Wright feels that the spirits were not necessarily evil, but only upset at having their peace disturbed, she vows never to broadcast again from a haunted building. And because of the notoriety occasioned by her visit, the tours of St. Mark's have been discontinued.

Father Todd takes a sanguine attitude toward the phenomena. He believes that his beautiful church is filled with the spirits of many deceased parishioners—men, women and children—and he hopes one day to join them.

Meanwhile, he has been asked if tests would ever be made to determine the location of the stonemason's body. He shakes his head. "That tower ghost . . . has a private chamber suite . . . he can and does play the carillon whenever he wishes."

Most ghosts never have it so good.

CANADA

The Portrait

In December 1965, artist Teresa Montgomery and her husband, Charles, moved into a stately twelve-room house in the Fraser Valley community of Chilliwack. Although the place had been used at one time as a boardinghouse, few major repairs were necessary. Cosmetic improvements alone would certainly go far in restoring the house to its earlier grandeur. The couple were fortunate to have found a house with such potential, and at a reasonable price, no less.

The story of what happened in the Montgomery's house was one of the most widely reported ghost stories in the British Columbia press of the 1960s. This is what happend to these surprised homeowners.

One afternoon while Teresa worked in the kitchen, she heard drawers opening and closing in an upstairs room. She was alone in the house. Dashing up the stairway, she threw open the doors to all the rooms. In an unused bedroom, she found an old chest that had come with the house, looking as if it had been ransacked; some drawers were partly open, and others were opened wide and jarred off their tracks. An iron bedstead, also left behind by the previous owners, sat in the middle of the floor. Teresa recalled seeing it against one wall on the day they'd moved in. The chest and the bed were the only furniture in the room.

Teresa didn't tell her husband, but as the days passed she became increasingly nervous in the huge house. Then came the frightening dreams in which she saw a woman lying on the hallway floor. The figure wore a red dress with a pattern of yellow flowers. "She is terrified," Teresa told a reporter.

The nightmares were making her ill. When her husband asked what was the matter, she said she must have become overly tired by the move. She continued to unpack trunks and boxes, arrange furniture, and hang pictures, but took little pleasure in the work. She cooked meals for Charles, but ate sparingly herself. Her husband wasn't overly concerned. He had lived long enough with his wife to recognize the artist's moods. He assumed she had been hard at work on some paintings, and on those occasions little else mattered. She disliked talking about her work, so Charles never asked.

Then, one morning in her studio, Teresa sat down at her easel to paint a portrait of the woman she'd seen in her dreams. Perhaps in this way she could rid herself of the ghastly dream. But something took control of the brush in her hand. Although she tried to paint the portrait of a woman, the face became that of a man—a man with strong, dark, virile features.

Nothing like this had ever happened to the artist before. Was she losing her talent? Her mind? Fright drove her from the studio that afternoon.

The next day Teresa found the portrait she'd left on the easel had changed. The man's dark eyes had become menacing, and deep shadows concealed one side of his face. Each morning thereafter Teresa would find the portrait altered in some way. She knew then that she would never be able to paint again, at least not in *this* house.

Then late one night a slight noise sent Teresa again into the unused bedroom. As she peered through the door, a dim light appeared in a window and in the center of the light she glimpsed a woman's face. Although the features were somewhat indistinct, Teresa felt certain that this was the woman in her nightmares. This was the ghost who haunted her house.

Soon after the actual sighting of the mysterious woman, other phenomena developed. The front door began to open and close by itself. Footfalls were heard on the stairs when no one was there, and sounds of heavy breathing came from empty rooms.

As Teresa became acquainted with her neighbors, they told her tales about her house—perhaps more than she wanted to hear. One account had it that a woman had been murdered in the house and her body cremated in the chimney. Another story was of a man who'd committed suicide in the house a decade earlier. He was said to have occupied the empty room. The worried homeowner wondered if that might account for the heavy breathing she had heard. No one seemed to know if there'd been any connection between the two people, or, indeed, if either story had any basis in fact.

However, the previous owners, Rebecca and Jackson Perkins, told the Montgomerys that an old man living in the house *had* committed suicide, but he drowned himself in a slough behind the house. Mr. and Mrs. Perkins noted that they'd experienced nothing unusual during the four years they had lived in the house, and dismissed the rumors of ghost business as "baloney."

By spring the media got wind of the strange goings-on in Chilliwack. Teresa eagerly accepted all requests by reporters and photographers to tour the house, and she took special pains to show them the four-by-six-foot portrait that she claimed was changing daily. She said the dark side of the picture had lightened, the outline of a cheek appeared, and a thin moustache was now visible.

One night during the last week of May 1966, Jess Odam, a staff reporter for the *Vancouver Sun*, and Ken Oakes, a *Sun* photographer, visited the house. They kept vigil in the unused bedroom, which was lit by one candle on the chest. A friend of Teresa Montgomery who did not wish to be identified sat with the two men. Teresa was in the kitchen preparing sandwiches.

At 12:25 A.M., Odam reported that he thought he heard a footstep out in the hallway. The friend said she'd heard a "sliding sound." Oakes, seated farthest from the doorway, heard nothing.

Moments later when Teresa came up the stairs with the tray of sandwiches, she discovered a piece of linoleum lying on the hallway floor. She took it into the room and showed her guests the place where it had been tacked to the wall. She'd seen it there on the day she and her husband had moved in and was certain that it was in place when the little group arrived.

Odam wrote, "We saw no ghost, we heard no ghost . . . or did we?"

The following week, at Teresa's request, Odam returned to the house to investigate a small turret at the corner of the building. Teresa had dreamed that the ghost lady "lived" in there. Perhaps the turret held a clue as to the woman's identity and her fate. Before Odam reached the house, Teresa had already broken an opening into the turret by removing some attic paneling. But fearing spiders, she dared not go in.

Odam armed himself with a flashlight and squeezed into the tiny space. Lying on his stomach, he swung the flashlight slowly in all directions. Nothing. Nothing but insulation material that had crumbled over the years and now littered the small floor. When Teresa saw it she said it looked similar to the white specks she'd seen in her dreams.

Shortly after Odam's visit, a former occupant telephoned the Montgomerys to report that there were secret chutes running from the top of the house to the bottom. For what purpose the caller did not know. Teresa suspected it was a prank call, but there were so many questions without answers that she scheduled a séance.

A hypnotist and a clairvoyant met at the house on an afternoon in June. Teresa had moved a table and chairs into the empty bedroom. As the men seated themselves, she pulled down the room-darkening shades at the windows and lit a candle in the center of the table. Charles Montgomery was posted in the front yard to keep sightseers away. (The newspaper articles had attracted some unwanted attention.)

"Is there anyone here?" asked the clairvoyant. "You may come forth now, please."

Silence.

The clairvoyant raised his voice. "We are here only to help you."

Teresa stared so intently at the candle that she saw multiple images of the flame.

"Do not fear us," said the hypnotist. "We bring you no harm."

There were no sounds save the rhythmic breathing of the three persons at the table.

The clairvoyant folded his hands together. "We implore you to go to the light. You are dead and on this earth plane there is nothing more for you. In the kingdom of light others will help you."

Teresa thought that one window shade rippled at the sill, but she couldn't be certain.

As the summer days stretched into weeks and the weeks into months, hundreds of people besieged the homeowners, all wanting tours of the "spook" house. Children told their wide-eyed classmates that caskets floated from room to room and skeletons rattled up and down the staircase. All nonsense, of course.

The Montgomerys finally posted a NO SIGHTSEERS sign on the door, but it had no effect. In one week alone two hundred cars a day disgorged noisy ghost hunters, and on one Sunday seven hundred people broke the front steps trying to gain entry to the house. Teresa, exhausted from the turbulent publicity, refused to admit anyone unless they had written her a letter first. And letters were arriving daily from all parts of Canada.

Charles Montgomery resented the flood of letters and the unruly strangers who banged at the door and peeked in the windows at all hours of the day and night. There could be only one solution. The couple would charge admission to tour their home! Surely anyone wishing to see a house "infested" with ghosts would be willing to pay for the privilege.

But Teresa Montgomery didn't reckon on the trouble she would have getting a trade license to operate a "haunted house."

Chilliwack's acting mayor, Al Holden, said that if the council granted her request then the entire neighborhood would have to be rezoned from residential to commercial. Alderman Bill Nickel said he felt Mrs. Montgomery only wanted to exploit the free publicity she'd received about her claims that ghosts were in her house.

One day Teresa and a friend discovered that the portrait was fading and also *shrinking* in size. They measured it to confirm their suspicions and wondered how such a feat could be accomplished.

Dr. Geoffrey Riddehough, a lecturer in classics at the University of British Columbia and a member of the Psychical Research Society of England, was invited to study the portrait. He came to no conclusions, other than to remark that there are some things happening in the world for which people have no explanation.

Eventually, Teresa grew sick of the portrait and threatened to get rid of it. She did. The Pacific National Exhibition displayed it for a while, and in 1973 it became the property of a Vancouver radio station. Press accounts do not mention the picture's condition at that time.

Were the accounts of the Chilliwack haunting genuine? That question is impossible to answer. The local journalist who first broke the story said Mrs. Montgomery told her the painting would put the little town on the map. That it certainly did. But the reporter spent many hours and days in the house and, according to an interview with her, "never saw anything or heard anything to suggest the place was haunted."

In 1972 the Montgomerys sold the house and moved to Vancouver Island to enjoy a more tranquil life in a house presumably free of unwanted guests.

The new owner stayed in the mansion for barely a year. He said that he and his family were moving for personal reasons. He did not elaborate. The house sold for $23,000 to a young Chilliwack couple who intended to renovate it and raise a family there. The new buyers knew the ghost legend, but didn't think much of it.

A Chilliwack real estate agent who handled the sale said the transaction was not that difficult, despite the house's history.

"It used to be that selling a haunted house was a real estate man's nightmare," he told a Canadian Press reporter. "But not anymore. Today, haunted houses seem to attract more interest than those that are not. . . ."

If the new owners ever did start seeing strange sights and hearing unusual noises in their notorious home, they had only to call the agent for reassurance that no one else shared their home. You see, the Realtor did not believe in ghosts.

NOTE: Certain names in this story have been changed.

The Amherst Demon

THE TIME:
The night of September 10, 1878

THE PLACE:
A bedroom in shoemaker Daniel Teed's two-story cottage at
6 Princess Street, Amherst, Nova Scotia

THE MESSAGE:
ESTHER COX—YOU ARE MINE TO KILL

The family watched in horrible fascination as the foot-high letters appeared on the plaster wall above the girl's bed. Words not written by human hand. Esther screamed. Her sister, Olive Teed, hugged her close. Several onlookers struggled to understand the meaning of the chilling phrase.

No one slept that September night. In the morning the bleary-eyed Daniel Teed staggered off to his foreman's job at the Amherst Shoe Factory. He could not foresee that forces unknown and unknowable would wreak havoc upon his home for the next eighteen months.

Daniel's household was a large one. He and his wife, Olive, were parents of two small boys, Willie, aged five, and George, aged one. Also living under his roof were Olive's two unmarried sisters, Esther Cox, aged eighteen, and Jennie Cox, aged twenty-two, and their brother, William. Daniel's brother, John Teed, boarded at the house and worked in the shoe factory. With eight people and only four upstairs bedrooms the house was obviously incommodious, but Daniel seldom complained. He'd been glad to offer a home to his wife's siblings after their mother's death and their father's remarriage and subsequent move to the United States.

Esther and Jennie shared one bedroom. They could not have been more different in appearance and in personality. Esther was short and heavyset with a pale, moon-shaped face and a child's naïveté in at least some aspects of life. However, she had a moody disposition when she didn't get her way. Jennie, however, was slender, with dark, cascading locks, flashing eyes, and the ability to get whatever she wanted. She could have any suitor in Amherst, but spurned them all.

The first intimations of strange happenings in the Teed home actually began about a week before the grim words appeared on Esther's wall. On the cold, rainy night of September 4, 1878, Esther awoke her sister.

"There's something in bed with us," she cried.

Jennie leaped out of bed and turned up the oil lamp. Something *did* seem to be moving inside the mattress, making faint scratching noises. But after several minutes of quiet, the girls shook out the bedclothes and punched the mattress, but neither saw nor felt any lumps. Jennie said Esther was probably dreaming. They went back to bed and slept fitfully until dawn.

The next night it was Jennie's turn to be frightened. She heard a rustling coming from beneath their bed. The girls had a carton of quilt pieces stored under there. Maybe a mouse had somehow gotten inside it. Jennie reached under the bed and pulled the box into the middle of the room. Seconds later it suddenly rose several inches into the air and then tipped over. Jennie stood it back up, but it flipped over again. The girls screamed in unison. Daniel Teed came rushing in, hitching up his trousers as he stumbled through the door. He laughed when Jennie stammered out the tale. He said they both must have been imagining things. He pushed the cavorting carton back under the bed and slammed the door behind him on his way out. Jennie didn't touch the box again. She lay quietly, not sleeping the rest of the night.

On the third night, Esther awoke gasping. "I'm dying . . . please help me!"

Jennie quickly lit the lamp. Her sister's face was bloodred, her eyes bulged, and her short hair stood on end. Esther's arms and legs began to swell and she cried out in pain. At the same moment something began banging on the walls.

Olive and Daniel awakened at the racket and rushed into the girls' bedroom. Jennie stood trembling in a corner, her hands covering her face. A terrible blow against the outside wall shook the room. Esther's body seemed to deflate, as if air were slowly being released from a balloon.

The incident was not discussed at breakfast the following morning. Could it be that for some reason Esther could not recall the events? No one knew. No one asked.

On the following night the heavy bed quilts rose from the girls' bed and landed in a corner of the room. Jennie retrieved them. As she started back to bed, she noticed her sister's body starting to swell again. Crashing blows shook the walls and Esther's body shrank back to its normal size.

Daniel Teed had seen and heard enough. He summoned a local physician, Dr. Thomas W. Caritte. The entire family gathered around as Dr. Caritte examined the besieged teenager. He shook his head. A diagnosis would be difficult; he thought she might have some sort of nervous problem. As he sat by her bedside, the girl's pillow rose up from beneath her head and inflated itself like a balloon. Flying through the air, the pillow smacked John Teed in the face.

Dr. Caritte hurried to his office and returned with a potent sedative. Esther gratefully took it and fell into a deep sleep. But now a steady hammering was coming from the roof, as if someone were putting down shingles with a sledgehammer. Family members could find no cause for it. Meanwhile, Dr. Caritte, alone in Esther's room, claimed he was hit on the head by a bushel of potatoes that Jennie had been peeling earlier in the evening. The blow sent him sprawling across the floor.

Daniel Teed had sworn his extended family, and Dr. Caritte, to secrecy about these incidents. However, townspeople soon learned what was going on. Passersby couldn't help but hear the weird sounds emanating daily from the house. Persons of insatiable curiosity trampled Teed's front lawn and his flower beds to get close enough to peer through the windows. Daniel was forced to ask for police protection.

Dr. Caritte returned to the Teed house every day for three weeks, keeping his patient in a semicomatose state to ease her suffering. And it was in this state that Esther first muttered a fragmented and terrifying tale to relatives gathered at her bedside. This was her story:

Although the weather had been unsettled with a storm rising on the western horizon, she'd agreed to go buggy riding one night the previous summer with Bob McNeal, an employee at the shoe factory. He'd tried to seduce her. When she refused his sexual advances, he pulled a pistol from his coat pocket, cocked the hammer, and took aim at her. Lightning slashed the sky, thunder roared, and rain pelted the buggy. Instead of pulling the trigger, the angry young man whipped the horses, heading into a deep woods. Esther feared that McNeal was going to make good on his threat by killing her and dumping her body in the forest. But he didn't get the chance. Just then she heard a wagon coming up behind them, its wooden wheels creaking over the rough terrain.

McNeal sharply swung the buggy around and, at breakneck speed, headed back to Amherst. He delivered Esther to her door—and was never again seen in the village. Esther hadn't told anyone of her frightful night.

Esther's ramblings finally stopped. She turned her head toward the wall and again lapsed into deep sleep. Daniel put one arm around his wife and the other around Jennie, who wept softly. As McNeal's boss at the shoe factory, Daniel had been as puzzled as anyone about the young man's sudden disappearance. He had known nothing, of course, about McNeal's "date" with Esther. The only thing Daniel had learned was what other villagers knew—that McNeal had paid up his rent to his landlady and vanished. Eventually he had been forgotten. But now the questions came back. Where had Bob McNeal gone? Had he been killed? Could his vengeful ghost have returned to punish Esther Cox for not giving in to him?

When her sister stirred again, Jennie asked if she recalled telling the story of the attempted rape. Esther looked away and nodded. Was it true, Jennie wanted to know. "It is true," whispered Esther, tears welling up in her eyes.

"Then it must be Bob McNeal who is responsible for this awful spirit," Jennie continued.

In quick succession, three loud taps sounded from the bedroom wall. The small group stared in fascination. "I think it understands what we're saying," Jennie whispered. Tap . . . tap . . . tap came the reply. Over the next several minutes, Dr. Caritte worked out a "code" with Esther's unseen tormentor. One tap meant "no," two taps signified a "maybe," and three taps a definite "yes." It is claimed that the spirit was able to answer such simple questions as the number of people in the room, and the time of day or night.

Despite his newfound "ability" to communicate with the supposed spirit, Dr. Caritte had exhausted his knowledge of conventional remedies for Esther's and the family's problems. Religion might provide a cure. A prominent Baptist minister, the Reverend Dr. Edwin Clay, was asked to visit the house. He agreed with Dr. Caritte that Esther was not producing the noises herself. After several visits, he posed an intriguing theory: since electricity had just come into wide usage, he wondered if the young woman had received an electric shock and been turned into a kind of "living battery." The noises that shook the house might be small claps of "thunder" coming from Esther's body. She said once that she felt electricity coursing through her. This fantastic hypothesis brought lots of attention, especially to the Reverend Dr. Clay, who spoke of it from the pulpit.

The Teeds' own minister, the Reverend A. Temple of the Methodist church, also came calling to see if he could lend any theological insight into the troubles. He sat in the kitchen visiting with the family. A bucket of cold water on the table started to boil. The minister excused himself and backed out the door. He did not return.

Meanwhile, lack of sleep and frayed nerves were telling on Daniel Teed. He was tired of the visitors, peeved with the sightseers in his yard, and frustrated with his strange sister-in-law—whom some people were now calling a faker. But a solution suddenly seemed to present itself in a most unexpected way. Esther contracted diphtheria, and the dreaded disease kept everyone away except Dr. Caritte. Curiously, and to the surprise and relief of the family, all phenomena ceased during the two weeks that Esther was ill.

Daniel sent Esther away to convalesce at the home of another of her married sisters, a Mrs. Snowden in Sackville, New Brunswick. No phenomena occurred at the Sackville house. Peace continued to reign in Amherst, and Daniel Teed was happier than he'd been in months. But Jennie and Olive wanted their sister back home, and Esther was eager to return. Daniel consented. The phenomena were gone. Daniel even shuffled the bedrooms around to provide a new room for Esther and Jennie. He wanted Esther to make a fresh start.

That start was more frightening than anyone could have imagined.

On the first night of Esther's return, small fireballs fell from the ceiling of her bedroom. One of Esther's dresses, hanging from a peg on the wall, was set afire. Daniel was in the room at the time and snuffed out the fire.

In the coming days, Olive's dresses were torched and small, spontaneous fires were discovered nearly every day in various parts of the house.

One afternoon a bucket of cedar shavings in the basement started to burn. Esther ran into the street, screaming for help. The fire department arrived and, although no charges were ever filed, many of the firemen suspected arson, perhaps by Esther. Olive knew better. She and her sister had been together, alone in the house; there had been no opportunity for Esther to have sneaked down to the basement.

That night, Jennie asked the spirit if it intended to burn down the house. "YES" came the raps!

Now, adult members of the family slept in shifts to keep constant watch for the flames that might destroy the house and all the sleeping occupants in it.

Within a week, Daniel Teed ordered Esther out of his house. He was sorry, he said, but her presence posed too great a danger to the rest of the family members.

This time Olive and Jennie could not save their sister despite their pleadings. Esther had to leave. She might have walked the streets had it not been for the generosity of one John W. White, a local restaurateur. He offered the penniless, frightened girl employment, and lodging with his own family. White didn't believe any of the tales he'd heard and read about the Teed house; besides, he had always been a champion of the underdog. His own life had been a struggle and he was always willing to help a young person. Esther would have a "new chance," as he put it, at his restaurant.

White's generosity nearly ruined him. Whenever Esther served customers, knives, forks, and spoons flew off tables and counters and clung to the girl's clothing. Doors opened and closed by themselves and the door to a large oven fell off its stout hinges. Heavy tables and chairs moved around the dining room whenever the girl was on duty, frightening customers who vowed never to come back. With regret, White realized that he could not keep Esther in his employ. He sent her back to 6 Princess Street.

Daniel did not have to take her back, as it happened. He'd just received a communication from a stranger, one Capt. James Beck of St. John, New Brunswick. The captain wrote that he'd been following the press accounts of Esther and was intrigued by the story. He said he'd like the opportunity for several of his physician friends to study the girl.

For three weeks Esther was a guest in the Captain and Mrs. Beck's home and for twenty-one days nothing happened. She did, however, entertain her hosts and their guests with stories of the ghosts who were threatening her. She identified them by the names "Peter Cox," "Maggie Fisher," and "Bob Nickle." The last one, a thinly veiled reference to Bob McNeal, threatened her with fires and stabbings, she said. Maggie Fisher was the name of an old school chum, long deceased. She didn't know who Peter Cox was.

In time, the Becks sent her back to Amherst, and again, Daniel Teed turned her away. Fortunately, another couple in the region, the Van Amberghs, were willing to provide her with room and board. Mr. Van Ambergh farmed. His wife was a sturdy, patient, hardworking woman who quickly developed an attachment to Esther.

Esther had never imagined such peace. She slept soundly every night and awoke refreshed each morning, anxious to help Mrs. Van Ambergh with the necessary chores.

But such good fortune did not last. Olive Teed wanted her sister back home, and had persuaded her husband to give Esther yet another chance.

That chance was ill advised. Esther had no sooner walked through the door of the Teeds' house than the poltergeist began its mischief—walls shook with heavy vibrations, while above their heads the roof reverberated as if it were being bombarded with hundreds of heavy bricks.

Daniel was prepared this time. He shipped Esther off immediately to Mr. and Mrs. Arthur Davidson, a rural couple who wanted a servant girl in their home.

Within days of her arrival, the Davidsons' barn was destroyed by fire. Esther was accused of arson, arrested, indicated, and convicted. She spent a month in jail. Only through the efforts of sympathetic friends in Amherst was she released. Daniel was at his wit's end.

Compounding the real fear that the Teeds had that their house *and their lives* might be destroyed by whatever haunted Esther Cox were the cries from various Amherst clergy that Satan had insinuated himself in their midst in the person of young Esther. There were calls from some quarters demanding that the entire family be driven from the village.

Stepping into this cauldron of fear and suspicion was one Walter Hubbell, a skeptical American magician who believed that he had the answer to the possession of Esther Cox: he would "lay the ghost," a nineteenth-century term for exorcising a spirit from the household. He told the Teeds that he would pay for his own food and lodging if he could visit the home and decide for himself if the young woman was indeed possessed—or a fraud.

The Teeds had little choice. Either they permanently banned Esther from the only home she really had, or, if she stayed, they faced the wrath of their superstitious neighbors. And, Hubbell's talents *were* well known; indeed he had performed across Canada. Perhaps, Daniel prayed, the magician could succeed where others had failed.

If there was any thought that the appearance of the famous magician would silence the ghost, Hubbell's first visit proved the opposite. On the rainy morning he walked through the front door, the umbrella he held was wrenched out of his hands, and a butcher knife hurtled through the air directly at him. He quickly ducked as the terrible missile embedded itself in the wall behind him. It had been thrown with such force, by whom or by what no one knew, that the handle vibrated for several seconds. No sooner had Hubbell recovered from his shocking introduction to the poltergeist than all the chairs in the dining room rocked backward and crashed to the floor.

After a few hours of quiet, Hubbell and the family sat down to their noonday meal. Quick raps came from the table. The magician said he knew the "code" and would carry on a conversation with the spirits. For several minutes, Hubbell rapped out a series of messages that appeared to be answered by the spirits. He told the mystified family that the spirits had told him the correct dates of the coins in his pocket and he produced the coins as evidence. The slick maneuverings of a professional magician, or evidence of spirit world communication? The question lingers.

During Hubbell's five-week stay he was an eyewitness to various sorts of flying missiles, but the self-styled debunker of ghostly phenomena couldn't explain the bizarre events he witnessed, including:

- At breakfast one morning a china sugar bowl vanishing from the table and ten minutes later falling from the ceiling.
- A blooming plant and a can filled with water apparently rising up from the kitchen floor and settling down on the floor of the parlor. No one had been in the kitchen at the time.
- A small German silver trumpet materializing out of nowhere and treating the family to blaring "music" day and night. It was said that no one in Amherst owned such an instrument.

Toward the end of Hubbell's "investigation," he approached Esther and the family with an idea. He suggested putting Esther on the stage, in vampire costume, and letting her summon the ghosts. She'd be a sensation in North America and the European capitals and he, Hubbell, would be her business manager.

Olive was violently opposed. The idea of her sister being displayed as some sort of "freak" was out of the question.

"Don't be silly," Daniel shot back. "We need the income this would bring." He grimly pointed out that William Cox and John Teed had already left the house in disgust and they were nearly bankrupt. Broken furniture littered the rooms, china had been smashed, the wallpaper was charred from the mysterious fires, and valuable silver had vanished.

Olive continued to protest, but to no avail. Daniel agreed with Hubbell that Esther should be put on the stage and that she should appear first in Amherst. Hubbell was by this point thoroughly convinced that some supernatural force inhabited Esther's body, and compared her "gifts" to those of the finest spiritualist mediums. He rented a public hall and spared no money to advertise the big event. What Esther's position was on all the decisions being made for her is not recorded. If she did not wholeheartedly endorse the project, she at least went along with the magician's scheme.

At her debut in Amherst, Esther Cox faced a hall jammed with curious spectators. She appeared in her absurd vampire costume, but the spirits were taking the night off. No supernatural manifestations occurred. Angry patrons demanded their money back. The evening was a humiliating experience for Esther and a great disappointment to Hubbell.

However, the magician was not easily discouraged. There were places all over Canada where Esther—The Girl with the Devils in Her—(as Hubbell billed her) could perform.

On June 18, 1879, in a Moncton, New Brunswick, auditorium, various household objects placed on the stage flew about when Esther appeared. Reports of the event claim spectators were unable to see any evidence of trickery or fraud.

Now certain of success, Hubbell booked Esther for a performance at the Moncton Baptist Church. There, loud rappings came from the church floor. The faithful were impressed enough to drive both Esther and Hubbell from the church.

Their "act" didn't receive any better reviews in Chatham, New Brunswick. The pair were chased out of town by stone-throwing citizens. Clearly, Esther's talents were not to be tolerated after all, and The Girl with the Devils in Her canceled all of her remaining performances in fear for her life.

Walter Hubbell performed one final, peculiar deed, however, before vanishing from Amherst and Esther's life forever. He summoned a Micmac Indian medicine man from Pictou, Nova Scotia, to "drive the devils out" of Esther Cox. The young woman agreed, though the rituals seemed weird and frightening.

The unnamed Indian succeeded where preachers and physicians had failed. He freed the spirits that had plagued her for so long.

Esther eventually married a man from Springdale, Nova Scotia, but the marriage was not a happy one. After her husband died Esther moved to the United States, where she married Peter Shannahan, a workman at the J. M. O'Donnell Shoe Factory in Brockton, Massachusetts. She bore one child, a son. He and his father were at Esther's bedside when she died at the age of fifty-two.

Meanwhile, Walter Hubbell wrote a book called *The Great Amherst Mystery* that would become a best-seller in both Canada and the United States. The book had gone through ten printings by 1916, as Hubbell dredged up increasing amounts of material from the copious notes he took of the events in which he had been so intimately involved. Olive Teed said that Hubbell sensationalized some incidents, but that it was a basically honest portrayal of her sister's long and agonizing "illness."

The case of Esther Cox was never solved, but a modern psychotherapist could posit some explanations.

Even though the young girl outwardly rebuked the darkly handsome Bob McNeal for even suggesting a romp in the woods, part of her certainly craved that intimacy. Esther was plain and plump and realized that suitors were not to be found with any degree of regularity in the isolated environs of Amherst, Nova Scotia. In turning McNeal aside, she may have unconsciously projected upon herself the torments that she suffered. Experts theorize that sexual frustration and confusion can initiate poltergeist activity.

There is also a question about the role that Daniel played in Esther's suffering. Although he never inflicted physical pain upon her (as far as is known), he verbally abused her and mistreated her badly by throwing her out of the house. Again, Esther may have unconsciously sought to be severely punished and degraded by her brother-in-law. Such masochism brings about sexual excitement and satisfaction in certain people.

All theories aside, the case of Esther Cox remains a classic account of poltergeist haunting and is certainly one of Canada's best-known ghost stories.

Mysterious Ontario

A young man with dark hair who wants to live with his old friends . . . the ghost whose likeness was immortalized in a gargoyle's face . . . a wandering singer in Yorkville . . . and a famous house whose spirits may be of the fictional variety. Ghosts and haunted places have been reported for many decades in Ontario Province and its largest city, Toronto.

An Unwanted Visitor

A pleasant avenue in suburban Toronto would seem an unlikely place to find the supernatural, but don't tell that to one young couple who moved into the basement apartment of a neat brick home on just such a boulevard several years ago.

The series of events that inexplicably plagued the pair were serious enough to warrant a "dehaunting" by Ian Currie and Carole Davis, two Canadian investigators of the paranormal.

Twenty-year-old Rob, his wife Cindy, nineteen, and their infant son had been in their new apartment barely a month when a growling sound coming from their child's room startled them awake late one night. The couple found the tyke standing up in bed staring at the wall. He seemed scared about something, his mother said. The source of the menacing growl remained a puzzlement.

Over the next few weeks, the child experienced further episodes of sudden crying and screaming. The couple were at a loss to explain his fearful outbursts.

Other freakish occurrences scared Rob and Cindy. A coffeemaker spurted hot water for no apparent reason, a window slammed shut on a still night, and, most incredible of all, a glass full of milk glided halfway across a table as the couple looked on in amazement. When a friend stayed overnight in the baby's room, she told Cindy about being awakened by a breeze across her face, and of seeing a pallid, yellow light shining down from above.

The couple found out about Ian Currie, an author and former professor, and

Carole Davis, a psychic who claimed to have helped police in Canada and the United States. Their little apartment needed, the parents decided, a professional ghost-cleansing.

Currie and Davis claimed to have dehaunted nearly sixty homes at the rate of $250 Canadian per house. "Satisfaction guaranteed," Currie told newspaper reporter Gerald Volgenau.

Davis was in the apartment only a short while when she pronounced it definitely haunted. But the ghost was not an evil presence, "just a poor person in distress," she said. Further, she sensed the presence was that of a dark haired young man killed in a traffic accident.

Psychic Davis went into a trance with Currie at her side. Within minutes, she was speaking for the ghost—of the driving rain, of the darkness and sudden headlights, of the trouble he had caused for his loved ones, and of his desire to go home. Meanwhile, Ian Currie was talking soothingly to his unseen listener, telling him that he was dead, that the accident was not his fault. He should "go into the light," Currie insisted.

Soon the psychic was quiet, her head jerking slightly as if to clear it of the last vestiges of the visiting spirit.

Cindy was stunned at the scene. She had known just such a man, a young acquaintance who had been drinking one night and stumbled in front of an oncoming car during a rainstorm. He was killed instantly.

It can only be surmised that his ghost had for some reason attached itself to the young couple. But now he was gone, Currie and Davis said. Rob and Cindy were relieved. The apartment was definitely *not* big enough for four.

Ivan the Ghost

No! It just wasn't possible, the surly master stonemason screamed, throwing down his chisel and hammer. His friend Sergei Ilyitch backed away. Maybe this hadn't been such a good idea, he thought. Sergei had only wanted to be helpful by pointing out that Ivan Reznikoff's face was being carved in a gargoyle on the central facade of University College. Another mason, Paul Diabolos, was the culprit. To him it was a big joke, but to Ivan the thought of *his* face on that of a grotesque and ugly statue was outrageous.

And now the insult had turned to rage. Sergei had just added the news that Diabolos was after Ivan's girlfriend, Susie.

"If you do not believe me," Sergei stammered as he backed away, fearful of the muscular Russian's temper, "come back tonight and wait at the Arcade. That's where they meet. You will see."

To this Ivan agreed. But until nightfall, he would start exacting his own revenge—the gargoyle upon which he, himself, was working would have a new feature . . . the face of the miscreant Diabolos!

The year was 1858. The Toronto architects Cumberland and Storm had the commission to design and build University College at the University of Toronto. When they had advertised for workmen, a squat, heavily muscled, bearded Russian named Ivan Reznikoff was among the applicants. He showed the architects his carvings. They were pleased with his work and hired him to create some of the gargoyles on the central facade.

Not a great deal was, or is, known about Reznikoff. He was born in Russia sometime in the early nineteenth century and had shown up in Canada in the mid-1840s. One version of his life claims he worked for Messrs. Cumberland and Storm on projects even before University College. He told them he had carved statues in cities all across Europe and worked for a while in Britain, bragging that he had carvings on buildings around Piccadilly Circus.

Though he was a good worker, Reznikoff was a sullen, solitary figure with few close friends. His disdain for human contact was the cause of his global wanderlust. Carving was his only pleasure, especially cutting stone into the gremlins and gargoyles and other vermin of the night. Some said the nightmares that plagued him led to his most creative work.

Reznikoff did not seek, nor was there extended to him, the friendship of others. Sergei Ilyitch, a fellow Russian émigré, was the only one in whom Reznikoff ever confided. So Ilyitch felt an obligation to point out that Paul Diabolos's gargoyle was turning into a likeness of Reznikoff—and to mention Diabolos's interest in the Russian's girlfriend. The girl's last name isn't known, nor is there any indication of how or why the gruff Russian and the Canadian girl got together, but Diabolos must have thought it great sport to steal the only woman in whom Reznikoff showed an interest, albeit an affection she did not save for him alone.

As night fell, Reznikoff hid in the arcade of the building. A few minutes later, Diabolos and Susie came into view, hand-in-hand and laughing gaily. It was all too much for Reznikoff. He charged at Diabolos, his mason's axe held high above his head. He swung a mighty blow, but Diabolos ducked and Reznikoff's axe struck an oaken door. The deep gash remains visible to this day.

Diabolos ran up the stairs of the central tower. He crouched in a dark corner, drew a small dagger from his waistband and waited. When the mad Russian appeared, Diabolos leaped out and plunged the knife into his attacker's heart. He pushed Reznikoff's corpse down the twelve-story, unfinished central tower well.

During the 1860s, 1870s, and 1880s, students, faculty, and visitors at the university sometimes reported seeing a dark figure wearing a conical hat suddenly appear in the vicinity of the tower. The story was told about how Reznikoff had died. Others said it was just a legend, until . . .

A fire swept through University College in 1890. In the rubble, searchers found a skull and bones and a silver buckle—at the bottom of the tower's well. Just where Ivan Reznikoff was said to have been deposited. His remains were reburied in a corner of the quadrangle.

Does Ivan Reznikoff still haunt University College? Any strange noise in the building is attributed to Reznikoff, but there have been no recent, verified reports. Staff and students treat the legend with a certain lighthearted air. A pub in the building's basement was even named after him. But, still, if you linger

long enough beneath one of the Reznikoff gargoyles on a moonlit night . . .
anything is possible.

The ROM

On Queen's Park Crescent, the Royal Ontario Museum may have two old ghosts
in addition to its eclectic collection of Canadiana.

The better known of the pair may be the ghost of the museum's former
director, Dr. Charles Currelly, who was eighty-two when he died in 1957. He
was director of the museum for thirty-two years, from 1914 until his retirement
in 1946.

Dr. Currelly isn't a frightening specter at all, just peculiarly dressed. He wears
a nightshirt and cap as he scurries down the corridor. Precisely why he is dressed
this way, or the reason for his haste, is not known.

A little curly-haired blond girl of about eight was seen in the planetarium section of the museum in the late 1970s. She wore a starched white
dress and looked very unhappy, according to one museum staff member. Unfortunately, as with many ghosts, no one knew her name or the nature of her
distress.

Yorkville Apparitions

Whenever old houses are converted to more modern uses, say offices or trendy
shops, incorporeal residents of those selfsame dwellings can put a chill into any
business climate. Such was the case in two circa-1900 Yorkville homes.

A house on Hazelton Avenue was remodeled into offices for a music production company, but that didn't stop the vocalizings of a female ghost. A company
executive working late heard the singing while locking up for the night. He said
it was quite a "beautiful" sound. So far as is known no attempt was made to
sign her to a contract.

A psychic who worked in the house some years ago said it may have been a
woman who lived there during World War II, and was still waiting for her
husband to return. The woman was once seen walking down a second-floor hallway, and thence through a wall and front window.

Another man claimed the alarm system, which used motion detectors and
infrared light beams, was always going off. The police eventually refused to respond to any alarms at the house, he said.

The people who built a house on Roxborough Street may be still looking after
the place. According to reports from 1986, the woman who then ran a business
there said her cat always acted strangely in the house. A medium was consulted,
and she said there were several friendly ghosts present. To a spirit, they were
happy with what the woman was doing with their old house, the medium said,
and only wanted to protect what had been theirs in life.

Mackenzie House

Did the ghost of Isabel Mackenzie really slap the caretaker at the historic William Lyon Mackenzie House?

The most often-told ghost story in Toronto concerns the mansion at 82 Bond Street where the Canadian statesman and Toronto's first mayor lived from 1859 until his death in 1861. He died an ill-tempered and disillusioned old man. Mackenzie himself was supposedly seen and heard hanging about his former home, running the hand-operated Washington flatbed printing press and playing the pump organ. But it is his wife, Isabel, who has been the subject of the most frequent supernatural tales. Are they true?

"The Mackenzie House is not haunted," Mrs. E. M. Drake, a curatorial assistant at Mackenzie House, said. "Such stories did circulate during the 1950s, but there have been absolutely no such manifestations since the Toronto Historical Board assumed management of the house in 1960. Despite this, a public perception that we are haunted does continue to persist, reinforced each Halloween by our local media, who conveniently ignore our assurances and the fact that the house was exorcised in 1960."

Exorcised?

The simple fact that it was deemed necessary to conduct such a religious ceremony may of itself suggest that there was more to the haunting than anyone cares to admit. And that's certainly not surprising considering the disputatious life of William Lyon Mackenzie.

A native of Dundee, Scotland, Mackenzie emigrated to Canada in 1820 at the age of twenty-five. With a partner, Mackenzie was soon in business operating a drug- and book-selling business in York, later the city of Toronto. He married Isabel Baxter, to whom he had become engaged in Scotland, in 1822.

Mackenzie began his career as a journalist in 1824 with the appearance of *The Colonial Advocate* newspaper in Queenston, where he had moved after his marriage. His career as a radical politician and proponent of Canadian self-rule ascended upon his move back to York, the provincial capital, and with his increasingly strident editorials criticizing the "Family Compact," a close-knit group of influential provincial families. His words stung so deeply that in 1826 the sons of some of the prominent families broke into his print shop and wrecked his presses.

The general public, however, rushed to his defense and elected him to a seat in the Assembly of Upper Canada in 1828 as a leader of the radical wing of the Reform Party. His firebrand rhetoric continued to get him into trouble. He was expelled from the Assembly on numerous occasions and finally denied his seat in that body.

His overall popularity remained high, however, and in 1834 he was elected alderman of the new city of Toronto and then mayor, becoming thereby the first chief executive of what is now Canada's largest city.

Mackenzie found the years following fraught with rejection and disillusionment. He was defeated for reelection in 1836, along with other members of the Reform Party.

It was at this point in his stormy career that Mackenzie began to advocate open rebellion against the government, which he criticized as unresponsive and unrepresentative. Not content to use words alone, he led seven hundred men in the ill-fated December 1837 coup attempt. He was just able to flee with his supporters to Navy Island in the Niagara River where he announced a provisional government that was rejected by Canadian, United States, and British authorities.

The United States tried and convicted Mackenzie of treason in 1839. Eventually the Canadian government pardoned Mackenzie, and the rebels and he returned home. He served seven more years in the Legislative Assembly and established a new newspaper, *Mackenzie's Weekly Message*. He published it until 1860.

His final years were full of bitterness over his failed political ambitions and his financial difficulties. His friends raised funds to purchase the house on Bond Street, and Mackenzie lived there from 1859 until he died on August 28, 1861.

The exorcism that reportedly took place in 1960 was probably aimed at persuading William's wife, Isabel, to leave the premises. Following her death in 1873, there were periodic reports in the press claiming Mrs. Mackenzie's ghost was seen marching down the stairs and out the front door. Those stories, of course, preceded the story of her slapping the caretaker, which has variously been reported as having occurred sometime in the 1950s or early 1960s. Her ghost was also said to have jealously guarded the kitchen. Employees said they, too, were sometimes slapped by nothing they could see when they came into the kitchen from the back door.

Sources say her ghost was finally put to rest when a minister was summoned by Col. Charles Lindsey, the Mackenzies' grandson. The unnamed minister held a service during which he asked Mrs. Mackenzie's ghost to relocate somewhere else.

The media continue to include the Mackenzie House on their annual Halloween Toronto "ghost tour," but it would seem that its days of being haunted are over. At least for now.

The Tombstone

Mike Cino's demolition firm had nearly finished ripping apart the second floor of the old building they'd been hired to raze in Hamilton during the fall of 1982. The work was progressing smoothly. Nothing untoward or terribly unusual had happened. The workers had found the customary odds and ends and bric-a-brac in the place, but certainly nothing that would set back their timetable.

On this particular day a worker thought he had heard a strange noise from within the building as the machines tore into the structure, but he attributed it to the groans of a well-made house reluctantly giving way to the wrecker's ball.

Then they found the tombstone.

Discovered secreted in a wall of the second floor, the stone bore the chiseled words OUR BABY at the top. Below, two names were still clearly discernible: *Martha Louise, 1888*; and *Emma Grace, Nov. 9, 1879*.

No one knew who the little children might have been, or why they died. Nor could Mike Cino guess why the stone was placed where it was found, other than the possibility that it might have been used to prop up the wall.

The discovery, however, was critical for helping to solve an eleven-year-old mystery: the possible cause of frightening visits from a ghost witnessed by two former residents.

Norm Bilotti worked in the composing room of the *Hamilton Spectator* in the early 1970s. He lived in the house with his wife, Sherrie. Their brush with the supernatural came quite unexpectedly, in the middle of the night. Twice.

The first time, Norm jerked awake when his wife screamed at the top of her lungs from the bed next to him. He blinked in the gloomy darkness until he was able to focus on what his wife saw—a human form wearing a long gown hovering above their bed. He couldn't see any face. He had no idea if it was male or female. Only that it was there.

"If she had only seen it herself, I would have thought she was crazy," Norm said in a Canadian Press account of the incident. "If it had only been me, I would have thought I was crazy. But both of us saw it."

The figure vanished when Norm turned on the light.

The second time they knew for *certain* neither was dreaming. Norm saw it first this night, and his cries awoke his wife. A legless woman hovered near them, her eyes protruding grotesquely from her face. And her hair . . . her hair stood on end as if she had stuck her finger in an electrical outlet. She said not a word and then was gone.

Despite the unnerving, middle-of-the-night episodes, the Bilottis had a certain curiosity about the identity of the ghost. They thought a ghost hunter might provide some clues and called Malcolm Bessent, of Rosary Hill College in Buffalo, New York.

Bessent visited the home and immediately sensed a "presence" in the house. "I think something is concealed in this area—what, I don't know," he said, pointing to a particular section of a wall. "I'm being drawn to it very strongly. It's the reason for the manifestation."

The Bilottis never again were visited by the mysterious woman and moved out of the house shortly thereafter. They thought nothing more would ever be heard about the ghost until . . .

. . . Mike Cino's crew began leveling the old house. He wasn't surprised at finding the nineteenth-century tombstone—after all, he had once found a *bomb* in one place—but it was a bit odd that such a marker would be used to shore up a wall.

Norm Bilotti found out about the discovery. It all made sense, and at the same time chilled the very marrow in his bones.

The tombstone was found *directly above* the bedroom in which the couple had seen the ghost. And further, Malcolm Bessent had pointed to nearly the *precise section of the wall* where the stone was discovered. Norm and Sherrie had seen a ghost . . . and it was somehow connected to the tombstone.

The identity of the two children memorialized on the stone was never established. Was it their mother the Bilottis saw? If so, there might be presented here further evidence that a mother takes care of her children—even after death.

Les Phénomènes du Québec

The uniqueness of a culture can be attributed to a variety of factors. A current dictionary defines them as "the totality of socially transmitted behavior patterns, arts, beliefs, institutions, and all other products of human work and thought."

Where do ghost stories fit in the concept of culture? Perhaps tales of the undead have as much to do with our *beliefs* as with any other aspect of human existence. For as long as there have been identifiable cultures, and in all contemporary cultures of the world, tales of ghosts and hauntings are commonplace. This may be especially true in those cultures that take uncommon measures to retain their history and cultural uniqueness.

French-speaking Canada, especially the province of Quebec, is such a society. Although its seven million people are outnumbered nearly four to one by English Canada, the Quebecois have been successful at remaining distinct and apart from the rest of Canada. From the banning of most signs in English to a requirement that all children study in French schools, Quebec is resolute that French language, culture, and history in North America will not only survive, but flourish.

Tales of the supernatural are as singular as any other aspect of Canadian French society. And that is another good indication that ghost stories have no geographical, cultural, or linguistic barriers.

Mon Père

Jocelyne Choquette makes her home on rue Saint-André in the exhilarating cosmopolitan city of Montreal. Until January 11, 1990, she lived at home with her elderly mother and father. On that day, Jocelyne's father, sixty-nine-year-old Phillippe Choquette, passed away.

But that is not quite correct. He passed *on* . . . but he is most definitely not *away*.

To begin with, the moment of Phillippe's death matches nearly exactly that of his sister. She died in July 1987 at the same age, on the same day of the year, and at the same hour as her brother three years later.

That was only the beginning of this curious story. Phillippe insists upon dropping in unexpectedly on his daughter and wife.

"All through [1993] my father . . . appeared either in dreams or in physical form, giving us advice or warning us of danger," Jocelyne said. "Everything he has said turned out to be true."

Jocelyne's father always appears with the clothes on he was wearing the day he died.

Not unexpectedly, Jocelyne and her mother didn't receive too much support from the rest of their family when they learned about Phillippe's continued presence.

Jocelyne doesn't mind the skepticism. She is content to have her father very near to her and her mother. She especially likes it when he explains things that later turn out to be true.

"For instance, I had a dream in 1991 about my father. It was two weeks before Christmas. In the dream, my father told me about a big surprise for my mother and me on Christmas Day. He assured us he could do everything and that nothing was refused to him. In anticipation, I was very curious and anxious," she said.

Christmas passed without any "surprise" that Jocelyne or her mother could identify. They didn't know why until a few days later.

"On New Year's Eve, my father appeared very clearly at my side with a look of disappointment. I immediately understood that he was hoping to come back for Christmas as flesh and blood."

Jocelyne's mother, Yvette Lamontagne Choquette, has seen her late husband several times, either in the kitchen or in the living room.

"Very often the sudden smell of his cologne could be detected throughout the room," Jocelyn said. "Sometimes it was followed or preceded by another scent which was very pleasant too."

The appearances of Phillippe happen most often in the morning or in the late afternoon, but rarely at night. Jocelyne's two brothers have never been visited by their late father.

The ghost is also quite insistent in giving advice to his daughter. When she has not followed it, she has had "to go through a lot of problems. Today, when my father gives me advice, I listen to him notwithstanding the fact that it is very difficult to understand everything that is happening to us."

As it would be for anyone.

Simon on a Sled

The most persistent ghost legend in Montreal dates to the eighteenth century and concerns one of the city's most colorful characters, the Scottish fur trading baron Simon McTavish. His ghost is said to rest uneasily in a mausoleum on Mount Royal.

To understand McTavish's continued longing for an earthly existence, it is necessary to know a little about his eccentric personality and extravagant life-style, which earned him the nickname of "Le Marquis."

McTavish landed in Canada after living for a number of years in New England during the late 1700s, and established himself in the fur trade. In his early years, he traveled by canoe as far as the Great Lakes buying pelts. He later became a principal owner, with Simon Fraser as one of his partners, of the North-West Company which, from 1780 to 1821, dominated the fur trade throughout most of the North American continent.

The business acumen McTavish exhibited is not what kept most Montrealers enthralled. The man's appetite for hard work was matched equally by his appetite for food—and for love! A bachelor most of his life, he said he was never happy unless he was *in* love, or *falling* in love. Apparently that happened quite frequently. He was equally famous for his grand parties, and for his craving for oysters and alcohol, both of which he consumed in prodigious quantities.

McTavish eventually married a beautiful French-Canadian woman, but it would not be a long union. Therein lies the beginning of the tale of Simon McTavish's ghost.

The old Scotsman promised his bride that atop Mount Royal he would build her the most fabulous mansion in all of Montreal. Today, Mount Royal is the principal landmark by which Montreal is known and a municipal park with a breathtaking view of the city, but in the early 1800s, it was quite possible for the richest man in the city to build his castle wherever he pleased.

McTavish did not live to enjoy either his marriage or his new home. He died in 1805 during the construction of the mansion and was buried in a mausoleum, which can still be seen inside the park on Mount Royal past the end of rue McTavish. The mansion was never completed.

The joie de vivre that made the rich fur trader one of Montreal's great men-about-town might be the reason legends persist that he continues to roam his old neighborhood.

His unfinished mansion came to be called the "haunted house of Mount Royal." Some said that for a long time after McTavish's death, the revelries of great parties could be heard from within its partly completed walls. Those with more fanciful imaginations swore that "fairies" danced on its tin roof. One or two of his old acquaintances whispered that he died after seeing the ghost of a former mistress in the mansion during one of his frequent forays to oversee its construction.

But it is outside, on the wintry slopes of Mount Royal, that Simon McTavish's ghost is in its element. The scene can be grim and quite startling: McTavish is sitting up in his coffin, the lid flung open, tobogganing pell-mell down the mountain!

There may be some truth in the reports that *something* ghoulish did at one time come sliding down Mount Royal. An anatomy professor is said to have lived near the abandoned McTavish mansion during the 1870s. He had a hard time acquiring corpses for class demonstrations and thus employed grave robbers to make forays into the newly built Mount Royal and Côte-des-Neiges cemeteries. They may have transported their "acquisitions" down the mountain aboard sleds and into the professor's waiting wagon. Witnesses could be correct in their assertions that a coffin occasionally came coasting down the snowy slopes, but it might not have been Simon McTavish along for the ride.

Then again, who is to say that his ghost might not have liked to have joined the disturbers of the dead for an impromptu, albeit gruesome, toboggan party?

Father Ghost

The Reverend Humphrey Oswald Slattery thought he was quite alone as he knelt at the altar of St. John the Evangelist Episcopal Church saying his evening devotions. Quite unexpectedly, a chair scraped across the worn stone floor from somewhere toward the back of the empty church. Footsteps came up the center aisle and paused, as if the person were genuflecting. Father Slattery was surprised at the unanticipated intrusion. He turned around to greet the visitor. No one was there.

The ghost of Father Edmund Wood was paying a visit.

During the late 1970s, stories circulated that Father Wood, who died in 1909, was making regular visits to the church he had founded over a hundred years ago. But unlike some encounters with departed souls, those churchmen who believed Father Wood was back did not feel threatened or frightened.

Father Slattery, for instance, said the ghost's presence gave him a feeling of "physical warmth." The damp, stone church would suddenly be filled with "something spiritual," he told reporter Ron Caylor, adding that "many times I have felt despondent, but after encountering Father Wood's presence I leave with a stronger feeling. It's almost like someone's patted you on the back."

Sometimes the priest's ghost would simply play practical jokes, such as hiding objects like devotional candles for several days and then putting them back exactly where they should have been.

Even though Father Wood did not terrorize or disrupt church activities, his occasional wanderings had the capacity to send unwary witnesses into flight. That is what happened to Pastor Harold Parsons. He had been ringing the steeple bells when he had the overwhelming sense that someone else was with him. "I could feel someone behind me get up," he said. At the same time the air seemed to warm significantly. The pastor stopped in mid-toll and left the church.

The Cursed House

Sometimes it is better not to question Providence. Yet the intervention of coincidence or chance or God or whatever one chooses to call it is not always heeded by prudent men and women.

Such was the case in nineteenth-century Montreal at a municipal facility that housed incorrigible children. Built in 1805 in the design of a secure but "homey" structure, the place was soon struck with tragedy. Two children killed the director and his wife and set the house ablaze to cover up their crime. They were soon apprehended and put on trial for murder. They were quickly found guilty of the slayings—and hanged.

That should have been the end of this particular brutality, but it wasn't. The house was rebuilt on its original foundation and passed from owner to owner for the next hundred years. If it is possible for a *locale* to be haunted by past events, this is one of those cases. Murder, suicide, and more unexplained fires plagued the numerous habitués of this cursed house. Zones of frigid air suddenly sprang up in the warmest of its rooms.

In 1905, author Paul Fortier, his pretty young wife Denise, and their lively five-year-old daughter Gisele bought the home and moved in. They knew little of its history. They should have been more careful.

Fortier's inaugural novel, *Fields of Amaranth*, had just been published to generally positive reviews. He had nearly completed a second book and was looking forward to spending his writing career in the distinctive old house.

Denise Fortier was the first to discover the true legacy of the home. Its role in a heinous crime early in the last century was well known in the neighborhood, and perhaps to the real estate agents as well, but everyone failed to warn the Fortiers. Perhaps this was an accident, perhaps it was something more. At any rate, when Denise spoke to neighbors about their home, the story of its past settled heavily on her conscience.

She grew more apprehensive with each passing week. Then her little daughter, Gisele, became affected. The child barely slept through the night; her bedroom seemed afflicted with gnawing cold spots. Perhaps too she sensed her mother's increasingly anxious moods. The poor tot could do little but worry that *"ma mère"* was upset about . . . something.

Denise's visit with her parish priest did little to absolve her of the gnawing fear; he thought the strain of keeping up the large house was too much for her. When she asked him to exorcise her home, he sent her away with more than a little skepticism in his dismissive tone.

Denise came home from the church with the almost palpable understanding that on this night there would come something truly horrible.

Paul seemed especially churlish at dinner. He consumed nearly a full bottle of wine and spoke little to either his wife or his daughter. His behavior had changed since moving into the house; he snapped at Denise whenever she tried to broach the subject of his erratic comportment. He just laughed when she tried to point out those rooms in the house that seemed unnaturally cold, or those in which there seemed to be several pairs of eyes watching her every move. She hardly dared mention those other times when she heard childish laughter that sent chills as cold as the grave itself through her entire body.

The evening was a disaster. Denise knew better than to let Gisele linger too long in such an atmosphere. She carried the child up to bed, whispering all the while that the bright morning sun would cheer them all.

Gisele shook her head. She held her mother tight, begging her to take her away from the house that night. A cold spot had been in her bed last night, she cried. She was afraid it would come back.

Denise tucked the child in and kissed her good-night. Gisele held on to her mother with all the might she could muster in her tiny arms. It was as if to let her mother go would mean the end of her small family.

The events of the next few hours were eventually pieced together from Gisele's tortured memories and the testimony of a few witnesses.

Some hours after she fell asleep, Gisele awoke to the smell of smoke. There were no flames visible nor any sense of extreme heat. She ran down the hallway. Smoke was coming from beneath her parents' bedroom door. She pushed the door open. The bedroom was an inferno. But there was a more horrible sight— her father's lifeless body sprawled on the floor, a pair of scissors buried in his throat; only the bloodied handles were visible. Gisele's eyes shifted to the bed where her frenzied mother was fighting off two small, naked boys who were shaking with soundless laughter as they drove their fists into Denise's bruised and bloody face.

Gisele ran next door for help. When the neighbors arrived the scene was not at all as she had breathlessly related to them. Yes, Paul Fortier's remains were on the floor and Denise was barely conscious on the bed—but there was no fire, no frenzied, naked boys, no smell of smoke. Only the indisputable signs of a murderous quarrel between husband and wife. Denise had apparently fought off her husband's attack by stabbing him in self-defense with the scissors.

That was the verdict of the police, anyway. They dismissed Gisele's account as the sad result of having seen her mother kill her father. Denise lived for several months before succumbing to her critical injuries. She never regained consciousness.

Gisele Fortier moved away to the United States to live with her grandparents.

The Fortiers were the last family to live in the damned house. It burned to the ground—for the last time—in 1906.

A Chance Encounter

Emile Charles Hamel was a prominent journalist, writer, and former Radio Canada employee in Montreal. So it was not surprising to Mlle. Pierrette Champoux, herself a celebrated author and television commentator, when she encountered her old friend at the 1961 convention of the Canadian Association of Journalists at the Queen Elizabeth hotel.

They exchanged pleasantries for several minutes and parted. The only oddity in the encounter was Mlle. Champoux's distinct impression that he had left something unsaid.

He certainly had. What he didn't tell her was that she had just completed a conversation with a ghost.

Pierrette Champoux has had a distinguished career as a writer, fashion analyst, broadcaster, and world traveler. Indeed, her journeys have taken her to the far corners of the world, allowed her to meet the famous and influential, and given her many fascinating adventures. She has written about her life in newspapers, magazines, and in her most recent books, *Parle-moi du Canada/Talk to me of Canada, Raconte-moi Montreal,* and *Les Pionnières.* Her unique style even extends to sending personal stationery embossed with her picture standing amidst a smiling group of Uganda pygmies during one of her African safaris.

Nothing in her public life, however, prepared her for the 1961 adventure with a ghost that she later recounted to author Eileen Sonin.

At about mid-afternoon of Saturday, November 18, 1961, Mlle. Champoux had left a pleasant gathering of fellow journalists attending the convention. The meetings were going well, lunch had been served, but Mlle. Champoux had decided to take her leave.

Just short of the exit, a hand reached out to touch her arm. She turned to see the writer Emile Charles Hamel, a good friend of both Mlle. Champoux and her sister. She had not seen M. Hamel for some time. He graciously kissed her hand and they chatted amiably about her recent experiences, and all the work he had to finish. When she asked if it was quite a lot, he nodded in agreement. "A great deal of work that I have at this time," he phrased it.

She declined his invitation to partake of the dwindling buffet—she had already lunched—and M. Hamel and Mlle. Champoux warmly shook hands. He said they ought to see more of each other and, she later recalled, it seemed that something else was on his mind. But he didn't say anything more and strode away.

The incident passed from Mlle. Champoux's mind. On Monday evening, two days hence, her sister chanced to mention that she had seen a news item in Saturday's newspaper about the sudden death that morning of their friend— Emile Charles Hamel.

Pierrette Champoux was flabbergasted. The newspaper must be in error, she said, because he had been alive and well Saturday afternoon.

"It isn't as if I merely recognized him across the dining room," she told writer Eileen Sonin. "He stopped me as I was leaving, he kissed my hand and we chatted together for quite a time. I know it was Emile. I surely recognize my friends when I meet them."

But her sister was just as insistent that it couldn't have been him because the newspaper said he had died at about 8:00 A.M., a half dozen hours *before* Mlle. Champoux said she had talked to him at the Queen Elizabeth Hotel.

Mlle. Champoux placed a telephone call to General de Verdun Hospital, where the newspaper said he had died. They confirmed the news. Emile Hamel had been an emergency admittance Friday night and had died quite unexpectedly Saturday morning.

Pierrette could not believe what all the evidence, and her respect for the facts, pointed to—that some*how* and for some *reason* she had chatted with Emile's ghost. It didn't make sense to this woman used to dealing with the real world and its verifiable details.

For the next week, Mlle. Champoux closely examined the many articles written in the Quebec press about M. Hamel's death. He had been a prominent member of the media, and thus his untimely passing attracted wide attention. The photographs of him in the articles were definitely of the man Pierrette saw at the hotel. But that was about all of which she was confident.

"I was so nervous and upset," she said. Even her parish priest assured her that he believed what had happened to her. In fact, he added, he wished the same experience would befall him!

Pierrette Champoux has had several other experiences with the supernatural since that 1961 meeting with Emile Charles Hamel's ghost. She intends to publish her experiences in a book.

Still, she is perplexed about that first incident. Why did he choose *her* to visit? Why was her conversation with a *ghost* so normal, so completely ordinary? It would seem that more important news would be passed between the corporeal and incorporeal.

The questions have never been answered. However, Mlle. Champoux has never disputed the reality of the chance encounter—she spoke with a man who had been dead for several hours and never once thought anything was out of the ordinary. Of that she is entirely and forever certain.

Heed Your Promises

When the troubles began, Catherine Longpre was alone with her young son in her house by the river. Her husband, Georges Cloutier, was away working at a logging camp.

The horses wouldn't settle down when she tried to bring them in one evening. They shied away from her, jumping and bucking at her every approach. Exhausted, frustrated, and not a little mystified by her usually docile animals' tumultuous behavior, Catherine paddled a small boat across the river to get help from her neighbor, Eva Duciaume.

The women finally succeeded in getting the horses corralled and went inside the Cloutiers' simple, rural home. Catherine sat down and lit a cigarette. As she snuffed out the match, her gaze shifted to the downstairs bedroom, which she could see through an open door. Her eyes widened. Stacked upon the bed was a pile of firewood normally kept by the stove. It was neatly placed, as if someone had mistaken the old bed with its feather mattress for the wood bin. Except no one other than Catherine and her young child, and now Eva, had been in the house all day. The wood hadn't been there an hour before.

Catherine told Eva that was it—she was truly frightened now and wasn't about to stay by herself in the house any longer.

Catherine Longpre and her husband Georges Cloutier had only one young son, Florian, in 1922, the year the puzzling incidents unfolded at their home not far from Notre-Dame-de-Pontmain in western Quebec.

During a period of several months in 1922, Georges and Catherine's home was possessed. The couple, along with several other witnesses, described a series of unimaginable events that seemed, for a time, to be without explanation.

The history of what happened to the couple and how the mystery was finally resolved by at last following a dying old woman's last request is recounted by Clovis Daoust, who knew some of the people involved and now lives on land once occupied by the Cloutier cabin in rural Notre-Dame-de-Pontmain.

Eva Duciaume had to return to her own home that night, so Catherine hurried to the house of Leon Dicaire and his family. She asked if the boys, Hermas, who was nine, and eleven-year-old Joseph, could keep her company that night. She explained what had transpired and their parents agreed that the boys could help her keep "guard" overnight.

Some years later, Hermas recalled that it was one of the most amazing nights of his life. As he slept in his bed, he saw a rocking chair moving from side to side in the kitchen. Hermas woke up both his brother and Catherine, and they, too, saw the rocker move.

The next morning, Catherine told the boys she hadn't slept the entire night. For most of the time, she said, the flame of an oil lamp that had been left on moved up and down at regular intervals.

Over the next several days, various phenomena were sighted. A large, wet rock rolled noisily down the stairs. Hermas said it looked as if it had come from the river. Georges and Catherine's dog didn't budge, even though the rock landed near him. Later, two other rocks seemed to come from nowhere and collided in midair.

Catherine was nearly hysterical. She sent word to her husband about what was happening in the house and begged him to return from the camp as soon as possible. In the meantime, Catherine moved in with Leon Dicaire and his wife, Rose de Lima Valiquett, the parents of young Hermas and Joseph. The boys were too frightened to stay another night in Catherine's own cabin. They had never seen such things—shoes and baskets would dance about the rooms, an egg-basket slid across the floor, potatoes placed in a sack bounced back out.

Leon and Rose genuinely doubted Catherine's story and looked upon their sons' tales with amusement—until Leon saw with his own eyes one of the most incredible sights he had ever beheld.

On the day after Catherine moved in, she and the Dicaires had gone back to the vacant house to finish some chores. Shortly after noon, they suddenly noticed several pieces of laundry zoom out an open bedroom window, caper down the clothesline and "dance" toward the river. "They came back jumping as if somebody was inside," Hermas recalled. Skirts, stockings, shirts, and trousers bounced back across the ground, up the clothesline, and retreated through the window into the house.

To say the little group was astonished is an understatement. Leon checked all around the house but found no accounting for what had happened.

Later that night, Catherine and the Dicaires observed lights going on and off in various parts of the cabin, sometimes downstairs, then upstairs, and back down and so forth for several minutes at a time.

Georges Cloutier came home the next day from the camp near "Carp's Creek," jesting that his wife was making up the whole story because she was jealous of the two young women cooking for the loggers. But when Leon told him what *he* had seen, Georges grew more serious.

He would soon see for himself that his wife and friends were not joking.

Leon Dicaire left to deliver some oxen he had sold to a man some miles away. Georges and the Dicaire boys spent the day cutting hay. While Catherine prepared supper that evening, Georges and his "apprentices" enjoyed a glass of poutine, an alcoholic brew that his wife made.

Catherine was turning a thick omelette when a loud crash came from the same downstairs bedroom in which she had earlier seen the stacked firewood. Georges rushed to open the door but found it partly blocked by one of the beds inside. He put his shoulder against the door and succeeded in opening it far enough so that he could peek inside—and cried out in astonishment.

The mattress was *floating* several feet above the bed!

The boys came running to the door and stared unbelievingly as the mattress rose to just below the ceiling, banked and crossed the room.

Catherine grabbed her child, and with Georges and the stricken boys ran out of the house and didn't stop until they had all reached the Dicaires'. Leon arrived home shortly thereafter. He went with Georges and another neighbor back to the house. They found the mattress slanted between the two beds in the room. It was stiff. When Leon tried to lift a corner of the mattress to put it back on the bed, it seemed to recoil "as if it had been attacked." Try as they might, the men could not get it out from between the beds.

They left for the night and returned the next day. The mattress was soft and malleable, and the men easily got it back on the bed.

Georges and Catherine had almost decided to move when someone suggested that perhaps the Church could help. Special masses might be said to relieve their home of whatever entity was plaguing it. This they had done; the phenomena vanished for a time, and the little family was allowed to live in peace.

What really happened in that house by the river?

The likeliest explanation of the phenomena was finally offered by Johnny Cloutier, Georges' elderly father. He had lived in the house before his son and daughter-in-law moved in.

He said with some regret that just before his wife, Julie, died in the house and in the bed in the downstairs bedroom, he had promised to have special masses said for her. He had not carried out his promise. Perhaps it was she who was calling attention to the broken pact by creating mischief in her old home.

Johnny also revealed that he often awoke at his new home in Pontmain with someone tugging on his hand. That, too, might have been Julie, he thought.

Georges had the masses sung for his late mother and the phenomena disappeared while he lived there.

In later years there were other stories of that house—of how one could see dancing couples through its windows even though it was unoccupied and the snow was piled halfway up the front door, of how utensils were sometimes found scattered over the kitchen floor, and of how the hand-wound wall clock was found working after an owner had been away for several months.

The house was torn down long ago, its materials used to build a barn and stables, and later a sturdy home that is lived in by Clovis Daoust. But the story of what happened in the old Longpre/Cloutier home remains as alive—and as mystifying—as if it were only yesterday.

The Moose Head Inn Mystery

A cold February night was descending on the Kenosee Lake region of southern Saskatchewan. The year was 1992. An occasional automobile driver passing the landmark Moose Head Inn would not have seen anything out of the ordinary. At seven o'clock on this evening, a few cars huddled in the parking lot, light spilled out of the bar windows onto the compacted snow, and perhaps the rhythms of a country song played on a jukebox might be heard drifting across the roadway. It was well known in the neighborhood that the new owner, Dale Orsted, was resolute in his determination to make the roadhouse the popular nightspot it had once been.

In the third-floor apartment of the inn, Dale and his girlfriend at the time, Adele Wyatt, rested on a couch watching a CBC television program. The faint sounds of bar conversation and music two stories below assured them that all was well.

That was a relief.

Over the past several weeks, as workmen replaced all the carpeting in the building and the other major renovations of the inn seemed to be finally coming to an end, the many small, unexplained annoyances and troublesome noises had frayed their nerves. Lights wouldn't stay off, doors banged open for no reason, and then there would be the footsteps, solid and distinct. The problem was there was no *body* connected to them.

Dale and Adele, along with Jeff Stephen, the manager, really didn't want to think about who—or what—might be causing these vexations. Burglars or trespassers had been discounted. There had even been those times when the trio had questioned their own sanity.

The young couple's serene evening of television and small talk was suddenly shattered. A loud, deep moan, the cry of someone in agony, arose from an adjoining room used as an office. The eerie wail lasted for a full ten seconds before it stopped as abruptly as it had begun.

When the couple gathered their wits about them, they cautiously looked into the room where the sound seemed to have come from. It was as empty as they had expected it to be. They were alone in the apartment, far removed from any of the bar patrons at the Moose Head Inn. The doors going downstairs were securely locked. No other *living* being could have possibly gained access to their apartment.

That was just the problem. The living weren't scaring Dale and Adele and Jeff. On that night in February, the haunting of Moose Head Inn by an entity they came to call "Stanley" became a reality for Dale Orsted and his companions.

The story of the Moose Head Inn begins early in this century. The Hungarian community near Kipling built a church and, a short distance away, a dance hall for the far-flung neighbors to gather on Saturday nights. That area, known as Bekavar, is about twenty miles northwest of Kenosee. For the next half century, teenagers and adults enjoyed weekly parties and dances at Bekavar Hall. But patterns of entertainment changed and attendance dropped off. Radio, and later television, along with quicker access to the metropolitan areas of Regina and Winnipeg, forced many rural community halls to close by the 1960s.

In 1966, Archebald and Ethel Grandison purchased over two acres of land in the popular summer resort of Kenosee Lake, in Moose Mountain Provincial Park of southeastern Saskatchewan. Two years later the couple began construction of what they called "Grandison Hall." They bought the Bekavar dance hall and added it atop their original building. A third-floor apartment was later built.

From 1970 to 1979, it was "one of the most popular and busiest places in Saskatchewan, because it [was] located in the provincial park," Dale Orsted said. As a teen, he spent nearly every summer at his family's cabin in Kenosee and attended many teen dances at Grandison's dance hall.

Illness forced the Grandisons to sell the place in 1979 to a group of buyers, including Reg Dlouhy. He is credited with the remodeling of the hall into the fine nightclub that came to be known as Moose Head Inn.

In 1989 Dale Orsted learned his old teen hangout was for sale and purchased the property. He took over the business in March 1990. Within weeks the puzzling adventures that Dale and others labeled a "haunting" began to occur.

"Immediately after taking possession, I began some renovations in the cabaret room, on the second floor," Dale remembered. "New bars were built, the deejay booth was removed and relocated."

After the renovations were begun, Dale said, small items would "go missing" only to mysteriously reappear a few weeks later in the same place in which they had last been seen. One of the oddest incidents involved a box of till tape for the cash register. Dale said three people searched for the box of tape several times. It later showed up right where it should have been.

"That also happened with other items in the bar," Dale said, adding that the bar was not open to the public until May 1990. "I thought perhaps previous employees had keys and had taken the items. I had every lock in the building rekeyed or replaced and it still happened."

Meanwhile, Dale and his girlfriend had moved into the third-floor apartment.

"We would be awakened to a series of loud bangings in the cabaret," Dale said. "[It] would continue on and off for more than half an hour. Because we believed someone must have been breaking in, we called the RCMP, but nothing could ever be found."

Most of the incidents happened at night.

"The loudness . . . was impossible to re-create during the daytime," Dale said. "We tried banging on doors and windows but couldn't create the intensity or violence of the [original]."

Security cameras were installed because Dale thought someone was trying to break in. The banging was recorded on one camera, but instead of sounding as if someone were trying to get *in*, the noise clearly came from *inside* the inn.

"We also added motion detectors connected to an alarm in the apartment," Dale said. "On one occasion when the banging was happening, I looked up the phone number of the police and a gust of wind blew across the phone book and moved the page."

The police did eventually arrive, but found absolutely no sign of intruders, nor any evidence of someone lurking about outside.

"As the police checked out the building downstairs," Dale remembered, "Adele heard footsteps come up to the apartment. She thought I was bringing the police upstairs. However, the door leading to the stairway was locked at the time and we were on a different floor when she heard the footsteps."

Adele waited for Dale to call out a greeting, or stick his head in the room. He didn't, of course, because it wasn't Dale she heard. And she *should* have known better—distinct footfalls coming up the stairway to the locked apartment door have been heard by three other people at different times. And never does anyone knock on the door.

Other Inn staff members had their own stories.

A kitchen worker said that one night the heavy door to a walk-in cooler was opened and then slammed shut.

"Before [the incident] I didn't believe in it," the man said. "And now you start second-guessing a lot of stuff. It's hard to say you don't believe in ghosts. The cooler opened and shut and there's no way it could have done that. I was there."

Dale Orsted said an incident in the bar "made firm believers out of some skeptics." A dishwasher suddenly started up by itself, ran for ten seconds and then shut off. As if it were a scene from an old western movie, everyone in the room suddenly stopped talking and stared at the machine, their mouths hanging open.

There were other, closer encounters. Something brushed against Jeff Stephen's arm when he reached for a light switch in a darkened room . . . Dale saw lights on one morning as he arrived for work, but by the time he got inside they were off, and no one else was there . . . doors locked one minute and unlocked the next became fairly "routine" for the owner and manager of the inn.

For some time after the completion of Orsted's renovations things seemed to quiet down at the Moose Head Inn. There were the occasional items that would go missing, or a footstep or two in the night, but the infernal booming and banging that seemed to threaten the very walls of the inn had disappeared.

Until the first week of February 1992. That's when all hell broke loose.

"I removed the old carpeting from the cabaret floor," Dale explained. "That night at approximately nine P.M. extreme loud banging began to happen. Jeff

Stephen . . . and myself were sound asleep when it began. We went downstairs and checked the building. No one was [there]. When we went back upstairs the banging started again. This occurred every night during the renovations at approximately the same time."

Not only did Jeff and Dale hear it, but so did Dale's girlfriend, Adele Wyatt, and another friend who was persuaded to spend the night in the inn.

"This is when we began to believe that there *must* be a ghost," Dale said.

The removal of the old carpeting took several weeks. All during that time, employees were subjected to nearly daily events attributed to the "ghost."

"Lights that were turned off, turned on," Dale said. "Doors with emergency panic hardware would bang open when people were in the cabaret. That happened at least ten different times with many different witnesses. The doors were always kept closed and needed a good push to open them."

Whatever pushed open the doors usually waited until after the crowds had gone and only a few employees were left cleaning up.

"When [the banging] was happening every night," Dale said, "I thought whatever it was, was too dangerous. [At times] there were almost explosionlike sounds."

The turning point came on that night when the new carpet was finally installed. That was the evening Dale and Adele were relaxing in their apartment's living room.

"From an adjoining room, a very eerie moaning sound lasted for about ten seconds, as if someone was in extreme pain," Dale said. That room is kept locked unless someone is using the office.

There would be more trouble that night. At about four o'clock in the morning, a tremendous crash just outside their locked apartment literally knocked the couple out of bed.

"It came from the same room as the moaning did earlier," Dale recalled. "It was as loud and as violent as if you were in a head-on car crash. The impact broke dishes in our sink, and water began running from the faucet. It was the first time the banging occurred upstairs where we lived. The actual crash was incredible. I can't even describe it. The panic we felt. You could feel a rush of energy."

Dale carefully crept out to check the room from which the noise had erupted.

"The room was exactly as it was before, nothing was out of place. I tried to re-create the crash by dropping items and jumping off a steel office desk, but it wasn't until I picked up an end of the desk and dropped it that the same crash sound was created. The only way the same *intensity* could be re-created would be to take four people to lift the desk above their heads and drop it."

The doors leading into the apartment from the lower floors were locked as usual, and, as usual, the door into the office was dead-bolted. "There is no way anyone was in that room because of all the locked doors," Dale insisted. That night was enough for Adele Wyatt. She never stayed overnight in the Moose Head Inn again.

On Monday, April 27, 1992, the daily newspaper in Regina, Saskatchewan, carried an account of the haunting at Moose Head Inn. So many people had heard about the events there, or had witnessed one or more of the episodes, that it was impossible to keep them secret.

But Dale Orsted disavows any ulterior motive. "We didn't do this as a publicity stunt," he said. "It really happened to us and the story got out."

In the article, Dale mentioned an earlier attempt to contact a Winnipeg investigator of the paranormal, Roy Bauer. While the haunting was at its peak in early February, Adele Wyatt had called Bauer when her local newspaper ran an article about his avocation of ghost-hunting. Unfortunately, Adele didn't leave her telephone number, and Bauer failed to write down the pertinent information about the haunting.

Bauer, who is a trained electronics engineer, received a copy of the April 27 Regina newspaper article and proceeded to contact Orsted. Although the inn had been relatively "haunt-free" for several weeks, Bauer thought the case sounded interesting enough to look into. Also, the CBC-TV program "News Magazine" had earlier asked permission to accompany Bauer on one of his investigations. Bauer warned the television crew "not to expect a ghost to walk by the camera."

"I believe in what we call ghosts today, that there is something going on," Bauer said at the time. "I wouldn't necessarily say it's the spirits of people who have died [and] who have somehow remained in that location and are still roaming around in the house. . . . On the surface, that's what it seems to be and there's a very good chance that's what it is. But I'm willing to explore all possibilities."

Bauer undertook his investigation of the inn over a period of several days beginning on Sunday, May 24, 1992. After extensive interviews with Dale Orsted, Adele Wyatt, Jeff Stephen, and others, Bauer concluded that the cause of the disturbances was probably a ghost because the incidents had happened to too many people, including numerous visitors.

"I have classified all paranormal into three categories which are: poltergeist, hauntings and apparitions," Bauer wrote in a letter to Dale summarizing his findings. "Each of these categories has characteristics particular to that type of event."

Bauer eliminated a poltergeist since the incidents had happened to visitors. He also ruled out what he termed a haunting.

What was going on was very possibly a "classic" apparition, Bauer said, adding that an apparition is similar to a haunting in that some form of "intelligence" survives after death.

"It can therefore react to events in its surroundings," Bauer said. "What most strongly indicates an intelligence is the mischievous nature of the events, seeming only to attract attention, but not repeating itself when people are waiting for things to happen."

The best example, Bauer said, was the banging that usually took place when people were asleep, but subsided when anyone got up to look around. It started up again when everyone went back to bed.

On Sunday night, May 24, Bauer began his search for the apparition at Moose Head Inn. With the CBC cameras recording his moves, he set up sophisticated recording equipment and sensitive microphones. He hoped to catch "ghost sounds" during the early morning hours.

"[The CBC] set up two cameras in the cabaret; one was just taping and the other was taping and also being monitored upstairs in the apartment," Bauer said. He would be staying all night in the apartment Dale Orsted by now had refused to occupy. "We stayed up until three-thirty watching the monitor and listening for sounds. I had set up my tape recorder in the dining room. It was connected to a timer which would turn on for an hour at four-thirty."

It was relatively quiet all night, Bauer said. A distant echo of footsteps recorded on tape he attributed to one of the crew members walking around. The CBC journalist on the scene, Sasa Petricic, did report that earlier in the evening some lights that had been turned *off* when the cabaret was closed and locked for the night were found *on* about ten minutes later. No one could explain how that happened.

By four-thirty, the CBC crew had retreated to their motel rooms and Bauer had called it a night.

"The next morning I was up by eight," Bauer said. "I checked on the tape recorder to see if it had recorded anything. I started playing back the tape and noticed something unusual. I was hearing two tracks simultaneously. I had previously recorded a talk show which could still be heard, along with the recording of the dining room. I tried to duplicate this effect, but could not. It seems as though the erase head had malfunctioned and the recorder recorded on one track only. I listened to the entire tape hearing various sounds which I attributed to the machinery in the room."

The CBC crew also watched and listened to their tapes but they, too, found nothing of significance.

Despite the haunt-hunters' failure to detect any ghostly visitors, Bauer considered the Moose Head Inn a good case. "I would say yes because of the multiple witnesses, especially since they weren't connected to each other."

Bauer has developed a grading system for the hauntings he's investigated. On the authenticity level, Bauer gives the inn a four rating out of a possible five. A zero would be a single witness, while a five represents many witnesses.

For severity, Bauer ranks the inn at about the middle of his scale because there wasn't a great deal of physical disruption during the times of peak activity.

During his interviews with Dale Orsted and Jeff Stephen on Sunday, Bauer had isolated two potential causes for the apparition.

The first theory had to do with local legends surrounding the church that had owned the community hall which Mr. and Mrs. Grandison had moved and rebuilt as the original dance hall. That hall is now incorporated into the inn's cabaret.

Some residents believe the church to be haunted. Automobiles allegedly lose power when passing nearby, two people are said to have been killed within weeks of visiting the church, and others claim an eerie glow emanates from the place on certain nights. Most interesting of all is the rumor that a minister committed suicide in its tower.

However, Bauer was doubtful of the church's relationship to the haunting because the community hall had never been a *physical* part of the church proper.

The accuracy of a minister's suicide is dubious. The son of the longest-serving minister at the church told CBC interviewers: "I'm sure there wasn't anyone committed suicide there. Not a minister. I don't know where that story came from, but there's nothing to it. It's actually not a fact at all."

Bauer was not able to pinpoint any unexplained deaths connected to the church. And as for the "eerie glow," Bauer said it "seems to stem from the fact that the church is almost white, with the roof practically black. This contrast, especially when the moon is out, would reflect off the church, making it visible for miles around."

The only other potential "suspect" Bauer identified was the original builder, the late Archebald Grandison. He quite literally put his entire life and fortune into the project. He suffered a heart attack shortly thereafter, never fully able to appreciate the business he had built with his own hands. He died over a decade ago.

"He did not have the opportunity to gradually give up the inn, but rather one day he was running it and the next day he wasn't," Bauer theorized. "Some portion of his consciousness and memories was drawn back to the inn. . . ."

Bauer said Archebald's ghost had been content to quietly roam the inn for twenty years, but then became more active when Dale Orsted undertook major renovations. "Now his hard work is being changed and it is not to his liking. He becomes active to let people know he's there. . . . After the renovations are complete his anger dissipates, but he still plays pranks on people to let them know he is around and will continue [to be] so long as the inn is standing," Bauer contended.

But the case for Archebald as ghost didn't sit well with his widow, Ethel.

"My husband loved that hall and he loved the kids that came there. He really enjoyed those dances. But he wouldn't haunt it," Mrs. Grandison firmly told CBC interviewer Sasa Petricic.

Ghost hunter Roy Bauer may be right in saying the haunting of Moose Head Inn has to do with the renovations Dale Orsted made to it, but he may have the *identity* of the ghost wrong. At least that's what Dale now believes.

At the time of the CBC interview and Bauer's visit to the inn, Dale didn't know about Reg Dlouhy's role in transforming the inn from the Grandisons' original dance hall into the nightclub it became in the early 1980s. Dlouhy, who died in 1983, and three partners, including Eleanor Sedger (Jeff Stephen's aunt), bought "Grandison's Hall" in 1979 after Archebald became ill. Mrs. Grandison could not operate the nightspot by herself.

Reg and his brother did most of the original remodeling. The men transformed what had been a large dance hall into a unique restaurant and nightclub. New rooms were built, expensive paneling installed, an entertainment system added to the cabaret, a large bar added, and dining facilities enlarged.

Unfortunately, a dispute among the owners led to Reg Dlouhy's being bought out by his partners. According to Dale Orsted, Reg had the carpentry skills for the remodeling and worked as the on-site manager—even living in the apartment for over a year—but he had no money invested in the project.

He was "bitter over the takeover," Dale said, noting that several people who knew Reg have told him that his anger over being bought out makes it reasonable to assume he might now be haunting the inn.

"He didn't have a reason to haunt the place until changes were made" to his original design, Dale said. "I tend to believe it is more possible the 'ghost' may be Reg Dlouhy than Mr. Grandison."

Ironically, Roy Bauer may have helped to pinpoint Reg as the source of the haunting without even knowing it.

In a letter to Dale and Jeff, dated June 23, 1992, Bauer recounted a telephone conversation he had with a psychic during which they discussed the Moose Head Inn case. Although Bauer still thought at that time that the ghost was Archebald Grandison, the psychic's comments could be interpreted as referring to Reg Dlouhy.

"Near the end of the conversation she started telling me things about the Inn and who was haunting it," Bauer said in his letter. "She related information which I was and was not familiar with. She had not seen the article in the *Regina Leader-Post* nor heard the CBC radio interview that Dale and I did. She claimed to have fallen asleep just minutes before the 'News Magazine' piece came on [although] she may have subconsciously remembered the show even when she was asleep." Bauer forwarded to Dale and Jeff those comments that he believed may have indicated that the psychic had "tuned in" to the haunting at the inn. The first set of comments related to the inn or events related to it:

- *Hardwood not original.* At one time the rooms had all-hardwood floors.
- *Stairs have been changed.* The stairway from the third-floor apartment to the cabaret has been changed.
- *Proud of the place.* Reg was very satisfied with his work. The building is unique. Everyone involved in the business is proud of it.
- *Ruffle sound.* There is often a noise like that of someone working in a wood-shop.
- *Cabinlike atmosphere.* The interior of the building is all wood, like that of a north woods cabin.
- *Female in charge/didn't like her at all.* The previous owner was a female. Reg had a falling out with the owners.
- *Western-style buffalo.* A moose head is hanging on one wall. The psychic also noted items such as "church in the distance," "won't hurt anyone—just hanging around," "brothers," "strong-willed," "opposite of the way he liked it before," which could relate to the ghost itself.

Roy Bauer listed twenty-five additional characteristics about the "ghost" that the psychic disclosed in her telephone call. It's not possible to relate *all* of them to Reg Dlouhy, but several seem to point in his direction, Dale Orsted believes, especially those that deal with his stubbornness and his desire to be recognized for the work he did at the inn.

*   *   *

Of the dozen or more hauntings he's investigated over the past decade, Bauer still considers the events at the Moose Head Inn some of his most mysterious encounters.

"I would rank it as one of the most severe cases because of the bangings," he said. "It definitely is paranormal. I don't think it can cause a lot of harm, it's just causing a lot of disruption."

Bauer has done less work investigating haunted houses in the past year.

"I'm more skeptical now than I was at the beginning. I think many cases are like telepathic hallucinations," he said. But he is quick to emphasize that this doesn't imply any "mental illness" on the part of witnesses, simply that what is going on doesn't occur "in our physical space." That's especially true, he said, when only one person in a group will "see" something the others don't.

Nothing even remotely matching the events of early 1992 has taken place at the Moose Head Inn. The last major "disruption" occurred in September 1993. Dale Orsted had installed a new center-island bar and changed the appearance of the second-floor cabaret. During the week after the work was completed, a caretaker heard chairs and tables being moved in that area after closing. He was alone in the building. Manager Jeff Stephen heard the same noises and he, too, failed to figure out their cause.

"It was just like the tables and chairs were being moved. It was like Reg was putting things back the way they were," Dale said.

The small peculiarities have become almost routine for him. A heavy fire door will swing open when no one is near it, or the occasional clatter of unidentified footsteps will stop a conversation in mid-sentence.

No one lives in the inn's apartment now. Dale Orsted and Jeff Stephen had enough of the infernal night sounds. They hired a caretaker to keep an eye on the inn.

"I was ready to walk away from the place after that first week of noises nearly every night," Dale said. He was mostly concerned that there really *was* a human source for the mystery. "I wasn't so much scared by any entity" as he was by a burglar, he said. The inn has been broken into once.

For now, Dale Orsted is content to maintain his ownership at a distance and let the tourists and locals enjoy the ambience and hospitality that the inn provides. The haunting doesn't seem to have disrupted the popularity the nightspot enjoys. But Dale is still wary after hours, never quite sure what to expect when the lights go out.

"It's more in the not knowing what you're scared of. You know there's *something* there—but you don't know what it is."

Personal Ghosts

Whether it's because of the long, cold winter nights they must endure or the great distances they must travel to visit friends and relatives, Canadians are great storytellers. Among the best tales are those recounting encounters with the supernatural, as told by the people involved.

Tarlton Maternity Home

Nearly sixty years ago, Marie Gibbs was a young girl of ten living in Swift Current, Saskatchewan, when her father announced that the family would be moving into a large old place he had found. Housing was scarce in the town during those Depression years, and the reasonable rent made the house doubly attractive.

But Marie's mother was not pleased. She and her husband argued over the plan. "I will not move into *that* house," Marie's mother insisted. She lost the argument, however. It was the only house they could afford, her husband insisted.

"Nothing more was said but I noticed that Mom would never stay in the house alone at night," Marie remembers. She grew to learn the reason for her mother's fears.

"As time went by I heard strange sounds throughout the house, but more so at night when footsteps . . . ascended the stairs and [then went] down an L-shaped hall which led to the bedroom I shared with my older sister," Marie says.

On one night in particular, Marie's father came bustling into the girls' bedroom.

"Are you all right?" he asked, his brow wrinkled in concern. "I heard someone walking around and then the door of your room opened."

The girls assured their worried father that they were both perfectly safe in their beds.

"I must have been dreaming." He smiled.

He said that "so as not to alarm us, I'm sure," Marie says now. It was clear to her that her mother's concerns were shared to some extent by her father.

The peculiar sounds in the night became almost routine for Marie's family, so much so that the matter was hardly discussed. Only after repeated attempts by Marie and her sister did their mother reveal her continued displeasure at being forced to live in the house.

At one time the house had been the "infamous" Tarlton Maternity Home, a private hospital designed solely for expectant mothers, and ruled over by an owner/matron known for her cold demeanor and unsympathetic ways, especially toward women whose babies had been stillborn.

"Eventually she went insane and died in a mental institution," Marie notes. Soon after that the maternity home was closed and the property put up for rent.

Ironically, Marie's sister had been born in the very same room she now shared with Marie. It had once been the Tarlton's delivery room. "Due to a very difficult pregnancy, Mom spent forty days there, and they were forty days in hell," Marie recalls her mother saying, attributing most of her suffering to the matron's cruelty.

Marie believes the ghostly footsteps and opening doors were the products of the ghosts of the many women who died in childbirth coming to claim their babies in the old delivery room.

Or perhaps, she avers, it might be the matron herself, continuing on her night rounds—always at eleven o'clock, the time when the footsteps were the most pronounced—checking on the young mothers in labor.

The old house once called the Tarlton Maternity Home still stands in Swift Current. Marie Gibbs said she has been told tenants are never retained for very long.

And she knows why.

The Cottage

During the late 1960s Jean Moore took her two children—then ages seven and four—to a cottage on Saskatchewan Beach for the summer. She was very happy to find such an idyllic warm-weather retreat, but a series of events that took place there one night were so "strange" that Jean remembers them clearly to this day.

The well-kept cabin had been in the same family for nearly sixty years. It was "marvelous," Jean recalled, noting that a rocking chair, a unique freestanding hammock, and several interesting pieces of wicker furniture remained in the living room. A china cabinet held an eccentric collection of teacups and saucers which Jean and her children used for "elegant" tea parties. "Some of the saucers even matched the cups!" she said.

A narrow staircase led to an attic room that the children called "the tower," in which they would play for hours on rainy summer afternoons.

"We had a good view of the lake from the living room windows," Jean said. "Many times that summer the three of us watched as a storm swept down the lake like a fury draped in gray mist, finally crashing in on us with howling winds and curtains of water."

The children were especially pleased if the electricity went out. Then they weie permitted to light the kerosene lamp with its beautiful china bowl and delicately fluted chimney.

On the night Jean Moore remembers so well, the children had been in bed only a short while when a storm rose over the lake. As it bore down on the snug little cottage by the shore, Jean secured the windows and doors more carefully than usual and then went to bed. Her bedroom opened off one side of the living room; her children's rooms were located directly across the living room from her.

"I lay awake in bed for some time, quite happily watching the living room light up with each flash of lightning, and when the thunder finally subsided I drifted off to sleep," Jean said.

"I don't know how long I slept, but the storm was over, and when I woke it was sudden, as though I'd been called from a deep and dreamless state. For a few seconds I was aware only of total silence, total darkness, and of a total, all-encompassing, senseless . . . fear. My heart was pounding violently. I was drenched in sweat."

The fear that paralyzed Jean Moore was caused by a sense that there was *something* in the darkness at the foot of her bed. Something in the blackness she could not see. Her eyes seemed to be on stems that reached out and through the night to identify whatever it was that lurked there.

"I couldn't speak or cry out," she said. It was not an intruder, Jean knew. "It wasn't that type of fear."

For what seemed like an eternity, the young mother was immobilized by this silent horror, unable to utter as much as a single syllable.

"Just when I thought my heart would burst, I had the sense that whatever it was, was moving out of my room. It seemed to be shuffling slowly across the living room toward the children's rooms."

Still she was unable to move, even though the thing was heading toward her sleeping tots.

"Mother, is that you?" Jean's seven-year-old son suddenly cried out from his room.

Minutes passed—or was it merely several seconds?—before Jean found her voice.

"Are . . . you . . . all right, son?" Jean's voice was strained as she called back.

"Yes, I'm okay, Mom," came his weak reply.

The sun was shining through the curtained windows when Jean awoke from her fitful sleep. Had she been dreaming? she wondered. A horrible nightmare kindled by the thunderstorm . . . She leaped from bed and ran barefoot across the living room. She threw open the doors to her children's separate rooms. Both were sleeping soundly. A quick check of the windows and outside doors showed they had not been disturbed. Surely there *had* been something about in the cabin last night . . . and yet . . .

At breakfast a few hours later, Jean casually asked her son why he had called out to her during the night.

He paused a few seconds before saying, "Something was in my room."

"What was it?" Jean coaxed.

"I don't know," the boy said thoughtfully, "but it was black and round. I was too scared to turn on the light so I turned over and pretended to be asleep."

The boy then added a peculiar afterthought. "I think it was smiling at me, though."

He told his mom that when he turned back over to look at where the thing had been, there was nothing there.

Jean Moore still wishes she knew what had been in her cottage.

Windcrest

The 1830 farmhouse known as the old Hagen Place had an almost mystical pull on the middle-aged couple. When it came on the market finally, it was a foregone conclusion that they would buy it for a combination summer/retirement retreat. Little did they know that a ghost they came to call the "old lady" would also share their lives in the home they renamed Windcrest.

The couple's daughter, M. R. Mulvale, of Greenwood, Nova Scotia, said that her mother described "only half in jest" the ghost's activities over the years.

"As they drove away to the city after a weekend at Windcrest," M. R. said, "my mother regularly noticed the curtains move in the window of the only unused room upstairs. The house's door was routinely hooked shut [because the door latch was broken] before they left—and just as routinely was found unhooked upon their return the following Friday." No other signs of disturbance were ever found, nor was there evidence of a break-in by burglars.

"My father also accepted the old lady's residence, but he never gave specific details of any encounters. But whenever he couldn't find a particular tool, he was quick to implicate her and her 'borrowing' habits."

But an incident in 1970 involving M. R. and her two children convinced everyone that Windcrest did, indeed, harbor a mysterious spirit.

"Kate, who was three, had long conversations with who-knows-whom at bedtime as a matter of course," M. R. said. Neither mother nor grandparents paid much attention to the child's patter, assuming she could see someone they couldn't.

The other child was Terry, a very active three-month-old who, according to his mother, was "the world champion kicker-off of blankets in his age group." She said he would chatter at length while kicking off his blankets and falling asleep.

"One evening I went upstairs and tucked him in after he had thrashed himself to sleep. Sometime later, he awoke and repeated his bedtime performance—heard by four adults. I told my mother we would let him wear himself out."

Within a few minutes the thumps and bumps and wails from his crib ceased. Wanting to make sure that her son was all right, M. R. went upstairs to the bedroom and peeked inside.

"He was sound asleep," M. R. said, "and tucked in tightly. Unless he had been bellowing full tilt without moving a muscle, somebody had soothed him and tucked him in again."

And, she concludes, "it wasn't any *physical* being in the house." Even ghosts must have a hard time sleeping through a toddler's cries.

Doctor Stewart

The inexperienced may find it strange that real-life hauntings are quite often nothing to be feared. To many people, the knowledge that there is someone *unseen* with them while they go about their daily tasks is a comfort, and brings a peacefulness that is difficult to explain.

Such is the case with Miriam Siwak, of Sydney, Nova Scotia. She works for a stevedoring firm housed in an old building on the Government Wharf in that Cape Breton Island city. During World War II, the structure was used as a naval hospital. It's no wonder that an occasional apparition would make an appearance where life and death walked hand-in-hand.

"I have seen images in different sections of the building," Miriam began. "So many times that I no longer think it strange. But one night something different happened. I was working late and alone when I smelled pipe tobacco. Not smoke, but fresh tobacco. I thought nothing about it at first . . . but then it happened again. Not only does no one smoke in our office, but there hadn't been a pipe smoker in it for months."

The stevedore company has the only offices in the building, so Miriam doubted the pipe smoke could be coming from elsewhere. Later, Miriam related the incident to a friend. He reported back to her that his own father said the pipe smoke was probably coming from "Doctor Stewart," a physician during the years the building had been a hospital. He was "always filling his pipe," Miriam was told. Although she hasn't been able to strictly confirm the identity of the doctor, Miriam points to several other incidents as proof that the good doctor, or someone, haunts the offices. She calls him—it?—her "friend."

"I was talking to my niece and the owner of the firm, 'Jim,' when he asked me if there was anyone else in the building. I told him that there wasn't. He then said my 'friend' had just walked into my office! He described [what he had seen] as a silhouette in the shape of a man gliding into my office. That is exactly how I had described my 'friend' to other people after I had seen him."

The firm's secretary was working late one afternoon when she heard a man cough in one of the lower offices. She didn't think anything of it until she left her office a few minutes later. No one else was in the building. Who, then, coughed? Fearful of answering her own question, the secretary grabbed her coat and left.

One of Miriam's friends has had two unsettling experiences in the old building. Once he stopped in his office on Saturday morning to check for incoming faxes. He had his dog with him. "He was walking down the hall and his dog came up to the . . . washroom door and started to growl," Miriam recalled. "My friend knew someone was in the washroom and suspected a burglar. The dog growled steadily and all the hair stood up on her back. My friend went in to check and there was nothing to be seen. He closed the washroom door, but the dog stayed out there until he left the office. He knew there was something there, but only the dog could see it."

Several times Miriam's friend has heard file cabinet drawers opening and papers being shuffled noisily about in offices that are dark and locked.

Miriam Siwak is one of those witnesses to the supernatural who take the experience in stride.

"I know my friend is here. I feel he will always protect me. I don't fear being alone in the office; the only thing that frightens me when I work at night are the living who hang around the wharf area. If the spirit that occupies this office *were* evil I would have been gone long ago. I feel only peace when I work alone."

For that, Doctor Stewart—or whoever—deserves to be commended!

Bibliography

Alabama

BOOKS

Steiger, Brad. *Real Ghosts, Restless Spirits and Haunted Minds.* New York: Award Books, Universal-Award House, Inc., 1968.
————. *True Ghost Stories.* Rockport, Mass.: Para Research, 1982.

PERIODICALS

Campbell, Dwayne, and Tim Willoughby. "There ain't no such thang as 'haints'. . ." *The Cullman Tribune,* June 23, 1977.
Dunnavant, Bob. "Yankee soldier is still lurking at old depot." *Birmingham Post-Herald,* July 26, 1979.
"The Face in the Window" or "The Ghost in the Garret." Account by Town of Carrollton, Alabama, n.d.
Hogan, Ann. "Rocky Hill Remembered for Its Grandeur." *Moulton Advertiser,* July 26, 1973 (reprinted from *The Huntsville Times,* March 12, 1967).
Mac Guire, Buster. "The Ghost House of Camden." Moulton *Advertiser* November 14, 1976.
"The McEntire House." The Decatur Chamber of Commerce, Decatur, Alabama, March 14, 1957.
Nagel, George. "Interesting Tale Told of Old McEntire House in Decatur." *The Birmingham News,* July 7, 1940.
————. "Mrs. Charles Waller Actually Has Seen a Real Apparition." *The Birmingham News,* September 29, 1940.
Rawls, Phillip, and Ginger Grantham. "South Alabama Abounds with Eerie Ghost Stories." *The Montgomery Advertiser/Alabama Journal,* December 31, 1976.
Salter, Charles. "A Ghostly Tale from Stover Creek." *The Atlanta Journal and Constitution,* May 28, 1978.
————. "Ghosts? No, but Footsteps Are There." *The Atlanta Journal and Constitution,* September 10, 1978.
Sentell, Lee. "The Ghosts of McEntire." *Decatur Daily,* June 20, 1971.
Sikora, Frank. "Dead man's face marks courthouse." *The Birmingham News,* December 6, 1981.
"Spirit 78." *Powergram,* October 1974.
Spotswood, Frances. "Fall cleanup seems assured at Homewood haunted house." *The Birmingham News,* October 27, 1966.
Truchon, Frank. "Ghostly goings-on in Alabama related by Mrs. Windham." *The Birmingham News,* November 21, 1977.

Watkins, Ed. "The face in the window still big draw in Carrollton." *Tuscaloosa News*, July 9, 1974.
Windham, Kathryn T. "The ghosts of Alabama." *The Sun*, July 15, 1971.

UNPUBLISHED WORKS

Eskridge, Dena Fay. Letter from Courtland Public Library, Courtland, Ala., September 4, 1984.
Interview with Don Turnipseed, February 1985.

Alaska

BOOKS

Pamphlet from Golden North Hotel, Skagway, Alaska, n.d.
Keithahn, Edward L. *Alaskan Igloo Tales*. Anchorage: Alaska Northwest Publishing Co., n.d.
Lokke, Carl L. *Klondike Saga*. Minneapolis: University of Minnesota Press, 1965. (Published for the Norwegian-American Historical Association.)

PERIODICALS

Carpenter, Tom. "This ghost is one of the family!" *Woman's World*, December 6, 1984.
Dirlam, Sharon. "Spirit of boom-town days lives again in Skagway." *The Milwaukee Journal*, July 21, 1985.

Arizona

BOOKS

Peterson, Thomas H., Jr. *Fort Lowell, A. T. Army Post During the Apache Campaigns*. Published by the Tucson Corral of the Westerners (Fall 1963, Revised 1976, No. 8).
Smith, Susy. *The Power of the Mind*. Chilton Book Co., Radnor, PA 1975.

PERIODICALS

Biere, Francine. "Ghosts of the Old West." *Accent*, October 1983.
Bowden, Charles. "When things go bump in the night." *Tucson Citizen*, October 29, 1982.
Collins, Christina. "Ghosts." *Tucson Citizen*, October 29, 1977.
Fowler, Larry. "Ghost in Catalina High halls?" *Tucson Citizen*, October 31, 1980.
Huff, Dan. " 'Ghost's' house is sold, but memories linger on." *Tucson Citizen*, n.d.
Hunt, Nancy Lee. "Old-time ghost in modern building." *Arizona Daily Wildcat*, October 31, 1989.
Knight, Susan M. "Reporter's past puts her in ghostly spirit." *Arizona Daily Star*, October 30, 1980.

——— . "Spooky goings-on send family fleeing to new home." *Arizona Daily Star*, October 30, 1980.

Loughran, Joe. "Old building reflects development of post." *The Huachuca Scout*, October 30, 1980.

———. "Will the ghost walk at Carleton House?" *The Huachuca Scout*, October 30, 1980.

McDaniel, Doug. "Things go bump in night at UA." *Arizona Daily Wildcat*, October 23, 1981.

Merrill, Debbi. "Ghost story on old post will not die." *Arizona Daily Star*, January 26, 1986.

———. "Ghost tale haunts Fort Huachuca." *Sierra Vista Herald*, February 13, 1986.

Negri, Sam. "The ghost of Fort Huachuca." *Arizona Republic*, March 23, 1986.

Porter, Claire. "Tucson 'haunts': spirits, places of local legend." *The Territorial*, October 25, 1984.

Rosenblum, Keith. "Ghosts—Hunt for spirits' haunts fruitless task in Tucson." *Arizona Daily Star*, October 28, 1979.

Schellie, Don. "Phantom hitchhiker time once again." *Tucson Citizen*, May 25, 1979.

———. "Where are the Tucson ghosts?" *Tucson Citizen*, June 28, 1979.

Shuttleworth, Stan. " 'Charlotte' lives on at Carleton House." *Sierra Vista Sunday News*, June 21, 1981.

Sinclair, Murray. "One of Tucson's Variety of Ghosts Doesn't Like Children or Dobermans." *Arizona Daily Star*, n.d.

Sorenson, Dan. "Guess who might be coming to dinner?" *Tucson Citizen*, December 5, 1983.

"The youthful ghost of Suarez house." *Tucson Citizen*, May 17, 1980.

UNPUBLISHED WORKS

Interview with Jerry LaBarre, July 28, 1989.
Interviews with Roy Strom, Nancy Todd, and Warren Todd, August 28, 1989.

Arkansas

BOOKS

Allsop, Fred W. *Allsop's Folklore of Romantic Arkansas*, Volume II. The Grolier Society, U.S.A., 1931.

Woolery, Dr. D. R. *The Grand Old Lady of the Ozarks*. Hominy, Okla.: Eagles' Nest Press, 1986.

PERIODICALS

Dickinson, Sam. "Tales of Ghosts." *Arkansas Democrat*, May 27, 1962.

Fletcher, Jim. "Crescent tests ghost theory." *Eureka Springs Times-Echo* Monthly Visitor's Guide, August Edition, Volume 13, Number 5.

Gravley, Ernestine. "The Crescent Hotel." *Eureka Springs Times-Echo*, April 21, 1966 (in the *Arkansas Gazette*, October 4, 1964, reprinted by permission).

Harper, Edward. "Eccentricity at an Old Spa in the Ozarks." *The New York Times*, May 28, 1989.

Shell, Lilith. "The Strains of a Violin." *Arcadian Magazine*, November 1931.

California

BOOKS

Albion, Robert G. *Five Centuries of Famous Ships.* New York: McGraw-Hill Book Co., 1978.

May, Antoinette. *Haunted Houses and Wandering Ghosts of California.* San Francisco: The San Francisco Examiner Division of The Hearst Corporation, 1977.

Smith, Susy. *Prominent American Ghosts.* Cleveland and New York: World Publishing Co., 1967.

Taylor, L. B. *Haunted Houses.* New York: Wanderer Books, 1983.

PERIODICALS

Arnold, Thomas K. "Investigative Team Stalks the Supernatural in San Diego Houses." *Los Angeles Times,* October 25, 1982.

———. "The Spirits of San Diego." *San Diego Magazine,* October 1985.

Bardacke, Frances. "The Swinging World of 'Yankee Jim.' " *San Diego and Point Magazine,* January 1966.

Burgess, Michele. "The Winchester House: A Marvelous Mystery." *Sky* (Delta Airlines Inflight Magazine), April 1982.

Dean, Andrea Oppenheimer. "*Queen Mary* Will Not Set Sail." *Historic Preservation News,* December 1992.

Randall, Gale. "Spirited Mansion." *Sonoma Press Democrat,* April 23, 1987.

Rogers, Paul. "Lodge that once was a celebrity haunt now may just be haunted." *St. Paul (Minn.) Pioneer Press,* January 14, 1991.

Rose, Frank. "Where the Mystical Meets the Bizarre." *The New York Times,* July 12, 1987.

Shoup, Mike. "Winchester House Was Built to Ward Off Evil Spirits." *Omaha (Neb.) World Herald,* July 10, 1986.

Shuster, Fred. " 'Haunted passages' of cruise ship spin some spooky yarns." *Star Tribune (Minneapolis),* March 3, 1991.

Sullivan, Gail Bernice. "How About a Ghost Story?" *San Francisco Sunday Examiner,* January 9, 1972.

Sweeney, Thomas W. "A Royal Dilemma." *Historic Preservation News,* June 1992.

Weisang, Myriam. "Hearts for Art's Sake (A profile of the San Francisco Art Institute and its second annual Artists Valentines Exhibition/Auction)." *The San Francisco Bay Guardian,* February 6, 1985.

UNPUBLISHED WORKS

Interview with Kim Gilbert, February 2, 1991, and March 28, 1991. Notes from anonymous booklet provided by Kim Gilbert on history of Brookdale Lodge.

Interviews with Richard Kerlin, Billy Thompson, Nancy Wozny, Tom Hennessy, Shawn Duke, Ellie May, Lester Hart, John Smith, July 1988.

Interview with Mrs. June Reading, San Diego, July 7, 1988.

Mulford, Harry. *Legends of a Ghost,* July 20, 1976.

San Francisco Art Institute séance press release, October 26, 1976.

"Unsolved Mysteries," Cosgrove-Meurer Productions, transcripts of interviews, July 1988.

Colorado

BOOKS

Bradley, Dorothy Bomar, and Robert A. Bradley, M.D. *Psychic Phenomena: Revelations and Experiences.* West Nyack, N.Y.: Parker Publishing Co., Inc., 1967.
Brandon, Jim. *Weird America.* New York: E. P. Dutton, 1978.
Gaddis, Vincent H. *Mysterious Fires and Lights.* New York: Dell, 1967.
Martin, MaryJoy. *Ghosts, Ghouls & Goblins: Twilight Dwellers of Colorado.* Boulder, Colo.: Pruett Publishing Company, 1985.
Smyth, Frank. *Ghosts and Poltergeists.* Garden City, N.Y.: Doubleday and Co., Inc., 1976.

PERIODICALS

Fry, Eleanor. "Townsite of Rosita officially abandoned." *Pueblo Star-Journal,* August 21, 1978.
Kelly, Bernard. "So you don't believe in GHOSTS!" *Denver Post Contemporary Magazine,* October 28, 1962.
Linehan, Edward J. "The Rockies' Pot of Gold: Colorado." *National Geographic* 136: 2 (August 1969).
Little, W. T. "County seat battle raged for years." *Canon City Daily Record,* October 6, 1980.
———. "Dancing Ghosts Carry Own Lights." *Rocky Mountain News,* April 19, 1956.
———. "Hunting Ghosts in a Ghost Town Out West." *The New York Times,* August 20, 1967.
"Old, new melds in Silver Cliff." *Pueblo Star-Journal and Sunday Chieftain,* March 18, 1979.
Parker, Dorothy. "Leadership encompasses 30 years." *Canon City Daily Record,* May 7, 1980.
"Three Brigands of Rosita." *The Denver Tribune,* August 28, 1881.
Wilkinson, Bruce M. "Silver Cliff Respects Heritage." *Pueblo Star-Journal and Sunday Chieftain,* October 24, 1965.

UNPUBLISHED WORKS

Interviews with Dr. Robert A. Bradley, November 3, 1987, and December 1, 1987.
Francis, Irene. "The Lights in the Silver Cliff Cemetery," tape recording, Westcliffe, Colorado, November 1987.
Local History Center of the Public Library, Canon City, Colorado.

Connecticut

BOOKS

Blackington, Alton H. *Yankee Yarns.* New York: Dodd, Mead & Company, 1954.
Bolté, Mary. *Haunted New England.* Riverside, Conn.: The Chatham Press, Inc., 1972.
Cahill, Robert Ellis. *New England's Ghostly Haunts.* Peabody, Mass.: Chandler-Smith Publishing House, 1983.

Federal Writers' Project. *American Guide Series for Connecticut*. Boston: Houghton Mifflin Co., 1938.
Stevens, Austin N. *Mysterious New England*. Dublin, N.H.: Yankee, Inc., 1971.
Wilcoxson, William Howard. *History of Stratford, Connecticut*. n.p., n.d.

PERIODICALS

"Death of Phelps Mansion." *The Stratford Bard*, February 17, 1972.
Decerbo, Esther. "Historical, Haunted Mansion Finally Ends Its Stormy Life." *Bridgeport Sunday Post*, March 5, 1972.
"Ghost Sightings at Hero's Homestead." *The Mexico City News*, August 20, 1987.
Jarman, Rufus. "Mystery House on Elm Street." *Yankee*, October 1971.

UNPUBLISHED WORKS

Notes by M. E. Baker, Hale Homestead Administrator for the Antiquarian and Landmarks Society of Connecticut.
Information from Franklin, Connecticut, Town Hall.

Delaware

BOOKS

Delaware: A Guide to the First State (American Guide Series). Compiled and written by the Federal Writers' Project of the Works Progress Administration for the State of Delaware. New York: The Viking Press, 1938.
Smith, Susy. *Ghosts Around the House*. Cleveland and New York: World Publishing Co., 1988.
———. *Haunted Houses for the Millions*. New York: Dell Publishing Co., Inc., 1967.

PERIODICALS

"Delaware Governor and Wife to Move to Haunted House." *The New York Times*, December 12, 1965.
Dover Evening Journal, March 24, 1972.
Dover Post, June 30, 1976.
"The Governor's Ghost." *Datsun Student Travel Guide*, 1978.
"Gubernatorial ghost-busting fails." *St. Paul (Minn.) Pioneer Press and Dispatch*, May 8, 1985.

UNPUBLISHED WORKS

The Governor's House State of Delaware (mimeographed report) n.d.
Interview with Jennifer Mackey, Staff Assistant, Office of Constituent Relations, State of Delaware, Office of the Governor, December 9, 1987.

District of Columbia

BOOKS

Alexander, John. *Ghosts: Washington's Most Famous Ghost Stories.* Washington, D.C.: Washingtonian Books, 1975.

Brandon, Jim. *Weird America.* New York: E. P. Dutton, 1978.

Datsun Student Travel Guide, 1978.

Greenhouse, Herbert B. *In Defense of Ghosts.* New York: Simon and Schuster, Inc., Essandess Special Editions, 1970.

Jeffrey, A. K. *Across the Land from Ghost to Ghost.* Lahaska, Pa.: New Hope Publishing Co., 1975.

The Octagon. Pamphlet printed in USA, November 1984.

Parks, Lillian Rogers, with Frances Spatz Leighton. *My Thirty Years Backstairs at the White House.* New York: Fleet Publishing Corp., 1961.

Scott, Beth, and Michael Norman. *Haunted Heartland.* Madison, Wis.: Stanton & Lee Publishers, Inc., 1985; rpt. New York: Warner Books, 1986, Dorset Press, 1991.

Smith, Susy. *Haunted Houses for the Millions.* New York: Dell Publishing Company, Inc., 1967.

Steiger, Brad. *Real Ghosts, Restless Spirits and Haunted Minds.* New York: Award Books, Universal-Award House, Inc., 1968.

Walker, Danton. *I Believe in Ghosts.* New York: Taplinger Publishing Co., 1969 (a revised version of *Spooks Deluxe,* published in 1956).

PERIODICALS

"Book quotes folks on Lincoln's ghost." *Milwaukee Sentinel,* November 1, 1978.

Conroy, Sarah Booth. "Tales from the Octagon: The Case of the Missing Plans." *The Washington Post,* August 13, 1989.

"5 'authentic' ghosts in Capitol." *The Montgomery Advertiser Alabama Journal,* October 30, 1977.

"Ghosts may haunt corridors of Capitol." *The Tuscaloosa (Ala.) News,* October 30, 1977.

"Who's whooo: Unexplained tales lure many tourists." *Cleveland Press,* October 31, 1978.

Florida

BOOKS

Kettelkamp, Larry. *Haunted Houses.* New York: William Morrow and Company, 1969.

Roll, William G. *The Poltergeist.* Metuchen, N.J.: Scarecrow Press, Inc., 1976.

Steiger, Brad. *Real Ghosts, Restless Spirits and Haunted Minds.* New York: Award Books, Universal-Award House, Inc., 1968.

———. *True Ghost Stories.* Rockport, Mass.: Para Research, 1982.

PERIODICALS

Achenbach, Joel. "For sale: Home with ghost." *Miami Herald,* May 1, 1985.

———. "Ghosts here? It's their night." *Miami Herald,* October 31, 1985.

Browning, Michael. "A Chance of a Ghost." *Miami Herald Tropic Magazine,* October 31, 1982.

Epstein, Warren. "Haunting grounds." *Tampa Tribune*, October 19, 1984.
Glass, Ian. "A cloud of smoke grabbed me . . . this is it." *Miami News*, May 30, 1974.
———. "Ghost house for sale—only $110,000." *Miami News*, March 22, 1976.
———. "Knock, knock, who's there at Villa Paula's?" *Miami News*, March 22, 1976.
———. "A pall of confusion called by séance and may be Paula." *Miami News*, April 5, 1976.
Grimes, Sandra. "A Ghost Story." *Tampa Tribune*, February 19, 1982.
Hall, H. Kevin. "Does late worker's ghost haunt theatre?" *The Neighbor*, June 16–22, 1983.
Nordheimer, Jon. "Even Police Can't Locate 'Spook in the Stockroom.'" *Miami Herald*, January 18, 1967.
Roberts, Jack. "I Paid a Visit to Our City's Spook House." *Miami News*, January 18, 1967.
———. "There Was a Boy, a Very Strange. . ." *Miami News*, March 2, 1967.
"Tampa theatre ghost is elusive creature." *Tampa Bay-Star*, October 29, 1980.
Warren, Bill. "Phantom of the Tampa Theatre." *Tampa Times*, September 28, 1978.
Werne, Jo. "I'm Not the Shelf Spook, 19-Year-Old Clerk Says." *Miami Herald*, February 3, 1967.

UNPUBLISHED WORKS

Interview with Angel Altuzarra, November 10, 1986.
Interview with Pat McElroy, May 1987.

Georgia

BOOKS

Perkerson, Medora Field. *White Columns in Georgia*. New York: Rinehart, n.d.
Roberts, Nancy, and Bruce Roberts. *This Haunted Land: Where Ghosts Still Roam*. Charlotte, N.C.: McNally and Loftin, Publishers, 1970.
Taylor, L. B. *Haunted Houses*. New York: Wanderer Books, 1983.
Windham, Kathryn Tucker. *Thirteen Georgia Ghosts and Jeffrey*. Huntsville, Ala.: The Strode Publishers, n.d.

PERIODICALS

Broussard, Richard. "The Ghost Of Orna Villa." *Atlanta Magazine*, October 1984.
Denholtz, David. "Old Faculty Members Never Die. . . ?" *The Spokesman* (Oxford College Student Newspaper), May 30, 1980.
Jordan, Vera. "The Alexander Means Home: Haunted House of Oxford." *The Spokesman* (Oxford College Student Newspaper), March 1972.
Smith, Jeanne. "The Ghost of Orna Villa." *Covington News*, August 30, 1977.
St. John, Wylly Folk. "Ghost That Eats Biscuits?" *The Atlanta Journal Magazine*, October 13, 1946.

UNPUBLISHED WORKS

Davis, M. L. "The Surrency Ghost." Special Collections Division, The University of Georgia Libraries, Athens, Georgia.

Correspondence from Katherine L. Tatum, June 20, 1988; interviews with Katherine L. Tatum, August 2, 1988.
Interview with James Watterson, May 1987.

Hawaii

BOOKS

Brandon, Jim. *Weird America.* New York: E. P. Dutton, 1978.
Coffin, Tristram Potter and Hennig Cohen. *The Parade of Heroes.* Garden City, N.Y.: Anchor Press/Doubleday, 1978.
Smith, Susy. *Prominent American Ghosts.* Cleveland and New York: World Publishing Co., 1967.
Westervelt, W. D. *Hawaiian Legends of Volcanoes.* Boston: Ellis Press, 1916.

PERIODICALS

"Al Pelayo 'Legendary' Host at Volcano House." *Hawaiian Times* 2:1.
Apple, Russ, and Peg Apple. "Pele's Signal to a Mother." *Honolulu Star Bulletin,* May 12, 1973.
Bruggencate, Jan Ten. "Pele is an old acquaintance for Sadie Brown." *Honolulu Advertiser,* December 6, 1986.
Gilmore, Alice. "The Lady in Red." *OAHU* 4: 3 (April 1980).
Hardy, Barlow. "Mme. Pele Re-appears." *Paradise of the Pacific,* February 1946.
Howard, Vol. A. "Fire Goddess Pele, Real or Imaginary?" *Paradise of the Pacific,* March 1944.
Maguire, Eliza D. "Madame Pele's Last Legend." *Paradise of the Pacific,* December 1926.
Martin, Marlene. "Pele's Fury." *Los Angeles Times,* October 18, 1987.
Tabrah, Ruth. "How Madam Pele Got 'The Word.'" *Honolulu Magazine,* n.d.

Idaho

BOOKS

d'Easum, Dick. *Sawtooth Tales.* Caldwell, Idaho: The Caxton Printers, Ltd., 1977.

PERIODICALS

Burrows, Ken. "Ghost in a Boise Home." *The Idaho Statesman,* September 23, 1973.
d'Easum, Dick. "Footsteps of Idaho Ghosts." *The Idaho Statesman,* November 3, 1963.

Illinois

PERIODICALS

"Eastern Folklore—Fact or Fiction?" *Old Main Line* (Eastern Illinois University), Summer 1985.

Hughes, T. Lee. "Peoria Library on 'Cursed' Site." *Peoria Journal Star*, October 31, 1974.

Knapp, Karen. "Myth of Pem ghost based on live coed." *Eastern News* (Eastern Illinois University), November 5, 1976.

Michael, William M. "I ain't afraid of no ghosts!" *Herald & Review* (Decatur, Ill.), n.d.

Norman, Frances. "Old Curse Dooms Library Site as Eternal Source of Ill Fortune to Owner." *Peoria Journal Star*, January 30, 1944, rpt. February 10, 1957.

" 'Old Book' . . . The Tragic Story of a Demented Soul and 'The Graveyard Elm.' " *Peoria Journal Star*, October 31, 1980.

O'Neill, Patty. "Was 'Mary' dorm's late-night visitor?" *Herald & Review* (Decatur, Ill.), n.d.

"True Tale of Peoria." *Peoria Herald*, September 15, 1895.

UNPUBLISHED WORKS

Bryan, William W. "Historical Sketch of the Peoria Public Library." Compiled 1980.

Interviews with William M. Michael and Shirley Von Bokel, November 16, 1992.

Indiana

BOOKS

Baker, Ronald L. *Hoosier Folk Legends*. Bloomington: Indiana University Press, 1982.

Bayless, Raymond. *The Exorcism Series, Book 1*. New York: Ace Books, 1967.

Ellis, Edward S., A.M. *The History of Our Country*. Vol. 3. Cincinnati: The Jones Brothers Publishing Company, 1918.

Panati, Charles. *Supersenses*. New York: Quadrangle/The New York Times Book Co., 1974.

Rogo, D. Scott. *Parapsychology: A Century of Inquiry*. New York: Taplinger Publishing Co., 1975.

Roll, William G. *The Poltergeist*. Metuchen, N.J.: The Scarecrow Press, Inc., 1976.

Smith, Warren. *Strange Hexes*. New York Popular Library Edition, 1970.

PERIODICALS

Bell, Steve. "Scary Places." *Indianapolis Monthly*, October 1984.

Clements, William M., and William E. Lightfoot. "The Legend of Stepp Cemetery." *Indiana Folklore* 5:1 (1972).

" 'Flying Glass' Terrorizes Trio." *Indianapolis Star*, March 13, 1962.

McLayea, Eunice. "This old house still has 'ghosts.' " *Indianapolis Star*, March 22, 1981.

Ward, Joe. "Ghost stories." *Louisville (Ky.) Courier-Journal*, October 29, 1974.

Whyde, Kathy. "Cities have their own folklore." Indianapolis *Star*, April 4, 1982.

Iowa

PERIODICALS

Annals of Iowa, Spring 1965.

Bluhm, Donald A. "The Duke of Winterset." *The Milwaukee Journal,* August 12, 1984.

Chanaud, Timothy. "Grand workers claim 'spirited' company." *Dubuque Telegraph Herald,* May 4, 1987.

The Festival Flyer. supplement to the *Winterset Madisonian,* Volume Six, October 11 and 12, 1975.

Hopkins, Julie. "Tales to make your blood run cold." *The Des Moines Register,* October 31, 1976.

Monson, Valerie. "Phantoms in Dubuque's opera house." *The Des Moines Register,* n.d.

Today's Dubuque, 1987.

UNPUBLISHED WORKS

Interview with Cathy Breitbach, February 23, 1991.

Interview with Helen Johnston, February 15, 1991.

Interviews with Jim Landis, Bill Stark, Jeff Schneider, Sue Riedel, January 12, 1991.

Interviews with Jim Meyer and Sue Lynch-Huerta, February 20, 1991.

Smeator, Mrs. Guy. WPA, Federal Writer's Project 1940 Ms., 240 Folklore.

Kansas

BOOKS

Ghost Stories of Fort Leavenworth, compiled by The Musettes, 1984.

PERIODICALS

Conley, Manuel A., Maj. USA. "Haunted Fort Leavenworth." *The Retired Officer,* October 1979.

Lazzarino, Evie. "Ghostly tale still haunts Sigma Nu house." *Lawrence Journal World,* October 31, 1982.

Mouze, Victoria, S.Sgt. "Getting into the Spirit." *Soldiers,* October 1982.

Seifert, Allen. "They're around, all right—in spirit." *St. Joseph News-Press/Gazette,* October 26, 1986.

"Wichita psychic probes legend of Theorosa's Bridge." *Valley News,* May 26, 1976.

UNPUBLISHED WORKS

Heffley, Deborah Anne. "Haunting Tales of Emporia, Kansas." Written for Studies in American Folklore EN 740 C, Emporia State University, July 15, 1983.

Koch, William E. The William E. Koch Folklore Collection, Kansas State University, Manhattan.

Kentucky

BOOKS

Rice, Alice Caldwell Hegan. *Flapdoodle, Trust & Obey*. (One chapter, "Mama Relates the Tale of a Conjured Chest," submitted to authors by Kentucky Historical Society, 1991.)

PERIODICALS

Brown, Anne Burnside. "One Headless Ghost." October 29, 1950. (Source missing on photocopy.)

Crawford, Byron. "Conjuring up tragedy." *Frankfort Courier-Journal*, April 28, 1982.

King, Gail. "Kentucky Ghosts: A Trilogy." October 30, 1977. (Source missing on photocopy.)

Reed, Billy. "Tales of Leah Smock's ghost haunt Meade, and you can visit her grave . . . If the spirit should move you." *Frankfort Courier-Journal*, October 31, 1975.

Stacy, Helen Price. "A Ball of Hair and a Pinch of Salt." *Re-discover Kentucky*, Department of Public Information, Frankfort, October 23, 1970.

———. "It's Time to Make Friends with Goblins." *Re-discover Kentucky*, Department of Public Information, Frankfort, October 20, 1972.

———. "Shades of Ghosts Provide Stories for October Reading." *Re-discover Kentucky*, Department of Public Information, Frankfort, January 12, 1973.

Louisiana

BOOKS

Botkin, B. A. *A Treasury of Southern Folklore*. New York: Crown Publishers, 1949.

Cohen, Daniel. *The World's Most Famous Ghosts*. New York: Pocket Books, 1978.

Hurwood, Bernhardt J. *Monsters and Nightmares*. New York: Belmont Productions, Inc., 1967.

Saxon, Lyle, et al. *Gumbo Ya-Ya*. New York: Bonanza Books, 1945.

Smith, Susy. *Prominent American Ghosts*. Cleveland and New York: World Publishing Co., 1967.

PERIODICALS

Alexander, Bill. "The Myrtles' Friendly Ghosts Provide Extra Entertainment for Some Overnight Guests." *The Old News Is Good News Antiques Gazette*, July 1990.

Burrough, Bryan. "As Spooky Places Go, an Inn in the Bayous Goes a Bit Too Far." *The Wall Street Journal*, October 31, 1984.

Foster, Mary. "Big Easy ghosts find many places to hang around." *New Orleans Times-Picayune*, October 28, 1989.

"The Haunted House, Its Interesting History and Strange Romance (Events in the Life of Madame Lalaurie Called to Mind)." *New Orleans Daily Picayune*, March 13, 1892.

Lewis, Joy Schaleben. "This Bed and Breakfast Is a Scream." *Los Angeles Times*, September 27, 1987.

Munson, Richard. "At the Zumo Home, Ghosts Just Move in with the Furniture." *Sunday Advocate*, March 5, 1978.

Rivers, Bill. "Louisiana's Gentle Ghosts." *Morning Advocate*, September 28, 1952.

Stasio, Marilyn. "New Orleans Lets the Scary Times Roll." *The New York Times*, October 27, 1991.

Veach, Damon, "Ghost Tales of Baton Rouge." *Baton Rouge Enterprise*, October 29, 1981.

Wonk, Dalt. "The Fall of the House of Orchard." *New Orleans Magazine*, June 1975.

Maine

BOOKS

Babcock, Blakely B. *Jonathan Buck of Bucksport*. Ellsworth, Maine: *The Ellsworth American*, n.d.

Bernard, Christine. *A Host of Ghosts*. Philadelphia and New York: J. B. Lippincott, 1976.

Bolté, Mary. *Haunted New England*. Riverside, Conn.: The Chatham Press, Inc., 1972.

Cahill, Robert Ellis. *New England's Ghostly Haunts*. Peabody, Mass.: Chandler-Smith Publishing House, 1983.

Federal Works Project. *American Guide Series for Maine*. Boston: Houghton Mifflin, 1937.

Smith, Susy. *Prominent American Ghosts*. Cleveland and New York: World Publishing Co., 1967.

Snow, Edward Rowe. *Fantastic Folklore and Fact*. New York: Dodd, Mead, 1968.

Maryland

BOOKS

Anderson, Elizabeth B., with Michael P. Parker. *Annapolis: A Walk Through History*. Centreville, Md.: Tidewater Publisher, n.d.

Ellis, Edward S., A.M. *The History of Our Country*. Cincinnati: The Jones Brothers Publishing Co., 1918.

Hammond, John Martin. *Colonial Mansions of Maryland and Delaware*. Philadelphia and London: J. B. Lippincott Co., 1914.

Merriam, Anne Van Ness, comp. *The Ghosts of Hampton*, n.d.

Skinner, Charles M. *Myths and Legends of Our Own Land*. Philadelphia: J. B. Lippincott Co., 1896.

Stevens, William O. *Unbidden Guests*. New York: Dodd, Mead, 1946.

Taylor, L. B. *Haunted Houses*. New York: Wanderer Books, 1983.

Winer, Richard, and Nancy Osborn Ishmael. *More Haunted Houses*. New York: Bantam Books, 1981.

PERIODICALS

AAA World, September/October 1986.

Brown, Chip. "Evermore: Roses, Cognac at Poe's Grave." *The Washington Post*, January 20, 1983.

Burdett, Hal. "Brice House ghost stories." *Evening Capital*, n.d.

Challmes, Joseph J., and Tom Horton, comps. "Marylanders compile rich legacy of ghostly tales and legendary lore." *Baltimore Sun*, October 31, 1972.

Colimore, Edward. "Ghostly Visits Enliven North Point House." *News American*, August 11, 1976.
Conboy, Don, and Marian Conboy. "Baltimore's Spookiest Ghost Stories." *Baltimore Magazine*, October 1979.
"Ever More." *The New York Times*, January 21, 1983.
Hillinger, Charles. "Campaign trying to squelch myth that Poe was an addict." *Minneapolis Star Tribune*, March 10, 1991.
———. "Park rangers campaign to restore the reputation of Edgar Allan Poe." *The Des Moines Register*, April 3, 1991.
Jackson, Elmer, Sr. "Jennings House." *Anne Arundel Times*, January 15, 1970.
"A night to remember at Poe's grave." *Baltimore Sun*, November 1, 1982.
"Poe Birthday Ritual." *The Washington Post*, January 20, 1990.
"Poe's mystery visitor filmed." *Minneapolis Star Tribune*, June 26, 1990.
Randolph, Evan. "The Spirit of Commodore Truxton." *Yankee*, June 1977.
Smith, Gary. "Once upon a Midnight Dreary." *Life*, July 1990.

UNPUBLISHED WORKS

Communication May 15, 1992, from Ellen Berkov, Anne Arundel County Public Library, Annapolis, Md.

Massachusetts

BOOKS

Botkin, B. A., ed. *A Treasury of American Folklore*. New York: Bantam Books, 1948.
———. *A Treasury of New England Folklore*. New York: Crown Publishers, 1947.
Brimblecom, Deborah. *The Screeching Lady of Marblehead*. Beverly, Mass.: Wilkscraft Inc., 1976.
Chamberlain, Samuel. *New England Legends and Folklore* (adapted with additions from *A Book of New England Legends and Folk Lore* by Samuel Adams Drake, 1884). New York: Hastings House, 1967.
Drake, Samuel Adams. *A Book of New England Legends and Folk Lore in Prose and Poetry*. Boston: Little, Brown and Co., 1901. Rpt. Detroit: Singing Tree Press, Book Tower, 1969.
Miles, Dorothy. *The Wizard of Orne Hill and Other Tales of Old Marblehead*. Privately published, 1985.
Snow, Edward Rowe. *Fantastic Folklore and Fact*. New York: Dodd, Mead, 1968.

PERIODICALS

Allmaker, Ali Martin. "Local Haunts." *The Berkshire Eagle*, July 6–12, 1984.
Coppage, Noel, and Walter D. Mosher. "A Mighty Hole in the Ground." *Yankee*, November 1973.
Drohan, Glenn. "Hoosac Tunnel's mysteries linger after century." Western Gateway Heritage State Park Grand Opening, a commemorative supplement by *The Transcript*, October 10, 1985.
"Even John Barnard Believed the Story of the Screeching Woman." *Marblehead Messenger*, January 26, 1938.
"Ghosts saved my life twice in haunted tunnel." *The Star*, August 31, 1976.
"Historic Marblehead." *Lynn (Mass.) Item*, July 22, 1952.
Kuperschmid, Eileen. Untitled article. *The Berkshire Sampler*, Sunday, October 30, 1977.

Mosher, Walter D. "The Legends of Hoosac Tunnel." Springfield (Mass.) *Sunday Republican*, March 19, 1972.
Schacht, Susan. "Miles' book chronicles local lore." *Marblehead Reporter*, September 26, 1985.
"The Screeching Woman." *The Boston Globe*, August 28, 1929.
Taft, Lewis A. "The Legend of Peter Rugg." *Yankee*, October 1960.

UNPUBLISHED WORKS

Interview with Joe and Peg Roberts, May 14, 1987.

Michigan

BOOKS

Eberle, Gary. *Haunted Houses of Grand Rapids*. Vol. 2. Ada, Mich.: Ivystone Publications, 1982.
Farrant, Don. *Haunted Houses of Grand Rapids*. Vol. 1. Ada, Mich.: Ivystone Publications, 1979.
Hurwood, Bernhardt J. *Monsters and Nightmares*. New York: Belmont Productions, Inc., 1967.

PERIODICALS

"Mysterious Incident Recalled." *The Evening News (Sault Ste. Marie)*, August 1952.
Oates, Morgan. "The Case of the Dead Man's Mirror." *The Detroit Free Press*, August 1952.

Minnesota

BOOKS

Blegen, Theodore C. *Minnesota: A History of the State*. Minneapolis: University of Minnesota Press, 1963.
Collections of the Minnesota Historical Society. Vol. 5. St. Paul: Minnesota Historical Society, 1902.
Minnesota: A State Guide (American Guide Series). New York: The Viking Press, 1938.

PERIODICALS

"Coroner to Probe House of Mystery." *The St. Paul Pioneer Press*, February 20, 1911.
El-Hai, Jack. "Nights of the Living Dead." *Minneapolis St. Paul Magazine*, October 1987.
" 'Ghost' Excites a St. Paul Family." *The St. Paul Pioneer Press*, February 18, 1911.
Philbrick, Andrea. "Area ghost tale lives on." *Mankato Free Press*, October 31, 1980.
Proctor, Angie. "Annie Mary lives on since 1886." *New Ulm Daily Journal*, October 31, 1979.
"Rosaries Increase Mystery of Ghost." *The St. Paul Pioneer Press*, February 19, 1911.
Ruff, Gwen. "Twente legend still has believers." *New Ulm Daily Journal*, October 31, 1981.

Weber, Donna. "The Legend of Annie Mary Twente." *New Ulm Daily Journal,* June 22, 1986.
"When 'things go bump in night,' Mack listens." *Plainview News,* October 30, 1984.

UNPUBLISHED WORKS

Interview with Tim Mack, August 14, 1990.

Mississippi

BOOKS

Botkin, B. A., ed. A *Treasury of Southern Folklore.* New York: Bonanza Books, n.d.
Colorful Moments from Mississippi's History. Meridian, Miss.: Junior Food Stores, Inc., n.d.
Crocker, Mary Wallace. *Historic Architecture in Mississippi.* Jackson: University Press of Mississippi, 1973.
Datsun Student Travel Guide, 1978.
Newton, Carolyn, and Patricia H. Coggin. *Meet Mississippi.* Huntsville, Ala.: Strode Publishers, Inc., 1976.
Roberts, Nancy, and Bruce Roberts. *This Haunted Land.* Charlotte, N.C.: Heritage Printers, Inc., 1984.
Windham, Katherine Tucker. *13 Mississippi Ghosts and Jeffrey.* Huntsville, Ala.: Strode Publishers, Inc., 1974.

PERIODICALS

Aden, Marky. "House is history plus mystery." *The Delta Democrat-Times (Greenville),* n.d.
Bergeron, Kat. "Gulf Coast spooks, old ones and new, still can produce a nightmare or two." *The Sun/The Daily Herald, Mississippi Gulf Coast,* n.d.
Brigham, Allegra. "Potpourri. . . " *Columbus Dispatch,* February 12, 1978.
Burdsal, Bill. "Ghost Stories." *Mississippi Magazine,* September–October 1985.
Campbell, Nanci. "Suspicion of Arson in Cahill Fire." *The Daily Herald (Biloxi-Gulfport),* July 19, 1970.
Chidsey, Judge Charles E. "The Mysterious Music of Pascagoula." In *Four Centuries on the Pascagoula.* (Article is an abridgment of author's article in *Popular Science Monthly,* 1890.)
Culbertson, Jean. "State Folklore Abounds in Ghosts." *The Clarion-Ledger,* October 31, 1967.
Ehrbright, Nan Patton. "Gentle Coast ghosts have haunted houses for years." *Mississippi Gulf Coast,* n.d.
Ewing, Jim. " 'Witch's Grave' still chief haunting site in spooky Yazoo City." *Jackson Daily News,* October 27, 1983.
Flynn, Pat. "Who's buried in the witch's grave?" *The Yazoo Daily Herald,* July 2, 1978.
Fox, Marion Laffey. "The Natchez Way." *Adventure Road,* Spring 1983.
Gerrard, Ben. "Did the Witch Cause the 1904 Fire?" In *Bookends* 1983, Yazoo City High School yearbook.
"Ghost Tales Include That of 'Miss Nellie.' " *Columbus Dispatch,* December 25, 1974.

Gorringe, Maybelle. " 'Spirits' Visit Haunted House." *Jackson Daily News*, December 19, 1969.

Harrison, Martha. "Madison Chapel Hallows Ground Where Pioneers Sleep." *Jackson Daily News*, February 20, 1938.

Mangum, David. "Graveyard—Where Ghosts Appear—at Chapel of Cross." *The Clarion-Ledger*, October 28, 1973.

Ryan, Pam. "Legend of Spirits Ends with Fire." *The Daily Herald (Biloxi-Gulfport)*, July 19, 1970.

Simmons, Rebecca. "Ghost's Hostess Won't Tempt Fate." *Columbus Dispatch*, November 26, 1978.

————. "Ghosts Find Conditions Favorable in Columbus." Columbus *Dispatch*, October 28, 1979.

Skipper, Deborah. "Boo or balderdash? We'll let you decide." *The Clarion-Ledger, Jackson Daily News*, October 30, 1983.

"Two ghosts at old King's Tavern blamed for erratic clock, eerie sounds, lights." *Press Register (Mobile)*, July 3, 1977.

"Where a Ghost Walks." *The Delta Democrat-Times (Greenville)*, December 31, 1943.

Wright, Carol von Pressentin. "Plantation Mansions on the Mississippi." *The New York Times*, February 10, 1991.

UNPUBLISHED WORKS

Wallace, Gil. "Haunted Houses of Columbus." Paper, May 17, 1972.

Missouri

BOOKS

Basler, Lucille. A *Tour of Old Ste. Genevieve*. Ste. Genevieve: Lucille Basler & Wehmeyer Printing Co., Inc., 1975.

Collins, Earl A. *Legends and Lore of Missouri*. San Antonio: The Naylor Co., 1951.

Missouri, a Guide to the "Show Me" State (American Guide Series). New York: Duell, Sloan & Pearce, 1941.

Moore, Tom. *Mysterious Tales and Legends of the Ozarks*. Philadelphia: Dorrance & Co., 1938.

Randolph, Vance. *Ozark Magic and Folklore*. New York: Dover Publications, Inc., 1964. (Originally titled *Ozark Superstitions*, published by Columbia University Press, 1947. Reprinted by special arrangement with Columbia University Press.)

Rayburn, Otto Ernest. *Ozark Country*. New York: Duell, Sloan & Pearce, 1941, from the American Folkways series edited by Erskine Caldwell.

Steiger, Brad. *True Ghost Stories*. Rockport, Mass.: Para Research, 1982.

Visit Historic Ste. Genevieve. Pamphlet from Tourist Information Center, South Third St., Ste. Genevieve, Mo. 63670, n.d.

PERIODICALS

Peterson, Charles E. "Rediscovering Old Ste. Genevieve." *Gone West!* 3: 2 (Spring 1985).

"Ste. Genevieve, a French Legacy in Middle America." *Country Home*, August 1985.

UNPUBLISHED WORKS

Interview with Kristine Basler, April 16, 1987.

Montana

BOOKS

Murray, Earl. *Ghosts of the Old West.* Chicago: Contemporary Books, Inc., 1988.

PERIODICALS

Liberty, Margot. "Ghost Herder's Battlefield." *Hardin Tribune-Herald,* June 22, 1961.
Palmer, Tom. "Helena's Haunted House." *The Independent Record,* October 29, 1984.
Robbins, Jim. "Assignment: Little Bighorn—113 years after Custer fell, spirits still roam grounds." *Chicago Tribune,* November 1, 1989.
Smyth, Mitchell, "Some visitors to Little Bighorn aren't ready to give up the ghost." *Chicago Tribune,* August 31, 1986.

UNPUBLISHED WORKS

Interview with Dorothy Card, May 14, 1987.
Interview with Mardell Plainfeather, April 6, 1990.

Nebraska

BOOKS

Vaughan, Alan. *Incredible Coincidence—The Baffling World of Synchronicity.* New York: J. B. Lippincott, 1979.

PERIODICALS

The Bridgeport News-Blade, October 10, 1913.
Chadron Citizen, February 9, 1893.
The Enterprise (Pawnee), July 7, 1880.
The Hastings Tribune, October 29, 1985.
Lincoln Evening News, November 22, 1892.
Madison County Reporter, March 8, 1900.

UNPUBLISHED WORKS

Files of Federal Writers' Project of the Works Progress Administration in Collections of Nebraska State Historical Society.
Nelson, Burton. Tape-recorded account of "Miss Anna," submitted to authors, February 28, 1988.

Nevada

BOOKS

McDonald, Douglas. *Camels in Nevada.* Las Vegas, Nevada Publications, 1983.
O'Brien, Dolores K. *Meet Virginia City's Ghosts.* Self-published. Virginia City, 1969.
Roberts, Bruce, and Nancy Roberts. *America's Most Haunted Places.* Garden City, N.Y.: Doubleday & Co., Inc , 1976.

PERIODICALS

Earl, Phillip I. "Lee Singleton: A man haunted by a ghostly past." *Nevada State Journal,* October 25, 1981.
———. "Nevada has its ghostly past." *Nevada State Journal,* October 31, 1982.
———. "Six-Mile's haunted treasure." *Sparks Tribune,* July 28, 1982.

New Hampshire

BOOKS

Beck, Horace. *Folklore and the Sea.* Brattleboro, Vt.: The Stephen Greene Press, 1983.
Botkin, B. A., ed. *A Treasury of New England Folklore.* New York: Crown Publishers, 1947.
Cahill, Robert Ellis. *New England's Ghostly Haunts.* Peabody, Mass.: Chandler-Smith, n.d.
Carmer, Carl. *The Hurricane's Children.* New York and Toronto: Farrar & Rinehart, Inc., 1937.
Drake, Samuel Adams. *New England Legends and Folk Lore in Prose and Poetry.* Boston: Roberts Brothers, 1884.
———. *Nooks and Corners of the New England Coast.* New York: Harper & Bros., 1875. Rpt. Detroit: Singing Tree Press, Book Tower, 1969.
Rutledge, Lyman V. *Ten Miles Out: Guidebook to the Isles of Shoals.* 4th ed. Boston: Isles of Shoals Unitarian Association, 1964.
Simpson, Dorothy. *The Maine Islands in Story and Legend.* Philadelphia and New York: J. B. Lippincott Co., 1960.
Smith, Susy. *Prominent American Ghosts.* Cleveland and New York: World Publishing Co., 1967.
———. *Worlds of the Strange.* New York: Pyramid Publications, 1963.
Steiger, Brad. *Real Ghosts, Restless Spirits and Haunted Minds.* New York: Universal-Award House, Inc., 1968.
———. *True Ghost Stories.* Rockport, Mass.: Para Research, 1982.
Taylor, L. B. *Haunted Houses.* New York: Wanderer Books, 1983.

PERIODICALS

AAA World, September/October 1986.
Napolitan, Joseph. "Season Is Open for New England Ghosts." *The New York Times,* July 28, 1957.
Roberts, D. W. "Star Island." *New Hampshire Profiles,* April 1986.

"Shoals Marine Laboratory." *Yankee*, February 1987.
"To Be a Legend in Your Own Time." *Yankee*, July 1972.

New Jersey

BOOKS

Cohen, David Steven. *The Folklore and Folklife of New Jersey*. New Brunswick: Rutgers University Press, 1983.
Fort, Charles. *The Complete Books of Charles Fort*. New York: Dover Publications, Inc., 1974.
McCloy, James F., and Ray Miller Jr. *The Jersey Devil*. Wallingford, Pa.: The Middle Atlantic Press, 1976.
McMahon, William. *South Jersey Towns: History and Legend*. New Brunswick: Rutgers University Press, 1973.
McPhee, John. *The Pine Barrens*. New York: Farrar, Straus & Giroux, 1967.
New Jersey: A Guide to Its Present and Past. Complied and written by the Federal Writers' Project of the Works Progress Administration for the State of New Jersey (American Guide Series). New York: Hastings House, 1939.
Skinner, Charles M. *American Myths and Legends*. Vol. 1. Philadelphia and London: J. B. Lippincott Company, 1903.

PERIODICALS

Axelrod, Robin Hope. "Don't wait for the spirit to move you." *The Spectator* (Somerset, N. J.), n.d.
Giarelli, Andrew. "Devil's Tale." *New Jersey Monthly*, January 1986.
"Jersey Demon Eludes Hunters." *Burlington (Vt.) Free Press*, November 15, 1982.
" 'Jersey Devil' Returns as Applejack Mellows, and Dry Agents Investigate the Coincidence." *The New York Times*, August 6, 1930.
Lewis, Peggy. "The Graisberry's Ghost." *Interact*, October 1976.
Marks, Peter. "Chronicles of Jersey's 'ghosties.' " *Sunday Star-Ledger*, October 28, 1979.
Szathmary, Richard. "Ghost of a Chance." *New Jersey Monthly*, October 1983.
Waldron, Martin. "The State's 'Bicentennial Ghost' Fades from Sight Again." *The New York Times*, November 21, 1976.
"The World Turned Upside Down." *Psychic: The Magazine of New Realities* 7:5 (n.d.).

UNPUBLISHED WORKS

Correspondence with David C. Munn, Cherry Hill, New Jersey, March 19, 1986; February 15, 1989.
Nowak, Gary. *The Story of the Jersey Devil, 1735–1976*. Ms. courtesy of University of Vermont Special Collections.

New Mexico

PERIODICALS

Friberg, Debra. "The 'grand damme' [sic] is on the way back." *Alamogordo Daily News*, August 3, 1983.

Gaines, Judith. "The Lodge is the main event in the mountains of New Mexico." *Chicago Tribune,* December 4, 1988.

The Lodge Lookout. Various issues 1990–1991.

Pilarte, Doralisa. "Mountain lodge features red-haired ghost, golf course." *Las Cruces Sun-News,* September 7, 1986.

Ripp, Bart. "Check into the Lodge for earthly delights, ghostly nights." *Los Angeles Herald-Examiner,* February 8, 1987.

Selcraig, Bruce. "In New Mexico, There's Life Below I-40." *The New York Times,* June 21, 1992.

Simmons, Jean. "Lodge in search of new heights." *The Dallas Morning News,* August 28, 1983.

"Splendid Isolation." *Diversion Travel Planner,* May 15, 1988.

Thompson, Fritz. "Enchanted Tales Ring Across State." *Albuquerque Journal,* October 30, 1988.

Wolcott, Jann Arrington. "Best-Kept Secret in New Mexico." *Southwest Profile,* February 1988.

UNPUBLISHED WORKS

Interviews with Jerry Sanders, Lisa Thomassie, Johnnie Adams, and Dick Adams, July 1988.

New York

BOOKS

Brandon, Jim. *Weird America.* New York: E. P. Dutton, 1978.

Jones, Louis. *Things That Go Bump in the Night.* New York: Hill and Wang, 1959.

Kettelkamp, Larry. *Haunted Houses.* New York: William Morrow and Co., 1969.

Roll, William G. *The Poltergeist.* Metuchen, N.J.: The Scarecrow Press, Inc., 1976.

PERIODICALS

Bracker, Milton, "Mystery in L. I. House Deepens; Family Experts, Police Stumped." *The New York Times,* March 3, 1958.

"Joint Still Jumpin' for L. I. Herrmanns." *The New York Times,* March 5, 1958.

"L. I. Family Returns to Mystery House." *The New York Times,* n.d.

"L. I. House Is Quiescent: No Spooks for 16 Days." *The New York Times,* n.d.

"L. I. 'Poltergeist' Stumps Duke Men." *The New York Times,* August 10, 1958.

"Lost: One Poltergeist." *The New York Times,* n.d.

Miller, Joy. "If Your House Has to Be Haunted, Pick an Entertaining Poltergeist." *Mobile Press Register,* February 7, 1960.

"Mysterious Force Routs L. I. Family." *The New York Times,* February 22, 1958.

"Professor Says Weird Events in L. I. House Are Not a Hoax." *The New York Times,* March 7, 1958.

"Professor Seeks L. I. Mystery Key." *The New York Times,* n.d.

Shanley, John P. "TV: Baffling Phenomena—'House of Flying Objects' Dramatizes Mysterious Movements in L. I. Home." *The New York Times,* October 30, 1958.

BIBLIOGRAPHY
North Carolina

BOOKS

Brandon, Jim. *Weird America*. New York: E. P. Dutton, 1978.

Gaddis, Vincent H. *Mysterious Fires and Lights*. New York: Dell Publishing Co., Inc., 1968.

Harden, John. *The Devil's Tramping Ground and Other North Carolina Mystery Stories*. Chapel Hill: The University of North Carolina Press, 1949.

————. *Tar Heel Ghosts*. Chapel Hill: The University of North Carolina Press, 1954.

Rankin, Hugh F. *The Pirates of Colonial North Carolina*. Raleigh, N.C.: Department of Cultural Resources, Division of Archives and History, 1977.

Roberts, Nancy. *Ghosts of the Carolinas*. Charlotte, N.C.: McNally and Loftin, Publishers, 1962.

Whedbee, Charles Harry. *Legends of the Outer Banks and Tar Heel Tidewater*. Winston-Salem, N.C.: John F. Blair, 1966.

Winer, Richard, and Nancy Osborn Ishmael. *More Haunted Houses*. New York: Bantam Books, 1981.

PERIODICALS

"At Night Do Spirits Stalk?" *Milwaukee Journal*, April 19, 1985.

Mintz, Frances. Untitled article. *Fayetteville (N.C.) Observer*, October 25, 1959.

Pressley, Sue Anne. "Things Go Bump in the Night at N.C. Capitol." *Charlotte Observer*, July 20, 1979.

"The Queer Lights on Brown Mountain." *Literary Digest*, November 7, 1925.

Schlosser, Jim. "State to celebrate its Capitol as wise 150-year investment." *Greensboro News & Record*, June 30, 1990.

UNPUBLISHED WORKS

Interview with Raymond Beck, December 8, 1987.

Interview with Owen Jackson, November 5, 1989.

Interview with Sam P. Townsend Sr., December 22, 1989.

North Dakota

BOOKS

Devils Lake Illustrated. Grand Forks, N.D.: W. L. Fudley, Publisher, Press of *Grand Forks Herald*, 1898.

Gaddis, Vincent H. *Mysterious Fires and Lights*. New York: Dell Publishing Co., Inc., 1968.

North Dakota: A Guide to the Northern Prairie State (American Guide Series). Written by Workers of the Federal Writers' Project of the Works Progress Administration for the State of North Dakota. Fargo: Knight Printing Company, 1938.

Skinner, Charles M. *Myths and Legends of Our Own Land*. Vol. 2. Philadelphia: J. B. Lippincott Co., 1896.

PERIODICALS

Hope Pioneer, Steele County, July 28, 1893.
North Dakota Historical Quarterly. Collections of the State Historical Society of North
    Dakota, Vol. 1, October 1926–July 1927.
North Dakota History, 13:4 (October 1946).

UNPUBLISHED WORKS

Federal Writers' Projects, Folklore Series, folder 38, Series 550 Box 88, State Historical
    Society of North Dakota.
Fannie Dunn Quain papers, State Historical Society of North Dakota manuscript collec-
    tion.
Interviews by Ann Alexander with Frank Vyzralek, Walter Bailey, Gloria Engel, Ron War-
    ner, and Jim Sperry, April 1986.

Ohio

BOOKS

Bromfield, Louis. *Pleasant Valley*. New York: Harper & Bros., 1943.
Woodyard, Chris. *Haunted Ohio*. Beavercreek, Ohio: Kestrel Publications, 1991.
———. *Haunted Ohio II*. Beavercreek, Ohio: Kestrel Publications, 1992.

PERIODICALS

" 'Ghost' Sightings Reported in Ohio State Parks." *Star-Beacon*, October 25, 1978.
Malabar Farm State Park brochure, n.d. Rt. 1, Box 469, Lucas, Ohio 44843.
Richland Shield and Banner, July 25, 1896; October 17, 1896; and October 24, 1896.
    Microfilmed edition of 1979, Ohio Historical Society, roll dated January 5, 1889,
    through December 5, 1896.

UNPUBLISHED WORKS

Interviews with Douglas and Pamela Campbell, Waynesville, Ohio, June 7, 1986, and
    September 15, 1990.
Interview with Dennis Dalton, Waynesville, Ohio, June 7, 1986.
Transcript of "Haunted House Investigation, Baily-Campbell House," October 26, 1988,
    by WKRC Channel 12 Television.
Interview with Bruno, Dorothy, and Pam Mallone, Hiram, Ohio, June 1986.

Oklahoma

PERIODICALS

Ruth, Kent. "Heard any ghost stories lately?" *Daily Oklahoman*, October 24, 1976.
———. "Oklahoma has ghost of its own." *Daily Oklahoman*, October 4, 1981.
Sarchet, Mark. "Eerie Sounds by Moonlight." *Daily Oklahoman*, April 14, 1957.

Wooley, John, Jeanne Forbis, and Tom Ewing. "Oklahoma Haunts: The Hills Are Alive." *Oklahoma Magazine*, October 31, 1982.
Woolf, Sue. "Dead Woman's Crossing." *The Chronicles of Oklahoma*, 1985.

Oregon

BOOKS

Finucane, Stephanie. *Heceta House: A History and Architectural Survey*. Printed jointly by Lane Community College and USFS for the Heceta House Development Fund. Revised February 6, 1980.
Helm, Mike. *Oregon's Ghosts and Monsters*. Eugene: Rainy Day Press, 1983.

PERIODICALS

Bauguess, John. "Lighthouse Tract Suits Pair." *Oregon Journal*, May 14, 1975.
Eals, Clay. "Spirits roam real haunted house." *The Oregonian*, October 31, 1977.
"Heceta Head" *Sunset Magazine*, February 1986.
Hesseldahl, Norman. "Heceta Head: A Picturesque Postcard with an Interesting Past." *Oregon Coast* magazine, April/May 1988.
Miller, Mark. "Oregon's Lovely, Lonely Coast." *National Geographic*, December 1979.
"Mystery Lures Duffy Home." *Minneapolis Tribune*, December 5, 1982. p. 26.
Trachtenberg, Bruce. "Murder/Suicide Orphans Five Children." *The Oregonian*, December 24, 1973.
Ward, Darrell E. "Lighthouse gets painstaking restoration." *The Oregonian*, November 8, 1983.

UNPUBLISHED WORKS

Interview with Carolyn Brown, August 23, 1992.
Letter from Michael Brown, February 26, 1991.
Interview with Loyd Collette, July 6, 1988.

Pennsylvania

BOOKS

Smith, Susy. *Haunted Houses for the Millions*. New York: Dell, 1967.
Steiger, Brad. *True Ghost Stories*. Rockport, Mass.: Para Research, 1982.

PERIODICALS

Adamic, Louis. "The Millvale Apparition." *Harper's Magazine*, April 1938.
"Artist Declares He Saw Ghost in Millvale Church." *The Pittsburgh Press*, March 19, 1938.
Bull, John V. R. "General Wayne Inn maintains a tradition of fine food." *The Philadelphia Inquirer*, April 27, 1986.

Carynnyk, Carol R. "A colonial inn with a penchant for surviving." *The Philadelphia Inquirer, September 16, 1984.*
Ciccarelli, Maura C. "A ghostly tour along Main Line." *Main Line Times (Ardmore, Pa.),* October 30, 1986.
Delahan, William. "Maxo Vanka and the Millvale Ghost." *The Pittsburgh Press,* October 8, 1967.
McManus, Betty. "The General Wayne Inn." *Main Line Times (Ardmore, Pa.),* January 22, 1987.
Mendte, J. Robert. "General Wayne Inn." Anthony Wayne Historical Association, Merion, Pa. (Originally printed in the *Main Line Chronicle* from a paper read before the Anthony Wayne Historical Society, n.d.)
Patterson, Doris. "Are Hessian Soldiers, Ghosts Floating Around Main Line?" *Main Line Times (Ardmore, Pa.),* October 30, 1986.
Thompson, R. E. S. "Scribe Disappointed (?) in Search for Ghost." *Post-Gazette,* March 21, 1938.

UNPUBLISHED WORKS

Interview with Barton Johnson, June 1986.
Interview with Billy and Linda Micklos, June 1986.

Rhode Island

BOOKS

Brandon, Jim. *Weird America.* New York: E. P. Dutton, 1978.
Chamberlain, Samuel. *New England Legends and Folklore* (adapted with additions from *A Book of New England Legends and Folk Lore* by Samuel Adams Drake, 1884). New York: Hastings House, 1967.
Reynolds, James. *Ghosts in American Houses.* New York: Bonanza Books, a division of Crown Publishers, by arrangement with the original publisher, Farrar, Straus and Cudahy, 1955.
Smyth, Frank. *Ghosts and Poltergeists.* Garden City, N.Y.: Doubleday and Co., Inc., 1976.
Steiger, Brad. *Real Ghosts, Restless Spirits and Haunted Minds.* New York: Award Books, Universal-Award House, Inc., 1968.

PERIODICALS

Powell, Noel. "Block Island's Fiery Ghost." *Yankee,* July 1956.
Rhode Island Collection, Providence Public Library, Providence, Rhode Island.

South Carolina

BOOKS

Graydon, Nell S. *South Carolina Ghost Tales.* Beaufort, S.C.: Beaufort Book Shop, Inc., 1969.

Greenhouse, Herbert B. *In Defense of Ghosts.* New York: Simon and Schuster, Inc., Essandess Special Editions, 1970.

Kellogg, Day Otis, ed. *The Encyclopedia Britannica.* Vol. 5. New York and Chicago: The Werner Co., 1900.

Rhyne, Nancy. *Coastal Ghosts.* Charlotte, N.C.: The East Woods Press, 1985.

Roberts, Bruce, and Nancy Roberts. *America's Most Haunted Places.* New York: Doubleday, 1976.

Roberts, Nancy. *Ghosts of the Carolinas.* Charlotte, N.C.: McNally and Loftin, Publishers, 1962.

Willcox, Clarke A. *Musings of a Hermit.* Charleston, S.C.: Walker, Evans & Cogswell Company, 1966.

PERIODICALS

Chadwick, Bruce. "The Charms of Charleston." *American Way,* March 18, 1986.

"Grand Strand Ghosts." Myrtle Beach Area Chamber of Commerce booklet, 1987.

"History of the Grand Strand." Myrtle Beach Area Chamber of Commerce booklet, 1987.

"Hugo didn't keep Gray Man from post." *Coastal Observer,* October 12, 1989.

Leland, Jack. "Ghosts Part of Lowcountry Lore." *The News and Courier (Charleston, S.C.),* October 28, 1985.

Prufer, Mona R. "Ghosts of the Grand Strand." *COAST,* September 6–12, 1987.

Ralston, Edwina. "Nineteenth Century Lady in White Is Resident of Twentieth Century." *Knoxville (Tenn.) News Sentinel,* April 9, 1989.

Sparks, Andrew. "I Spent the Night in a Haunted House." *The Atlanta Journal and Constitution Magazine,* October 29, 1961.

Yancey, Kitty Bean. "The Laid-Back Life on Pawleys Island." *USA Today,* December 6, 1985.

UNPUBLISHED WORKS

Letter from Robert J. Thomas, November 9, 1989.
Letter from Clarke A. Willcox, October 18, 1988.

South Dakota

BOOKS

Karolevitz, Robert F. *Paper Mountain.* n.p., n.d.

PERIODICALS

Lollar, Kevin. "Halloween spirit lurks in theater." *Sioux Falls Argus-Leader,* October 31, 1985.

UNPUBLISHED WORKS

Interview with Marlene Akhtar, November 3, 1990.
Interview with Ray Loftesness, May 19, 1987.
Interview with Jack Mortenson, May 24, 1987.

Tennessee

BOOKS

Winer, Richard, and Nancy Osborn Ishmael. *More Haunted Houses.* New York: Bantam Books, 1981.

PERIODICALS

Coppock, Paul R. Untitled article. *Memphis Commercial Appeal,* January 1, 1978.

Dawson, David. "The Ghost in Seat C-5." *Memphis Magazine,* n.d.

Donohue, Michael. "Plan to Reconstruct House Revives Talk of Memphis Ghost." *Memphis Press-Scimitar,* October 31, 1980.

Finger, Michael. "What Really Happened to Clara Robertson?" *Memphis Magazine,* October 1984.

"Ghost of 1871 May Vanish in Removal of Old Mansion." *Memphis Commercial Appeal,* July 14, 1972.

Randall, Nancy R. "Memphis Ghosts Don't Always Wait for Halloween to Make Appearance." *Daily News (Memphis),* October 31, 1985.

Talley, Robert. "Ghost Story." *Memphis Commercial Appeal,* October 29, 1939.

Texas

BOOKS

Brandon, Jim. *Weird America.* New York: E. P. Dutton, 1978.

Gaddis, Vincent H. *Mysterious Fires and Lights.* New York: Dell Publishing Co., Inc., 1968.

Greenway, John, ed. *Folklore of the Great West.* Palo Alto, Calif.: American West Publishing Co., 1969.

Roberts, Nancy. *Ghosts of the Wild West.* New York: Doubleday, 1976.

Syers, Ed. *Ghost Stories of Texas.* Waco: Texian Press, 1981.

PERIODICALS

Stipp, David. "Marfa, Texas, Finds a Flickering Fame in Mystery Lights." *The Wall Street Journal,* March 21, 1984.

Utah

BOOKS

Brunvand, Jan Harold. *Studies in Western Folklore and Fiction.* Prepared by the Printing Service, University of Utah, for sale through the University Bookstore to students in the Folklore of the West course, Salt Lake City, Utah, 1972.

Coffin, Tristram Potter, and Henning Cohen, eds. *The Parade of Heroes.* Garden City, N.Y.: Anchor Press/Doubleday, 1978.

Coleman, Loren. *Mysterious America.* London and Boston: Faber and Faber, 1983.

Dorson, Richard M. *Buying the Wind: Regional Folklore in the United States.* Chicago: University of Chicago Press, 1964.

Greenway, John, ed. *Folklore of the Great West.* Palo Alto, Calif.: American West Publishing Company, 1969.

Kraut, Ogden, comp. *The Three Nephites.* New York: Arno Press, 1977.

Smith, Joseph, Jr., trans. *The Book of Mormon.* Salt Lake City: The Church of Jesus Christ of Latter-day Saints, 1950.

Stegner, Wallace. *Mormon Country.* New York: Bonanza Books, 1942.

PERIODICALS

Kapaloski, Gayle. "Ghost Stories." *Utah Holiday,* October 1984.

Vermont

BOOKS

Doyle, Arthur Conan. *The History of Spiritualism.* 2 vols. New York: Arno Press, 1975. A facsimile of the 1924 edition.

Stevens, Austin N., ed. *Mysterious New England.* Dublin, N.H.: Yankee Publishing, Inc., 1971.

PERIODICALS

Brainerd, Barbara. "Stowe Hollow Bridge." *The Potash Kettle* 23:2 (Winter 1975).

Fagan, Tom. "State Sprinkled with Evil Curses, Spooky Goings-On (Eddys of Chittenden Were Focus of Occult)." *The Sunday Rutland Herald* and the *Sunday Times Argus,* October 29, 1978.

Green Mountain Whittlin's. Published by Green Mountain Folklore Society, Volume XXXIV, 1982–83.

Rubin, Cynthia. "State Sprinkled with Evil Curses, Spooky Goings-On (Emily's Bridge Haunted by Several Odd Legends)." *The Sunday Rutland Herald* and the *Sunday Times Argus,* October 29, 1978.

UNPUBLISHED WORKS

Low, Gilman. "Superstition and the Supernatural as they pertain to Folk Cultures in Vermont," 1977. Ms. courtesy of the University of Vermont Special Collections.

Correspondence with Richard Sweterlitsch, Assistant Professor of Folklore, University of Vermont, Burlington, May 1987.

Virginia

BOOKS

Greenhouse, Herbert B. *In Defense of Ghosts.* New York: Simon and Schuster, Inc., Essandess Special Editions, 1970.

Lee, Marguerite DuPont. *Virginia Ghosts.* Berryville, Va.: Virginia Book Company, 1966.
Olmert, Michael. *Official Guide to Colonial Williamsburg.* Williamsburg: The Colonial Williamsburg Foundation, 1985.
Taylor, L. B. *The Ghosts of Williamsburg . . . and Nearby Environs.* Williamsburg; self-published. Printed in the USA by Progress Printing Co., Inc., 1983.
————. *Haunted Houses.* New York: Wanderer Books, 1983.

PERIODICALS

Bonko, Larry. "M'lady is invisible." *Norfolk Ledger Star,* April 17, 1978.
Briel, David. "Ghost Hunt." *America,* Spring 1987.
Carpenter, Bill. "Are Spirits of Historic Persons Walking Williamsburg's Streets?" *Richmond Daily Press,* October 31, 1965.
Dietz, F. Meredith. "Ghost of 'Antique Virgin' Said to Haunt Westover." *Richmond Times-Dispatch,* September 17, 1950.
Farkas, Harold M. "The V.I.P. Ghosts in Virginia: A Spectral Who's Who." *The New York Times,* January 24, 1971.
"Happy Halloween." *College of William and Mary News,* October 30, 1979.
Howard, Tom. "State Ghosts Are Legendary." *Richmond Times-Dispatch,* n.d.
Mahoney, Mary Reeves. "Virginia's Haunted House Highway." *Ford Times,* October 1979.
McLaughlin, Bill. "Who frequents rooms and stairwells within CW's long-empty buildings?" *Richmond Times-Herald,* October 30, 1981.
Spano, Susan. "Their Old Virginia Homes." *The New York Times,* March 22, 1992.
Virginia Travel News. Department of Economic Development, Fall 1984.
"Who's whoo: Unexplained tales lure many tourists." *Cleveland Press,* October 31, 1978.
Worldwide Travel Planner, March 1990.

UNPUBLISHED WORKS

Information given to authors by guide at Peyton Randolph House, August 14, 1989.

Washington

PERIODICALS

Andrews, Page. "Ghost Stories." *The Seattle Times/Seattle Post-Intelligencer,* October 30, 1983.
Morris, Dan. "Jesuit Challenges 'Force' Haunting Old Mansion." *The National Observer,* May 3, 1975.
Robinson, Kathryn. "Haunted Seattle." *theWeekly,* October 28–November 3, 1983.

UNPUBLISHED WORKS

Interview with Nan Cauthorn Cooper, December 4, 1987.

West Virginia

BOOKS

Brown, Stephen D. *Ghosts of Harpers Ferry.* Harpers Ferry, W. Va.: The Little Brown House Publishing Co., 1981.
———. *Haunted Houses of Harpers Ferry.* Harpers Ferry, W. Va.: The Little Brown House Publishing Co., 1976.
Musick, Ruth. *The Telltale Lilac Bush.* Lexington: University of Kentucky Press, 1965.

PERIODICALS

Dykeman, Wilma. "John Brown's Landscape." *The New York Times,* November 1, 1987.
Thomas, Dana. "On a Tour of Harpers Ferry's Favorite Haunts." *The Washington Post,* October 31, 1989.

Wisconsin

BOOKS

Skinner, Charles M. *Myths and Legends of Our Native Land.* Philadelphia: J. B. Lippincott, 1896.

PERIODICALS

Anastasi, Rachel N. "Expert ties family stress to poltergeist in Horicon." *Milwaukee Sentinel,* August 22, 1988.
———. "Parapsychologist links stress, psychic events." *Milwaukee Sentinel,* February 1, 1988.
Bruch, Gloria. "Spooky roommates." *Stevens Point Journal,* October 26, 1988.
Brunsman, Barrett J. "Ghost story—Reporting on the haunted house of Horicon." *The Quill,* April 1988.
Coon, Laura Sumner. "Haunting melody." *The Milwaukee Journal,* October 26, 1984.
DeShaney, Ginger, and United Press International. "Psychic 'Experts' Lend Credence to Story." *Milwaukee Sentinel,* January 29, 1988.
Dornfeld, Connie Polzin. "Experts: Show Compassion for Troubled Family." *Beaver Dam Daily Citizen,* February 1, 1988.
———. "Family Strives to Put Lives Back in Order." *Beaver Dam Daily Citizen,* February 26, 1988.
———. "Film crew stirs spirits in Horicon." *Beaver Dam Daily Citizen,* August 22, 1988.
———. "Haunted House in Horicon?" *Beaver Dam Daily Citizen,* January 25, 1988.
———. "Pastor Helps Silence Rumor Mill." *Beaver Dam Daily Citizen,* February 19, 1988.
Dullum, Randall. "Horicon haunting recreated." *Fond du Lac Reporter,* October 27, 1988.
Erickson, Lisa. "This house really is haunted." *Antigo Daily Journal,* October 31, 1984.
"FmHA Gets Horicon House." *Beaver Dam Daily Citizen,* February 19, 1988.
Hayes, Paul G. "Horicon calm amid a ghostly flurry." *The Milwaukee Journal,* n.d.
"Horicon ghosts gone?" *Madison Capital Times,* February 19, 1988.
"Horicon 'spirits' will show up on TV." *Madison Capital Times,* August 19, 1988.

"The Horicon, Wisconsin, 'Haunted House.' " *New Frontiers (Oregon, Wis.)* 26 and 27 (Spring–Summer 1988).

Jaeger, Richard W. "Horicon ghosts gone for good." *Wisconsin State Journal,* June 14, 1988.

———. "Paranormal revisited." *Wisconsin State Journal,* February 22, 1993.

Janz, William. "Who ya gonna call? Police chief of 'ghost town' haunted by havoc." *Milwaukee Sentinel,* January 30, 1988.

Nelson, James B. "Horicon couple say apparitions, noises drove them from home." *Milwaukee Sentinel,* January 27, 1988.

———. "Horicon family finds relief after beds buried." *Milwaukee Sentinel,* February 19, 1988.

———. "Horicon ghosts: Rumors of eerie events draw curious crowds." *Milwaukee Sentinel,* January 27, 1988.

———. " 'Hot spots' found in Horicon home." *Milwaukee Sentinel,* February 1, 1988.

———. "Official fears Horicon may scare off film projects." *Milwaukee Sentinel,* August 25, 1988.

———. "Re-created ghost story haunts Horicon neighbors." *Milwaukee Sentinel,* August 23, 1988.

———."Uneasy couple visit their 'ghost house.' " *Milwaukee Sentinel,* January 28, 1988.

Petricka, Pat. "Remodeling reveals 110-year-old newspaper." *River Falls Journal,* September 22, 1988.

UNPUBLISHED WORKS

Interview with Jeff Bils, May 3, 1990.
Interview with Gloria Bruch, March 31, 1990.
Interview with Douglas Glamann, June 22, 1988.
Interview with Jacki, a psychic, September 30, 1990.
Interview with Douglas O'Brien family, June 12, 1989.
Interview with Allen and Deborah Tallmann, June 22 and 23, 1988.
Manuscript written and submitted to authors by Deborah Tallman, May 1988.

Wyoming

BOOKS

Munn, Debra D. *Ghosts on the Range: Eerie True Tales of Wyoming.* Boulder, Colo.: Pruett Publishing Company, 1989.

Murray, Earl. *Ghosts of the Old West.* Chicago and New York: Contemporary Books, 1988.

PERIODICALS

Hamilton, Brad. "Story of St. Mark's Ghost Tower Re-Told." *Wyoming State Tribune,* October 21, 1979.

UNPUBLISHED WORKS

Fifield, Dorothy H. "The Ghost Rides Again." Wyoming State Archives, Museums and Historical Department, Cheyenne.

Canada

BOOKS

Blundell, Nigel and Roger Boar. *The World's Greatest Ghosts.* New York: Berkeley, 1988.
Fink-Cline, Beverly and Leigh Cline. *The Terrific Toronto Trivia Book.* Toronto: Personal Library Publishers, 1979.
Guiley, Rosemary. *Encyclopedia of Ghosts and Spirits.* New York, NY: Facts on File, 1992.
Haining, Peter. *A Dictionary of Ghosts.* New York, NY: Dorset Press, 1993.
Kevan, Martin. *The Best of Montreal and Quebec City.* New York: Crown, 1992.
MacKenzie House. Pamphlet published by Toronto Historical Board, Toronto, Ontario, n.d.
Notre-Dame-de-Pontmain, 1884–1984. n.d. (translated by Anthony Baechle for the authors).
Russell, Paul and Jeffrey Robert. *Toronto's Top 10.* Toronto: Methuen, 1984.
Sherwood, Roland H. *Maritime Mysteries.* Windsor, N. S.: Lancelot Press, 1976.
Singer, Kurt (ed.) *The Unearthly.* New York, NY: Belmont Books, 1965.
Smith, Susy. *Haunted Houses for the Millions.* New York, NY: Dell, 1967.
Sonin, Eileen. *ESP-ecially Ghosts.* Toronto: Clarke, Irwin and Company, 1970.

PERIODICALS

Caylor, Ron. "Priest Haunts Church," *National Enquirer,* January 31, 1978.
Clark, Victor. "Metro's Ghostliest Places," *The Subway Link,* Vol. 1, No. 2, October 31–November 20, 1986.
Cobb, Michael. "She's Hostess With Ghostess," Vancouver *Sun,* May 30, 1966.
"Escape in a haunted house," n.d., n.s. June 17, 1966.
"Ghost Fee Ruled Out," Vancouver *Sun,* July 21, 1966.
"Ghosts host haunted," The *Province,* June 24, 1966.
"Haunted house sold," Vancouver *Sun,* April 2, 1973.
Herman, Wendy. "Ghost town Toronto," Toronto *Star,* April 27, 1980.
"Not a Chance," The *Province,* July 20, 1966.
Odam, Jess. "Hetty's Haunted by Ghost Fans," Vancouver *Sun,* June 8, 1966.
———. "Sun Team Sees No Ghost—But What Was That In Hall?" Vancouver *Sun,* June 2, 1966.
"Scare Still On," Vancouver *Sun,* June 1, 1966.
Stroud, Carstens. "The Case of the Missing Snipe," Toronto *Star,* December 9, 1979.
"Sunday Seance Seeks Shy Spook," Vancouver *Sun,* June 3, 1966.
Sutter, Trevor. "Ghost in Nightclub," Regina *Leader-Post,* April 27, 1992.
"Two visits by 'phantom' tied to wall's tombstone," Vancouver *Sun,* October 26, 1982.
Volgenau, Gerald. "Ghostbusters: Pair Claims to Banish Spirit From Home," Montreal *Free Press,* n.d.
White, Scott. "Legislature's Past Spooky," Vancouver *Sun,* July 5, 1984.
"Who Wants Haunted House?" The *Province,* March 31, 1973.

UNPUBLISHED WORKS

Bauer, Roy. Letters to Dale Orsted, May–June, 1992.
Canadian Broadcasting Corporation, "News Magazine." "The Moosehead Inn Ghost Story," n.d.
Correspondence from Pierrette Champoux, Montreal, November–December, 1993.

Correspondence from Jocelyne Choquette, Montreal, December 1993. (translated by Anthony Baechle).

Correspondence from Judy Curry, Metropolitan Toronto Library Board, November 1986

Correspondence from Clovis Daoust, Notre-Dame-de-Pontmain, Quebec, December 1993. (translated by Anthony Baechle).

Correspondence from Mrs. E. M. Darke, curatorial assistant for historic houses, Toronto Historical Board, January 1987.

Correspondence from Marie V. Gibbs, Moose Jaw, Saskatchewan, October 1993.

Correspondence from Laura Jantek, coordinator of reference services, Halifax City Regional Library, n.d.

Correspondence from Jean Moore, Regina, Saskatchewan, n.d.

Correspondence from M. R. Mulvale, Greenwood, Nova Scotia, December 1993.

Correspondence from Dale Orsted, Estevan, Saskatchewan, November 1993.

Correspondence from Miriam Siwak, Sydney, Nova Scotia, October 1993.

Interview with Dale Orsted, Estevan, Saskatchewan, February 1994.

Interview with Roy Bauer, Winnipeg, Manitoba, February 1994.